The Merriam-Webster Instant Speller

The Merriam-Webster Instant Speller

A Merriam-Webster®

MERRIAM-WEBSTER INC., *Publishers*
Springfield, Massachusetts

ISBN 0-87779-907-5

MADE IN THE UNITED STATES OF AMERICA

123456AG/B949392

Contents

Preface

The major feature of The Merriam-Webster Instant Speller is an alphabetical word list intended for use by writers, secretaries, and typists as a handy guide to spelling and to the division of words at the end of lines.

The division of words in English dictionaries has a long, somewhat complicated history, and the traditions upon which such division is based have developed gradually, not to say haphazardly, over a period of about a century and a half. It is commonly thought that word division is based primarily on pronunciation. In actuality, spelling, etymology (the history of a word), common sense, and occasionally arbitrary choice also play important roles. Since the question of end-of-line division occurs only in written contexts, it is perhaps unreasonable to expect the spoken form of the language to dictate a workable set of principles to solve a largely mechanical problem. For one thing, there are many words with perfectly acceptable variant pronunciations. Take *homicide* as an example. Those who pronounce the first syllable of *homicide* to rhyme with *home* may prefer an end-of-line division before the *m*, while those who rhyme it with *bomb* may prefer a division after the *m*. Both divisions are correct, but in this book only one of them is shown since an entry such as *ho · m · i · cide* would be confusing to many. In order to be consistent in the large number of cases which fall into this category, we show only the leftmost division in each instance. Thus, the entry appears as *ho · mi · cide* in this book.

Etymology is taken into account in the division of such words as *accordance* and *dictionary.* These words were not formed by adding suffixes to the English words *accord* and *diction;* rather they are derived from the early French *acordance* and medieval Latin *dictionarium* respectively. Thus, we show the divisions *ac · cor · dance* and *dic · tio · nary* (rather than *ac · cord · ance* and *dic · tion · ary*). Common sense and the established practice of most typists and printers are followed in this book in that a single letter at the beginning or end of a word is not separated from the rest of the word.

While there are acceptable alternative end-of-line divisions just as there are acceptable variant spellings and pronunciations, we recognize that the purpose of showing divisions in this book is to save the user the time and trouble of making a choice in what is essentially a minor matter. Our general recommendation to those concerned about end-of-line division is to choose a reliable up-to-date dictionary or speller such as this and to rely on it without worrying about divisions shown elsewhere. Other books may not be wrong, just different. Greater consistency of division will result from the regular use of a single work.

The Merriam-Webster Instant Speller also shows variant spellings for many words, as well as irregular inflections of verbs, adjectives, and nouns. Short identifying glosses and cross-references are provided to help distinguish words of similar sound or spelling that might otherwise be confused, such as *allusive, elusive,* and *illusive* or *straight* and *strait.* Variant spellings preceded by *or* are found in frequent use. Those preceded by *also* are found less frequently though often enough to be included in this book. All of the variant spellings given are acceptable in standard English writing.

The following labels and abbreviations are used in the glosses and cross-references which distinguish between entries:

adj (adjective)
adverb
biol (biology)
chem (chemistry)
comp (comparative)
conj (conjunction)
fem (feminine)
masc (masculine)
math (mathematics)
noun
pl (plural)
prep (preposition)
var (variant)
verb

For ease of reference, guide words are printed in boldface type at the top left and right hand corners of each two-page spread. Following the A to Z vocabulary list are four back-matter sections: Abbreviations, Handbook of Style, Forms of Address, and Weights and Measures.

A

aard·vark

aba·cus
pl aba·ci *or* aba·cus·es

ab·a·lo·ne

aban·don

aban·doned

aban·don·ment

abase

abase·ment

abash

abate

abate·ment

ab·a·tis
pl ab·a·tis *or* ab·a·tis·es

ab·at·toir

ab·ax·i·al

ab·ba·cy

ab·bé

ab·bess

ab·bey

ab·bot

ab·bre·vi·ate

ab·bre·vi·a·tion

ab·di·cate

ab·di·ca·tion

ab·do·men

ab·dom·i·nal

ab·duct

ab·duc·tion

ab·duc·tor

abe·ce·dar·i·an

abed

ab·er·rant

ab·er·ra·tion

abet
abet·ted
abet·ting

abet·tor
or abet·ter

abey·ance

ab·hor
ab·horred
ab·hor·ring

ab·hor·rence

ab·hor·rent

abide

abil·i·ty
pl abil·i·ties

ab·ject

ab·jec·tion

ab·ject·ly

ab·ject·ness

ab·ju·ra·tion

ab·jure

ab·late

ab·la·tion

ab·la·tive

ablaze

able

able-bod·ied

ab·lu·tion

ab·ne·gate

ab·ne·ga·tion

ab·nor·mal

ab·nor·mal·i·ty

ab·nor·mal·ly

aboard

abode

aboil

abol·ish

ab·o·li·tion

ab·o·li·tion·ist

A-bomb

abom·i·na·ble

abom·i·nate

abom·i·na·tion

ab·orig·i·nal

ab·orig·i·ne

aborn·ing

abort

abor·tion

abor·tion·ist

abor·tive

abound

about

about-face

above

above·board

ab·ra·ca·dab·ra

abrade

abra·sion

abra·sive

ab·re·act

abreast

abridge

abridg·ment
or abridge·ment

abroad

ab·ro·gate

ab·ro·ga·tion

abrupt

ab•scess
ab•scis•sa
ab•scis•sion
ab•scond
ab•sence
ab•sent
ab•sen•tee
ab•sen•tee•ism
ab•sent•mind•ed
ab•sinthe
or ab•sinth
ab•so•lute
ab•so•lute•ly
ab•so•lu•tion
ab•so•lut•ism
ab•solve
ab•sorb
ab•sor•ben•cy
ab•sor•bent
ab•sorp•tion
ab•sorp•tive
ab•stain
ab•ste•mi•ous
ab•sten•tion
ab•sti•nence
ab•stract
ab•strac•tion
ab•struse
ab•surd
ab•sur•di•ty
abun•dance
abun•dant
abuse
abu•sive
abut
abut•ted
abut•ting
abut•ment
abut•tals
abys•mal
abys•mal•ly
abyss
abys•sal
aca•cia
ac•a•deme
ac•a•dem•ic
also ac•a•dem•i•cal
ac•a•dem•i•cal•ly
ac•a•de•mi•cian
ac•a•dem•i•cism
acad•e•my
acan•thus
a cap•pel•la
also a ca•pel•la
ac•cede
agree (*see* exceed)
ac•ce•le•ran•do
ac•cel•er•ate
ac•cel•er•a•tion
ac•cel•er•a•tor
ac•cent
ac•cen•tu•al
ac•cen•tu•ate
ac•cen•tu•a•tion
ac•cept
receive (*see* except)
ac•cept•abil•i•ty
ac•cept•able
ac•cep•tance
ac•cep•ta•tion
ac•cess
approach (*see* excess)
ac•ces•si•bil•i•ty
ac•ces•si•ble
ac•ces•sion
ac•ces•so•ry
also ac•ces•sa•ry
pl ac•ces•so•ries
also ac•ces•sa•ries
ac•ci•dence
ac•ci•dent
ac•ci•den•tal
ac•ci•den•tal•ly
also ac•ci•dent•ly
ac•claim
ac•cla•ma•tion
ac•cli•mate
ac•cli•ma•ti•za•tion
ac•cli•ma•tize
ac•cliv•i•ty
ac•co•lade
ac•com•mo•date
ac•com•mo•dat•ing
ac•com•mo•da•tion
ac•com•pa•ni•ment
ac•com•pa•nist
ac•com•pa•ny
ac•com•plice
ac•com•plish
ac•com•plished
ac•com•plish•ment
ac•cord
ac•cor•dance
ac•cor•dant
ac•cord•ing•ly

ac·cor·di·on
ac·cost
ac·count
ac·count·abil·i·ty
ac·count·able
ac·coun·tan·cy
ac·coun·tant
ac·count·ing
ac·cou·tre
or ac·cou·ter
ac·cou·tre·ment
or ac·cou·ter·ment
ac·cred·it
ac·cred·i·ta·tion
ac·cre·tion
ac·cru·al
ac·crue
ac·cru·ing
ac·cul·tur·ate
ac·cul·tur·a·tion
ac·cu·mu·late
ac·cu·mu·la·tion
ac·cu·mu·la·tor
ac·cu·ra·cy
ac·cu·rate
ac·cu·rate·ly
ac·cu·rate·ness
ac·cursed
ac·cus·al
ac·cu·sa·tion
ac·cu·sa·tive
ac·cuse
ac·cus·er
ac·cus·tom
ac·cus·tomed
acer·bi·ty
ac·et·al·de·hyde
ac·et·an·i·lide
or ac·et·an·i·lid
ac·e·tate
ace·tic
chem (*see* ascetic)
ac·e·tone
acet·y·lene
ache
achieve
achieve·ment
ach·ing
ach·ro·mat·ic
ac·id
acid·ic
acid·i·fi·ca·tion
acid·i·fy
acid·i·ty
ac·i·do·sis
acid·u·late
acid·u·lous
ack-ack
ac·knowl·edge
ac·knowl·edg·ment
also ac·knowl·edge·ment
ac·me
ac·ne
ac·o·lyte
ac·o·nite
acorn
acous·tic
acous·ti·cal
acous·ti·cal·ly
acous·tics
ac·quaint
ac·quain·tance
ac·quain·tance·ship
ac·qui·esce
ac·qui·es·cence
ac·qui·es·cent
ac·quire
ac·quire·ment
ac·qui·si·tion
ac·quis·i·tive
ac·quis·i·tive·ness
ac·quit
ac·quit·ted
ac·quit·ting
ac·quit·tal
acre
acre·age
ac·rid
acrid·i·ty
ac·ri·mo·ni·ous
ac·ri·mo·ny
ac·ro·bat
ac·ro·bat·ic
ac·ro·nym
ac·ro·pho·bia
acrop·o·lis
across
across-the-board
acros·tic
ac·ry·late
acryl·ic
act·ing
ac·tin·ic

ac·tin·i·um
ac·tion
ac·tion·able
ac·ti·vate
ac·ti·va·tion
ac·tive
ac·tive·ly
ac·tiv·ism
ac·tiv·ist
ac·tiv·i·ty
ac·tor
ac·tress
ac·tu·al
ac·tu·al·i·ty
ac·tu·al·ize
ac·tu·al·ly
ac·tu·ar·i·al
ac·tu·ary
ac·tu·ate
ac·tu·a·tor
acu·ity
acu·men
acu·punc·ture
acute
acute·ly
acute·ness
ad·age
ada·gio
pl **ada·gios**
ad·a·mant
ad·a·man·tine
ad·a·mant·ly
adapt
to fit (*see* **adept, adopt**)
adapt·abil·i·ty
adapt·able
ad·ap·ta·tion
adapt·er
also **adapt·or**
ad·dend
ad·den·dum
pl **ad·den·da**
ad·der
snake
add·er
one that adds
ad·dict
ad·dic·tion
ad·dic·tive
ad·di·tion
ad·di·tion·al
ad·di·tion·al·ly
ad·di·tive
ad·dle
ad·dress
ad·dress·ee
ad·duce
ad·e·noid
ad·e·noi·dal
ad·ept
an expert
adept
proficient (*see* **adapt, adopt**)
adept·ly
adept·ness
ad·e·qua·cy
ad·e·quate
ad·e·quate·ly
ad·here
ad·her·ence
ad·her·ent
ad·he·sion
ad·he·sive
ad·he·sive·ness
ad hoc
adi·a·bat·ic
adieu
pl **adieus** *or* **adieux**
ad in·fi·ni·tum
ad in·ter·im
adi·os
ad·i·pose
ad·i·pos·i·ty
ad·ja·cent
ad·jec·ti·val
ad·jec·ti·val·ly
ad·jec·tive
ad·join
ad·join·ing
ad·journ
ad·journ·ment
ad·judge
ad·ju·di·cate
ad·ju·di·ca·tion
ad·junct
ad·ju·ra·tion
ad·jure
ad·just
ad·just·able
ad·just·er
also **ad·jus·tor**
ad·just·ment
ad·ju·tant
ad·ju·vant

ad-lib
ad•libbed
ad•lib•bing

ad lib
adverb

ad li•bi•tum
ad•man
ad•min•is•ter
ad•min•is•tra•ble
ad•min•is•trant
ad•min•is•trate
ad•min•is•tra•tion
ad•min•is•tra•tive
ad•min•is•tra•tor
ad•mi•ra•ble
ad•mi•ra•bly
ad•mi•ral
ad•mi•ral•ty
ad•mi•ra•tion
ad•mire
ad•mir•er
ad•mis•si•bil•i•ty
ad•mis•si•ble
ad•mis•sion
ad•mit
ad•mit•ted
ad•mit•ting
ad•mit•tance
ad•mit•ted•ly
ad•mix
ad•mix•ture
ad•mon•ish
ad•mo•ni•tion
ad•mon•i•to•ry

ad nau•se•am
ado
ado•be
ad•o•les•cence
ad•o•les•cent
adopt
to accept (*see* adapt, adept)

adop•tion
adop•tive
ador•able
ad•o•ra•tion
adore
adorn
adorn•ment
ad•re•nal
adren•a•line
adrift
adroit
adroit•ly
adroit•ness
ad•sorb
ad•sor•bent
ad•sorp•tion
ad•sorp•tive
ad•u•late
ad•u•la•tion
adult
adul•ter•ant
adul•ter•ate
adul•ter•a•tion
adul•ter•er
adul•ter•ess
adul•ter•ous
adul•tery

adult•hood
ad•um•brate
ad•um•bra•tion
ad va•lo•rem
ad•vance
ad•vance•ment
ad•van•tage
ad•van•ta•geous
ad•vent
ad•ven•ti•tious
ad•ven•ture
ad•ven•tur•er
ad•ven•ture•some
ad•ven•tur•ess
ad•ven•tur•ous
ad•verb
ad•ver•bi•al
ad•ver•bi•al•ly
ad•ver•sary
ad•ver•sa•tive
ad•ver•sa•tive•ly
ad•verse
unfavorable (*see* averse)

ad•verse•ly
ad•ver•si•ty
ad•vert
ad•ver•tise
ad•ver•tise•ment
ad•ver•tis•er
ad•ver•tis•ing
ad•vice
noun (*see* advise)

ad•vis•abil•i•ty
ad•vis•able

ad·vise
verb (*see* advice)

ad·vis·er
or ad·vi·sor

ad·vise·ment

ad·vi·sory

ad·vo·ca·cy

ad·vo·cate

ae·gis
or egis

ae·o·lian

ae·on

aer·ate

aer·a·tion

ae·ri·al
adj

aer·i·al
noun

ae·ri·al·ist

ae·rie

aero

aer·o·bat·ics

aer·obe

aer·o·bic

aero·drome

aero·dy·nam·i·cal·ly

aero·dy·nam·ics

aer·o·log·i·cal

aer·ol·o·gist

aer·ol·o·gy

aero·naut

aero·nau·ti·cal
or aero·nau·tic

aero·nau·tics

aer·o·nom·ic
or aer·o·nom·i·cal

aer·on·o·mist

aer·on·o·my

aero·pause

aero·sol

aero·space

aery

aes·thete
or es·thete

aes·thet·ic
or es·thet·ic

aes·thet·i·cal·ly

aes·thet·i·cism

aes·thet·ics
or es·thet·ics

aes·ti·vate

aes·ti·va·tion

af·fa·bil·i·ty

af·fa·ble

af·fa·bly

af·fair

af·fect
to influence (*see* effect)

af·fec·ta·tion

af·fect·ed

af·fect·ing

af·fec·tion

af·fec·tion·ate

af·fer·ent

af·fi·ance

af·fi·da·vit

af·fil·i·ate

af·fil·i·a·tion

af·fin·i·ty

af·firm

af·fir·ma·tion

af·fir·ma·tive

af·fix

af·fla·tus

af·flict

af·flic·tion

af·flic·tive

af·flu·ence

af·flu·ent

af·ford

af·fray

af·fright

af·front

af·ghan

af·ghani

Af·ghan·i·stan

afi·cio·na·do
pl afi·cio·na·dos

afield

afire

aflame

afloat

aflut·ter

afoot

afore·men·tioned

afore·said

afore·thought

a for·ti·o·ri

afraid

afresh

Af·ri·can

Af·ri·kaans

Af·ro

af·ter

af·ter·birth

af·ter·burn·er
af·ter·care
af·ter·deck
af·ter·ef·fect
af·ter·glow
af·ter·life
af·ter·math
af·ter·noon
af·ter·taste
af·ter·tax
af·ter·thought
af·ter·ward
or af·ter·wards

again
against
Aga·na
agape
adj, gaping

aga·pe
noun, love

ag·ate
ag·ate·ware
aga·ve
age·less
agen·cy
agen·da
agent
age-old
ag·gior·na·men·to
pl ag·gior·na·men·tos

ag·glom·er·ate
ag·glom·er·a·tion
ag·glu·ti·nate
ag·glu·ti·na·tion
ag·gran·dize
ag·gran·dize·ment
ag·gra·vate
ag·gra·va·tion
ag·gre·gate
ag·gre·ga·tion
ag·gres·sion
ag·gres·sive
ag·gres·sive·ness
ag·gres·sor
ag·grieve
aghast
ag·ile
agil·i·ty
ag·i·tate
ag·i·ta·tion
ag·i·ta·tor
agleam
aglit·ter
aglow
ag·nos·tic
ag·nos·ti·cism
ago
agog
ag·o·nize
ag·o·niz·ing·ly
ag·o·ny
ag·o·ra
marketplace, pl ag·o·ras *or* ag·o·rae

ago·ra
coin, pl ago·rot

ag·o·ra·pho·bia
ag·o·ra·pho·bic
agrar·i·an
agree
agree·abil·i·ty
agree·able
agree·able·ness
agree·ably
agree·ment
ag·ri·cul·tur·al
ag·ri·cul·ture
ag·ri·cul·tur·ist
ag·ro·nom·ic
or ag·ro·nom·i·cal

ag·ro·nom·i·cal·ly
agron·o·mist
agron·o·my
aground
ague
ahead
ahoy
aid
help

aide
assistant

aide-de-camp
pl aides-de-camp

ai·grette
ail
to be ill (*see* ale)

ai·le·ron
ail·ment
aim·less
aim·less·ness
air
gas (*see* heir)

air·borne
air·brush

air•bus
air-con•di•tion
air-cool
air•craft
air•crew
air•drome
air•drop
air-dry
air•field
air•flow
air•foil
air•frame
air•glow
air•lift
air•line
air•lin•er
air•mail
air•man
air mile
air-mind•ed
air•mo•bile
air•plane
air•port
air•post
air•ship
air•sick
air•sick•ness
air•space
air•speed
air•stream
air•strip
air•tight
air-to-air
air•wave
air•way

air•wor•thi•ness
air•wor•thy
airy
aisle
passage (*see* isle)
ajar
akim•bo
Ak•ron
Al•a•bama
al•a•bas•ter
a la carte
alac•ri•ty
a la mode
alarm
also ala•rum
alarm•ist
Alas•ka
al•ba•core
Al•ba•nia
Al•ba•nian
Al•ba•ny
al•ba•tross
al•be•it
Al•ber•ta
al•bi•nism
al•bi•no
al•bum
al•bu•men
egg white
al•bu•min
protein
al•bu•min•ous
Al•bu•quer•que
al•cal•de
al•ca•zar

al•che•mist
al•che•my
al•co•hol
al•co•hol•ic
al•co•hol•ism
al•cove
al•der
al•der•man
ale
beverage (*see* ail)
ale•a•tor•ic
ale•house
ale•wife
alert
alert•ness
Al•ex•an•dria
al•ex•an•drine
al•fal•fa
al•fres•co
al•ga
pl al•gae *also* al•gas
al•ge•bra
al•ge•bra•ic
Al•ge•ria
Al•ge•ri•an
al•go•rithm
alias
al•i•bi
alien
alien•able
alien•ate
alien•ation
alien•ist
alight

align
also aline

align•ment
also aline•ment

alike

al•i•ment

al•i•men•ta•ry

al•i•mo•ny

al•i•quot

alive

al•ka•li

al•ka•line

al•ka•lin•i•ty

al•ka•lin•ize

al•ka•loid

al•kyd

all
the whole (*see* awl)

Al•lah

all-Amer•i•can

all-around

al•lay

al•le•ga•tion

al•lege

al•leg•ed•ly

Al•le•ghe•ny

al•le•giance

al•le•gor•i•cal

al•le•go•ry

al•le•gro

al•le•lu•ia

Al•len•town

al•ler•gen

al•ler•gen•ic

al•ler•gic

al•ler•gist

al•ler•gy

al•le•vi•ate

al•le•vi•a•tion

al•ley
passage (*see* ally)

al•ley•way

All•hal•lows

al•li•ance

al•lied

al•li•ga•tor

al•lit•er•ate

al•lit•er•a•tion

al•lit•er•a•tive

al•lo•cate

al•lo•ca•tion

al•lo•ge•ne•ic

al•lot
al•lot•ted
al•lot•ting

al•lot•ment

al•lot•tee

all-out

all•over

al•low

al•low•able

al•low•ance

al•loy

all-round

All Saints' Day

All Souls' Day

all•spice

al•lude
to refer (*see* elude)

al•lure

al•lure•ment

al•lu•sion
reference (*see* illusion)

al•lu•sive
suggestive (*see* elusive, illusive)

al•lu•sive•ness

al•lu•vi•al

al•lu•vi•um

al•ly
to unite, friend (*see* alley)

al•ma ma•ter

al•ma•nac

al•mighty

al•mond

al•mo•ner

al•most

alms

alms•house

al•ni•co

al•oe

aloft

alo•ha

alone

along

along•shore

along•side

aloof

aloof•ness

aloud

al•paca

al•pen•stock

al•pha

al•pha•bet

al·pha·bet·ic
or al·pha·bet·i·cal

al·pha·bet·ize

al·pha·nu·mer·ic
also al·pha·nu·mer·i·cal

Al·pine

al·ready

al·so

al·so-ran

al·tar
noun (*see* alter)

al·tar·piece

al·ter
verb (*see* altar)

al·ter·ation

al·ter·cate

al·ter·ca·tion

al·ter ego

al·ter·nate

al·ter·nate·ly

al·ter·nat·ing

al·ter·na·tion

al·ter·na·tive

al·ter·na·tor

al·though
also al·tho

al·tim·e·ter

al·ti·tude

al·to
pl al·tos

al·to·geth·er

al·tru·ism

al·tru·ist

al·tru·is·tic

al·um

alu·mi·na

alu·mi·num

alum·na
pl alum·nae

alum·nus
pl alum·ni

al·ways

amal·gam

amal·gam·ate

amal·gam·ation

aman·u·en·sis
pl aman·u·en·ses

am·a·ranth

am·a·ran·thine

Am·a·ril·lo

am·a·ryl·lis

amass

am·a·teur

am·a·to·ry

amaze

amaze·ment

amaz·ing·ly

am·a·zon

am·a·zo·nian

am·bas·sa·dor

am·bas·sa·do·ri·al

am·bas·sa·dress

am·ber

am·ber·gris

am·bi·dex·trous

am·bi·ence
or am·bi·ance

am·bi·ent

am·bi·gu·ity

am·big·u·ous

am·bi·tion

am·bi·tious

am·biv·a·lence

am·biv·a·lent

am·ble

am·bro·sia

am·bro·sial

am·bu·lance

am·bu·lant

am·bu·la·to·ry

am·bus·cade

am·bush

ame·ba
var of amoeba

ame·ban
var of amoeban

ame·bic
var of amoebic

ame·lio·rate

ame·lio·ra·tion

ame·na·ble

amend
to change (*see* emend)

amend·ment

ame·ni·ty

amerce

amerce·ment

Amer·i·can

Amer·i·ca·na

Amer·i·can·ism

Amer·i·can·iza·tion

Amer·i·can·ize

am·er·i·ci·um

Am·er·ind

Am•er•in•di•an

am•e•thyst

ami•a•bil•i•ty

ami•a•ble

ami•a•bly

am•i•ca•bil•i•ty

am•i•ca•ble

am•i•ca•bly

amid
or amidst

amid•ships

ami•no

amiss

am•i•ty

am•me•ter

am•mo

am•mo•nia

am•mo•nite

am•mo•ni•um

am•mu•ni•tion

am•ne•sia

am•ne•si•ac
or am•ne•sic

am•nes•ty

amoe•ba
or ame•ba
pl amoe•bas *or* amoe•bae *or* ame•bas

amoe•bic
or ame•bic *also* amoe•ban *also* ame•ban

amoe•boid

amok

among
also amongst

amon•til•la•do
pl amon•til•la•dos

amor•al

amor•al•ly

am•o•rous

amor•phous

am•or•ti•za•tion

am•or•tize

amount

amour

amour pro•pre

am•per•age

am•pere

am•per•sand

am•phet•amine

am•phib•i•an

am•phib•i•ous

am•phi•the•ater

am•pho•ra
pl am•pho•rae *or* am•pho•ras

am•ple

am•pli•fi•ca•tion

am•pli•fi•er

am•pli•fy

am•pli•tude

am•ply

am•pul
or am•pule *or* am•poule

am•pul•la
pl am•pul•lae

am•pu•tate

am•pu•ta•tion

am•pu•tee

am•u•let

amuse

amuse•ment

anach•ro•nism

anach•ro•nis•tic

an•a•con•da

an•a•dem

anae•mia
var of anemia

anae•mic
var of anemic

an•aer•o•bic

an•aes•the•sia
var of anesthesia

an•aes•thet•ic
var of anesthetic

ana•gram

An•a•heim

anal

an•al•ge•sia

an•al•ge•sic

anal•o•gous

an•a•logue
or an•a•log

anal•o•gy

anal•y•sis
pl anal•y•ses

an•a•lyst
one who analyzes (*see* annalist)

an•a•lyt•ic
or an•a•lyt•i•cal

an•a•lyze

an•a•pest

an•a•pes•tic

an•ar•chic

an•ar•chism

an·ar·chist
an·ar·chis·tic
an·ar·chy
an·astig·mat·ic
anath·e·ma
anath·e·ma·tize
an·a·tom·ic
or an·a·tom·i·cal
anat·o·mist
anat·o·mize
anat·o·my
an·ces·tor
an·ces·tral
an·ces·try
an·chor
an·chor·age
an·cho·ress
or an·cress
an·cho·rite
an·cho·vy
an·cien ré·gime
an·cient
an·cil·lary
an·dan·te
and·iron
and/or
An·dor·ra
An·dor·ran
an·dro·gen
an·ec·dote
ane·mia
or anae·mia
ane·mic
or anae·mic
an·e·mom·e·ter
anem·o·ne
an·er·oid
an·es·the·sia
or an·aes·the·sia
an·es·the·si·ol·o·gist
an·es·the·si·ol·o·gy
an·es·thet·ic
or an·aes·thet·ic
anes·the·tist
anes·the·tize
an·gel
spiritual being (*see* angle)
an·gel·ic
or an·gel·i·cal
an·gel·i·cal·ly
An·ge·lus
an·ger
an·gi·na
an·gle
math (*see* angel)
an·gler
an·gle·worm
An·gli·can
an·gli·cism
an·gli·ci·za·tion
an·gli·cize
an·gling
an·glo·phile
an·glo·phobe
An·glo-Sax·on
An·go·la
an·go·ra
an·gri·ly
an·gry
angst
ang·strom
an·guish
an·gu·lar
an·gu·lar·i·ty
an·hy·drous
an·i·line
an·i·mad·ver·sion
an·i·mad·vert
an·i·mal
an·i·mal·cule
or an·i·mal·cu·lum
pl an·i·mal·cules *or* an·i·mal·cu·la
an·i·mal·ism
an·i·mate
an·i·mat·ed
an·i·ma·tion
an·i·mism
an·i·mist
an·i·mis·tic
an·i·mos·i·ty
an·i·mus
an·ion
an·ise
an·is·ette
ankh
an·kle
an·klet
an·nal·ist
recorder of events (*see* analyst)
An·nap·o·lis
an·neal
an·nex
an·nex·ation
an·ni·hi·late

an·ni·hi·la·tion
an·ni·ver·sa·ry
an·no Do·mi·ni
an·no·tate
an·no·ta·tion
an·no·ta·tor
an·nounce
an·nounce·ment
an·nounc·er
an·noy
an·noy·ance
an·nu·al
an·nu·al·ly
an·nu·itant
an·nu·ity
an·nul
an·nu·lar
an·nul·ment
an·nun·ci·ate
an·nun·ci·a·tion
an·nun·ci·a·tor
an·ode
an·od·ize
an·o·dyne
anoint
anom·a·lous
anom·a·ly
an·o·nym·i·ty
anon·y·mous
anoph·e·les
an·oth·er
an·ovu·lant
an·ovu·la·to·ry
an·swer
an·swer·able
ant·ac·id
an·tag·o·nism
an·tag·o·nist
an·tag·o·nis·tic
an·tag·o·nize
ant·arc·tic
Ant·arc·ti·ca
an·te
ant·eat·er
an·te·bel·lum
an·te·ced·ent
an·te·cham·ber
an·te·date
an·te·di·lu·vi·an
an·te·lope
an·te me·ri·di·em
an·te·mor·tem
an·te·na·tal
an·ten·na
pl an·ten·nae *or* an·ten·nas
an·te·pe·nult
an·te·pen·ul·ti·mate
an·te·ri·or
an·te·room
an·them
an·ther
ant·hill
an·thol·o·gy
an·thra·cite
an·thrax
an·thro·po·cen·tric
an·thro·poid
an·thro·po·log·i·cal
an·thro·pol·o·gist
an·thro·pol·o·gy
an·thro·po·mor·phic
an·thro·po·mor·phism
an·ti
an·ti·air·craft
an·ti·bac·te·ri·al
an·ti·bal·lis·tic mis·sile
an·ti·bi·ot·ic
an·ti·body
an·tic
An·ti·christ
an·tic·i·pate
an·tic·i·pa·tion
an·tic·i·pa·to·ry
an·ti·cli·mac·tic
an·ti·cli·max
an·ti·de·pres·sant
an·ti·dote
an·ti·freeze
an·ti·gen
an·ti·grav·i·ty
an·ti·his·ta·mine
an·ti·knock
an·ti·log·a·rithm
an·ti·ma·cas·sar
an·ti·mag·net·ic
an·ti·mis·sile
an·ti·mo·ny
an·ti·pas·to
an·ti·pa·thet·ic
an·tip·a·thy
an·ti·per·son·nel
an·ti·phon

an·tiph·o·nal
an·tip·o·dal
an·ti·pode
pl an·tip·o·des
an·ti·pov·er·ty
an·ti·quar·i·an
an·ti·quary
an·ti·quat·ed
an·tique
an·tiq·ui·ty
an·ti-Se·mit·ic
an·ti-Sem·i·tism
an·ti·sep·sis
an·ti·sep·tic
an·ti·sep·ti·cal·ly
an·ti·so·cial
an·tith·e·sis
pl an·tith·e·ses
an·ti·thet·i·cal
an·ti·thet·i·cal·ly
an·ti·tox·in
an·ti·trust
ant·ler
ant·lered
ant·onym
an·trum
anus
an·vil
anx·i·ety
anx·ious
any·body
any·how
any·more
any·one
any·place
any·thing
any·way
any·where
any·wise
aor·ta
aor·tic
apace
apart
apart·heid
apart·ment
ap·a·thet·ic
ap·a·thet·i·cal·ly
ap·a·thy
aper·i·tif
ap·er·ture
apex
pl apex·es *or* api·ces
apha·sia
aph·elion
pl aph·elia
aphid
aphis
pl aphi·des
aph·o·rism
aph·o·ris·tic
aph·ro·dis·i·ac
api·a·rist
api·ary
api·cal
apiece
aplomb
apoc·a·lypse
apoc·a·lyp·tic
apoc·ry·pha
apoc·ry·phal
apo·gee
apo·lit·i·cal
apol·o·get·ic
apol·o·get·i·cal·ly
ap·o·lo·gia
apol·o·gist
apol·o·gize
ap·o·logue
apol·o·gy
ap·o·plec·tic
ap·o·plexy
apos·ta·sy
apos·tate
a pos·te·ri·o·ri
apos·tle
apos·to·late
ap·os·tol·ic
apos·tro·phe
apos·tro·phize
apoth·e·cary
ap·o·thegm
apo·the·o·sis
Ap·pa·la·chian
ap·pall
also ap·pal
ap·pa·nage
ap·pa·ra·tus
pl ap·pa·ra·tus·es *or* ap·pa·ra·tus
ap·par·el
ap·par·ent
ap·pa·ri·tion
ap·peal
ap·pear

ap·pear·ance
ap·pease
ap·pease·ment
ap·pel·lant
ap·pel·late
ap·pel·la·tion
ap·pel·lee
ap·pend
ap·pend·age
ap·pen·dec·to·my
ap·pen·di·ci·tis
ap·pen·dix
pl **ap·pen·dix·es** *or* **ap·pen·di·ces**
ap·per·cep·tion
ap·per·tain
ap·pe·tite
ap·pe·tiz·er
ap·pe·tiz·ing
ap·plaud
ap·plause
ap·ple
ap·ple·jack
ap·pli·ance
ap·pli·ca·bil·i·ty
ap·pli·ca·ble
ap·pli·cant
ap·pli·ca·tion
ap·pli·ca·tor
ap·plied
ap·pli·qué
ap·ply
ap·point
ap·poin·tee
ap·point·ive
ap·point·ment
ap·por·tion
ap·por·tion·ment
ap·po·site
ap·po·si·tion
ap·pos·i·tive
ap·prais·al
ap·praise
value (*see* apprise)
ap·prais·er
ap·pre·cia·ble
ap·pre·ci·ate
ap·pre·ci·a·tion
ap·pre·cia·tive
ap·pre·hend
ap·pre·hen·sion
ap·pre·hen·sive
ap·pren·tice
ap·pren·tice·ship
ap·prise
inform (*see* appraise)
ap·proach
ap·proach·able
ap·pro·ba·tion
ap·pro·pri·ate
ap·pro·pri·ate·ly
ap·pro·pri·ate·ness
ap·pro·pri·a·tion
ap·prov·al
ap·prove
ap·prox·i·mate
ap·prox·i·mate·ly
ap·prox·i·ma·tion
ap·pur·te·nance
ap·pur·te·nant
apri·cot
April
a pri·o·ri
apron
ap·ro·pos
ap·ti·tude
apt·ly
apt·ness
aqua·cade
aqua·ma·rine
aqua·naut
aqua·plane
aquar·i·um
pl **aquar·i·ums** *or* **aquar·ia**
aquat·ic
aq·ue·duct
aque·ous
aq·ui·line
ar·a·besque
Ara·bi·an
Ar·a·bic
ar·a·ble
ar·ba·lest
or **ar·ba·list**
ar·bi·ter
ar·bit·ra·ment
ar·bi·trari·ly
ar·bi·trari·ness
ar·bi·trary
ar·bi·trate
ar·bi·tra·tion
ar·bi·tra·tor
ar·bor
ar·bo·re·al

ar·bo·re·tum
pl ar·bo·re·tums *or* ar·bo·re·ta

ar·bor·vi·tae

ar·bu·tus

arc
curve (*see* ark)

ar·cade

ar·cane

ar·chae·o·log·i·cal

ar·chae·ol·o·gist

ar·chae·ol·o·gy

ar·cha·ic

ar·cha·i·cal·ly

arch·an·gel

arch·bish·op

arch·bish·op·ric

arch·dea·con

arch·di·o·cese

arch·duch·ess

arch·duke

arch·en·e·my

ar·cher

ar·chery

ar·che·type

arch·fiend

ar·chi·epis·co·pal

ar·chi·pel·a·go
pl ar·chi·pel·a·goes *or* ar·chi·pel·a·gos

ar·chi·tect

ar·chi·tec·ton·ic

ar·chi·tec·tur·al

ar·chi·tec·ture

ar·chi·trave

ar·chive

ar·chi·vist

arch·ly

arch·ness

arch·way

arc·tic

ar·dent

ar·dor

ar·du·ous

ar·ea
space (*see* aria)

area·way

are·na

Ar·gen·ti·na

Ar·gen·tine

ar·gon

ar·go·sy

ar·got

ar·gu·able

ar·gue

ar·gu·ment

ar·gu·men·ta·tion

ar·gu·men·ta·tive
also ar·gu·men·tive

ar·gyle

aria
song (*see* area)

ar·id

arid·i·ty

arise
arose
aris·en
aris·ing

ar·is·toc·ra·cy

aris·to·crat

aris·to·crat·ic

arith·me·tic
noun

ar·ith·met·ic
or ar·ith·met·i·cal
adj

arith·me·ti·cian

Ar·i·zo·na

ark
boat (*see* arc)

Ar·kan·sas

ar·ma·da

ar·ma·dil·lo

Ar·ma·ged·don

ar·ma·ment

ar·ma·ture

arm·chair

Ar·me·nian

arm·hole

ar·mi·stice

arm·let

ar·mor

ar·mored

ar·mor·er

ar·mo·ri·al

ar·mory

arm·pit

arm·rest

ar·my

ar·ni·ca

aro·ma

ar·o·mat·ic

ar·o·mat·i·cal·ly

around

arous·al

arouse

ar·peg·gio
ar·raign
ar·raign·ment
ar·range
ar·range·ment
ar·rant
ar·ras
pl ar·ras
ar·ray
ar·rears
ar·rest
ar·ri·ère-pen·sée
ar·riv·al
ar·rive
ar·ro·gance
ar·ro·gant
ar·ro·gate
ar·row
ar·row·head
ar·row·root
ar·royo
ar·se·nal
ar·se·nic
noun
ar·sen·ic
adj
ar·son
ar·te·fact
var of artifact
ar·te·ri·al
ar·te·ri·ole
ar·te·rio·scle·ro·sis
ar·te·rio·scle·rot·ic
ar·tery
ar·te·sian well
art·ful
art·ful·ly
ar·thrit·ic
ar·thri·tis
pl ar·thrit·i·des
ar·thro·pod
ar·ti·choke
ar·ti·cle
ar·tic·u·lar
ar·tic·u·late
ar·tic·u·late·ly
ar·tic·u·la·tion
ar·ti·fact
or ar·te·fact
ar·ti·fice
ar·ti·fi·cer
ar·ti·fi·cial
ar·ti·fi·ci·al·i·ty
ar·ti·fi·cial·ly
ar·til·lery
art·i·ly
art·i·ness
ar·ti·san
art·ist
ar·tiste
ar·tis·tic
ar·tis·ti·cal·ly
art·ist·ry
art·less
arty
ar·um
Ary·an
as·bes·tos
also as·bes·tus
as·cend
as·cen·dan·cy
also as·cen·den·cy
as·cen·dant
also as·cen·dent
as·cen·sion
as·cent
upward slope (*see* assent)
as·cer·tain
as·cet·ic
austere (*see* acetic)
as·cet·i·cism
ascor·bic acid
as·cot
as·crib·able
as·cribe
as·crip·tion
asep·tic
asex·u·al
ashamed
ash·en
ash·lar
ashore
ashy
Asian
aside
as·i·nine
as·i·nin·i·ty
askance
askew
aslant
asleep
aso·cial
as·par·a·gus
as·pect

as•pen
as•per•i•ty
as•per•sion
as•phalt
as•phyx•ia
as•phyx•i•ate
as•phyx•i•a•tion
as•pic
as•pi•dis•tra
as•pi•rant
as•pi•rate
as•pi•ra•tion
as•pire
as•pi•rin
as•sail
as•sail•ant
as•sas•sin
as•sas•si•nate
as•sas•si•na•tion
as•sault
as•say
to try (*see* essay)
as•sem•blage
as•sem•ble
as•sem•bly
as•sem•bly•man
as•sent
agree (*see* ascent)
as•sert
as•ser•tion
as•sert•ive
as•sess
as•sess•ment
as•ses•sor
as•set

as•sev•er•ate
as•sev•er•a•tion
as•si•du•ity
as•sid•u•ous
as•sign
as•sign•able
as•sig•na•tion
as•sign•ment
as•sim•i•late
as•sim•i•la•tion
as•sist
as•sis•tance
as•sis•tant
as•size
as•so•ci•ate
verb
as•so•ciate
adj, noun
as•so•ci•a•tion
as•so•cia•tive
as•so•nance
as•so•nant
as•sort
as•sort•ed
as•sort•ment
as•suage
as•sume
as•sump•tion
as•sur•ance
as•sure
as•sured
pl as•sured *or* as•sureds
as•ta•tine
as•ter

as•ter•isk
as•ter•oid
asth•ma
asth•mat•ic
as•tig•mat•ic
as•tig•mat•i•cal•ly
astig•ma•tism
as•ton•ish
as•ton•ish•ment
as•tound
astrad•dle
as•tra•khan
or as•tra•chan
as•tral
astride
as•trin•gen•cy
as•trin•gent
as•tro•bi•ol•o•gist
as•tro•bi•ol•o•gy
as•tro•labe
as•trol•o•ger
as•tro•log•i•cal
as•trol•o•gy
as•tro•naut
as•tro•nau•tic
or as•tro•nau•ti•cal
as•tro•nau•tics
as•tron•o•mer
as•tro•nom•i•cal
or as•tro•nom•ic
as•tron•o•my
as•tro•phys•i•cist
as•tro•phys•ics
as•tute
asun•der

asy·lum

asym·met·ric
or **asym·met·ri·cal**

at
coin, pl **at**

at·a·vism

at·a·vis·tic

ate·lier

athe·ism

athe·ist

athe·is·tic

ath·e·nae·um
or **ath·e·ne·um**

ath·lete

ath·let·ic

ath·let·i·cal·ly

ath·let·ics

athwart

At·lan·ta

At·lan·tic

at·las

at·mo·sphere

at·mo·spher·ic

at·mo·spher·ics

atoll

at·om

atom·ic

atom·ics

at·om·ize

at·om·iz·er

aton·al

ato·nal·i·ty

aton·al·ly

atone

atone·ment

atri·um
pl **atria** *also* **atri·ums**

atro·cious

atroc·i·ty

at·ro·phy

at·ro·pine

at·tach

at·ta·ché

at·tach·ment

at·tack

at·tain

at·tain·abil·i·ty

at·tain·able

at·tain·der

at·tain·ment

at·taint

at·tar

at·tempt

at·tend

at·ten·dance

at·ten·dant

at·ten·tion

at·ten·tive

at·ten·u·ate

at·ten·u·a·tion

at·test

at·tes·ta·tion

at·tic

at·tire

at·ti·tude

at·ti·tu·di·nize

at·tor·ney

at·tract

at·trac·tion

at·trac·tive

at·trib·ut·able

at·tri·bute
noun

at·trib·ute
verb

at·tri·bu·tion

at·trib·u·tive

at·tri·tion

at·tune

atyp·i·cal

au·burn

au cou·rant

auc·tion

auc·tion·eer

auc·to·ri·al

au·da·cious

au·dac·i·ty

au·di·bil·i·ty

au·di·ble

au·di·bly

au·di·ence

au·dio

au·dio·phile

au·dio·vi·su·al

au·dit

au·di·tion

au·di·tor

au·di·to·ri·um

au·di·to·ry

au·ger
tool (see **augur***)*

aught
zero (see **ought***)*

aug·ment

aug·men·ta·tion
au gra·tin
au·gur
foretell (*see* auger)
au·gu·ry
au·gust
Au·gust
Au·gus·ta
auk
au·ra
au·ral
hearing (*see* oral)
au·re·ate
au·re·ole
or au·re·o·la
au re·voir
au·ri·cle
heart chamber (*see* oracle)
au·ric·u·lar
au·rif·er·ous
au·ro·ra
pl au·ro·ras *or* au·ro·rae
au·ro·ra aus·tra·lis
au·ro·ra bo·re·al·is
aus·pice
aus·pi·cious
aus·tere
aus·ter·i·ty
Aus·tin
aus·tral
Aus·tra·lia
Aus·tra·lian
Aus·tria
Aus·tri·an
au·then·tic
au·then·ti·cal·ly
au·then·ti·cate
au·then·ti·ca·tion
au·then·tic·i·ty
au·thor
au·thor·ess
au·thor·i·tar·i·an
au·thor·i·ta·tive
au·thor·i·ty
au·tho·ri·za·tion
au·tho·rize
au·thor·ship
au·to
au·to·bahn
au·to·bi·og·ra·pher
au·to·bio·graph·i·cal
also auto·bio·graph·ic
au·to·bi·og·ra·phy
au·toch·tho·nous
au·toc·ra·cy
au·to·crat
au·to·crat·ic
au·to·crat·i·cal·ly
au·to·graph
au·to·in·tox·i·ca·tion
au·to·mate
au·to·mat·ic
au·to·mat·i·cal·ly
au·to·ma·tion
au·tom·a·ti·za·tion
au·tom·a·tize
au·tom·a·ton
pl au·tom·a·tons *or* au·tom·a·ta
au·to·mo·bile
au·to·mo·bil·ist
au·to·mo·tive
au·ton·o·mous
au·ton·o·my
au·top·sy
au·to·stra·da
au·tumn
au·tum·nal
aux·il·ia·ry
aux·in
avail
avail·abil·i·ty
avail·able
av·a·lanche
avant-garde
av·a·rice
av·a·ri·cious
avenge
aveng·er
av·e·nue
aver
averred
aver·ring
av·er·age
averse
reluctant (*see* adverse)
aver·sion
avert
avi·an
avi·ary

avi·a·tion
avi·a·tor
avi·a·trix
av·id
avid·ity
av·id·ly
av·o·ca·do
av·o·ca·tion
avoid
avoid·able
avoid·ance
av·oir·du·pois
avow
avow·al
avun·cu·lar
await
awake
  awoke
  awak·en
award
aware
aware·ness
awash
away
  from this place
aweigh
  raised
awe·some
awe·strick·en
  or awe·struck
aw·ful
  objectionable (*see* offal)
aw·ful·ly
awhile
awhirl
awk·ward
awk·ward·ness
awl
  tool (*see* all)
aw·ning
awry
ax
  or axe
ax·i·al
  or ax·al
ax·i·om
ax·i·om·at·ic
ax·is
  pl ax·es
ax·le
axle·tree
aza·lea
az·i·muth
Az·tec
azure

B

bab·bitt
bab·ble
ba·bel
ba·boon
ba·bush·ka
ba·by
ba·by-sit
ba·by-sit·ter
bac·ca·lau·re·ate
bac·ca·rat
bac·cha·nal
bac·cha·na·lia
bac·cha·na·lian
bach·e·lor
ba·cil·lus
  pl ba·cil·li
back·ache
back-bench·er
back·bite
back·bit·er
back·board
back·bone
back·drop
back·er
back·field
back·fire
back·gam·mon
back·ground
back·hand
back·hand·ed
back·ing
back·lash
back·log
back·rest
back·side
back·slap
back·slap·per
back·slide
back·slid·er
back·spin
back·stage
back·stairs
back·stop
back·stretch
back·stroke
back talk

back·track

back·up
noun

back·ward
or back·wards

back·ward·ness

back·wash

back·wa·ter

back·woods

ba·con

bac·te·ri·al

bac·te·ri·cid·al

bac·te·ri·o·log·ic
or bac·te·ri·o·log·i·cal

bac·te·ri·ol·o·gist

bac·te·ri·ol·o·gy

bac·te·ri·um
pl bac·te·ria

badge

bad·ger

ba·di·nage

bad·land

bad·min·ton

bad·ness

Bae·de·ker

baf·fle

bag
bagged
bag·ging

bag·a·telle

ba·gel

bag·gage

bag·gy

ba·gnio
pl ba·gnios

bag·pipe

ba·guette

Ba·ha·ma

Bah·rain
or Bah·rein

baht
pl bahts *or* baht

bail
security (*see* bale)

bai·liff

bai·li·wick

bails·man

bait
lure (*see* bate)

bai·za

baize

bak·er

bak·er's doz·en

bak·ery

bak·sheesh

bal·a·lai·ka

bal·ance

bal·boa

bal·brig·gan

bal·co·ny

bal·da·chin
or bal·da·chi·no

bal·der·dash

bald·ness

bale
bundle (*see* bail)

bal·er

bale·ful

balk

Bal·kan

balky

ball
rounded body (*see* bawl)

bal·lad

bal·last

ball·car·ri·er

bal·le·ri·na

bal·let

bal·let·o·mane

bal·lis·tic

bal·lis·tics

bal·loon

bal·loon·ist

bal·lot

ball-point pen

ball·room

bal·ly·hoo
pl bal·ly·hoos

balmy

bal·sa

bal·sam

Bal·tic

Bal·ti·more

bal·us·ter

bal·us·trade

bam·boo

bam·boo·zle

ban
prohibit (*see* band)
banned
ban·ning

ban
pl ba·ni
coin

ba·nal

ba·nal·i·ty

ba·nana

band
strip (*see* ban)

ban·dage

ban·dan·na
or ban·dana

band box

ban·de·role
or ban·de·rol

ban·dit

ban·dit·ry

band·mas·ter

ban·do·lier
or ban·do·leer

band·stand

band·wag·on

ban·dy

bane·ful

Ban·gla·desh

ban·gle

bang·tail

bang-up
adj

bang up
verb

ban·ish

ban·ish·ment

ban·is·ter
also ban·nis·ter

ban·jo
pl ban·jos

ban·jo·ist

bank·book

bank·er

bank·roll

bank·rupt

bank·rupt·cy

ban·ner

ban·nock

banns
marriage

ban·quet

ban·quette

ban·shee

ban·tam

ban·ter

Ban·tu

Ban·tu·stan

ban·yan

ban·zai

bao·bab

bap·tism

bap·tis·mal

Bap·tist

bap·tis·tery
or bap·tis·try

bap·tize

bar
exclude (*see* bard)
barred
bar·ring

Bar·ba·di·an

Bar·ba·dos

bar·bar·ian

bar·bar·ic

bar·ba·rism

bar·bar·i·ty

bar·ba·rous

bar·be·cue

bar·bell

bar·ber

bar·ber·shop

bar·ber·ry

bar·bi·tal

bar·bi·tu·rate

bar·ca·role
or bar·ca·rolle

bard
poet (*see* bar)

bare
naked (*see* bear)

bare·back
or bare·backed

bare·faced

bare·foot
or bare·foot·ed

bare-hand·ed

bare·head·ed

bare·ly

bar·gain

barge·man

bari·tone

bar·i·um

bar·keep·er

bark·er

bar·ley

bar·maid

bar·man

bar mitz·vah

bar·na·cle

barn·storm

barn·yard

baro·graph

ba·rom·e·ter

baro·met·ric

bar·on
a noble (*see* barren)

bar·on·age

bar·on·ess

bar·on·et

bar·on·et·cy

ba·ro·ni·al

bar·ony

ba·roque

ba·rouche

bar·rack

bar·ra·cu·da

bar·rage

bar·ra·try

bar·rel

bar·ren
sterile (*see* baron)

bar·ren·ness

bar·rette

bar·ri·cade

bar·ri·er

bar·ris·ter

bar·room

bar·row

bar·tend·er

bar·ter

bas·al

ba·salt

ba·sal·tic

base
foundation (*see* bass)

base·ball

base·board

base·born

base·less

base·ly

base·ment

base·ness

base·run·ning

bash·ful

bash·ful·ness

ba·sic

ba·si·cal·ly

ba·sil

ba·sil·i·ca

bas·i·lisk

ba·sin

ba·sis
pl ba·ses

bask

bas·ket

bas·ket·ball

bas·ket·work

bas mitz·vah

Basque

bas-re·lief

bass
fish, deep voice (*see* base)

bas·si·net

bas·so
pl bas·sos *or* bas·si

bas·soon

bass·wood

bas·tard

bas·tard·ize

baste

bas·tion

bas·tioned

bat
bat·ted
bat·ting

batch

bate
restrain (*see* bait)

ba·teau
pl ba·teaux

bath

bathe

bath·er

ba·thet·ic

bath·house

ba·thos

bath·robe

bath·room

bath·tub

bathy·scaphe
also bathy·scaph

bathy·sphere

ba·tik

ba·tiste

bat·man

ba·ton

Bat·on Rouge

bats·man

bat·tal·ion

bat·ten

bat·ter

bat·tery

bat·ting

bat·tle

bat·tle-ax

bat·tle·field

bat·tle·ment

bat•tle•ship

bau•ble

baux•ite

Ba•var•i•an

bawd•i•ly

bawd•i•ness

bawdy

bawl
cry (*see* ball)

bay•ber•ry

bay•o•net
bay•o•net•ed
also bay•o•net•ted
bay•o•net•ing
also bay•o•net•ting

bay•ou

ba•zaar
marketplace (*see* bizarre)

ba•zoo•ka

beach
shore (*see* beech)

beach•comb•er

beach•head

bea•con

bead

bead•ing

bea•dle

beady

bea•gle

bea•ker

bean•ie

bear
animal, carry (*see* bare, born)
bore
borne
also born
bear•ing

bear•able

beard•less

bear•er

bear•ish

bé•ar•naise sauce

bear•skin

beast•ly

beat
to strike (*see* beet)
beat
beat•en
or beat
beat•ing

be•atif•ic

be•at•i•fi•ca•tion

be•at•i•fy

be•at•i•tude

beat•nik

beau
pl beaux *or* beaus
suitor (*see* bow)

Beau•jo•lais

beau monde

Beau•mont

beau•te•ous

beau•ti•cian

beau•ti•fi•ca•tion

beau•ti•fi•er

beau•ti•ful

beau•ti•ful•ly

beau•ti•fy

beau•ty

bea•ver

be•calm

be•cause

beck•on

be•cloud

be•come
be•came
be•come
be•com•ing

be•com•ing•ly

bed
bed•ded
bed•ding

be•daz•zle

be•daz•zle•ment

bed•bug

bed•clothes

bed•ding

be•deck

be•dev•il

bed•fel•low

bed•lam

bed•ou•in
or bed•u•in

be•drag•gled

bed•rid•den
or bed•rid

bed•rock

bed•roll

bed•room

bed•side

bed·sore
bed·spread
bed·stead
bed·time
beech
tree (*see* beach)
beech·nut
beef
pl beefs *or* beeves
beef·steak
beefy
bee·hive
bee·keep·er
bee·keep·ing
bee·line
beer
beverage (*see* bier)
beery
bees·wax
beet
vegetable (*see* beat)
bee·tle
be·fall
be·fell
be·fall·en
be·fit
be·fog
be·fore
be·fore·hand
be·friend
be·fud·dle
beg
begged
beg·ging
be·get
be·got
be·got·ten
or be·got
be·get·ting
beg·gar
beg·gar·ly
be·gin
be·gan
be·gun
be·gin·ning
be·gin·ner
be·gone
be·go·nia
be·grime
be·grudge
be·guile
be·guine
be·gum
be·half
be·have
be·hav·ior
be·hav·ior·al
be·hav·ior·ism
be·hav·ior·ist
be·head
be·he·moth
be·hest
be·hind
be·hind·hand
be·hold
be·held
be·hold·ing
be·hold·en
be·hold·er
be·hoove
or be·hove
be·hooved
or be·hoved
be·hoov·ing
or be·hov·ing
beige
be·ing
be·la·bor
be·lat·ed
be·lay
belch
be·lea·guer
bel·fry
Bel·gian
Bel·gium
be·lie
be·lied
be·ly·ing
be·lief
be·liev·able
be·lieve
be·liev·er
be·lit·tle
bel·la·don·na
bell·boy
belles let·tres
bell·hop
bel·li·cose
bel·li·cos·i·ty
bel·lig·er·ence
bel·lig·er·en·cy
bel·lig·er·ent
bel·low

bel·lows
bell·weth·er
bel·ly
be·long
be·long·ings
be·loved
be·low
belt·way
be·mire
be·moan
be·muse
bend
  bent
  bend·ing
ben·day
be·neath
ben·e·dict
bene·dic·tion
bene·fac·tion
bene·fac·tor
bene·fac·tress
ben·e·fice
be·nef·i·cence
be·nef·i·cent
ben·e·fi·cial
ben·e·fi·cial·ly
ben·e·fi·cia·ry
ben·e·fit
  ben·e·fit·ed
    or **ben·e·fit·ted**
  ben·e·fit·ing
    or **ben·e·fit·ting**
be·nev·o·lence
be·nev·o·lent
be·night·ed
be·nign
be·nig·nant
be·nig·ni·ty
be·nign·ly
ben·i·son
Be·nin
ben·thic
  or **ben·thal**
ben·thos
be·numb
Ben·ze·drine
ben·zene
ben·zine
ben·zo·ic acid
ben·zo·in
ben·zol
be·queath
be·queath·al
be·quest
be·rate
Ber·ber
ber·ceuse
be·reave
  be·reaved
    or **be·reft**
  be·reav·ing
be·reave·ment
be·ret
beri·beri
Berke·ley
Ber·mu·da
Ber·mu·di·an
  or **Ber·mu·dan**
ber·ry
  fruit (*see* **bury**)
ber·serk
berth
  distance, bed (*see* **birth**)
ber·yl
be·ryl·li·um
be·seech
  be·sought
    or **be·seeched**
  be·seech·ing
be·set
be·set·ting
be·side
be·sides
be·siege
be·sieg·er
be·smirch
be·sot·ted
bes·tial
bes·ti·al·i·ty
bes·ti·ary
be·stir
be·stow
bet
  bet
    also **bet·ted**
  bet·ting
be·ta
bête noire
  pl **bêtes noires**
be·tray
be·tray·al
be·tray·er
be·troth
be·troth·al

be·trothed

bet·ter
comp of good, well
(*see* bettor)

bet·ter·ment

bet·tor
or bet·ter
one that bets
(*see* better)

be·tween

be·twixt

bev·el

bev·eled
or bev·elled

bev·el·ing
or bev·el·ling

bev·er·age

bevy

be·wail

be·ware

be·wil·der

be·wil·der·ment

be·witch

be·yond

be·zel

bi·an·nu·al

bi·as

bi·ased
or bi·assed

bi·as·ing
or bi·as·sing

bi·be·lot

bi·ble

bib·li·cal

bib·li·og·ra·pher

bib·lio·graph·ic

bib·lio·graph·i·cal

bib·li·og·ra·phy

bib·lio·phile

bib·u·lous

bi·cam·er·al

bi·car·bon·ate

bi·cen·te·na·ry

bi·cen·ten·ni·al

bi·ceps

bi·chlo·ride

bick·er

bi·cus·pid

bi·cy·cle

bid

bade
or bid

bid·den
or bid *also* bade

bid·ding

bid·da·ble

bid·der

bide

bode
or bid·ed

bid·ed

bid·ing

bi·en·ni·al

bi·en·ni·al·ly

bi·en·ni·um
pl bi·en·ni·ums *or* bi·en·nia

bier
coffin stand (*see* beer)

bi·fo·cals

bi·fur·cate

bi·fur·ca·tion

big·a·mist

big·a·mous

big·a·my

big·horn

bight

big·ness

big·ot

big·ot·ed

big·ot·ry

big·wig

bi·jou
pl bi·joux

bike·way

bi·ki·ni

bi·lat·er·al

bi·lat·er·al·ly

bilge

bi·lin·gual

bil·ious

bill·board

bil·let

bil·let-doux
pl bil·lets-doux

bill·fold

bill·head

bil·liards

bill·ing

bil·lings·gate

bil·lion

bil·lionth

bil·low

bil·lowy

bil·ly

bil·ly goat

bi·met·al·lism

bi·month·ly

bi·na·ry
bin·au·ral
bind
  bound
  bind·ing
bind·er
binge
bin·na·cle
bin·oc·u·lar
bi·no·mi·al
bio·as·tro·nau·tics
bio·chem·i·cal
bio·chem·ist
bio·chem·is·try
bio·de·grad·abil·i·ty
bio·de·grad·able
bio·geo·graph·ic
bio·ge·og·ra·phy
bi·og·ra·pher
bio·graph·i·cal
bi·og·ra·phy
bi·o·log·i·cal
bi·ol·o·gist
bi·ol·o·gy
bio·med·i·cal
bio·med·i·cine
bi·on·ics
bio·phys·ics
bi·op·sy
bio·sphere
bio·syn·thet·ic
bio·syn·thet·i·cal·ly
bio·syn·the·sis
bi·ot·ic
bi·o·tin
bi·par·ti·san
bi·par·tite
bi·ped
bi·plane
bi·ra·cial
bird·bath
bird·house
bird·ie
bird·lime
bird·seed
bird's-eye
bi·ret·ta
Bir·ming·ham
birth
  nativity (*see* berth)
birth·day
birth·mark
birth·place
birth·rate
birth·right
birth·stone
bis·cuit
bi·sect
bi·sex·u·al
bish·op
bish·op·ric
Bis·marck
bis·muth
bi·son
  pl bi·son
bisque
bis·tro
  pl bis·tros
bitch
bite
  bit
  bit·ten
    also bit
  bit·ing
bit·ter
bit·tern
bit·ter·ness
bit·ter·sweet
bi·tu·men
bi·tu·mi·nous
bi·valve
  also bi·valved
biv·ouac
  biv·ouacked
  biv·ouack·ing
bi·week·ly
bi·zarre
  odd (*see* bazaar)
bi·zarre·ly
bi·zon·al
blab
  blabbed
  blab·bing
black·a·moor
black·ball
black·ber·ry
black·bird
black·board
black·en
black·guard
black·head
black·jack
black·list

black•mail
black•out
black•smith
black•thorn
black•top
blad•der
blame•less
blame•wor•thi•ness
blame•wor•thy
blanc•mange
blan•dish•ment
blan•ket
blar•ney
bla•sé
blas•pheme
blas•phe•mous
blas•phe•my
blast off
bla•tan•cy
bla•tant
blath•er
blaz•er
bla•zon
bleach•ers
bleak•ly
bleed
  bled
  bleed•ing
blem•ish
bless•ed•ness
blight
blind•fold
blink•er
blin•tze
  or blintz

bliss•ful
bliss•ful•ly
blis•ter
blithe•ly
blithe•some
blitz
blitz•krieg
bliz•zard
bloat•er
bloc
  group
block
  solid piece
block•ade
block•bust•er
block•head
block•house
blond
  or blonde
blood•cur•dling
blood•hound
blood•less
blood•mo•bile
blood•shed
blood•shot
blood•stain
blood•stone
blood•stream
blood•suck•er
blood•thirst•i•ly
blood•thirsty
bloody
bloop•er
blos•som

blot
  blot•ted
  blot•ting
blotch
blot•ter
blouse
blow-by-blow
blow•gun
blow•out
blow•pipe
blow•sy
  also blow•zy
blow•torch
blowy
blub•ber
blu•cher
blud•geon
blue•bell
blue•ber•ry
blue•bird
blue•fish
blue•grass
blue•nose
blue•point
blue•print
blue•stock•ing
blu•et
bluff•er
blu•ing
  or blue•ing
blu•ish
blun•der
blun•der•buss
blunt•ly
blunt•ness

blur
  blurred
  blur•ring
blur•ry
blus•ter
blus•tery
boa
boar
  animal (*see* bore)
board•er
  lodger (*see* border)
board•ing•house
board•walk
boast•ful
boast•ful•ly
boat hook
boat•man
boat•swain
  or bo•s'n *or* bo'•s'n *or* bo•sun *or* bo'•sun
bob
  bobbed
  bob•bing
bob•bin
bob•ble
bob•by-sox•er
bob•cat
bob•o•link
bob•sled
bob•white
boc•cie
  or boc•ci *or* boc•ce
bode
bod•ice
bodi•less
bodi•ly
bod•kin
body•guard
Boer
bog
  bogged
  bog•ging
bo•gey
  also bo•gy *or* bo•gie
  pl bo•geys *also* bo•gies
bo•gey•man
bo•gus
Bo•he•mi•an
boil•er
boil•er•mak•er
Boi•se
bois•ter•ous
bold•face
bold-faced
bold•ly
bold•ness
bo•le•ro
bo•li•var
  pl bo•li•vars *or* bo•li•va•res
Bo•liv•ia
Bo•liv•i•an
bo•lo
  pl bo•los
bo•lo•gna
Bol•she•vik
bol•she•vism
bol•ster
bo•lus
bom•bard
bom•bar•dier
bom•bard•ment
bom•bast
bom•bas•tic
bom•ba•zine
bomb•er
bomb•proof
bomb•shell
bomb•sight
bo•na fide
bo•nan•za
bon•bon
bond•age
bond•hold•er
bonds•man
bone•less
bon•er
bon•fire
bon•go
  pl bon•gos *also* bon•goes
bon•ho•mie
bo•ni•to
  pl bo•ni•tos *or* bo•ni•to
bon mot
  pl bons mots *or* bon mots
bon•net
bon•ny
bon•sai
  pl bon•sai
bo•nus
bon vi•vant
  pl bons vi•vants *or* bon vi•vants

bon voy·age

bony
or bon·ey

boo·by

boo·dle

book·case

book·end

book·ie

book·ish

book·keep·er

book·keep·ing

book·let

book·mak·er

book·mak·ing

book·mark

book·mo·bile

book·plate

book·sell·er

book·shelf

boo·mer·ang

boon·dog·gle

boor·ish

boost·er

boot·black

boo·tee
or boo·tie
baby's sock (*see* booty)

booth
pl booths

boot·leg

boo·ty
loot (*see* bootee)

booze

boozy

bo·rac·ic acid

bo·rax

bor·der
edge (*see* boarder)

bor·der·land

bor·der·line

bore
drill, tire (*see* boar)

bo·re·al

bore·dom

bor·er

bo·ric

born
given birth to (*see* bear)

bo·ron

bor·ough
town (*see* burro, burrow)

bor·row

borscht
or borsch

bo·s'n, bo'·s'n
var of boatswain

bo·som

boss·i·ness

bossy

Bos·ton

Bos·to·nian

bo·sun, bo'·sun
var of boatswain

bo·tan·i·cal

bot·a·nist

bot·a·ny

botch

both·er

both·er·some

Bo·tswa·na

bot·tle

bot·tle·neck

bot·tom

bot·tom·less

bot·u·lism

bou·doir

bouf·fant

bough
tree branch (*see* bow)

bought

bouil·lon
soup (*see* bullion)

boul·der

bou·le·vard

bounce

bounc·er

bound

bound·a·ry

bound·en

bound·less

boun·te·ous

boun·ti·ful

boun·ti·ful·ly

boun·ty

bou·quet

bour·bon

bour·geois
pl bour·geois

bour·geoi·sie

bourse

bou·tique

bou·ton·niere

bo·vine

bow
submit (*see* bough)

bow
knot (*see* beau)

bowd·ler·ize

bow·el

bow·er

bowl·ful

bow·legged

bowl·er
one that bowls

bow·ler
hat

bowl·ing

bow·man

bow·sprit

bow·string

box·car

box·er

box·ing

box·wood

boy
male child (*see* buoy)

boy·cott

boy·hood

boy·ish

boy·sen·ber·ry

brace·let

brack·en

brack·et

brack·ish

brag
bragged
brag·ging

brag·ga·do·cio

brag·gart

Brah·man
or Brah·min

braid

braille

brain·child

brain·less

brain·storm

brain·wash·ing

brainy

braise
cook (*see* braze)

brake
slow (*see* break)

brake·man

bram·ble

bran·dish

brand-new

bran·dy

bras·siere

brassy

bra·va·do
pl bra·va·does *or* bra·va·dos

brave·ly

brav·ery

bra·vo
pl bra·vos *or* bra·voes

bra·vu·ra

brawl

brawl·er

brawny

braze
solder (*see* braise)

bra·zen

bra·zen·ness

bra·zier

Bra·zil

Bra·zil·ian

breach
break (*see* breech)

bread·bas·ket

bread·board

breadth
width (*see* breath)

bread·win·ner

break
rupture (*see* brake)
broke
bro·ken
break·ing

break·able

break·age

break·down

break·er

break·fast

break·front

break·out

break·through

break·wa·ter

breast·bone

breast·plate

breast·stroke

breast·work

breath
air (*see* breadth)

breathe

breath·er

breath·less

breath·tak·ing

breech
trousers, rear part (*see* breach)

breed
bred
breed•ing

breed•er
breeze•way
breezy
breth•ren
bre•vet
bre•vet•ted
or brev•et•ed
bre•vet•ting
or brev•et•ing

bre•via•ry
brev•i•ty
brew•ery
brib•ery
bric-a-brac
brick•bat
brick•lay•er
brid•al
wedding (*see* bridle)

bride•groom
brides•maid
bridge•head
Bridge•port
bridge•work
bri•dle
restrain (*see* bridal)

brief•case
bri•er
or bri•ar

bri•gade
brig•a•dier
brig•and
brig•an•tine
bright•en
bright•ly
bright•ness
bril•liance
bril•lian•cy
bril•liant
bril•lian•tine
brim•ful
brim•stone
brin•dled
bring
brought
bring•ing

briny
bri•oche
bri•quette
or bri•quet

bris•ket
brisk•ly
bris•ling
or bris•tling
herring (*see* bristle)

bris•tle
stand erect (*see* brisling)
bris•tled
bris•tling

bris•tly
Brit•ain
country (*see* Briton)

Bri•tan•nic
Brit•ish
Brit•on
person (*see* Britain)

brit•tle
broach
to open (*see* brooch)

broad•band
broad•cast
broad•cast
also broad•cast•ed
broad•cast•ing

broad•cloth
broad•en
broad-mind•ed
broad•side
broad•sword
bro•cade
broc•co•li
or broc•o•li

bro•chette
bro•chure
bro•gan
brogue
broil•er
bro•ken
bro•ken•heart•ed
bro•ker
bro•ker•age
bro•mide
bro•mid•ic
bro•mine
bron•chi•al
bron•chi•tis
bron•chus
pl bron•chi

bron•co
pl bron•coes

brooch
ornament (see broach)

brood·er

brook·let

Brook·lyn

broom·stick

broth·el

broth·er

broth·er·hood

broth·er-in-law
pl broth·ers-in-law

broth·er·li·ness

broth·er·ly

brougham

brought

brou·ha·ha

brow·beat

brown·ie

brown·stone

browse

bru·in

bruise

bruis·er

bru·net
or bru·nette

brush-off

brush·wood

brusque
also brusk

brusque·ly

brus·sels sprout

bru·tal

bru·tal·i·ty

bru·tal·ly

brut·ish

bub·ble

bub·bly

bu·bon·ic

buc·ca·neer

buck·board

buck·et

buck·et·ful

buck·le

buck·ler

buck·ram

buck·saw

buck·shot

buck·skin

buck·wheat

bu·col·ic

bud
bud·ded
bud·ding

Bud·dha

Bud·dhism

Bud·dhist

bud·dy

budge

bud·get

Buf·fa·lo

buf·fa·lo
pl buf·fa·lo *or* buf·fa·loes

buff·er

buf·fet

buf·foon

buf·foon·ery

bug·a·boo

bug·bear

bug·gy

bu·gle

bu·gler

build
built
build·ing

build·er

build·ing

built-in

bul·bous

Bul·gar·ia

Bul·gar·i·an

bulge

bulg·ing

bulk·head

bulk·i·ly

bulk·i·ness

bulky

bull·dog

bull·doze

bull·doz·er

bul·let

bul·le·tin

bul·let·proof

bull·fight

bull·finch

bull·frog

bull·head·ed

bul·lion
precious metal (see bouillon)

bull·ish

bul·lock

bul·ly

bul·rush
also bull·rush

bul·wark

bum
bummed
bum·ming

bum·ble·bee

bump·er

bump·kin

bump·tious

bumpy

bun·co
or bun·ko
pl bun·cos *or* bun·kos

bun·dle

bun·ga·low

bung·hole

bun·gle

bun·gler

bun·ion

bun·ker

bun·kum
or bun·combe

bun·ting

buoy
float (*see* boy)

buoy·an·cy

buoy·ant

buq·sha

bur·den

bur·den·some

bur·dock

bu·reau
pl bu·reaus *also* bu·reaux

bu·reau·cra·cy

bu·reau·crat

bu·reau·crat·ic

bur·geon

bur·gess

bur·gher

bur·glar

bur·glar·ize

bur·gla·ry

bur·go·mas·ter

Bur·gun·dy

buri·al

bur·lap

bur·lesque

bur·ly

Bur·ma

Bur·man

Bur·mese

burn
burned
or burnt
burn·ing

burn·er

bur·nish

bur·noose
or bur·nous

burn·out

burr

bur·ro
donkey (*see* burrow, borough)

bur·row
hole (*see* burro, borough)

bur·sar

bur·si·tis

burst
burst
or burst·ed
burst·ing

Bu·run·di

Bu·run·di·an

bury
to inter (*see* berry)

bus
pl bus·es *or* bus·ses
vehicle (*see* buss)

bus·boy

bus·by

bush·el

bush·ing

bush·whack

busi·ly

busi·ness

busi·ness·man

bus·ing
or bus·sing

bus·kin

buss
kiss (*see* bus)

bus·tle

busy

busy·body

but
conj, prep (*see* butt)

butch·er

butch·ery

but·ler

butt
strike (*see* but)

but·ter

but·ter·cup

but·ter·fat
but·ter·fin·gered
but·ter·fin·gers
but·ter·fly
but·ter·milk
but·ter·nut
but·ter·scotch
but·tery
but·tocks
but·ton
but·ton·hole
but·ton·hook
but·tress
bu·tut
bux·om
buy
  bought
  buy·ing
buy·er
buz·zard
buzz·er
by·gone
by·law
  or bye·law
by-line
by·pass
by·path
by·play
by-prod·uct
by·stand·er
byte
by·way
by·word
Byz·an·tine

C

ca·bal
  ca·balled
  ca·bal·ling
ca·bana
cab·a·ret
cab·bage
cab·by
  or cab·bie
cab·in
cab·i·net
cab·i·net·mak·er
cab·i·net·mak·ing
cab·i·net·work
ca·ble
ca·ble·gram
cab·man
cab·o·chon
ca·boose
cab·ri·o·let
cab·stand
ca·cao
  pl ca·caos
cache
ca·chet
cack·le
ca·coph·o·nous
ca·coph·o·ny
cac·tus
  pl cac·ti *or* cac·tus·es
ca·dav·er
ca·dav·er·ous
cad·die
  or cad·dy
  golf (*see* caddy)
cad·dish
cad·dish·ness
cad·dy
  small box (*see* caddie)
ca·dence
ca·den·za
ca·det
cadge
cad·mi·um
cad·re
ca·du·ceus
  pl ca·du·cei
Cae·sar
cae·su·ra
ca·fé
  also ca·fe
ca·fé au lait
caf·e·te·ria
caf·feine
caf·tan
ca·gey
  also ca·gy
ca·gi·ly
ca·gi·ness
  also ca·gey·ness
ca·hoot
cais·son
cai·tiff
ca·jole
ca·jole·ment
ca·jol·ery

Ca·jun
also Ca·jan

cal·a·bash

cal·a·boose

cal·a·mine

ca·lam·i·tous

ca·lam·i·ty

cal·car·e·ous

cal·ci·fi·ca·tion

cal·ci·fy

cal·ci·mine

cal·ci·na·tion

cal·cine

cal·ci·um

cal·cu·la·ble

cal·cu·late

cal·cu·lat·ing

cal·cu·la·tion

cal·cu·la·tor

cal·cu·lus

cal·dron
or caul·dron

cal·en·dar
time (*see* calender)

cal·en·der
press (*see* calendar)

cal·ends

calf
pl calves *also* calfs

calf·skin

Cal·ga·ry

cal·i·ber
or cal·i·bre

cal·i·brate

cal·i·bra·tion

cal·i·co
pl cal·i·coes *or* cal·i·cos

Cal·i·for·nia

cal·i·per
or cal·li·per

ca·liph
or ca·lif

ca·liph·ate

cal·is·then·ics

calk

cal·la

call·back

call-board

call·er

cal·lig·ra·pher

cal·lig·ra·phy

call·ing

cal·li·o·pe

cal·lous
unfeeling (*see* callus)

cal·low

cal·lus
skin (*see* callous)

calm·ly

cal·o·mel

ca·lo·ric

cal·o·rie
also cal·o·ry

cal·o·rim·e·ter

cal·u·met

ca·lum·ni·ate

ca·lum·ni·a·tion

ca·lum·ni·a·tor

ca·lum·ni·ous

cal·um·ny

calve

Cal·vin·ism

Cal·vin·is·tic

ca·lyp·so

ca·lyx

ca·ma·ra·de·rie

cam·ber

cam·bi·um

Cam·bo·dia

Cam·bo·di·an

cam·bric

Cam·bridge

Cam·den

cam·el

ca·mel·lia
also ca·me·lia

Cam·em·bert

cam·eo
pl cam·eos

cam·era

Cam·er·oon

Cam·er·oo·nian

cam·i·sole

cam·o·mile
var of chamomile

cam·ou·flage

cam·paign

cam·pa·nile

camp·er

cam·phor

cam·phor·ate

camp·o·ree

camp·stool

cam·pus

cam·shaft

can
  canned
  can•ning
Can•a•da
Ca•na•di•an
ca•naille
ca•nal
can•a•li•za•tion
can•a•lize
can•a•pé
  food (*see* canopy)
ca•nard
ca•nary
ca•nas•ta
can•can
can•cel
  can•celed
    or can•celled
  can•cel•ing
    or can•cel•ling
can•cel•la•tion
  also can•cel•ation
can•cel•lous
can•cer
can•cer•ous
can•de•la•bra
can•de•la•brum
  pl can•de•la•bra *also* can•de•la•brums
can•des•cence
can•des•cent
can•did
candi•da•cy
can•di•date
can•died
can•dle
can•dle•light
Can•dle•mas
can•dle•pin
can•dle•stick
can•dle•wick
can•dor
can•dy
cane•brake
ca•nine
can•is•ter
  also can•nis•ter
can•ker
can•ker•ous
can•ker•worm
can•nel coal
can•nery
can•ni•bal
can•ni•bal•ism
can•ni•bal•is•tic
can•ni•bal•ize
can•ni•ly
can•ni•ness
can•non
  gun (*see* canon)
can•non•ade
can•non•ball
can•non•eer
can•not
can•ny
ca•noe
can•on
  principle (*see* cannon)
ca•non•i•cal
can•on•iza•tion
can•on•ize
can•o•py
  shelter (*see* canapé)
can•ta•bi•le
can•ta•loupe
can•tan•ker•ous
can•ta•ta
can•teen
can•ter
  gallop (*see* cantor)
can•ti•cle
can•ti•le•ver
can•to
  pl can•tos
Can•ton
can•ton
can•ton•al
can•ton•ment
can•tor
  singer (*see* canter)
can•vas
  also can•vass
  cloth (*see* canvass)
can•vas•back
can•vass
  also can•vas
  solicit (*see* canvas)
can•yon
caou•tchouc
cap
  capped
  cap•ping
ca•pa•bil•i•ty
ca•pa•ble
ca•pa•bly

ca·pa·cious
ca·pac·i·tance
ca·pac·i·tor
ca·pac·i·ty
ca·par·i·son
ca·per
cape·skin
Cape Verde
cap·il·lar·i·ty
cap·il·lary
cap·i·tal
city, wealth (*see* capitol)
cap·i·tal·ism
cap·i·tal·ist
cap·i·tal·is·tic
cap·i·tal·is·ti·cal·ly
cap·i·tal·iza·tion
cap·i·tal·ize
cap·i·tal·ly
cap·i·ta·tion
cap·i·tol
building (*see* capital)
ca·pit·u·late
ca·pit·u·la·tion
ca·pon
ca·pric·cio
pl ca·pric·cios
ca·price
ca·pri·cious
cap·ri·ole
cap·size
cap·stan
cap·su·lar
cap·su·late
or cap·su·lat·ed
cap·sule
cap·tain
cap·tain·cy
cap·tion
cap·tious
cap·ti·vate
cap·ti·va·tion
cap·tive
cap·tiv·i·ty
cap·tor
cap·ture
Cap·u·chin
car·a·bao
car·a·cole
ca·rafe
car·a·mel
car·a·pace
car·at
weight (*see* caret, carrot, karat)
car·a·van
car·a·van·sa·ry
or car·a·van·se·rai
car·a·vel
car·a·way
car·bide
car·bine
car·bo·hy·drate
car·bol·ic acid
car·bon
car·bon·ate
car·bon·ation
car·bon·ic
car·bon·if·er·ous
car·bon·iza·tion
car·bon·ize
Car·bo·run·dum
car·boy
car·bun·cle
car·bu·re·tor
car·cass
car·cin·o·gen
car·cin·o·gen·ic
car·ci·no·ma
car·da·mom
card·board
card-car·ry·ing
car·di·ac
car·di·gan
car·di·nal
car·di·nal·i·ty
car·dio·gram
car·dio·graph
car·di·og·ra·phy
car·di·ol·o·gy
car·dio·vas·cu·lar
ca·reen
ca·reer
care·free
care·ful
care·ful·ly
care·less
ca·ress
car·et
insert mark (*see* carat, carrot, karat)
care·tak·er
care·worn
car·fare

car•go
pl car•goes *or* car•gos

car•hop

Ca•rib•be•an

car•i•bou

car•i•ca•ture

car•i•ca•tur•ist

car•ies

car•il•lon

car•load

car•mi•na•tive

car•mine

car•nage

car•nal

car•nal•i•ty

car•nal•ly

car•na•tion

car•nau•ba

car•ne•lian

car•ni•val

car•ni•vore

car•niv•o•rous

car•ol
song (*see* carrel)

car•om

car•o•tene

ca•rot•id

ca•rous•al
revel (*see* carousel)

ca•rouse

ca•rou•sel
or car•rou•sel
merry-go-round (*see* carousal)

car•pel

car•pen•ter

car•pen•try

car•pet

car•pet•bag

car•pet•bag•ger

car•pet•ing

car•port

car•rel
library study (*see* carol)

car•riage

car•ri•er

car•ri•on

car•rot
vegetable (*see* carat, caret, karat)

car•rou•sel
var of carousel

car•ry

car•ry•all

car•ry•on

car•ry-over

car•sick

Car•son City

cart•age

carte blanche

car•tel

car•ti•lage

car•ti•lag•i•nous

car•to•gram

car•tog•ra•pher

car•to•graph•ic

car•tog•ra•phy

car•ton

car•toon

car•toon•ist

car•tridge

cart•wheel

carv•er

carv•ing

cary•at•id
pl cary•at•ids *or* cary•at•i•des

ca•sa•ba

cas•cade

cas•cara

ca•sein

case•ment

ca•shew

cash•ier

cash•mere

cas•ing

ca•si•no
also cas•si•no
pl ca•si•nos *also* cas•si•nos

cas•ket

cas•sa•va

cas•se•role

cas•sette
or ca•sette

cas•sia

cas•sock

cast
throw (*see* caste)
cast
cast•ing

cas•ta•net

cast•away

caste
class (*see* cast)

cas•tel•lat•ed

cast·er
or cas·tor

cas·ti·gate

cas·ti·ga·tion

cast·ing

cast iron

cas·tle

cast-off
adj

cast·off
noun

cas·tor

cas·trate

cas·tra·tion

ca·su·al

ca·su·al·ly

ca·su·al·ty

ca·su·ist

ca·su·is·tic

ca·su·is·ti·cal

ca·su·ist·ry

ca·sus bel·li

cat·a·clysm

cat·a·clys·mal
or cat·a·clys·mic

cat·a·comb

cat·a·falque

Cat·a·lan

cat·a·lep·sy

cat·a·lep·tic

cat·a·log
or cat·a·logue

cat·a·log·er
or cat·a·logu·er

ca·tal·pa

ca·tal·y·sis

cat·a·lyst

cat·a·ma·ran

cat·a·pult

cat·a·ract

ca·tarrh

ca·tarrh·al

ca·tas·tro·phe

cat·a·stroph·ic

cat·call

catch
caught
catch·ing

catch·all

catch·er

catch·ing

catch·ment

catch·pen·ny

catch·word

catchy

cat·e·chism

cat·e·chist

cat·e·chize

cat·e·chu·men

cat·e·gor·i·cal
also cat·e·gor·ic

cat·e·gor·i·cal·ly

cat·e·go·rize

cat·e·go·ry

ca·ter

cat·er·cor·ner
or cat·er-cor·nered
or cat·ty-cor·ner
or cat·ty-cor·nered
or kit·ty-cor·ner
or kit·ty-cor·nered

ca·ter·er

cat·er·pil·lar

cat·er·waul

cat·fish

cat·gut

ca·thar·sis

ca·thar·tic

ca·the·dral

cath·e·ter

cath·ode

ca·thod·ic

cath·o·lic

Ca·thol·i·cism

cath·o·lic·i·ty

cat·ion

cat·kin

cat·like

cat·nap

cat·nip

cat-o'-nine-tails
pl cat-o'-nine-tails

cat's-paw

cat·sup
or ketch·up

cat·tail

cat·ti·ly

cat·ti·ness

cat·tle

cat·ty

cat·ty-cor·ner
or cat·ty-cor·nered
var of catercorner

cat·walk

Cau·ca·sian

Cau·ca·soid

cau·cus
cau·dal
caul·dron
var of caldron
cau·li·flow·er
caulk
or calk
caus·al
cau·sal·i·ty
caus·al·ly
cau·sa·tion
caus·ative
cause cé·lè·bre
pl causes cé·lè·bres
cau·se·rie
cause·way
caus·tic
caus·ti·cal·ly
cau·ter·i·za·tion
cau·ter·ize
cau·tion
cau·tion·ary
cau·tious
cav·al·cade
cav·a·lier
cav·al·ry
cav·al·ry·man
ca·ve·at
cave-in
cave·man
cav·ern
cav·ern·ous
cav·i·ar
or cav·i·are
cav·il
cav·iled
or cav·illed
cav·il·ing
or cav·il·ling
cav·i·ty
ca·vort
ca·vy
cay·enne
cay·use
cease-fire
cease·less
ce·cum
pl ce·ca
ce·dar
Ce·dar Rap·ids
ce·di
ce·dil·la
ceil·ing
cel·an·dine
cel·e·brant
cel·e·brate
cel·e·brat·ed
cel·e·bra·tion
ce·leb·ri·ty
ce·ler·i·ty
cel·ery
ce·les·ta
ce·les·tial
ce·li·ac
cel·i·ba·cy
cel·i·bate
cel·lar
cel·lar·age
cel·lar·ette
or cel·lar·et
cel·list
cel·lo
cel·lo·phane
cel·lu·lar
cel·lu·loid
cel·lu·lose
Cel·sius
Celt·ic
cem·ba·lo
pl cem·ba·li
or cem·ba·los
ce·ment
ce·men·ta·tion
cem·e·tery
cen·o·bite
cen·o·bit·ic
ceno·taph
cen·ser
vessel (*see* censor)
cen·sor
suppressor (*see* censer)
cen·so·ri·al
cen·so·ri·ous
cen·sor·ship
cen·sur·able
cen·sure
cen·sur·er
cen·sus
cent
coin (*see* send)
cen·taur
cen·ta·vo
cen·te·nar·i·an
cen·te·na·ry
cen·ten·ni·al

cen·ten·ni·al·ly
cen·ter
cen·ter·board
cen·ter·piece
cen·tes·i·mal
cen·tes·i·mo
pl cen·tes·i·mi
cen·ti·grade
cen·ti·gram
cen·time
cen·ti·me·ter
cen·ti·mo
cen·ti·pede
cen·tral
cen·tral·iza·tion
cen·tral·ize
cen·trif·u·gal
cen·tri·fuge
cen·trip·e·tal
cen·trist
cen·tu·ri·on
cen·tu·ry
ce·phal·ic
ce·ram·ic
ce·ra·mist
or ce·ram·i·cist
ce·re·al
grain (*see* serial)
cer·e·bel·lum
ce·re·bral
cer·e·brate
cer·e·bra·tion
ce·re·brum
cer·e·mo·ni·al
cer·e·mo·ni·al·ly
cer·e·mo·ni·ous
cer·e·mo·ny
ce·rise
ce·ri·um
cer·met
cer·tain
cer·tain·ly
cer·tain·ty
cer·tif·i·cate
cer·ti·fi·ca·tion
cer·ti·fy
cer·ti·tude
ce·ru·le·an
cer·vi·cal
cer·vix
pl cer·vi·ces
ce·sar·e·an
also ce·sar·i·an
ce·si·um
ces·sa·tion
ces·sion
a yielding (*see* session)
cess·pool
ces·ta
Cha·blis
cha-cha
Chad
Chad·ian
chafe
rub (*see* chaff)
chaff
husks (*see* chafe)
chaf·finch
chaf·ing
cha·grin
cha·grined
cha·grin·ing
chain-re·act
chair·man
chaise longue
chal·ced·o·ny
cha·let
chal·ice
chalk·board
chalky
chal·lenge
chal·lis
cham·ber
cham·ber·lain
cham·ber·maid
cham·bray
cha·me·leon
cham·fer
cham·ois
also cham·my
or sham·my
cham·o·mile
or cam·o·mile
cham·pagne
wine (*see* champaign)
cham·paign
open country (*see* champagne)
cham·pi·on
cham·pi·on·ship
chan·cel
chan·cel·lery
or chan·cel·lory
chan·cel·lor
chan·cery

chan•cre
chancy
chan•de•lier
chan•dler
change•able
change•ful
change•less
change•ling
chang•er
chan•nel
chan•neled
or **chan•nelled**
chan•nel•ing
or **chan•nel•ling**
chan•nel•iza•tion
chan•nel•ize
chan•son
chan•teuse
chan•tey
or **chan•ty**
chan•ti•cleer
chan•try
Cha•nu•kah
var of Hanukkah
cha•os
cha•ot•ic
cha•ot•i•cal•ly
chap
chapped
chap•ping
chap•book
chap•el
chap•er•on
or **chap•er•one**
chap•fall•en
chap•lain
chap•let
chap•ter
char
charred
char•ring
char•ac•ter
char•ac•ter•is•tic
char•ac•ter•is•ti•cal•ly
char•ac•ter•iza•tion
char•ac•ter•ize
cha•rade
char•coal
charge•able
charge-a-plate
or **charge plate**
char•gé d'af•faires
pl **char•gés d'af•faires**
char•ger
cha•ri•ly
char•i•ness
char•i•ot
char•i•o•teer
cha•ris•ma
char•is•mat•ic
char•i•ta•ble
char•i•ty
char•la•tan
Charles•ton
char•ley horse
Char•lotte
charm•er
charm•ing
char•nel
char•ter
char•treuse
char•wom•an
chary
chase
pursue (*see* chaste)
chased
chas•ing
chas•er
chasm
chas•sis
chaste
virtuous (*see* chase)
chas•ten
chas•tise
chas•tise•ment
chas•ti•ty
cha•su•ble
châ•teau
pl **châ•teaus** *or* **châ•teaux**
chat•e•laine
Chat•ta•noo•ga
chat•tel
chat•ter
chat•ter•box
chat•ty
chauf•feur
chau•vin•ism
chau•vin•ist
chau•vin•is•tic
chau•vin•is•ti•cal•ly
cheap
inexpensive (*see* cheep)

cheap·en
cheap·skate
cheat·er
check·book
check·er
check·er·board
check·ers
check·list
check·mate
check·off
check·out
check·point
check·room
check·up
ched·dar
cheek·bone
cheek·i·ly
cheek·i·ness
cheeky
cheep
peep (*see* cheap)
cheer·ful
cheer·ful·ly
cheer·i·ly
cheer·i·ness
cheer·lead·er
cheer·less
cheery
cheese·burg·er
cheese·cake
cheese·cloth
cheesy
chee·tah
chef d'oeu·vre
pl chefs d'oeu·vre

chem·i·cal
chem·i·cal·ly
che·mise
chem·ist
chem·is·try
che·mo·ther·a·py
chem·ur·gy
che·nille
cher·ish
che·root
cher·ry
cher·ub
pl cher·ubs *or* cher·u·bim
ches·ter·field
chest·nut
che·va·lier
chev·i·ot
chev·ron
chewy
Chey·enne
Chi·an·ti
chiao
pl chiao
coin (*see* ciao)
chiar·oscu·ro
chic
stylish (*see* chick)
Chi·ca·go
chi·ca·nery
chi·chi
chick
young bird (*see* chic)
chick·a·dee
chick·en
chick·en·heart·ed

chick·weed
chic·o·ry
chide
chid
or chid·ed
chid
or chid·den *or* chid·ed
chid·ing
chief·ly
chief·tain
chif·fon
chif·fo·nier
chig·ger
chi·gnon
chil·blain
child
pl chil·dren
child·birth
child·hood
child·like
Chi·le
Chil·ean
chill·er
chill·i·ness
chilly
chi·me·ra
or chi·mae·ra
chi·me·ri·cal
chim·ney
chim·pan·zee
chin
chinned
chin·ning
Chi·na

chi·na
chin·chil·la
Chi·nese
chi·no
chintz
chip
  chipped
  chip·ping
chip·munk
chip·per
chi·rog·ra·pher
chi·ro·graph·ic
chi·rog·ra·phy
chi·ro·man·cy
chi·rop·o·dist
chi·rop·o·dy
chi·ro·prac·tic
chi·ro·prac·tor
chis·el
  chis·eled
    or **chis·elled**
  chis·el·ing
    or **chis·el·ling**
chis·el·er
chit·chat
chit·ter·lings
  or **chit·lings** *or* **chit·lins**
chi·val·ric
chiv·al·rous
chiv·al·ry
chlo·ral
chlor·dane
chlo·ric
chlo·ride
chlo·ri·nate
chlo·ri·na·tion
chlo·rine
chlo·ro·form
chlo·ro·phyll
chock·a·block
chock-full
choc·o·late
choir
  singers (*see* quire)
choir·boy
choir·mas·ter
cho·ler
chol·era
cho·ler·ic
cho·les·ter·ol
chon
  pl **chon**
choose
  chose
  cho·sen
  choos·ing
choos·er
choosy
  or **choos·ey**
chop
  chopped
  chop·ping
chop·house
chop·per
chop·pi·ly
chop·pi·ness
chop·py
chop·stick
chop su·ey
cho·ral
  of a choir (*see* chorale, coral)
cho·rale
  also **cho·ral**
  hymn (*see* choral, coral)
cho·ral·ly
chord
  music (*see* cord)
chore
cho·rea
cho·reo·graph
cho·re·og·ra·pher
cho·reo·graph·ic
cho·reo·graph·i·cal·ly
cho·re·og·ra·phy
cho·ris·ter
chor·tle
chorus
cho·sen
chow·chow
  relish (*see* chow chow)
chow chow
  dog (*see* chowchow)
chow·der
chow mein
chrism
chris·ten
Chris·ten·dom
chris·ten·ing
Chris·tian
chris·ti·ania
Chris·tian·i·ty

Chris·tian·ize

chris·tie
or chris·ty

Christ·mas

Christ·mas·tide

chro·mat·ic

chro·ma·tic·i·ty

chro·mato·graph·ic

chro·mato·graph·i·cal·ly

chro·ma·tog·ra·phy

chrome

chro·mic

chro·mite

chro·mi·um

chro·mo·som·al

chro·mo·some

chron·ic

chron·i·cal·ly

chron·i·cle

chron·i·cler

chro·no·graph

chro·no·log·i·cal

chro·nol·o·gist

chro·nol·o·gy

chro·nom·e·ter

chrys·a·lis

chry·san·the·mum

chrys·o·lite

chub·bi·ness

chub·by

chuck·hole

chuck·le

chug
chugged
chug·ging

chuk·ka
boot (*see* chukker)

chuk·ker
or chuk·kar
or chuk·ka
polo (*see* chukka)

chum
chummed
chum·ming

chum·mi·ness

chum·my

chunky

church·go·er

church·less

church·man

church·war·den

church·yard

churl

churl·ish

churn

chute
slide (*see* shoot)

chut·ney

chutz·pah
or chutz·pa

ciao
greeting (*see* chiao)

ci·ca·da

cic·a·trix
pl cic·a·tri·ces

ci·ce·ro·ne

ci·der

ci·gar

cig·a·rette
also cig·a·ret

cin·cho·na

Cin·cin·nati

cinc·ture

cin·der

cin·e·ma

cin·e·mat·ic

cin·e·mat·o·graph

cin·e·ma·tog·ra·pher

cin·e·mat·o·graph·ic

cin·e·ma·tog·ra·phy

cin·er·ar·i·um
pl cin·er·ar·ia

cin·na·bar

cin·na·mon

ci·pher

cir·ca

cir·cle

cir·clet

cir·cuit

cir·cu·itous

cir·cuit·ry

cir·cu·ity

cir·cu·lar

cir·cu·lar·i·ty

cir·cu·lar·iza·tion

cir·cu·lar·ize

cir·cu·late

cir·cu·la·tion

cir·cu·la·to·ry

cir·cum·am·bi·ent

cir·cum·am·bu·late

cir·cum·cise
cir·cum·ci·sion
cir·cum·fer·ence
cir·cum·flex
cir·cum·lo·cu·tion
cir·cum·lu·nar
cir·cum·nav·i·gate
cir·cum·nav·i·ga·tion
cir·cum·po·lar
cir·cum·scribe
cir·cum·scrip·tion
cir·cum·spect
cir·cum·spec·tion
cir·cum·stance
cir·cum·stan·tial
cir·cum·stan·tial·ly
cir·cum·vent
cir·cum·ven·tion
cir·cus
cir·rho·sis
cir·ro·cu·mu·lus
cir·ro·stra·tus
cir·rus
cis·lu·nar
cis·tern
cit·a·del
ci·ta·tion
cite
quote (*see* sight, site)
citi·fy
cit·i·zen
cit·i·zen·ry
cit·i·zen·ship
ci·trate
cit·ric acid
cit·ron
cit·ro·nel·la
cit·rus
city
city-state
civ·et
civ·ic
civ·ics
civ·il
ci·vil·ian
ci·vil·i·ty
civ·i·li·za·tion
civ·i·lize
civ·il·ly
claim·ant
clair·voy·ance
clair·voy·ant
clam·bake
clam·ber
clam·mi·ness
clam·my
clam·or
clam·or·ous
clam·shell
clan·des·tine
clan·gor
clan·gor·ous
clan·nish
clans·man
clap
clapped
also clapt
clap·ping
clap·board
clap·per
clap·trap
claque
clar·et
clar·i·fi·ca·tion
clar·i·fy
clar·i·net
clar·i·net·ist
clar·i·on
clar·i·ty
clas·sic
clas·si·cal
clas·si·cal·ly
clas·si·cism
clas·si·cist
clas·si·fi·able
clas·si·fi·ca·tion
clas·si·fy
clas·si·fied
clas·si·fy·ing
class·mate
class·room
clat·ter
clause
claus·tro·pho·bia
clav·i·chord
clav·i·cle
cla·vier
clay·ey
clay·more
clean-cut
clean·er
clean·li·ness
clean·ly

clean•ness
cleanse
cleans•er
clear•ance
clear-cut
clear•head•ed
clear•ing
clear•ing•house
cleav•age
cleave
cling
cleaved
or **clove**
also **clave**
cleav•ing

cleave
split
cleaved
also **cleft** *or* **clove**
cleaved
also **cleft** *or* **clo•ven**
cleav•ing

cleav•er
cle•ma•tis
clem•en•cy
clem•ent
clere•sto•ry
or **clear•sto•ry**

cler•gy
cler•gy•man
cler•ic
cler•i•cal
cler•i•cal•ism
Cleve•land
clev•er
clev•er•ness
clew
or **clue**

cli•ché
cli•ent
cli•en•tele
cliff-hang•er
cli•mac•tic
of a climax (*see* climatic)

cli•mate
cli•mat•ic
weather (*see* climactic)

cli•ma•to•log•i•cal
cli•ma•tol•o•gist
cli•ma•tol•o•gy
cli•max
climb•er
clinch•er
cling
clung
cling•ing

clin•ic
clin•i•cal
clin•i•cal•ly
cli•ni•cian
clin•ker
clip
clipped
clip•ping

clip•board
clip•per
clip•ping
clip•sheet
clique
cli•to•ral
or **cli•tor•ic**

cli•to•ris
cloche
clock•wise
clock•work
clod•hop•per
clog
clogged
clog•ging

cloi•son•né
clois•ter
closed-end
close•fist•ed
close•ly
close•mouthed
close•ness
clos•et
close-up
clo•sure
clot
clot•ted
clot•ting

cloth
fabric (*see* clothe)

clothe
to dress (*see* cloth)
clothed
or **clad**
cloth•ing

clothes•horse
clothes•line
clothes•pin
clothes•press
cloth•ier

clothing
clo•ture
cloud•burst
cloud•i•ness
clo•ver
clo•ver•leaf
pl clo•ver•leafs
or clo•ver•leaves
clown•ish
club
clubbed
club•bing
club•foot
club•house
clue
var of clew
clum•si•ly
clum•si•ness
clum•sy
clus•ter
clut•ter
coach•er
coach•man
co•ad•ju•tor
co•ag•u•lant
co•ag•u•late
co•ag•u•la•tion
co•ag•u•lum
pl co•ag•u•la
co•alesce
co•ales•cence
coal•field
co•ali•tion
coarse
rough (see course)

coars•en
coarse•ness
coast•al
coast•er
coast guard
coast•line
coat•ing
co•au•thor
co•ax•i•al
co•balt
cob•ble
cob•bler
cob•ble•stone
co•bra
cob•web
co•ca
co•caine
coc•cus
pl coc•ci
coc•cyx
pl coc•cy•ges *also*
coc•cyx•es
coch•i•neal
co•chlea
pl co•chle•as *or*
co•chle•ae
cock•ade
cock•a•too
cock•crow
cock•er•el
cock•eyed
cock•fight
cock•i•ly
cock•i•ness
cock•le
cock•le•shell

cock•ney
cock•pit
cock•roach
cock•sure
cock•tail
cocky
co•coa
co•co•nut
co•coon
co•da
cod•dle
co•deine
co•dex
pl co•di•ces
cod•fish
cod•ger
cod•i•cil
cod•i•fi•ca•tion
cod•i•fy
co•ed•u•ca•tion
co•ed•u•ca•tion•al
co•ef•fi•cient
co•equal
co•erce
co•er•cion
co•er•cive
co•eval
co•ex•ist
co•ex•is•tence
co•ex•ten•sive
cof•fee
cof•fee•house
cof•fee•pot
cof•fer
cof•fer•dam

cof·fin
co·gen·cy
co·gent
cog·i·tate
cog·i·ta·tion
co·gnac
cog·nate
cog·ni·tion
cog·ni·tive
cog·ni·zance
cog·ni·zant
cog·no·men
cog·wheel
co·hab·it
co·hab·i·ta·tion
co·heir
co·here
co·her·ence
co·her·ent
co·he·sion
co·he·sive
co·hort
coif·feur
coin·age
co·in·cide
co·in·ci·dence
co·in·ci·dent
co·in·ci·den·tal
co·ition
co·itus
co·la
col·an·der
cold-blood·ed
cold·ly
cold·ness
cole·slaw
col·ic
col·i·se·um
or col·os·se·um
arena (*see* Colosseum)
co·li·tis
col·lab·o·rate
col·lab·o·ra·tion
col·lab·o·ra·tor
col·lage
col·lapse
col·laps·ible
col·lar
col·lar·bone
col·lard
col·late
col·lat·er·al
col·la·tion
col·la·tor
col·league
col·lect
col·lect·ed
col·lect·ible
or col·lect·able
col·lec·tion
col·lec·tive
col·lec·tive·ly
col·lec·tiv·ism
col·lec·tiv·is·tic
col·lec·tiv·ize
col·lec·tor
col·leen
col·lege
col·le·gi·al·i·ty
col·le·gian
col·le·giate
col·le·gi·um
col·lide
col·lie
col·lier
col·liery
col·li·sion
col·lo·ca·tion
col·lo·di·on
col·loid
col·loi·dal
col·lo·qui·al
col·lo·qui·al·ism
col·lo·qui·um
col·lo·quy
col·lu·sion
col·lu·sive
co·logne
Co·lom·bia
Co·lom·bi·an
co·lon
biol, punctuation
co·lon
pl co·lo·nes
currency
col·o·nel
military (*see* kernel)
co·lo·ni·al
co·lo·nial·ism
col·o·nist
col·o·ni·za·tion
col·o·nize
col·o·niz·er
col·on·nade
col·o·ny

col·o·phon
col·or
Col·o·ra·do
col·or·ation
col·or·a·tu·ra
col·or-blind
col·or·cast
col·ored
col·or·fast
col·or·fast·ness
col·or·ful
col·or·less
co·los·sal
Col·os·se·um
or Col·i·se·um
amphitheater in Rome
(*see* coliseum)
co·los·sus
Co·lum·bia
col·um·bine
Co·lum·bus
col·umn
co·lum·nar
col·um·nist
co·ma
unconsciousness (*see* comma)
co·ma·tose
com·bat
com·bat·ant
com·bat·ive
comb·er
com·bi·na·tion
com·bine
comb·ings

com·bo
pl com·bos
com·bus·ti·ble
com·bus·tion
come
came
come
com·ing
come·back
co·me·di·an
co·me·di·enne
come·down
com·e·dy
come·li·ness
come·ly
come-on
co·mes·ti·ble
com·et
come·up·pance
com·fit
com·fort
com·fort·able
com·fort·ably
com·fort·er
com·ic
com·i·cal
com·i·ty
com·ma
punctuation (*see* coma)
com·mand
com·man·dant
com·man·deer
com·mand·er
com·mand·ment

com·man·do
pl com·man·dos *or* com·man·does
com·mem·o·rate
com·mem·o·ra·tion
com·mem·o·ra·tive
com·mence
com·mence·ment
com·mend
com·mend·able
com·men·da·tion
com·men·su·ra·bil·i·ty
com·men·su·ra·ble
com·men·su·rate
com·ment
com·men·tary
com·men·ta·tor
com·merce
com·mer·cial
com·mer·cial·ism
com·mer·cial·iza·tion
com·mer·cial·ize
com·mer·cial·ly
com·mi·na·tion
com·mi·na·to·ry
com·min·gle
com·mis·er·ate
com·mis·er·a·tion
com·mis·sar
com·mis·sar·i·at
com·mis·sary
com·mis·sion
com·mis·sion·er

com·mit
  com·mit·ted
  com·mit·ting
com·mit·ment
com·mit·tal
com·mit·tee
com·mit·tee·man
com·mit·tee·wom·an
com·mode
com·mo·di·ous
com·mod·i·ty
com·mo·dore
com·mon
com·mon·al·i·ty
  commonness
com·mon·al·ty
  common people
com·mon·er
com·mon·ly
com·mon·ness
com·mon·place
com·mon·weal
com·mon·wealth
com·mo·tion
com·mu·nal
com·mune
com·mu·ni·ca·ble
com·mu·ni·cant
com·mu·ni·cate
com·mu·ni·ca·tion
com·mu·ni·ca·tive
com·mu·nion
com·mu·ni·qué
com·mu·nism
com·mu·nist

com·mu·nis·tic
com·mu·nis·ti·cal·ly
com·mu·ni·ty
com·mu·nize
com·mut·able
com·mu·ta·tion
com·mu·ta·tive
com·mu·ta·tor
com·mute
com·mut·er
Com·o·ro
com·pact
com·pac·tor
  or **com·pact·er**
com·pan·ion
com·pan·ion·able
com·pan·ion·ship
com·pan·ion·way
com·pa·ny
com·pa·ra·ble
com·par·a·tive
com·par·a·tive·ly
com·pare
com·par·i·son
com·part·ment
com·part·men·tal·ize
com·pass
com·pas·sion
com·pas·sion·ate
com·pat·i·bil·i·ty
com·pat·i·ble
com·pa·tri·ot
com·peer

com·pel
  com·pelled
  com·pel·ling
com·pen·di·um
  pl **com·pen·di·ums** *or* **com·pen·dia**
com·pen·sate
com·pen·sa·tion
com·pen·sa·to·ry
com·pete
com·pe·tence
com·pe·ten·cy
com·pe·tent
com·pe·ti·tion
com·pet·i·tive
com·pet·i·tor
com·pi·la·tion
com·pile
com·pil·er
com·pla·cence
com·pla·cen·cy
com·pla·cent
  self-satisfied (*see* **complaisant**)
com·plain
com·plain·ant
com·plaint
com·plai·sance
com·plai·sant
  affable (*see* **complacent**)
com·ple·ment
  full quantity (*see* **compliment**)
com·ple·men·ta·ry
com·plete

com•plete•ness
com•ple•tion
com•plex
com•plex•ion
com•plex•i•ty
com•pli•ance
com•pli•an•cy
com•pli•ant
com•pli•cate
com•pli•cat•ed
com•pli•ca•tion
com•plic•i•ty
com•pli•er
com•pli•ment
flattery (*see* complement)
com•pli•men•ta•ry
com•ply
com•po•nent
com•port
com•port•ment
com•pose
com•posed
com•pos•er
com•pos•ite
com•po•si•tion
com•pos•i•tor
com•post
com•po•sure
com•pote
com•pound
com•pre•hend
com•pre•hen•si•ble
com•pre•hen•sion
com•pre•hen•sive
com•press
com•pressed
com•pres•sion
com•pres•sor
com•prise
com•pro•mise
comp•trol•ler
com•pul•sion
com•pul•sive
com•pul•so•ry
com•punc•tion
com•pu•ta•tion
com•pute
com•put•er
com•put•er•iz•able
com•put•er•iza•tion
com•put•er•ize
com•rade
con
conned
con•ning
con brio
con•cat•e•na•tion
con•cave
con•cav•i•ty
con•ceal
con•ceal•ment
con•cede
con•ceit
con•ceit•ed
con•ceiv•able
con•ceiv•ably
con•ceive
con•cel•e•brant
con•cen•trate
con•cen•tra•tion
con•cen•tric
con•cept
con•cep•tion
con•cep•tu•al
con•cep•tu•al•iza•tion
con•cep•tu•al•ize
con•cep•tu•al•ly
con•cern
con•cerned
con•cern•ing
con•cern•ment
con•cert
con•cert•ed
con•cer•ti•na
con•cert•mas•ter
or con•cert•meis•ter
con•cer•to
pl con•cer•ti *or* con•cer•tos
con•ces•sion
con•ces•sion•aire
con•ces•sive
conch
pl conchs *or* conch•es
con•cierge
con•cil•i•ate
con•cil•i•a•tion
con•cil•ia•to•ry
con•cise
con•cise•ness
con•ci•sion

con•clave
con•clude
con•clu•sion
con•clu•sive
con•coct
con•coc•tion
con•com•i•tant
con•cord
con•cor•dance
con•cor•dant
con•cor•dat
con•course
con•cres•cence
con•cres•cent
con•crete
con•cre•tion
con•cu•bi•nage
con•cu•bine
con•cu•pis•cence
con•cur
  con•curred
  con•cur•ring
con•cur•rence
con•cur•rent
con•cus•sion
con•demn
con•dem•na•tion
con•dem•na•to•ry
con•den•sa•tion
con•dense
con•dens•er
con•de•scend
con•de•scend•ing•ly
con•de•scen•sion
con•dign
con•di•ment
con•di•tion
con•di•tion•al
con•di•tioned
con•dole
con•do•lence
con•do•min•i•um
con•do•na•tion
con•done
con•dor
con•duce
con•du•cive
con•duct
con•duc•tance
con•duc•tion
con•duc•tive
con•duc•tiv•i•ty
con•duc•tor
con•duit
Con•es•to•ga
co•ney
con•fab•u•la•tion
con•fec•tion
con•fec•tion•er
con•fec•tion•ery
con•fed•er•a•cy
con•fed•er•ate
con•fed•er•a•tion
con•fer
  con•ferred
  con•fer•ring
con•fer•ee
con•fer•ence
con•fess
con•fessed•ly
con•fes•sion
con•fes•sion•al
con•fes•sor
con•fet•ti
con•fi•dant
  friend (*see* confident)
con•fide
con•fi•dence
con•fi•dent
  assured (*see* confidant)
con•fi•den•tial
con•fi•den•tial•ly
con•fid•ing
con•fig•u•ra•tion
con•fine
con•fine•ment
con•fin•er
con•firm
con•fir•ma•tion
con•fir•ma•to•ry
con•firmed
con•fis•cate
con•fis•ca•tion
con•fis•ca•to•ry
con•fla•gra•tion
con•flict
con•flu•ence
con•flu•ent
con•flux
con•form
con•form•able
con•for•mance

con•for•ma•tion
con•form•ist
con•for•mi•ty
con•found
con•fra•ter•ni•ty
con•frere
con•front
con•fron•ta•tion
Con•fu•cian•ism
con•fuse
con•fus•ed•ly
con•fu•sion
con•fu•ta•tion
con•fute
con•ga
con•geal
con•ge•nial
con•gen•i•tal
con•ger
con•ge•ries
con•gest
con•ges•tion
con•glom•er•ate
con•glom•er•a•tion
Con•go
Con•go•lese
con•grat•u•late
con•grat•u•la•tion
con•grat•u•la•to•ry
con•gre•gate
con•gre•ga•tion
con•gre•ga•tion•al
con•gre•ga•tion•al•ism
con•gre•ga•tion•al•ist
con•gress
con•gres•sio•nal
con•gress•man
con•gress•wom•an
con•gru•ence
con•gru•en•cy
con•gru•ent
con•gru•ity
con•gru•ous
con•ic
con•i•cal
co•ni•fer
co•nif•er•ous
con•jec•tur•al
con•jec•ture
con•join
con•joint
con•ju•gal
con•ju•gate
con•ju•ga•tion
con•junct
con•junc•tion
con•junc•tive
con•junc•ti•vi•tis
con•junc•ture
con•ju•ra•tion
con•jure
con•jur•er
or con•ju•ror
con•nect
Con•nect•i•cut
con•nec•tion
con•nec•tive
con•nec•tor
also con•nect•er
con•nip•tion
con•niv•ance
con•nive
con•nois•seur
con•no•ta•tion
con•no•ta•tive
con•note
con•nu•bi•al
con•quer
con•quer•or
con•quest
con•quis•ta•dor
pl con•quis•ta•do•res
or con•quis•ta•dors
con•san•guin•e•ous
con•san•guin•i•ty
con•science
con•sci•en•tious
con•scious
con•scious•ness
con•script
con•scrip•tion
con•se•crate
con•se•cra•tion
con•sec•u•tive
con•sen•sus
con•sent
con•se•quence
con•se•quent
con•se•quen•tial
con•se•quent•ly
con•ser•va•tion
con•ser•va•tion•ist

con•ser•va•tism
con•ser•va•tive
con•ser•va•tor
con•ser•va•to•ry
con•serve
con•sid•er
con•sid•er•able
con•sid•er•ably
con•sid•er•ate
con•sid•er•ation
con•sid•ered
con•sid•er•ing
con•sign
con•sign•ee
con•sign•ment
con•sign•or
con•sist
con•sis•tence
con•sis•ten•cy
con•sis•tent
con•sis•to•ry
con•so•la•tion
con•so•la•to•ry
con•sole
con•sol•i•date
con•sol•i•da•tion
con•som•mé
con•so•nance
con•so•nant
con•so•nan•tal
con•sort
con•sor•tium
con•spec•tus
con•spic•u•ous
con•spir•a•cy
con•spir•a•tor
con•spire
con•sta•ble
con•stab•u•lary
con•stan•cy
con•stant
con•stel•la•tion
con•ster•na•tion
con•sti•pate
con•sti•pa•tion
con•stit•u•en•cy
con•stit•u•ent
con•sti•tute
con•sti•tu•tion
con•sti•tu•tion•al
con•sti•tu•tion•al•i•
ty
con•sti•tu•tion•al•ly
con•sti•tu•tive
con•strain
con•straint
con•strict
con•stric•tion
con•stric•tive
con•stric•tor
con•struct
con•struc•tion
con•struc•tion•ist
con•struc•tive
con•struc•tor
con•strue
con•sub•stan•ti•a•
tion
con•sul
con•sul•ar
con•sul•ate
con•sult
con•sul•tant
con•sul•ta•tion
con•sul•ta•tive
con•sume
con•sum•er
con•sum•er•ism
con•sum•mate
con•sum•ma•tion
con•sump•tion
con•sump•tive
con•tact
con•ta•gion
con•ta•gious
con•tain
con•tain•er
con•tain•er•iza•tion
con•tain•er•ize
con•tain•ment
con•tam•i•nant
con•tam•i•nate
con•tam•i•na•tion
con•temn
con•tem•plate
con•tem•pla•tion
con•tem•pla•tive
con•tem•po•ra•ne•
ous
con•tem•po•rary
con•tempt
con•tempt•ible
con•temp•tu•ous
con•tend
con•tend•er

con·tent
con·tent·ed
con·ten·tion
con·ten·tious
con·tent·ment
con·ter·mi·nous
con·test
con·tes·tant
con·text
con·tex·tu·al
con·ti·gu·ity
con·tig·u·ous
con·ti·nence
con·ti·nent
con·ti·nen·tal
con·tin·gen·cy
con·tin·gent
con·tin·u·al
con·tin·u·al·ly
con·tin·u·ance
con·tin·u·a·tion
con·tin·ue
con·ti·nu·ity
con·tin·u·ous
con·tin·u·um
pl con·tin·ua *or* con·tin·u·ums
con·tort
con·tor·tion
con·tor·tion·ist
con·tour
con·tra·band
con·tra·cep·tion
con·tra·cep·tive
con·tract
con·trac·tile
con·trac·til·i·ty
con·trac·tion
con·trac·tor
con·trac·tu·al
con·trac·tu·al·ly
con·tra·dict
con·tra·dic·tion
con·tra·dic·to·ry
con·tra·dis·tinc·tion
con·trail
con·tral·to
pl con·tral·tos
con·trap·tion
con·tra·pun·tal
con·tra·ri·ety
con·trari·ly
con·trari·wise
con·trary
con·trast
con·tra·vene
con·tra·ven·tion
con·tre·temps
con·trib·ute
con·tri·bu·tion
con·trib·u·tor
con·trib·u·to·ry
con·trite
con·tri·tion
con·triv·ance
con·trive
con·triv·er
con·trol
con·trolled
con·trol·ling
con·trol·ler
con·tro·ver·sial
con·tro·ver·sy
con·tro·vert
con·tro·vert·ible
con·tu·ma·cious
con·tu·ma·cy
con·tu·me·li·ous
con·tu·me·ly
con·tuse
con·tu·sion
co·nun·drum
con·ur·ba·tion
con·va·lesce
con·va·les·cence
con·va·les·cent
con·vec·tion
con·vene
con·ve·nience
con·ve·nient
con·vent
con·ven·ti·cle
con·ven·tion
con·ven·tion·al
con·ven·tion·al·i·ty
con·ven·tion·al·ize
con·ven·tu·al
con·verge
con·ver·gence
con·ver·gent
con·ver·sant
con·ver·sa·tion
con·ver·sa·tion·al
con·verse
con·verse·ly

con·ver·sion

con·vert

con·vert·er
or con·ver·tor

con·vert·ible

con·vex

con·vex·i·ty

con·vey

con·vey·ance

con·vey·er
or con·vey·or

con·vict

con·vic·tion

con·vince

con·vinc·ing

con·viv·ial

con·viv·i·al·i·ty

con·viv·ial·ly

con·vo·ca·tion

con·voke

con·vo·lut·ed

con·vo·lu·tion

con·voy

con·vulse

con·vul·sion

con·vul·sive

cook·book

cook·ery

cook·ie
or cooky

cook·out

cool·ant

cool·er

coo·lie
laborer (*see* coolly)

cool·ly
also cooly
chillily (*see* coolie)

cool·ness

co-op

coo·per

coo·per·age

co·op·er·ate

co·op·er·a·tion

co·op·er·a·tive

co·op·er·a·tor

co-opt

co·or·di·nate

co·or·di·na·tion

co·or·di·na·tor

co·part·ner

copi·er

co·pi·lot

cop·ing

co·pi·ous

cop·per

cop·per·as

cop·per·head

cop·pice

co·pra

cop·u·la

cop·u·late

cop·u·la·tion

cop·u·la·tive

copy·book

copy·boy

copy·cat

copy·desk

copy·ist

copy·read·er

copy·right

co·quet
or co·quette

co·quet·ted

co·quet·ting

co·que·try

co·quette
noun

co·quett·ish

co·qui·na

cor·a·cle

cor·al
marine skeleton (*see* choral, chorale)

cor·bel

cord
string (*see* chord)

cord·age

cor·dial

cor·dial·i·ty

cor·dial·ly

cor·dil·le·ra

cord·less

cor·do·ba

cor·don

cor·do·van

cor·du·roy

core
center (*see* corps)

co·re·spon·dent
law (*see* cor·re·spon·dent)

co·ri·an·der

cork

cork·screw

cor•mo•rant
corn•cob
corn•crib
cor•nea
cor•ner
cor•ner•stone
cor•net
corn•flow•er
cor•nice
corn•meal
corn•stalk
corn•starch
cor•nu•co•pia
corny
co•rol•la
cor•ol•lary
co•ro•na
cor•o•nary
cor•o•na•tion
cor•o•ner
cor•o•net
cor•po•ral
cor•po•rate
cor•po•ra•tion
cor•po•ra•tive
cor•po•re•al
corps
group (*see* core, corpse)
corpse
dead body (*see* corps)
cor•pu•lence
cor•pu•lent
cor•pus
cor•pus•cle
cor•pus de•lic•ti
Cor•pus Chris•ti
cor•ral
cor•rect
cor•rec•tion
cor•rec•tive
cor•re•late
cor•re•la•tion
cor•rel•a•tive
cor•re•spond
cor•re•spon•dence
cor•re•spon•dent
writer (*see* corespondent)
cor•ri•dor
cor•ri•gen•dum
cor•rob•o•rate
cor•rob•o•ra•tion
cor•rob•o•ra•tive
cor•rob•o•ra•to•ry
cor•rode
cor•ro•sion
cor•ro•sive
cor•ru•gate
cor•ru•ga•tion
cor•rupt
cor•rupt•ible
cor•rup•tion
cor•sair
cor•set
cor•tege
also cor•tège
cor•tex
pl cor•ti•ces *or* cor•tex•es
cor•ti•cal
cor•ti•sone
co•run•dum
cor•us•cate
cor•us•ca•tion
cor•vette
co•ry•za
co•sig•na•to•ry
cos•met•ic
cos•me•tol•o•gist
cos•me•tol•o•gy
cos•mic
also cos•mi•cal
cos•mog•o•ny
cos•mo•log•i•cal
cos•mol•o•gy
cos•mo•naut
cos•mo•pol•i•tan
cos•mop•o•lite
cos•mos
cos•sack
Cos•ta Ri•ca
Cos•ta Ri•can
cost•li•ness
cost•ly
cos•tume
cos•tum•er
cos•tu•mi•er
co•te•rie
co•ter•mi•nous
co•til•lion
also co•til•lon
cot•tage
cot•ter
cot•ton
cot•ton•seed

cot·ton·tail
cot·ton·wood
cot·y·le·don
couch·ant
cou·gar
cough
cou·lomb
coun·cil
assembly (*see* counsel)
coun·cil·lor
or coun·cil·or
council member (*see* counselor)
coun·cil·man
coun·sel
advice (*see* council)
coun·sel
coun·seled
or coun·selled
coun·sel·ing
or coun·sel·ling
coun·sel·or
or coun·sel·lor
adviser (*see* councillor)
count·able
count·down
coun·te·nance
count·er
coun·ter·act
coun·ter·ac·tive
coun·ter·at·tack
coun·ter·bal·ance
coun·ter·claim
coun·ter·clock·wise
coun·ter·es·pi·o·nage
coun·ter·feit
coun·ter·feit·er
coun·ter·in·tel·li·gence
coun·ter·in·sur·gen·cy
count·er·man
coun·ter·mand
coun·ter·mea·sure
coun·ter·of·fen·sive
coun·ter·pane
coun·ter·part
coun·ter·point
coun·ter·poise
coun·ter·rev·o·lu·tion
coun·ter·sig·na·ture
coun·ter·sign
coun·ter·sink
coun·ter·ten·or
coun·ter·weight
count·ess
count·less
coun·tri·fied
also coun·try·fied
coun·try
coun·try·man
coun·try·side
coun·ty
coup de grace
coup d'etat
cou·pé
or coupe
cou·ple
cou·plet
cou·pling
cou·pon
cour·age
cou·ra·geous
cou·ri·er
course
track (*see* coarse)
cours·er
cour·te·ous
cour·te·san
cour·te·sy
court·house
court·ier
court·li·ness
court·ly
court-mar·tial
pl courts-martial
court·room
court·ship
court·yard
cous·in
cov·en
cov·e·nant
cov·er
cov·er·age
cov·er·all
cov·er·let
co·vert
cov·et
cov·et·ous
cov·ey
cow·ard
cow·ard·ice

cow·ard·li·ness
cow·bell
cow·boy
cow·er
cow·hide
cow·lick
cowl·ing
co-work·er
cow·poke
cow·punch·er
cow·slip
cox·comb
cox·swain
coy·ly
coy·ness
coy·ote
coz·en
co·zi·ly
co·zi·ness
co·zy
crab·bed
crab·by
crack·down
crack·er
crack·er·jack
  also crack·a·jack
crack·le
crack·pot
crack-up
cra·dle
craft·i·ness
crafts·man
crafty
crag·gy

cram
  crammed
  cram·ming
cran·ber·ry
cra·ni·al
cra·ni·um
  pl cra·ni·ums *or* cra·nia
crank·case
crank·i·ly
crank·i·ness
crank·shaft
cranky
cran·ny
crap·shoot·er
crash-land
crass·ly
cra·ter
cra·vat
cra·ven
crav·ing
craw·fish
cray·fish
cray·on
cra·zi·ly
cra·zi·ness
cra·zy
creak
  squeak (*see* creek)
creaky
cream·ery
creamy
cre·ate
cre·ation
cre·ative

cre·ativ·i·ty
cre·ator
crea·ture
crèche
cre·dence
cre·den·tial
cred·i·bil·i·ty
cred·i·ble
cred·it
cred·it·able
cred·it·ably
cred·i·tor
cre·do
  pl cre·dos
cre·du·li·ty
cred·u·lous
creek
  stream (*see* creak)
creel
creep
  crept
  creep·ing
creep·er
creepy
cre·mate
cre·ma·tion
cre·ma·to·ry
cren·el·late
  or cren·el·ate
cren·el·la·tion
Cre·ole
cre·o·sote
crepe
  or crêpe
cre·pus·cu·lar

cre•scen•do
pl cre•scen•dos
or cre•scen•does
cres•cent
crest•fall•en
cre•ta•ceous
cre•tin
cre•tonne
cre•vasse
crev•ice
crib
cribbed
crib•bing
crib•bage
crick•et
cri•er
crim•i•nal
crim•i•nal•i•ty
crim•i•nal•ly
crim•i•no•log•i•cal
crim•i•nol•o•gist
crim•i•nol•o•gy
crim•son
cringe
crin•kle
crin•kly
crin•o•line
crip•ple
cri•sis
crisp•ly
crisp•ness
crispy
criss•cross
cri•te•ri•on
pl cri•te•ria

crit•ic
crit•i•cal
crit•i•cal•ly
crit•i•cism
crit•i•cize
cri•tique
crit•ter
croak
cro•chet
crock•ery
croc•o•dile
cro•cus
pl cro•cus•es *also* cro•ci
crois•sant
cro•ny
crook•ed
croon•er
crop
cropped
crop•ping
crop•land
crop•per
cro•quet
game (*see* croquette)
cro•quette
food (*see* croquet)
cro•sier
cross•bar
cross•bow
cross•breed
cross-coun•try
cross•cur•rent
cross•cut

cross-ex•am•i•na•tion
cross-ex•am•ine
cross-eye
cross-eyed
cross•hatch
cross•ing
cross•over
cross•piece
cross-pol•li•nate
cross-pol•li•na•tion
cross-pur•pose
cross-ques•tion
cross-re•fer
cross-ref•er•ence
cross•road
cross•walk
cross•wise
crotch
crotch•et
crotch•et•i•ness
crotch•ety
crou•pi•er
crou•ton
crow•bar
crow•foot
cru•cial
cru•ci•ble
cru•ci•fix
cru•ci•fix•ion
cru•ci•form
cru•ci•fy
crude•ly
cru•el
cru•el•ly

cru•el•ty
cru•et
cruis•er
crul•ler
crum•ble
crum•bly
crum•pet
crum•ple
cru•sade
cru•sad•er
crus•ta•cean
crust•al
crusty
crutch
crux
pl **crux•es**
also **cru•ces**
cru•zei•ro
pl **cru•zei•ros**
cry•ba•by
cryo•bi•o•log•i•cal
cryo•bi•ol•o•gist
cryo•bi•ol•o•gy
cryo•gen•ic
cryo•gen•i•cal•ly
cryo•gen•ics
cryo•sur•gery
crypt
cryp•tic
cryp•to•gram
cryp•tog•ra•pher
cryp•tog•ra•phy
crys•tal
crys•tal•line
crys•tal•li•za•tion
crys•tal•lize
Cu•ba
Cu•ban
cub•by•hole
cu•bic
cu•bi•cal
like a cube (*see* **cubicle**)
cu•bi•cle
compartment (*see* **cubical**)
cu•bit
cuck•old
cuck•oo
pl **cuck•oos**
cu•cum•ber
cud•dle
cud•gel
cue
signal (*see* **queue**)
cui•sine
cul-de-sac
pl **culs-de-sac** *also* **cul-de-sacs**
cu•li•nary
cull
cul•mi•nate
cul•mi•na•tion
cul•pa•ble
cul•prit
cult•ist
cul•ti•va•ble
cul•ti•vat•able
cul•ti•vate
cul•ti•va•tion
cul•ti•va•tor
cul•tur•al
cul•tur•al•ly
cul•ture
cul•tured
cul•vert
cum•ber•some
cum•brous
cum•mer•bund
cu•mu•la•tive
cu•mu•lus
cu•ne•i•form
cun•ning
cup•bear•er
cup•board
cup•cake
cup•ful
cu•pid
cu•pid•i•ty
cu•po•la
cur•able
cu•rate
cu•ra•tive
cu•ra•tor
curb•ing
cur•dle
cu•ré
cure-all
cur•few
cu•ria
cu•rio
pl **cu•ri•os**
cu•ri•os•i•ty
cu•ri•ous
cu•ri•ous•ly
cu•ri•um

curl•er
curli•cue
curly
cur•rant
berry (*see* current)
cur•ren•cy
cur•rent
present, stream (*see* currant)
cur•ric•u•lum
pl cur•ric•u•la *also* cur•ric•u•lums
cur•ry
cur•ry•comb
cur•sive
cur•so•ri•ly
cur•so•ry
cur•tail
cur•tain
curt•ly
curt•sy
or curt•sey
cur•va•ture
curve
cush•ion
cus•pi•dor
cus•tard
cus•to•di•al
cus•to•di•an
cus•to•dy
cus•tom
cus•tom•ari•ly
cus•tom•ary
cus•tom-built
cus•tom•er
cus•tom•house
cus•tom-made
cut
cut
cut•ting
cut-and-dried
cu•ta•ne•ous
cut•back
cu•ti•cle
cut•lass
cut•lery
cut•let
cut•off
cut•ter
cut•throat
cut•ting
cut•tle•bone
cut•tle•fish
cut•up
cut•worm
cy•a•nide
cy•ber•nat•ed
cy•ber•na•tion
cy•ber•net•ics
cy•cla•mate
cy•cla•men
cy•cle
cy•clic
cy•cli•cal
cy•clist
cy•clom•e•ter
cy•clone
cy•clon•ic
cy•clo•pe•dia
or cy•clo•pae•dia
cy•clo•tron
cyg•net
cyl•in•der
cy•lin•dri•cal
or cy•lin•dric
cym•bal
musical instrument (*see* symbol)
cyn•ic
cyn•i•cal
cyn•i•cism
cy•no•sure
cy•press
Cyp•ri•ot
or Cyp•ri•ote
Cy•prus
cyst
cys•tic
cy•to•plasm
czar
or tsar *or* tzar
cza•ri•na
czar•ism
czar•ist
Czech
Czecho•slo•vak
Czecho•slo•va•kia
Czecho•slo•va•ki•an

D

dab
dabbed
dab•bing
dab•ble
dab•bler

dachs·hund
dac·tyl
dac·tyl·ic
dad·dy
daf·fo·dil
daf·fy
dag·ger
da·guerre·o·type
dahl·ia
dai·ly
dain·ti·ly
dain·ti·ness
dain·ty
dai·qui·ri
dairy
dairy·maid
dairy·man
da·is
dai·sy
da·la·si
Dal·las
dal·li·ance
dal·ly
  dal·lied
  dal·ly·ing
dal·ma·tian
dam
  stop up (*see* damn)
  dammed
  dam·ming
dam·age
dam·a·scene
dam·ask
damn
  condemn (*see* dam)
dam·na·ble
dam·na·bly
dam·na·tion
damp·en
damp·en·er
damp·er
damp·ness
dam·sel
dam·son
danc·er
dan·de·li·on
dan·der
dan·di·fy
dan·dle
dan·druff
dan·dy
dan·dy·ish
dan·ger
dan·ger·ous
dan·gle
Dan·ish
dan·seuse
dap·per
dap·ple
dare·dev·il
dar·ing
dark·en
dark·room
dar·ling
dash·board
dash·ing
das·tard·ly
da·ta
date·less
date·line
da·tive
da·tum
  pl da·ta *or* da·tums
daugh·ter
daugh·ter-in-law
  pl daugh·ters-in-law
daunt·less
dau·phin
dav·en·port
da·vit
daw·dle
daw·dler
day·bed
day·book
day·break
day·dream
day·light
day·time
Day·ton
daz·zle
daz·zling·ly
dea·con
dea·con·ess
de·ac·ti·vate
de·ac·ti·va·tion
dead·beat
dead·en
dead·line
dead·li·ness
dead·lock
dead·ly
dead·pan
dead·weight
dead·wood
deaf·en

deaf-mute
deaf·ness
deal
  dealt
  deal·ing
dean·ery
Dear·born
dear·ly
dearth
death·bed
death·blow
death·less
death·ly
death's-head
death·watch
de·ba·cle
de·bar
de·bark
de·bar·ka·tion
de·base
de·bat·able
de·bate
de·bat·er
de·bauch
de·bauch·ery
de·ben·ture
de·bil·i·tate
de·bil·i·ta·tion
de·bil·i·ty
deb·it
deb·o·nair
de·bouch
de·brief
de·bris
  pl de·bris

debt·or
de·bunk
de·but
deb·u·tante
de·cade
dec·a·dence
dec·a·dent
de·cal
de·cal·co·ma·nia
deca·logue
de·camp
de·cant
de·cant·er
de·cap·i·tate
de·cap·i·ta·tion
deca·syl·lab·ic
de·cath·lon
de·cay
de·cease
de·ceased
de·ce·dent
de·ceit
de·ceit·ful
de·ceit·ful·ly
de·ceive
de·ceiv·er
de·cel·er·ate
de·cel·er·a·tion
de·cel·er·a·tor
De·cem·ber
de·cen·cy
de·cen·ni·al
de·cen·ni·al·ly

de·cent
  proper (*see* descent, dissent)
de·cen·tral·iza·tion
de·cen·tral·ize
de·cep·tion
de·cep·tive·ly
deci·bel
de·cide
de·cid·ed
de·cid·u·ous
dec·i·mal
dec·i·mal·ize
dec·i·mal·ly
dec·i·mate
de·ci·pher
de·ci·pher·able
de·ci·sion
de·ci·sive
de·ci·sive·ness
deck·hand
deck·le
de·claim
dec·la·ma·tion
de·clam·a·to·ry
dec·la·ra·tion
de·clar·a·tive
de·clar·a·to·ry
de·clare
de·clar·er
de·clas·si·fy
de·clen·sion
de·clin·able
dec·li·nate
dec·li·na·tion

de·cline
de·cliv·i·ty
de·code
dé·col·le·tage
dé·col·le·té
de·col·o·ni·za·tion
de·com·mis·sion
de·com·pose
de·com·po·si·tion
de·com·press
de·com·pres·sion
de·con·tam·i·nate
de·con·tam·i·na·tion
de·con·trol
de·cor
or dé·cor
dec·o·rate
dec·o·ra·tion
dec·o·ra·tive
dec·o·ra·tor
dec·o·rous
de·co·rum
de·coy
de·crease
de·cree
dec·re·ment
de·crep·it
de·crep·i·tate
de·crep·i·tude
de·cre·scen·do
de·cry
ded·i·cate
ded·i·ca·tion
ded·i·ca·to·ry
de·duce
de·duc·ible
de·duct
de·duct·ible
de·duc·tion
de·duc·tive
deep·en
deep·ly
deep-root·ed
deep-sea
deep-seat·ed
deer·skin
de-es·ca·late
de-es·ca·la·tion
de·face
de·face·ment
de fac·to
de·fal·cate
de·fal·ca·tion
de·fal·ca·tor
def·a·ma·tion
de·fam·a·to·ry
de·fame
de·fault
de·fault·er
de·feat
de·feat·ism
de·feat·ist
def·e·cate
def·e·ca·tion
de·fect
de·fec·tion
de·fec·tive
de·fec·tor
de·fend
de·fen·dant
de·fend·er
de·fense
or de·fence
de·fense·less
de·fen·si·ble
de·fen·sive
de·fer
de·ferred
de·fer·ring
def·er·ence
respect (*see* difference)
def·er·en·tial
de·fer·ment
de·fer·ra·ble
de·fi·ance
de·fi·ant
de·fi·cien·cy
de·fi·cient
def·i·cit
de·file
de·file·ment
de·fin·able
de·fine
de·fin·er
def·i·nite
def·i·ni·tion
de·fin·i·tive
de·flate
de·fla·tion
de·fla·tion·ary
de·flect
de·flec·tion
de·flec·tor
de·fo·li·ant

de•fo•li•ate
de•fo•li•a•tion
de•for•es•ta•tion
de•form
de•for•ma•tion
de•for•mi•ty
de•fraud
de•fray
de•fray•al
de•frost
deft•ly
de•funct
de•fy
de•gen•er•a•cy
de•gen•er•ate
de•gen•er•a•tion
de•gen•er•a•tive
de•grad•able
deg•ra•da•tion
de•grade
de•gree
de•gree-day
de•hu•man•iza•tion
de•hu•man•ize
de•hu•mid•i•fy
de•hy•drate
de•hy•dra•tion
de•hy•dro•ge•nate
de•hy•dro•ge•na•tion
de•ice
de•ic•er
de•i•fi•ca•tion
de•i•fy
deign
de•ism
de•is•tic
de•i•ty
de•ject•ed
de•jec•tion
de ju•re
Del•a•ware
de•lay
de•le
de•lec•ta•ble
de•lec•ta•tion
del•e•gate
del•e•ga•tion
de•lete
del•e•te•ri•ous
de•le•tion
delft•ware
de•lib•er•ate
de•lib•er•ate•ness
de•lib•er•a•tion
de•lib•er•a•tive
del•i•ca•cy
del•i•cate
del•i•cate•ly
del•i•ca•tes•sen
de•li•cious
de•light
de•light•ed
de•light•ful•ly
de•lim•it
de•lin•eate
de•lin•ea•tion
de•lin•quen•cy
de•lin•quent
del•i•quesce
del•i•ques•cent
de•lir•i•ous
de•lir•i•um tre•mens
de•liv•er
de•liv•er•ance
de•liv•er•er
de•liv•ery
de•louse
del•phin•i•um
del•ta
de•lude
del•uge
de•lu•sion
de•lu•sive
de•luxe
delve
de•mag•ne•tize
dem•a•gog•ic
dem•a•gogue
or dem•a•gog
dem•a•gogu•ery
dem•a•gogy
de•mand
de•mar•cate
de•mar•ca•tion
de•marche
de•mean
de•mean•or
de•ment•ed
de•men•tia
de•mer•it
de•mesne
demi•god
demi•john
de•mil•i•tar•i•za•tion
de•mil•i•ta•rize

de·mi·monde
de·mise
demi·tasse
de·mo·bi·li·za·tion
de·mo·bi·lize
de·moc·ra·cy
dem·o·crat
dem·o·crat·ic
dem·o·crat·i·cal·ly
Dem·o·crat·ic Kam·pu·chea
de·moc·ra·ti·za·tion
de·moc·ra·tize
de·mog·ra·pher
de·mo·graph·ic
de·mo·graph·i·cal·ly
de·mog·ra·phy
de·mol·ish
de·mo·li·tion
de·mon
or dae·mon
de·mon·e·ti·za·tion
de·mon·e·tize
de·mo·ni·ac
de·mo·ni·a·cal·ly
de·mon·ic
de·mon·i·cal·ly
de·mon·ol·o·gy
de·mon·stra·ble
dem·on·strate
dem·on·stra·tion
de·mon·stra·tive
dem·on·stra·tor
de·mor·al·iza·tion
de·mor·al·ize

de·mote
de·mot·ic
de·mo·tion
de·mul·cent
de·mur
object (*see* demure)
de·murred
de·mur·ring
de·mure
prim (*see* demur)
de·mur·rage
de·mur·rer
de·na·tion·al·iza·tion
de·na·tion·al·ize
de·nat·u·ral·iza·tion
de·nat·u·ral·ize
de·na·tur·ant
de·na·ture
den·dri·form
den·dro·chron·o·log·i·cal·ly
den·dro·chro·nol·o·gy
den·dro·log·ic
den·drol·o·gist
den·drol·o·gy
den·gue
de·ni·al
de·ni·er
one that denies
de·nier
coin
den·i·grate
den·im

den·i·zen
Den·mark
de·nom·i·nate
de·nom·i·na·tion
de·nom·i·na·tor
de·no·ta·tion
de·no·ta·tive
de·note
de·noue·ment
de·nounce
dense·ly
den·si·ty
den·tal
den·tal·ly
den·ti·frice
den·tin
or den·tine
den·tist
den·tist·ry
den·ti·tion
den·ture
de·nu·da·tion
de·nude
de·nun·ci·a·tion
Den·ver
de·ny
de·odor·ant
de·odor·ize
de·odor·iz·er
de·ox·i·dize
de·ox·i·diz·er
de·oxy·ri·bo·nu·cle·ic acid
de·part
de·part·ment

de•part•men•tal
de•part•men•tal•ize
de•par•ture
de•pend
de•pend•abil•i•ty
de•pend•able
de•pen•dence
also de•pen•dance
de•pen•den•cy
de•pen•dent
de•per•son•al•iza•tion
de•per•son•al•ize
de•pict
de•pic•tion
de•pil•a•to•ry
de•plane
de•plete
de•ple•tion
de•plor•able
de•plore
de•ploy
de•po•lar•iza•tion
de•po•lar•ize
de•po•nent
de•pop•u•late
de•pop•u•la•tion
de•port
de•por•ta•tion
de•por•tee
de•port•ment
de•pose
de•pos•it
de•po•si•tion
de•pos•i•tor
de•pos•i•to•ry
de•pot
de•pra•va•tion
corruption (*see* deprivation)
de•prave
de•praved
de•prav•i•ty
dep•re•cate
dep•re•ca•tion
dep•re•ca•to•ry
de•pre•ci•ate
de•pre•ci•a•tion
dep•re•da•tion
de•press
de•pres•sant
de•pres•sion
dep•ri•va•tion
loss (*see* depravation)
de•prive
depth
dep•u•ta•tion
de•pute
dep•u•tize
dep•u•ty
de•rail
de•range
de•range•ment
der•by
der•e•lict
der•e•lic•tion
de•ride
de ri•gueur
de•ri•sion
de•ri•sive
der•i•va•tion
de•riv•a•tive
de•rive
der•ma•ti•tis
der•ma•tol•o•gist
der•ma•tol•o•gy
der•mis
der•o•gate
der•o•ga•tion
de•rog•a•to•ri•ly
de•rog•a•to•ry
der•rick
der•ri•ere
or der•ri•ère
der•ring-do
der•rin•ger
der•vish
de•sal•i•nate
de•sal•i•na•tion
de•sal•i•ni•za•tion
de•sal•i•nize
de•salt
des•cant
de•scend
de•scen•dant
or de•scen•dent
de•scent
decline (*see* decent, dissent)
de•scrib•able
de•scribe
de•scrip•tion
de•scrip•tive
de•scrip•tor
de•scry

des·e·crate
des·e·cra·tion
de·seg·re·gate
de·seg·re·ga·tion
de·sen·si·ti·za·tion
de·sen·si·tize
de·sen·si·tiz·er
des·ert
barren area (*see* dessert)
de·sert
leave (*see* dessert)
de·sert·er
de·ser·tion
de·serve
de·served·ly
de·serv·ing
des·ic·cant
des·ic·cate
des·ic·ca·tion
des·ic·ca·tor
de·sid·er·a·tum
pl de·sid·er·a·ta
de·sign
des·ig·nate
des·ig·na·tion
de·sign·er
de·sign·ing
de·sir·abil·i·ty
de·sir·able
de·sire
de·sir·ous
de·sist
Des Moines
des·o·late
des·o·late·ly
des·o·la·tion
des·oxy·ri·bo·nu·cle·ic acid
de·spair
de·spair·ing·ly
des·patch
var of dispatch
des·per·a·do
pl des·per·a·does *or* des·per·a·dos
des·per·ate
hopeless (*see* disparate)
des·per·ate·ly
des·per·a·tion
de·spi·ca·ble
des·pi·ca·bly
de·spise
de·spite
de·spoil
de·spoil·ment
de·spo·li·a·tion
de·spond
de·spon·den·cy
de·spon·dent
des·pot
des·pot·ic
des·pot·i·cal·ly
des·po·tism
des·sert
sweet food (*see* desert)
des·ti·na·tion
des·tine
des·ti·ny
des·ti·tute
des·ti·tu·tion
de·stroy
de·stroy·er
de·struct
de·struc·ti·bil·i·ty
de·struc·ti·ble
de·struc·tion
de·struc·tive
de·struc·tive·ness
de·struc·tor
de·sue·tude
des·ul·to·ry
de·tach
de·tach·able
de·tached
de·tach·ment
de·tail
de·tain
de·tain·ee
de·tect
de·tect·able
de·tec·tion
de·tec·tive
de·tec·tor
dé·tente
de·ten·tion
de·ter
de·terred
de·ter·ring
de·ter·gent
de·te·ri·o·rate
de·te·ri·o·ra·tion
de·ter·min·able

de·ter·min·ably
de·ter·mi·na·cy
de·ter·mi·nant
de·ter·mi·nate
de·ter·mi·na·tion
de·ter·mine
de·ter·mined
de·ter·mined·ly
de·ter·mined·ness
de·ter·min·ism
de·ter·min·ist
de·ter·rence
de·ter·rent
de·test
de·test·able
de·test·ably
de·tes·ta·tion
de·throne
de·throne·ment
det·o·nate
det·o·na·tion
det·o·na·tor
de·tour
de·tract
de·trac·tion
de·trac·tor
de·train
det·ri·ment
det·ri·men·tal·ly
de·tri·tus
De·troit
deuce
deu·te·ri·um
deut·sche mark
de·val·u·a·tion

de·val·ue
dev·as·tate
dev·as·ta·tion
de·vel·op
de·vel·op·er
de·vel·op·ment
de·vel·op·men·tal·ly
de·vi·ant
de·vi·ate
de·vi·a·tion
de·vice
mechanism (*see* devise)

dev·il
dev·iled
or dev·illed
dev·il·ing
or dev·il·ling

dev·il·ish
dev·il·ment
dev·il·ry
or dev·il·try
de·vi·ous
de·vis·able
de·vise
invent (*see* device)

de·vi·tal·ize
de·vit·ri·fy
de·void
de·vo·lu·tion
de·volve
de·vote
de·vot·ed
dev·o·tee
de·vo·tion
de·vo·tion·al

de·vour
de·vour·er
de·vout
de·vout·ness
dew
dew·ber·ry
dew·drop
dew·lap
dewy
dex·ter·i·ty
dex·ter·ous
or dex·trous

dex·trose
dhow
di·a·be·tes
di·a·bet·ic
di·a·bol·ic
or di·a·bol·i·cal

di·a·bol·i·cal·ly
di·a·crit·ic
di·a·crit·i·cal
di·a·dem
di·aer·e·sis
or di·er·e·sis
pl di·aer·e·ses
or di·er·e·ses

di·ag·nose
di·ag·no·sis
pl di·ag·no·ses

di·ag·nos·tic
di·ag·nos·ti·cal·ly
di·ag·nos·ti·cian
di·ag·o·nal
di·ag·o·nal·ly

di·a·gram
di·a·gramed
or di·a·grammed
di·a·gram·ing
or di·a·gram·ming
di·a·gram·mat·ic
di·a·gram·mat·i·cal·ly
di·al
di·aled
or di·alled
di·al·ing
or di·al·ling
di·a·lect
di·a·lec·tic
di·a·logue
or di·a·log
di·am·e·ter
di·a·met·ri·cal·ly
di·a·mond
di·a·mond·back
di·a·pa·son
di·a·per
di·aph·a·nous
di·a·phragm
di·a·phrag·mat·ic
di·a·rist
di·ar·rhea
or di·ar·rhoea
di·a·ry
di·as·to·le
di·a·stroph·ic
di·as·tro·phism
dia·ther·my
dia·ton·ic
dia·ton·i·cal·ly

di·a·tribe
dib·ble
dice
di·chot·o·my
dick·er
dick·ey
or dicky
di·cot·y·le·don
di·cot·y·le·don·ous
Dic·ta·phone
dic·tate
dic·ta·tion
dic·ta·tor
dic·ta·to·ri·al
dic·ta·tor·ship
dic·tion
dic·tio·nary
Dic·to·graph
dic·tum
pl dic·ta *also* dic·tums
di·dac·tic
di·dac·ti·cal·ly
di·dac·ti·cism
die
expire (*see* dye)
died
dy·ing
die
pl dice *or* dies
spotted cube, tool (*see* dye)
die·hard
di·elec·tric
di·er·e·sis
var of diaeresis

die·sel
di·et
di·etary
di·etet·ic
di·etet·ics
di·eti·tian
or di·eti·cian
dif·fer
dif·fer·ence
unlikeness (*see* deference)
dif·fer·ent
dif·fer·en·tial
dif·fer·en·ti·ate
dif·fer·en·ti·a·tion
dif·fi·cult
dif·fi·cul·ty
dif·fi·dence
dif·fi·dent
dif·frac·tion
dif·fuse
dif·fu·sion
dig
dug
dig·ging
di·gest
di·gest·ibil·i·ty
di·gest·ible
di·ges·tion
di·ges·tive
dig·ger
dig·it
dig·i·tal
dig·i·tal·is
dig·i·tal·ly

dig·ni·fied
dig·ni·fy
dig·ni·tary
dig·ni·ty
di·gress
di·gres·sion
di·gres·sive
di·lap·i·dat·ed
di·lap·i·da·tion
di·la·ta·tion
di·late
di·la·tion
dil·a·to·ry
di·lem·ma
dil·et·tante
pl dil·et·tantes *or* dil·et·tan·ti
dil·i·gence
dil·i·gent
dil·ly·dal·ly
dil·u·ent
di·lute
di·lu·tion
dim
dimmed
dim·ming
di·men·sion
di·men·sion·al
di·min·ish
di·min·u·en·do
dim·i·nu·tion
di·min·u·tive
dim·i·ty
dim·ly
dim·mer
dim·out
dim·ple
di·nar
din·er
one that dines (*see* dinner)
di·nette
din·ghy
boat (*see* dingy)
din·gi·ness
din·gy
shabby (*see* dinghy)
din·ky
din·ner
meal (*see* diner)
din·ner·ware
di·no·saur
di·oc·e·san
di·o·cese
di·ora·ma
di·ox·ide
dip
dipped
dip·ping
diph·the·ria
diph·thong
di·plo·ma
di·plo·ma·cy
dip·lo·mat
dip·lo·mat·ic
dip·lo·mat·i·cal·ly
di·plo·ma·tist
dip·per
dip·so·ma·nia
dip·so·ma·ni·ac
dip·stick
dip·ter·an
dip·ter·ous
di·rect
di·rec·tion
di·rec·tion·al
di·rec·tive
di·rect·ly
di·rec·tor
di·rec·tor·ate
di·rec·tor·ship
di·rec·to·ry
dire·ful
dirge
dir·ham
di·ri·gi·ble
dirndl
dirt·i·ness
dirty
dis·abil·i·ty
dis·able
dis·abuse
dis·ad·van·tage
dis·ad·van·ta·geous
dis·af·fect
dis·af·fec·tion
dis·agree
dis·agree·able
dis·agree·ably
dis·agree·ment
dis·al·low
dis·al·low·ance
dis·ap·pear
dis·ap·pear·ance
dis·ap·point

dis·ap·point·ment
dis·ap·pro·ba·tion
dis·ap·prov·al
dis·ap·prove
dis·arm
dis·ar·ma·ment
dis·ar·range
dis·ar·range·ment
dis·ar·ray
dis·as·sem·ble
dis·as·so·ci·ate
di·sas·ter
di·sas·trous
dis·avow
dis·avow·al
dis·band
dis·bar
dis·bar·ment
dis·be·lief
dis·be·lieve
dis·be·liev·er
dis·bur·den
dis·burse
pay out (*see* disperse)
dis·burse·ment
disc
var of disk
dis·card
dis·cern
dis·cern·ible
dis·cern·ing
dis·cern·ment
dis·charge
dis·charge·able
dis·ci·ple
dis·ci·pli·nar·i·an
dis·ci·plin·ary
dis·ci·pline
dis·claim
dis·claim·er
dis·close
dis·clo·sure
dis·cog·ra·pher
dis·cog·ra·phy
dis·col·or
dis·col·or·ation
dis·com·bob·u·late
dis·com·fit
dis·com·fi·ture
dis·com·fort
dis·com·mode
dis·com·pose
dis·com·po·sure
dis·con·cert
dis·con·nect
dis·con·nect·ed
dis·con·so·late
dis·con·tent
dis·con·tinu·ance
dis·con·tin·ue
dis·con·ti·nu·ity
dis·con·tin·u·ous
dis·co·phile
dis·cord
dis·cor·dant
dis·co·theque
dis·count
dis·count·able
dis·coun·te·nance
dis·cour·age
dis·cour·age·ment
dis·course
dis·cour·te·ous
dis·cour·te·sy
dis·cov·er
dis·cov·er·er
dis·cov·ery
dis·cred·it
dis·cred·it·able
dis·creet
prudent (*see* discrete)
dis·crep·an·cy
dis·crep·ant
dis·crete
distinct (*see* discreet)
dis·cre·tion
dis·cre·tion·ary
dis·crim·i·nate
dis·crim·i·nat·ing
dis·crim·i·na·tion
dis·crim·i·na·to·ry
dis·cur·sive
dis·cus
disk (*see* discuss)
dis·cuss
argue (*see* discus)
dis·cus·sant
dis·cus·sion
dis·dain
dis·dain·ful·ly
dis·ease
dis·em·bark
dis·em·bar·ka·tion
dis·em·body
dis·em·bow·el

dis•em•bow•el•ment
dis•en•chant
dis•en•cum•ber
dis•en•gage
dis•en•tan•gle
dis•es•tab•lish
dis•es•tab•lish•ment
dis•es•teem
dis•fa•vor
dis•fig•ure
dis•fig•ure•ment
dis•fran•chise
dis•gorge
dis•grace
dis•grace•ful•ly
dis•grun•tle
dis•guise
dis•gust
dis•gust•ed•ly
dis•ha•bille
dis•har•mo•ny
dish•cloth
dis•heart•en
di•shev•el
  di•shev•eled
    or di•shev•elled
  di•shev•el•ing
    or di•shev•el•ling
dis•hon•est
dis•hon•es•ty
dis•hon•or
dis•hon•or•able
dis•hon•or•ably
dish•rag
dish•wash•er
dish•wa•ter
dis•il•lu•sion
dis•il•lu•sion•ment
dis•in•cli•na•tion
dis•in•cline
dis•in•fect
dis•in•fec•tant
dis•in•fec•tion
dis•in•gen•u•ous
dis•in•her•it
dis•in•te•grate
dis•in•te•gra•tion
dis•in•ter
dis•in•ter•est•ed
dis•in•ter•est•ed•ness
dis•join
dis•joint
dis•joint•ed
disk
  or disc
dis•like
dis•lo•cate
dis•lo•ca•tion
dis•lodge
dis•loy•al
dis•loy•al•ty
dis•mal
dis•mal•ly
dis•man•tle
dis•may
dis•mem•ber
dis•mem•ber•ment
dis•miss
dis•miss•al
dis•mount
dis•obe•di•ence
dis•obe•di•ent
dis•obey
dis•or•der
dis•or•der•ly
dis•or•ga•ni•za•tion
dis•or•ga•nize
dis•own
dis•par•age
dis•par•age•ment
dis•par•ag•ing•ly
dis•pa•rate
  dissimilar (*see* desperate)
dis•par•i•ty
dis•pas•sion•ate
dis•pas•sion•ate•ly
dis•patch
  or des•patch
dis•patch•er
dis•pel
  dis•pelled
  dis•pel•ling
dis•pens•able
dis•pen•sa•ry
dis•pen•sa•tion
dis•pense
dis•pens•er
dis•pers•al
dis•perse
  spread (*see* disburse)
dis•per•sion
dispir•it
dis•place

dis•place•ment
dis•play
dis•please
dis•plea•sure
dis•port
dis•pos•able
dis•pos•al
dis•pose
dis•pos•er
dis•po•si•tion
dis•pos•sess
dis•pos•ses•sion
dis•proof
dis•pro•por•tion
dis•pro•por•tion•ate
dis•prove
dis•pu•ta•ble
dis•pu•tant
dis•pu•ta•tion
dis•pu•ta•tious
dis•pute
dis•put•er
dis•qual•i•fi•ca•tion
dis•qual•i•fy
dis•qui•et
dis•qui•etude
dis•qui•si•tion
dis•re•gard
dis•re•gard•ful
dis•re•pair
dis•rep•u•ta•ble
dis•rep•u•ta•bly
dis•re•pute
dis•re•spect
dis•re•spect•ful
dis•robe
dis•rupt
dis•rup•tion
dis•rup•tive
dis•sat•is•fac•tion
dis•sat•is•fy
dis•sect
dis•sect•ed
dis•sec•tion
dis•sem•ble
dis•sem•bler
dis•sem•i•nate
dis•sem•i•na•tion
dis•sen•sion
also dis•sen•tion
dis•sent
disagree (*see* decent, descent)
dis•sent•er
dis•sen•tient
dis•ser•ta•tion
dis•ser•vice
dis•sev•er
dis•si•dence
dis•si•dent
dis•sim•i•lar
dis•sim•i•lar•i•ty
dis•sim•u•late
dis•sim•u•la•tion
dis•si•pate
dis•si•pat•ed
dis•si•pa•tion
dis•so•ci•ate
dis•so•ci•a•tion
dis•sol•u•ble
dis•so•lute
dis•so•lute•ness
dis•so•lu•tion
dis•solve
dis•so•nance
dis•so•nant
dis•suade
dis•sua•sion
dis•taff
dis•sym•me•try
dis•tance
dis•tant
dis•taste
dis•taste•ful
dis•tem•per
dis•tend
dis•ten•sion
or dis•ten•tion
dis•tich
dis•ti•chous
dis•till
also dis•til
dis•til•late
dis•til•la•tion
dis•till•er
dis•till•ery
dis•tinct
dis•tinc•tion
dis•tinc•tive
dis•tin•guish
dis•tin•guish•able
dis•tin•guish•ably
dis•tort
dis•tor•tion
dis•tract

dis•trac•tion
dis•train
dis•trait
dis•traught
dis•tress
dis•tress•ful•ly
dis•trib•ute
dis•tri•bu•tion
dis•trib•u•tive
dis•trib•u•tor
dis•trict
Dis•trict of Co•lum•bia
dis•trust
dis•trust•ful•ly
dis•turb
dis•tur•bance
dis•turbed
dis•union
dis•unite
dis•uni•ty
dis•use
ditch
dith•er
dit•to
  pl dit•tos
dit•ty
di•uret•ic
di•ur•nal
di•va
  pl di•vas *or* di•ve
di•va•gate
di•va•ga•tion
di•van
dive
  dived
    or dove
  dived
  div•ing
div•er
di•verge
di•ver•gence
di•ver•gent
di•vers
  various (*see* diverse)
di•verse
  unlike (*see* divers)
di•ver•si•fi•ca•tion
di•ver•si•fy
di•ver•sion
di•ver•sion•ary
di•ver•si•ty
di•vert
di•vest
di•vide
div•i•dend
di•vid•er
div•i•na•tion
di•vine
di•vin•er
di•vin•i•ty
di•vis•i•bil•i•ty
di•vis•i•ble
di•vi•sion
di•vi•sion•al
di•vi•sive
di•vi•sor
di•vorce
di•vor•cée
div•ot
di•vulge
diz•zi•ly
diz•zi•ness
diz•zy
Dji•bou•ti
do
  did
  done
  do•ing
  does
dob•bin
do•cent
doc•ile
do•cil•i•ty
dock•age
dock•et
dock•hand
dock•yard
doc•tor
doc•tor•al
doc•tor•ate
doc•tri•naire
doc•trin•al
doc•trine
doc•u•ment
doc•u•men•ta•ry
doc•u•men•ta•tion
dod•der
dodge
do•do
  pl do•does *or* do•dos
doe•skin
doff

dog
hunt (*see* dogged)
dogged
dog·ging

dog·cart
dog·catch·er
doge
dog-ear
dog·fight
dog·fish
dog·ged
determined (*see* dog)
dog·ger·el
dog·house
dog·ma
dog·mat·ic
dog·mat·i·cal·ly
dog·ma·tism
dog·ma·tist
dog·trot
doi·ly
do·ing
do-it-your·self
dol·drums
dole·ful
dole·ful·ly
dol·lar
dol·lop
dol·ly
dol·men
do·lor
do·lor·ous
dol·phin
dolt·ish
do·main

do·mes·tic
do·mes·ti·cal·ly
do·mes·ti·cate
do·mes·ti·ca·tion
do·mes·tic·i·ty
do·mi·cile
do·mi·cil·i·ary
dom·i·nance
dom·i·nant
dom·i·nate
dom·i·na·tion
dom·i·neer
Dom·in·i·ca
Do·min·i·can Re·
pub·lic
do·min·ion
dom·i·no
pl dom·i·noes *or* dom·i·nos
don
donned
don·ning
do·nate
do·na·tion
dong
don·key
don·ny·brook
do·nor
doo·dad
doo·dle
doo·dler
dooms·day
door·jamb
door·keep·er
door·knob

door·man
door·mat
door·plate
dou·ble-quick
dou·ble-space
dou·blet
dou·ble-talk
dou·ble·think
dou·bloon
dou·bly
doubt
doubt·ful
doubt·ful·ly
doubt·less
douche
dough
dough·boy
dough·nut
dough·ty
doughy
dour
douse
dove·cote
or dove·cot
Do·ver
dove·tail
dow·a·ger
dowd·i·ly
dowd·i·ness
dowdy
dow·el
dow·er
down·beat
down·cast
down·fall

down•fall•en
down•grade
down•heart•ed
down•hill
down•pour
down•range
down•right
down•stage
down•stairs
down•stream
down•stroke
down•swing
down-to-earth
down•town
down•trod•den
down•turn
down•ward
  or down•wards
down•wind
downy
dow•ry
dox•ol•o•gy
doze
doz•en
doz•enth
drach•ma
dra•co•ni•an
draft•ee
drafts•man
drafty
drag
  dragged
  drag•ging
drag•net
drag•o•man
  pl drag•o•mans *or* drag•o•men
drag•on
drag•on•fly
dra•goon
drain•age
drain•pipe
dra•ma
dra•mat•ic
dra•mat•i•cal•ly
dra•ma•tist
dra•ma•ti•za•tion
dra•ma•tize
dra•ma•tur•gy
drap•er
drap•ery
dras•tic
dras•ti•cal•ly
draw
  drew
  drawn
  draw•ing
draw•back
draw•bridge
draw•er
draw•ing
drawl
draw•string
dread•ful
dread•ful•ly
dread•nought
dream
  dreamed
    or dreamt
  dream•ing
dream•er
dream•i•ly
dream•land
dream•like
dream•world
dreamy
drea•ri•ly
drea•ry
dredge
dredg•er
dress•mak•er
dress•mak•ing
dres•sage
dress•er
dress•ing
dressy
drib•ble
drib•let
dri•er
  or dry•er
  noun (*see* dry)
drift•er
drift•wood
drill•er
drill•mas•ter
drily
drink
  drank
  drunk
    or drank
  drink•ing

drink·able
drip
  dripped
  drip·ping
drip-dry
drive
  drove
  driv·en
  driv·ing
drive-in
driv·el
  driv·eled
    or **driv·elled**
  driv·el·ing
    or **driv·el·ling**
driv·el·er
  or **driv·el·ler**
driv·er
drive·way
driz·zle
droll·ery
drol·ly
drom·e·dary
drop
  dropped
  drop·ping
drop·kick
drop·let
drop·out
drop·per
drop·sy
dross
drought
  or **drouth**
drov·er
drowse
drows·i·ly
drows·i·ness
drowsy
drub
  drubbed
  drub·bing
drudge
drudg·ery
drug
  drugged
  drug·ging
drug·gist
drug·store
dru·id
drum
  drummed
  drum·ming
drum·beat
drum·mer
drum·stick
drunk·ard
drunk·en·ness
dry
  adj (*see* **drier**)
  dri·er
  dri·est
dry-clean
dry·er
  noun, var of **drier**
dry·ly
dry·ness
dry-rot
du·al
  double (*see* **duel**)
du·al·ism
du·al·i·ty
du·al·ly
dub
  dubbed
  dub·bing
du·bi·ety
du·bi·ous
du·bi·ous·ness
du·cal
duc·at
duch·ess
duchy
duck·bill
duck·board
duck·ling
duck·pin
duc·tile
duc·til·i·ty
duct·less
dud·geon
du·el
  combat (*see* **dual**)
du·el·ist
du·en·de
du·et
duf·fel
  or **duf·fle**
duf·fer
dug·out
duke·dom
dul·cet
dul·ci·mer

dull·ard
dull·ness
or **dul·ness**
dul·ly
Du·luth
du·ly
dumb·bell
dumb·found
or **dum·found**
dumb·ly
dumb·wait·er
dum·dum
dum·my
dump·ling
dumpy
dun
dunned
dun·ning
dun·der·head
dun·ga·ree
dun·geon
dung·hill
du·o·de·nal
du·o·de·num
pl **du·o·de·na** *or* **du·o·de·nums**
du·plex
du·pli·cate
du·pli·ca·tion
du·pli·ca·tor
du·plic·i·ty
du·ra·bil·i·ty
du·ra·ble
du·rance
du·ra·tion
du·ress
dur·ing
dusk·i·ly
dusk·i·ness
dusky
dust·er
dust·i·ly
dust·i·ness
dust·less
dust·pan
dusty
Dutch
du·te·ous
du·ti·able
du·ti·ful
du·ti·ful·ly
du·ty
dwarf
pl **dwarfs** *or* **dwarves**
dwarf·ish
dwell
dwelt
or **dwelled**
dwell·ing
dwin·dle
dyb·buk
pl **dyb·bu·kim** *also* **dyb·buks**
dye
color (*see* **die**)
dyed
dye·ing
dye·stuff
dy·nam·ic
dy·nam·i·cal·ly
dy·na·mism
dy·na·mite
dy·na·mo
pl **dy·na·mos**
dy·nast
dy·nas·tic
dy·nas·ty
dyne
dy·node
dys·en·tery
dys·pep·sia
dys·pep·tic
dys·pep·ti·cal·ly
dys·tro·phic
dys·tro·phy

E

ea·ger
ea·ger·ly
ea·ger·ness
ea·gle
ea·glet
ear·ache
ear·drum
ear·li·ness
ear·lobe
ear·ly
ear·mark
ear·muff
ear·nest
ear·nest·ly
ear·nest·ness
earn·ings
ear·phone

ear·ring
ear·shot
ear·split·ting
earth·en
earth·en·ware
earth·i·ness
earth·ling
earth·ly
earth·quake
earth·shak·ing
earth·work
earth·worm
earthy
ear·wax
ea·sel
ease·ment
eas·i·ly
eas·i·ness
east·er·ly
east·ern
East·ern·er
east·ward
easy
easy·go·ing
eat
  ate
  eat·en
  eat·ing
eat·able
eat·er
eau de co·logne
  pl eaux de co·logne
eaves
eaves·drop
eaves·drop·per
eb·o·ny
ebul·lience
ebul·lient
eb·ul·li·tion
ec·cen·tric
ec·cen·tri·cal·ly
ec·cen·tric·i·ty
ec·cle·si·as·tic
ec·cle·si·as·ti·cal
ech·e·lon
echo
  pl ech·oes
echo·lo·ca·tion
éclair
éclat
eclec·tic
eclec·ti·cism
eclipse
eclip·tic
ec·logue
eco·log·i·cal
  also eco·log·ic
eco·log·i·cal·ly
ecol·o·gist
ecol·o·gy
eco·nom·ic
eco·nom·i·cal
eco·nom·i·cal·ly
eco·nom·ics
econ·o·mist
econ·o·mize
econ·o·my
eco·sphere
eco·sys·tem
eco·tone
ecru
ec·sta·sy
ec·stat·ic
ec·stat·i·cal·ly
Ec·ua·dor
Ec·ua·dor·an
Ec·ua·dor·ian
ec·u·men·i·cal
ec·u·men·i·cal·ly
ec·u·me·nic·i·ty
ec·ze·ma
ec·zem·a·tous
Edam
ed·dy
edel·weiss
ede·ma
edem·a·tous
edge
edge·ways
edge·wise
edg·i·ness
edg·ing
edgy
ed·i·bil·i·ty
ed·i·ble
edict
ed·i·fi·ca·tion
ed·i·fice
ed·i·fy
ed·it
edi·tion
ed·i·tor
ed·i·to·ri·al
ed·i·to·ri·al·iza·tion
ed·i·to·ri·al·ize

ed·i·to·ri·al·iz·er
ed·i·to·ri·al·ly
ed·i·tor·ship
Ed·mon·ton
ed·u·ca·ble
ed·u·cate
ed·u·ca·tion
ed·u·ca·tion·al·ly
ed·u·ca·tor
educe
educ·ible
educ·tion
ee·rie
also **ee·ry**
ee·ri·ly
ef·face
ef·face·able
ef·face·ment
ef·fect
result (*see* **affect**)
ef·fec·tive
ef·fec·tive·ly
ef·fec·tive·ness
ef·fec·tu·al
ef·fec·tu·al·ly
ef·fec·tu·ate
ef·fem·i·na·cy
ef·fem·i·nate
ef·fer·ent
ef·fer·vesce
ef·fer·ves·cence
ef·fer·ves·cent
ef·fete
ef·fi·ca·cious
ef·fi·ca·cy
ef·fi·cien·cy
ef·fi·cient
ef·fi·cient·ly
ef·fi·gy
ef·flo·resce
ef·flo·res·cence
ef·flu·ence
ef·flu·ent
ef·flu·vi·um
pl **ef·flu·via** *or* **ef·flu·vi·ums**
ef·fort
ef·fort·less·ly
ef·fron·tery
ef·ful·gence
ef·ful·gent
ef·fuse
ef·fu·sion
ef·fu·sive
egal·i·tar·i·an
egal·i·tar·i·an·ism
egg·beat·er
egg·head
egg·nog
egg·plant
egg·shell
egis
var of **aegis**
ego
pl **egos**
ego·cen·tric
ego·cen·tric·i·ty
ego·ism
ego·ist
ego·is·tic
also **ego·is·ti·cal**
ego·is·ti·cal·ly
ego·tism
ego·tist
ego·tis·tic
or **ego·tis·ti·cal**
ego·tis·ti·cal·ly
egre·gious
egress
egret
Egypt
Egyp·tian
ei·der
eigh·teen
eigh·teenth
eighth
eight·i·eth
eighty
ei·ther
ejac·u·late
ejac·u·la·tion
eject
ejec·tion
ejec·tor
eke
ekis·tics
elab·o·rate
elab·o·rate·ly
elab·o·rate·ness
elab·o·ra·tion
élan
elapse
elas·tic
elas·tic·i·ty
elate
ela·tion

el·bow
el·bow·room
el·der·ber·ry
el·der·ly
el·dest
El Do·ra·do
elect·able
elec·tion
elec·tion·eer
elec·tive
elec·tor
elec·tor·al
elec·tor·ate
elec·tric
elec·tri·cal
elec·tri·cal·ly
elec·tri·cian
elec·tric·i·ty
elec·tri·fi·ca·tion
elec·tri·fy
elec·tro·anal·y·sis
elec·tro·an·a·lyt·ic
elec·tro·car·dio·gram
elec·tro·car·dio·graph
elec·tro·car·di·og·ra·phy
elec·tro·chem·i·cal·ly
elec·tro·chem·is·try
elec·tro·cute
elec·tro·cu·tion
elec·trode
elec·tro·en·ceph·a·lo·gram
elec·tro·en·ceph·a·lo·graph
elec·trol·y·sis
elec·tro·lyte
elec·tro·lyt·ic
elec·tro·lyze
elec·tro·mag·net
elec·tro·mag·net·ic
elec·tro·mag·ne·tism
elec·trom·e·ter
elec·tro·mo·tive force
elec·tron
elec·tron·ic
elec·tron·i·cal·ly
elec·tron·ics
elec·tro·plate
elec·tro·shock
elec·tro·ther·a·py
elec·tro·ther·mal
or elec·tro·ther·mic
elec·tro·type
el·ee·mos·y·nary
el·e·gance
el·e·gant
ele·gi·ac
also el·e·gi·a·cal
el·e·gize
el·e·gy
el·e·ment
el·e·men·tal
el·e·men·ta·ry
el·e·phant
el·e·phan·ti·a·sis
el·e·phan·tine
el·e·vate
el·e·va·tion
el·e·va·tor
elev·en
elev·enth
elf
pl elves
elf·in
elf·ish
elic·it
draw out (*see* illicit)
elide
el·i·gi·bil·i·ty
el·i·gi·ble
elim·i·nate
elim·i·na·tion
eli·sion
elite
elit·ism
elit·ist
elix·ir
Eliz·a·beth
Eliz·a·be·than
el·lipse
el·lip·sis
pl el·lip·ses
el·lip·tic
or el·lip·ti·cal
el·o·cu·tion
el·o·cu·tion·ist
elon·gate

elon·ga·tion
elope
elope·ment
el·o·quence
el·o·quent
El Paso
El Sal·va·dor
else·where
elu·ci·date
elu·ci·da·tion
elude
evade (*see* allude)
elu·sive
evasive (*see* allusive)
elu·sive·ly
elu·sive·ness
ely·sian
Ely·si·um
ema·ci·ate
ema·ci·a·tion
em·a·nate
em·a·na·tion
eman·ci·pate
eman·ci·pa·tion
eman·ci·pa·tor
emas·cu·late
emas·cu·la·tion
em·balm
em·balm·er
em·bank
em·bank·ment
em·bar·go
pl em·bar·goes
em·bark
em·bar·ka·tion
em·bar·rass
em·bar·rass·ment
em·bas·sy
em·bat·tle
em·bed
or im·bed
em·bel·lish
em·bel·lish·ment
em·ber
em·bez·zle
em·bez·zle·ment
em·bez·zler
em·bit·ter
em·bla·zon
em·blem
em·blem·at·ic
also em·blem·at·i·cal
em·bodi·ment
em·body
em·bold·en
em·bol·ic
em·bo·lism
em·boss
em·bou·chure
em·brace
em·brace·able
em·bra·sure
em·bro·cate
em·bro·ca·tion
em·broi·der
em·broi·dery
em·broil
em·broil·ment
em·bryo
pl em·bry·os
em·bry·o·log·ic
or em·bry·o·log·i·cal
em·bry·ol·o·gist
em·bry·ol·o·gy
em·bry·on·ic
em·cee
emend
correct (*see* amend)
emen·da·tion
em·er·ald
emerge
emer·gence
emer·gen·cy
emer·gent
emer·i·ta
emer·i·tus
pl emer·i·ti
em·ery
emet·ic
em·i·grant
em·i·grate
leave one's country (*see* immigrate)
em·i·gra·tion
émi·gré
or emi·gré
em·i·nence
em·i·nent
outstanding (*see* immanent, imminent)
emir
em·is·sary
emis·sion
emis·siv·i·ty

emit
emit•ted
emit•ting
emol•lient
emol•u•ment
emote
emo•tion
emo•tion•al
emo•tion•al•ly
emo•tive
em•path•ic
em•pa•thy
em•pen•nage
em•per•or
em•pha•sis
pl em•pha•ses
em•pha•size
em•phat•ic
em•phat•i•cal•ly
em•phy•se•ma
em•pire
em•pir•i•cal
also em•pir•ic
em•pir•i•cal•ly
em•pir•i•cism
em•pir•i•cist
em•place•ment
em•ploy
em•ploy•abil•i•ty
em•ploy•able
em•ploy•ee
or em•ploye
em•ploy•er
em•ploy•ment
em•po•ri•um
pl em•po•ri•ums *also* em•po•ria
em•pow•er
em•press
emp•ti•ness
emp•ty
emp•ty-hand•ed
em•py•re•an
emu
em•u•late
em•u•la•tion
em•u•lous
emul•si•fi•able
emul•si•fi•ca•tion
emul•si•fi•er
emul•si•fy
emul•sion
en•able
en•abled
en•abling
en•act
en•act•ment
enam•el
enam•eled
or enam•elled
enam•el•ing
or enam•el•ling
enam•el•ware
en•am•or
en bloc
en•camp
en•camp•ment
en•cap•su•late
en•case
en•ceph•a•lit•ic
en•ceph•a•li•tis
en•ceph•a•lo•my•eli•tis
en•chain
en•chant
en•chant•er
en•chant•ment
en•chant•ress
en•chi•la•da
en•ci•pher
en•cir•cle
en•cir•cle•ment
en•clave
en•close
en•clo•sure
en•code
en•co•mi•um
pl en•co•mi•ums *or* en•co•mia
en•com•pass
en•core
en•coun•ter
en•cour•age
en•cour•age•ment
en•croach
en•croach•ment
en•crust
or in•crust
en•cum•ber
en•cum•brance
en•cyc•li•cal
en•cy•clo•pe•dia
also en•cy•clo•pae•dia

en·cy·clo·pe·dic
also en·cy·clo·pae·dic
en·cyst
en·dan·ger
en·dear
en·dear·ment
en·deav·or
en·dem·ic
end·ing
en·dive
end·less
end·most
en·do·crine
en·do·cri·nol·o·gy
en·dog·a·mous
en·dog·a·my
en·dorse
or in·dorse
en·dorse·ment
en·do·scope
en·do·scop·ic
en·dos·co·py
en·dow
en·dow·ment
en·dur·able
en·dur·ance
en·dure
end·ways
en·e·ma
en·e·my
en·er·get·ic
en·er·get·i·cal·ly
en·er·gize
en·er·giz·er
en·er·gy
en·er·vate
en·er·va·tion
en·fee·ble
en·fee·ble·ment
en·fi·lade
en·fold
en·force
en·force·able
en·force·ment
en·fran·chise
en·fran·chise·ment
en·gage
en·gaged
en·gag·ing
en·gage·ment
en·gen·der
en·gine
en·gi·neer
En·gland
En·glish
en·graft
en·grave
en·graved
en·grav·ing
en·grav·er
en·gross
en·gulf
en·hance
en·hance·ment
enig·ma
enig·mat·ic
also enig·mat·i·cal
enig·mat·i·cal·ly
en·jamb·ment
or en·jambe·ment
en·join
en·joy
en·joy·able
en·joy·ably
en·joy·ment
en·large
en·large·ment
en·larg·er
en·light·en
en·light·en·ment
en·list
en·list·ment
en·liv·en
en masse
en·mesh
en·mi·ty
en·no·ble
en·no·ble·ment
en·nui
enor·mi·ty
enor·mous
enough
en·plane
en·quire
en·qui·ry
en·rage
en·rap·ture
en·rich
en·rich·ment
en·roll
or en·rol
en·rolled
en·roll·ing

en•roll•ment
en route
en•sconce
en•sem•ble
en•sheathe
en•shrine
en•shroud
en•sign
en•si•lage
en•slave
en•slave•ment
en•snare
en•sue
en•sure
en•tail
en•tan•gle
en•tan•gle•ment
en•tente
en•ter
en•ter•i•tis
en•ter•prise
en•ter•pris•ing
en•ter•tain
en•ter•tain•er
en•ter•tain•ment
en•thrall
or en•thral
en•thralled
en•thrall•ing
en•throne
en•thuse
en•thu•si•asm
en•thu•si•ast
en•thu•si•as•tic
en•thu•si•as•ti•cal•ly
en•tice
en•tice•ment
en•tire
en•tire•ly
en•tire•ty
en•ti•tle
en•ti•ty
en•tomb
en•tomb•ment
en•to•mo•log•i•cal
en•to•mol•o•gist
en•to•mol•o•gy
en•tou•rage
en•tr'acte
en•trails
en•train
en•trance
en•trant
en•trap
en•trap•ment
en•treat
en•treaty
en•trée
or en•tree
en•trench
en•trench•ment
en•tre•pre•neur
en•tro•py
en•trust
en•try
en•twine
enu•mer•ate
enu•mer•a•tion
enu•mer•a•tive
enu•mer•a•tor
enun•ci•ate
enun•ci•a•tion
enun•ci•a•tor
en•ure•sis
en•vel•op
en•ve•lope
en•vel•op•ment
en•ven•om
en•vi•able
en•vi•ably
en•vi•ous
en•vi•ous•ly
en•vi•ous•ness
en•vi•ron•ment
en•vi•ron•men•tal
en•vi•rons
en•vis•age
en•voy
en•vy
en•wreathe
en•zy•mat•ic
also en•zy•mic
en•zyme
eon
ep•au•let
also ep•au•lette
epergne
ephed•rine
ephem•er•al
ephem•er•on
pl ephem•era *also* ephem•er•ons
ep•ic
poem (*see* epoch)
epi•cen•ter

ep·i·cure
ep·i·cu·re·an
ep·i·dem·ic
epi·der·mal
also epi·der·mic
epi·der·mis
epi·glot·tis
ep·i·gram
ep·i·gram·mat·ic
ep·i·gram·mat·i·cal·ly
ep·i·graph
epig·ra·pher
ep·i·graph·ic
also ep·i·graph·i·cal
epig·ra·phy
ep·i·lep·sy
ep·i·lep·tic
ep·i·logue
epiph·a·ny
epis·co·pa·cy
epis·co·pal
Epis·co·pa·lian
epis·co·pate
ep·i·sode
ep·i·sod·ic
also epi·sod·i·cal
ep·i·sod·i·cal·ly
epis·tle
epis·to·lary
ep·i·taph
ep·i·tha·la·mi·um
or ep·i·tha·la·mi·on
pl ep·i·tha·la·mi·ums
or ep·i·tha·la·mia
ep·i·the·li·al
ep·i·the·li·um
ep·i·thet
epit·o·me
epit·o·mize
ep·och
era (*see* epic)
ep·och·al
ep·oxy
eq·ua·bil·i·ty
equa·ble
equa·bly
equal
equaled
or equalled
equal·ing
or equal·ling
equal·i·ty
equal·iza·tion
equal·ize
equal·iz·er
equal·ly
equa·nim·i·ty
equate
equa·tion
equa·tor
equa·to·ri·al
Equa·to·ri·al Guin·ea
equer·ry
eques·tri·an
eques·tri·enne
equi·an·gu·lar
equi·dis·tant
equi·lat·er·al
equil·i·brate
equil·i·bra·tion
equi·lib·ri·um
pl equi·lib·ri·ums *or* equi·lib·ria
equine
equi·noc·tial
equi·nox
equip
equipped
equip·ping
eq·ui·page
equip·ment
equi·poise
eq·ui·ta·ble
eq·ui·ta·bly
eq·ui·ta·tion
eq·ui·ty
equiv·a·lence
equiv·a·lent
equiv·o·cal
equiv·o·cal·ly
equiv·o·cate
equiv·o·ca·tion
equiv·o·ca·tor
era
erad·i·ca·ble
erad·i·cate
erad·i·ca·tion
erad·i·ca·tor
eras·able
erase
eras·er
era·sure
erect

erec•tion
erec•tor
ere•long
Erie
er•mine
erode
erog•e•nous
also er•o•gen•ic
ero•sion
ero•sive
erot•ic
erot•i•ca
erot•i•cal•ly
erot•i•cism
er•ran•cy
er•rand
er•rant
er•ra•ta
er•rat•ic
er•rat•i•cal•ly
er•ra•tum
pl er•ra•ta
er•ro•ne•ous
er•ror
er•satz
erst•while
er•u•dite
er•u•di•tion
erupt
to force out (*see* irrupt)
erup•tion
erup•tive
er•y•sip•e•las
es•ca•late
es•ca•la•tion
es•ca•la•tor
es•cal•lop
es•ca•pade
es•cape
es•cap•ee
es•cap•ism
es•cap•ist
es•ca•role
es•carp
es•carp•ment
es•char
es•cha•rot•ic
es•cha•to•log•i•cal•ly
es•cha•tol•o•gy
es•cheat
es•chew
es•cort
es•cri•toire
es•crow
es•cu•do
es•cutch•eon
Es•ki•mo
esoph•a•ge•al
esoph•a•gus
es•o•ter•ic
es•o•ter•i•cal•ly
es•pa•drille
es•pal•ier
es•pe•cial
es•pe•cial•ly
Es•pe•ran•to
es•pi•o•nage
es•pla•nade
es•pous•al
es•pouse
espres•so
es•prit de corps
es•py
es•quire
es•say
attempt (*see* assay)
es•say•ist
es•sence
es•sen•tial
es•sen•tial•ly
es•tab•lish
es•tab•lish•ment
es•tate
es•teem
es•ter
es•thete
var of aesthete
es•thet•ic
var of aesthetic
es•thet•ics
var of aesthetics
es•ti•ma•ble
es•ti•mate
es•ti•ma•tion
es•ti•ma•tor
Es•to•nia
Es•to•ni•an
es•trange
es•trange•ment
es•tro•gen
es•tu•ary
etch
etch•er
etch•ing

eter·nal
eter·nal·ly
eter·ni·ty
eth·ane
ether
ethe·re·al
ethe·re·al·ly
eth·i·cal
also eth·ic
eth·i·cal·ly
eth·ics
Ethi·o·pia
Ethi·o·pi·an
eth·nic
eth·ni·cal·ly
eth·no·cen·tric
eth·no·cen·tri·cal·ly
eth·no·cen·trism
eth·nog·ra·pher
eth·no·graph·ic
eth·no·graph·i·cal·ly
eth·nog·ra·phy
eth·no·log·ic
eth·no·log·i·cal·ly
eth·nol·o·gist
eth·nol·o·gy
etho·log·i·cal
ethol·o·gist
ethol·o·gy
ethos
eth·yl
eti·o·log·ic
eti·ol·o·gy
et·i·quette
étude
et·y·mo·log·i·cal
et·y·mol·o·gist
et·y·mol·o·gy
eu·ca·lyp·tus
Eu·cha·rist
eu·cha·ris·tic
eu·chre
eu·gen·ic
eu·gen·i·cal·ly
eu·gen·ics
eu·lo·gis·tic
eu·lo·gize
eu·lo·gy
eu·nuch
eu·phe·mism
eu·phe·mis·tic
eu·phe·mis·ti·cal·ly
eu·phon·ic
eu·pho·ni·ous
eu·pho·ny
eu·pho·ria
eu·phor·ic
Eur·asian
eu·re·ka
Eu·ro·bond
Eu·ro·dol·lar
Eu·rope
Eu·ro·pe·an
eu·sta·chian tube
eu·tha·na·sia
eu·then·ics
evac·u·ate
evac·u·a·tion
evac·u·ee
evade
eval·u·ate
eval·u·a·tion
ev·a·nes·cence
ev·a·nes·cent
evan·gel·i·cal
also evan·gel·ic
Evan·gel·i·cal·ism
evan·gel·i·cal·ly
evan·ge·lism
evan·ge·list
evan·ge·lis·tic
evan·ge·lis·ti·cal·ly
evan·ge·lize
Ev·ans·ville
evap·o·rate
evap·o·ra·tion
evap·o·ra·tor
eva·sion
eva·sive
even·hand·ed
eve·ning
even·ly
even·ness
even·song
event
event·ful
even·tide
even·tu·al
even·tu·al·i·ty
even·tu·al·ly
even·tu·ate
ev·er

ev·er·bloom·ing
ev·er·glade
ev·er·green
ev·er·last·ing
ev·er·more
ev·ery
ev·ery·body
ev·ery·day
ev·ery·one
ev·ery·thing
ev·ery·where
evict
evic·tion
ev·i·dence
ev·i·dent
ev·i·den·tial
ev·i·den·tial·ly
evil·do·er
evil·ly
evil-mind·ed
evince
evis·cer·ate
evis·cer·a·tion
evo·ca·tion
evoke
evo·lu·tion
evo·lu·tion·ary
evo·lu·tion·ist
evolve
ewe
female sheep (*see* yew)
ew·er
ex·ac·er·bate
ex·ac·er·ba·tion
ex·act
ex·act·ing
ex·ac·tion
ex·ac·ti·tude
ex·act·ly
ex·act·ness
ex·ag·ger·ate
ex·ag·ger·a·tion
ex·ag·ger·a·tor
ex·alt
ex·al·ta·tion
ex·am·i·na·tion
ex·am·ine
ex·am·in·er
ex·am·ple
ex·as·per·ate
ex·as·per·a·tion
ex·ca·vate
ex·ca·va·tion
ex·ca·va·tor
ex·ceed
surpass (*see* accede)
ex·ceed·ing·ly
ex·cel
ex·celled
ex·cel·ling
ex·cel·lence
ex·cel·len·cy
ex·cel·lent
ex·cel·si·or
ex·cept
also ex·cep·ting
leave out (*see* accept)
ex·cep·tion
ex·cep·tion·able
ex·cep·tion·al
ex·cep·tion·al·ly
ex·cerpt
ex·cerp·tion
ex·cess
surplus (*see* access)
ex·ces·sive
ex·ces·sive·ly
ex·change
ex·change·able
ex·che·quer
ex·cis·able
ex·cise
ex·ci·sion
ex·cit·abil·i·ty
ex·cit·able
ex·ci·tant
ex·ci·ta·tion
ex·cite
ex·cit·ed·ly
ex·cite·ment
ex·claim
ex·cla·ma·tion
ex·clam·a·to·ry
ex·clude
ex·clu·sion
ex·clu·sive
ex·clu·sive·ness
ex·clu·siv·i·ty
ex·com·mu·ni·cate
ex·com·mu·ni·ca·tion
ex·co·ri·ate
ex·co·ri·a·tion
ex·cre·ment

ex·cres·cence
ex·cres·cent
ex·crete
ex·cre·tion
ex·cre·to·ry
ex·cru·ci·at·ing
ex·cul·pate
ex·cul·pa·tion
ex·cul·pa·to·ry
ex·cur·sion
ex·cur·sion·ist
ex·cur·sive
ex·cus·able
ex·cus·ably
ex·cuse
ex·e·cra·ble
ex·e·crate
ex·e·cra·tion
ex·e·cute
ex·e·cu·tion
ex·e·cu·tion·er
ex·ec·u·tive
ex·ec·u·tor
ex·ec·u·trix
ex·e·ge·sis
pl ex·e·ge·ses
ex·e·gete
ex·em·plar
ex·em·pla·ry
ex·em·pli·fi·ca·tion
ex·em·pli·fy
ex·empt
ex·emp·tion
ex·er·cis·able
ex·er·cise
exert (*see* exorcise)
ex·er·cis·er
ex·ert
ex·er·tion
ex·ha·la·tion
ex·hale
ex·haust
ex·haust·ibil·i·ty
ex·haust·ible
ex·haus·tion
ex·haus·tive
ex·haust·less
ex·hib·it
ex·hi·bi·tion
ex·hi·bi·tion·ism
ex·hib·i·tor
ex·hil·a·rate
ex·hil·a·ra·tion
ex·hort
ex·hor·ta·tion
ex·hu·ma·tion
ex·hume
ex·i·gen·cy
ex·i·gent
ex·i·gu·i·ty
ex·ig·u·ous
ex·ile
ex·ist
ex·is·tence
ex·is·tent
ex·is·ten·tial
ex·is·ten·tial·ism
ex·it
ex·o·dus
ex of·fi·cio
ex·og·a·mous
ex·og·a·my
ex·og·e·nous
ex·on·er·ate
ex·on·er·a·tion
ex·or·bi·tant
ex·or·cise
expel (*see* exercise)
ex·or·cism
ex·or·cist
ex·o·ter·ic
ex·o·ter·i·cal·ly
ex·ot·ic
ex·ot·i·cal·ly
ex·ot·i·cism
also ex·o·tism
ex·pand
ex·pand·able
ex·pand·er
ex·panse
ex·pan·sion
ex·pan·sive
ex par·te
ex·pa·ti·ate
ex·pa·ti·a·tion
ex·pa·tri·ate
ex·pa·tri·a·tion
ex·pect
ex·pect·able
ex·pect·ably
ex·pec·tan·cy
ex·pec·tant
ex·pec·ta·tion
ex·pec·to·rant

ex•pec•to•rate
ex•pec•to•ra•tion
ex•pe•di•ence
ex•pe•di•en•cy
ex•pe•di•ent
ex•pe•dite
ex•pe•dit•er
also ex•pe•di•tor
ex•pe•di•tion
ex•pe•di•tion•ary
ex•pe•di•tious
ex•pel
ex•pelled
ex•pel•ling
ex•pend
ex•pend•abil•i•ty
ex•pend•able
ex•pen•di•ture
ex•pense
ex•pen•sive
ex•pen•sive•ly
ex•pe•ri•ence
ex•pe•ri•enced
ex•pe•ri•en•tial
ex•pe•ri•en•tial•ly
ex•per•i•ment
ex•per•i•men•tal
ex•per•i•men•tal•ly
ex•per•i•men•ta•tion
ex•per•i•ment•er
ex•pert
ex•per•tise
ex•pert•ly
ex•pert•ness
ex•pi•a•ble
ex•pi•ate
ex•pi•a•tion
ex•pi•a•tor
ex•pi•a•to•ry
ex•pi•ra•tion
ex•pire
ex•plain
ex•plain•able
ex•pla•na•tion
ex•plan•a•to•ry
ex•ple•tive
ex•pli•ca•ble
ex•pli•cate
ex•pli•ca•tion
ex•pli•ca•tor
ex•pli•ca•to•ry
ex•plic•it
ex•plode
ex•ploit
ex•ploit•able
ex•ploi•ta•tion
ex•ploit•ative
ex•ploit•er
ex•plo•ra•tion
ex•plor•ato•ry
ex•plore
ex•plor•er
ex•plo•sion
ex•plo•sive
ex•po•nent
ex•po•nen•tial
ex•port
ex•por•ta•tion
ex•port•er
ex•pose
ex•po•sé
ex•po•si•tion
ex•pos•i•tor
ex•pos•i•to•ry
ex post fac•to
ex•pos•tu•late
ex•pos•tu•la•tion
ex•po•sure
ex•pound
ex•press
ex•press•ible
ex•pres•sion
ex•pres•sion•ism
ex•pres•sion•ist
ex•pres•sion•is•tic
ex•pres•sive
ex•press•man
ex•press•way
ex•pro•pri•ate
ex•pro•pri•a•tion
ex•pul•sion
ex•punge
ex•pur•gate
ex•pur•ga•tion
ex•qui•site
ex•tant
existent (*see* extent)
ex•tem•po•ra•ne•ous
ex•tem•po•rary
ex•tem•po•re
ex•tem•po•rize
ex•tend
ex•ten•sion
ex•ten•sive

ex·tent
size (*see* extant)

ex·ten·u·ate

ex·ten·u·a·tion

ex·te·ri·or

ex·ter·mi·nate

ex·ter·mi·na·tion

ex·ter·mi·na·tor

ex·tern

ex·ter·nal

ex·ter·nal·ly

ex·ter·ri·to·ri·al

ex·ter·ri·to·ri·al·i·ty

ex·tinct

ex·tinc·tion

ex·tin·guish

ex·tin·guish·able

ex·tin·guish·er

ex·tir·pate

ex·tir·pa·tion

ex·tol
also ex·toll
ex·tolled
ex·tol·ling

ex·tort

ex·tor·tion

ex·tor·tion·ate

ex·tor·tion·er

ex·tor·tion·ist

ex·tra

ex·tract

ex·tract·able
or ex·tract·ible

ex·trac·tion

ex·trac·tive

ex·trac·tor

ex·tra·cur·ric·u·lar

ex·tra·dit·able

ex·tra·dite

ex·tra·di·tion

ex·tra·ga·lac·tic

ex·tra·le·gal

ex·tra·le·gal·ly

ex·tral·i·ty

ex·tra·mar·i·tal

ex·tra·mu·ral

ex·tra·ne·ous

ex·traor·di·nari·ly

ex·traor·di·nary

ex·trap·o·late

ex·trap·o·la·tion

ex·tra·sen·so·ry

ex·tra·ter·res·tri·al

ex·tra·ter·ri·to·ri·al

ex·tra·ter·ri·to·ri·al·i·ty

ex·trav·a·gance

ex·trav·a·gant

ex·trav·a·gan·za

ex·tra·ve·hic·u·lar

ex·tra·ver·sion
or ex·tro·ver·sion

ex·tra·vert
or ex·tro·vert

ex·tra·vert·ed
or ex·tro·vert·ed

ex·treme

ex·treme·ly

ex·trem·ism

ex·trem·ist

ex·trem·i·ty

ex·tri·cate

ex·tri·ca·tion

ex·trin·sic

ex·trin·si·cal·ly

ex·trude

ex·tru·sion

ex·u·ber·ance

ex·u·ber·ant

ex·u·da·tion

ex·ude

ex·ult

ex·ul·tant

ex·ul·ta·tion

ex·urb

ex·ur·ban·ite

ex·ur·bia

eye
eyed
eye·ing
or ey·ing

eye·ball

eye·brow

eye·ful

eye·glass

eye·lash

eye·let
hole (*see* islet)

eye·lid

eye-open·er

eye·piece

eye·sight

eye·sore

eye·spot

eye·strain

eye·tooth

eye·wash

eye·wit·ness

ey·rir
pl au·rar

F

Fa·bi·an

Fa·bi·an·ism

fa·ble

fa·bled

fab·ric

fab·ri·cate

fab·ri·ca·tion

fab·ri·ca·tor

fab·u·lous

fa·cade
also fa·çade

face·down

face-lift·ing

fac·et

fa·ce·tious

fa·ce·tious·ness

fa·cial

fac·ile

fa·cil·i·tate

fa·cil·i·ty

fac·ing

fac·sim·i·le

fac·tion

fac·tion·al·ism

fac·tion·al·ly

fac·tious

fac·ti·tious
artificial (*see* fictitious)

fac·tor

fac·tor·able

fac·to·ri·al

fac·to·ry

fac·to·tum

fac·tu·al

fac·tu·al·ly

fac·ul·ty

fad·dish

fad·dist

fade·less

fag
fagged
fag·ging

fag·ot
or fag·got

fag·ot·ing
or fag·got·ing

Fahr·en·heit

fa·ience
or fa·ïence

fail·ing

faille
silk (*see* file)

fail-safe

fail·ure

faint
weak (*see* feint)

faint·heart·ed

faint·ness

fair·ground

fair·ing

fair·ly

fair-mind·ed

fair·ness

fair-spok·en

fair-trade

fair·way

fair-weath·er

fairy

fairy·land

fait ac·com·pli
pl faits ac·com·plis

faith·ful

faith·ful·ly

faith·ful·ness

faith·less

faith·less·ness

fak·er
imposter (*see* fakir)

fa·kir
dervish (*see* faker)

fal·con

fal·con·er

fal·con·ry

fall
fell
fall·en
fall·ing

fal·la·cious

fal·la·cy

fal·li·bil·i·ty

fal·li·ble

fal·li·bly

fall·ing-out
pl fall·ings-out
or fall·ing-outs

fal·lo·pi·an tube
fall·out
fal·low
false·hood
false·ly
false·ness
fal·set·to
pl fal·set·tos
fal·si·fi·ca·tion
fal·si·fi·er
fal·si·fy
fal·si·ty
fal·ter
fal·ter·ing·ly
fa·mil·ial
fa·mil·iar
fa·mil·iar·i·ty
fa·mil·iar·iza·tion
fa·mil·iar·ize
fam·i·ly
fam·ine
fam·ish
fa·mous
fa·mous·ly
fan
fanned
fan·ning
fa·nat·ic
or fa·nat·i·cal
fa·nat·i·cal·ly
fa·nat·i·cism
fan·ci·er
fan·ci·ful
fan·ci·ful·ly
fan·ci·ly

fan·cy
fan·cy-free
fan·cy·work
fan·dan·go
pl fan·dan·gos
fan·fare
fan-jet
fan·light
fan·tail
fan·ta·sia
fan·tas·tic
fan·tas·ti·cal
fan·tas·ti·cal·ly
fan·ta·sy
far·ad
far·a·day
far·away
far·ceur
far·ci·cal
far·ci·cal·ly
fare·well
far·fetched
far-flung
fa·ri·na
far·i·na·ceous
farm·er
farm·hand
farm·house
farm·ing
farm·land
farm·stead
farm·yard
far-off
far-out

far·ra·go
pl far·ra·goes
far-reach·ing
far·row
far·see·ing
far·sight·ed
far·sight·ed·ness
far·ther
far·thest
far·thing
fas·ci·cle
fas·ci·nate
fas·ci·na·tion
fas·ci·na·tor
fas·cism
fas·cist
fas·cis·tic
fash·ion
fash·ion·able
fash·ion·ably
fast·back
fas·ten
fas·ten·er
fas·ten·ing
fas·tid·i·ous
fas·tid·i·ous·ness
fast·ness
fast-talk
fa·tal
fa·tal·ism
fa·tal·ist
fa·tal·is·tic
fa·tal·is·ti·cal·ly
fa·tal·i·ty
fa·tal·ly

fat·back
fat·ed
fate·ful
fate·ful·ly
fa·ther
fa·ther·hood
fa·ther-in-law
pl fa·thers-in-law
fa·ther·land
fa·ther·less
fa·ther·li·ness
fa·ther·ly
fath·om
fath·om·able
fath·om·less
fa·tigue
fat·ten
fat·ty
fa·tu·ity
fat·u·ous
fau·ces
fau·cet
fault·find·er
fault·find·ing
fault·i·ly
fault·less
faulty
faun
deity (*see* fawn)
fau·na
pl fau·nas *also* fau·nae
faux pas
pl faux pas
fa·vor
fa·vor·able
fa·vor·ably
fa·vored
fa·vor·ite
fa·vor·it·ism
fawn
grovel, deer (*see* faun)
faze
daunt (*see* phase)
fe·al·ty
fear·ful
fear·ful·ly
fear·less
fear·less·ness
fear·some
fea·si·bil·i·ty
fea·si·ble
fea·si·bly
feat
deed (*see* foot)
feath·er
feath·er·bed
feath·er·bed·ding
feath·ered
feath·er·edge
feath·er·weight
feath·ery
fea·ture
fea·tured
fea·tur·ing
fea·ture·less
feb·ri·fuge
fe·brile
Feb·ru·ary
fe·cal
fe·ces
feck·less
fe·cund
fec·un·date
fec·un·da·tion
fe·cun·di·ty
fed·er·al
fed·er·al·ism
fed·er·al·ist
fed·er·al·iza·tion
fed·er·al·ize
fed·er·ate
fed·er·a·tion
fed·er·a·tive
fe·do·ra
fee·ble
fee·ble·mind·ed
fee·ble·mind·ed·ness
fee·ble·ness
fee·bly
feed
fed
feed·ing
feed·back
feed·er
feel
felt
feel·ing
feel·er
feel·ing·ly
feign
feint
feigned (*see* faint)

fe•lic•i•tate
fe•lic•i•ta•tion
fe•lic•i•tous
fe•lic•i•ty
fe•line
fel•lah
pl fel•la•hin *or* fel•la•heen
fel•low
fel•low•man
fel•low•ship
fel•on
fe•lo•ni•ous
fel•o•ny
fe•male
fem•i•nine
fem•i•nin•i•ty
fem•i•nism
fem•i•nist
fe•mur
pl fe•murs *or* fem•o•ra
fen
pl fen
fenc•er
fenc•ing
fend•er
fen•es•tra•tion
fen•nel
fer•ment
fer•men•ta•tion
fe•ro•cious
fe•ro•cious•ness
fe•roc•i•ty
fer•ret
fer•ric
Fer•ris wheel
fer•rous
fer•rule
metal ring (see ferule)
fer•ry
fer•ry•boat
fer•tile
fer•til•i•ty
fer•til•iza•tion
fer•til•ize
fer•til•iz•er
fer•ule
rod (see ferrule)
fer•ven•cy
fer•vent
fer•vid
fer•vor
fes•tal
fes•ter
fes•ti•val
fes•tive
fes•tiv•i•ty
fes•toon
fe•tal
fetch
fetch•ing
fete
or fête
fet•id
fe•tish
also fe•tich
fe•tish•ism
fe•tish•ist
fet•lock
fet•ter
fet•tle
fe•tus
feu•dal
feu•dal•ism
feu•dal•is•tic
feu•da•to•ry
fe•ver
fe•ver•ish•ly
fez
pl fez•zes
fi•an•cé
masc
fi•an•cée
fem
fi•as•co
pl fi•as•coes
fi•at
fib
fibbed
fib•bing
fib•ber
fi•ber
or fi•bre
fi•ber•board
fi•ber•glass
fi•bril•late
fi•bril•la•tion
fi•brin
fi•bri•nous
fi•broid
fi•brous
fib•u•la
pl fib•u•lae *or* fib•u•las

fib·u·lar
fiche
fick·le
fick·le·ness
fic·tion
fic·tion·al
fic·ti·tious
imaginary (*see* factitious)

fid·dle
fid·dler
fid·dle·stick
fi·del·i·ty
fid·get
fid·gety
fi·du·cia·ry
field·er
field·piece
fiend·ish
fierce·ly
fierce·ness
fi·ery
fi·es·ta
fif·teen
fif·teenth
fifth
fif·ti·eth
fif·ty
fif·ty-fif·ty
fight
fought
fight·ing

fight·er
fig·ment
fig·u·ra·tion
fig·u·ra·tive
fig·ure
fig·ure·head
fig·u·rine
Fi·ji
fil·a·ment
fil·a·men·tous
fil·bert
filch
file
tool, cabinet (*see* faille)

fi·let
lace (*see* fillet)

fi·let mi·gnon
pl fi·lets mi·gnons

fil·ial
fil·i·bus·ter
fil·i·bus·ter·er
fil·i·gree
fil·ing
Fil·i·pi·no
fill·er
one that fills

fil·ler
pl fil·lers *or* fil·ler
coin

fil·let
also fi·let
strip, slice (*see* filet)

fill·ing
fil·lip
fil·ly
film·card
film·dom
film·strip
filmy
fils
pl fils

fil·ter
strainer (*see* philter)

fil·ter·able
also fil·tra·ble

filth·i·ness
filthy
fil·trate
fil·tra·tion
fi·na·gle
fi·na·gler
fi·nal
fi·na·le
fi·nal·ist
fi·nal·i·ty
fi·nal·ize
fi·nal·ly
fi·nance
fi·nan·cial
fi·nan·cial·ly
fi·nan·cier
find
found
find·ing

find·er
fin de siè·cle
find·ing
fine·ly
fine·ness
fin·ery
fine·spun
fi·nesse
fin·ger

fin·ger·board
fin·gered
fin·ger·ing
fin·ger·nail
fin·ger·post
fin·ger·print
fin·ger·tip
fin·i·al
fin·i·cal
fin·i·cal·ly
fin·ick·i·ness
fin·ick·ing
fin·icky
fi·nis
fin·ish
fin·ished
fin·ish·er
fi·nite
Fin·land
Fin·land·er
Finn
fin·nan had·die
Finn·ish
fiord
var of **fjord**
fir
tree (*see* **fur**)
fire·arm
fire·ball
fire·boat
fire·box
fire·brand
fire·break
fire·brick
fire·bug
fire·clay
fire·crack·er
fire·damp
fire-eat·er
fire·fly
fire·house
fire·light
fire·man
fire·place
fire·plug
fire·pow·er
fire·proof
fire·side
fire·stone
fire·trap
fire·wa·ter
fire·wood
fire·work
fir·ing
fir·ma·ment
firm·ly
firm·ness
first·born
first·fruits
first·hand
first·ly
first-rate
first-string
firth
fis·cal
fis·cal·ly
fish
pl **fish** *or* **fish·es**
fish-and-chips
fish·er
fish·er·man
fish·ery
fish·hook
fish·ing
fish·mong·er
fish·tail
fish·wife
fishy
fis·sion
fis·sion·able
fis·sure
fist·i·cuffs
fis·tu·la
pl **fis·tu·las** *or* **fis·tu·lae**
fis·tu·lous
fit
fit·ted
also **fit**
fit·ting
fit·ful
fit·ful·ly
fit·ly
fit·ness
fit·ter
fit·ting
fix·a·tion
fix·a·tive
fixed·ly
fixed·ness
fix·i·ty
fix·ture
fiz·zle
fjord
or **fiord**

flab·ber·gast
flab·bi·ly
flab·bi·ness
flab·by
flac·cid
fla·con
flag
  flagged
  flag·ging
fla·gel·lant
flag·el·late
flag·el·la·tion
fla·gel·lum
  pl **fla·gel·la** *also* **fla·gel·lums**
fla·geo·let
flag·ging
flag·on
flag·pole
fla·gran·cy
fla·grant
fla·gran·te de·lic·to
fla·grant·ly
flag·ship
flag·staff
flag·stone
flag-wav·ing
flair
  aptitude (*see* **flare**)
flak·i·ness
flaky
flam·beau
  pl **flam·beaux** *or* **flam·beaus**
flam·boy·ance
flam·boy·an·cy
flam·boy·ant
fla·men·co
flame·out
flame·proof
flam·er
flame·throw·er
flam·ing
fla·min·go
  pl **fla·min·gos** *also* **fla·min·goes**
flam·ma·bil·i·ty
flam·ma·ble
flange
flang·er
flank·er
flan·nel
flan·nel·ette
flap
  flapped
  flap·ping
flap·jack
flap·per
flap·py
flare
  flame (*see* **flair**)
flare·back
flar·ing
flare-up
flash·back
flash·bulb
flash·cube
flash·gun
flash·i·ly
flash·i·ness
flash·ing
flash·light
flashy
flask
flat
  flat·ted
  flat·ting
flat·bed
flat·boat
flat·car
flat·fish
flat-foot·ed
flat·iron
flat·ly
flat·ness
flat·ten
flat·ter
flat·ter·er
flat·tery
flat·top
flat·u·lence
flat·u·lent
fla·tus
flat·ware
flat·work
flat·worm
flaunt
flau·tist
fla·vor
fla·vored
fla·vor·ful
fla·vor·ing
fla·vor·less

fla·vor·some
flaw
flaw·less
flax·en
flea-bit·ten
fledg·ling
flee
  fled
  flee·ing
fleecy
fleet·ing
fleet·ly
fleet·ness
Flem·ing
Flem·ish
flesh·i·ness
flesh·ly
flesh·pot
fleshy
fleur-de-lis
  or **fleur-de-lys**
  pl **fleurs-de-lis** *or* **fleur-de-lis** *or* **fleurs-de-lys** *or* **fleur-de-lys**
flex·i·bil·i·ty
flex·i·ble
flex·i·bly
flex·or
flex·ure
flick·er
fli·er
  or **fly·er**
flight·i·ness
flight·less
flighty
flim·flam
flim·si·ly
flim·si·ness
flim·sy
fling
  flung
  fling·ing
Flint
flint·i·ly
flint·i·ness
flint·lock
flinty
flip
  flipped
  flip·ping
flip-flop
flip·pan·cy
flip·pant
flip·per
flir·ta·tion
flir·ta·tious
flit
  flit·ted
  flit·ting
flit·ter
fliv·ver
float·er
float·ing
flock·ing
floe
  ice (*see* **flow**)
flog
  flogged
  flog·ging
flog·ger
flood·gate
flood·light
flood·plain
flood·wa·ter
flood·way
floor·board
floor·ing
floor-length
floor·walk·er
floo·zy
  or **floo·zie**
flop
  flopped
  flop·ping
flop·py
flo·ra
  pl **flo·ras** *also* **flo·rae**
flo·ral
flo·res·cence
  flourishing (*see* **fluorescence**)
flo·res·cent
flo·ri·cul·ture
flor·id
Flor·i·da
Flo·rid·i·an
flo·rin
flo·rist
flossy
flo·ta·tion
flo·til·la
flot·sam
flounc·ing
flouncy

floun·der
flour·ish
flout
flow
stream (*see* floe)
flow·chart
flow·er
flow·ered
flow·er·i·ness
flow·er·pot
flow·ery
flu
influenza (*see* flue)
flub
flubbed
flub·bing
fluc·tu·ate
fluc·tu·a·tion
flue
chimney (*see* flu)
flu·en·cy
flu·ent
fluff·i·ness
fluffy
flu·id
flu·id·ic
flu·id·i·ty
flu·id·ounce
flu·idram
flum·mox
flun·ky
or flun·key
flu·o·resce
flu·o·res·cence
light (*see* florescence)
flu·o·res·cent
flu·o·ri·date
flu·o·ri·da·tion
flu·o·ride
flu·o·ri·nate
flu·o·ri·na·tion
flu·o·rine
flu·o·ro·scope
flu·o·ros·co·py
flur·ry
flus·ter
flut·ed
flut·ing
flut·ist
flut·ter
flut·tery
fly
move in air
flew
flown
fly·ing
fly
hit a fly ball
flied
fly·ing
fly·able
fly·blown
fly·by
fly-by-night
fly·catch·er
fly·er
var of flier
fly·leaf
fly·over
fly·pa·per
fly·speck
fly·weight
fly·wheel
foam·i·ly
foam·i·ness
foamy
fob
fobbed
fob·bing
fo·cal
fo·cal·ly
fo·cal·iza·tion
fo·cal·ize
fo·cus
pl fo·cus·es *or* fo·ci
fo·cus
fo·cused
also fo·cussed
fo·cus·ing
also fo·cus·sing
fod·der
foe
foe·tal
var of fetal
foe·tus
var of fetus
fog
fogged
fog·ging
fog·bound
fog·gi·ly
fog·gi·ness
fog·gy
fog·horn

fo·gy
also fo·gey

foi·ble

fold·away

fold·er

fol·de·rol

fo·liage

fo·li·ate

fo·li·at·ed

fo·li·a·tion

fo·lio
pl fo·li·os

folk·lore

folk·lor·ist

folksy

folk·way

fol·li·cle

fol·low

fol·low·er

fol·low·ing

fol·low-through

fol·low-up

fol·ly

fo·ment

fo·men·ta·tion

fon·dant

fon·dle

fond·ly

fond·ness

fon·due
also fon·du

food·stuff

fool·har·di·ly

fool·har·di·ness

fool·har·dy

fool·ish

fool·ish·ly

fool·ish·ness

fool·proof

fools·cap
or fool's cap

foot
(*see* feat)
pl feet
also foot

foot·age

foot·ball

foot·board

foot·bridge

foot·can·dle

foot·ed

foot·fall

foot·hill

foot·hold

foot·ing

foot·lights

foot·lock·er

foot·loose

foot·man

foot·mark

foot·note

foot·pad

foot·path

foot-pound

foot·print

foot·race

foot·rest

foot·sore

foot·step

foot·stool

foot·wear

foot·work

fop·pery

fop·pish

for·age

for·ag·er

for·ay

for·bear
abstain (*see* forebear)
for·bore
for·borne
for·bear·ing

for·bear·ance

for·bid
for·bade
or for·bad
for·bid·den
for·bid·ding

force·ful

force·ful·ly

for·ceps
pl for·ceps

forc·ible

forc·ibly

fore-and-aft

fore·arm

fore·bear
or for·bear
ancestor (*see* forbear)

fore·bode
also for·bode

fore·bod·ing

fore·cast
fore·cast
or fore·cast·ed
fore·cast·ing

fore•cast•er
fore•cas•tle
fore•close
fore•clo•sure
fore•deck
fore•doom
fore•fa•ther
fore•fin•ger
fore•foot
fore•front
fore•go
precede (*see* forgo)
fore•went
fore•gone
fore•go•ing
fore•ground
fore•hand
fore•hand•ed
fore•head
for•eign
for•eign•er
fore•know
fore•knowl•edge
fore•la•dy
fore•land
fore•leg
fore•limb
fore•lock
fore•man
fore•mast
fore•most
fore•name
fore•named
fore•noon
fo•ren•sic
fo•ren•si•cal•ly
fore•or•dain
fore•or•di•na•tion
fore•play
fore•quar•ter
fore•run•ner
fore•sad•dle
fore•said
fore•sail
fore•see
fore•saw
fore•seen
fore•see•ing
fore•see•able
fore•shad•ow
fore•sheet
fore•shore
fore•short•en
fore•sight
fore•sight•ed•ness
fore•skin
for•est
fore•stall
for•es•ta•tion
for•est•ed
for•est•er
for•est•ry
fore•taste
fore•tell
fore•told
fore•tell•ing
fore•thought
fore•to•ken
fore•top
for•ev•er
for•ev•er•more
fore•warn
fore•wom•an
fore•word
preface (*see* forward)
for•feit
for•fei•ture
for•gath•er
or fore•gath•er
forg•er
forg•ery
for•get
for•got
for•got•ten
or for•got
for•get•ting
for•get•ful
for•get•ta•ble
forg•ing
for•giv•able
for•give
for•gave
for•giv•en
for•giv•ing
for•give•ness
for•giv•ing
for•go
or fore•go
renounce (*see* forego)
for•went
or fore•went
for•gone
or fore•gone
for•go•ing
or fore•go•ing

fo·rint

forked

fork·lift

for·lorn

for·mal

form·al·de·hyde

for·mal·ism

for·mal·i·ty

for·mal·iza·tion

for·mal·ize

for·mal·ly

for·mat

for·ma·tion

for·ma·tive

for·mer

for·mer·ly

form·fit·ting

for·mi·da·ble

for·mi·da·bly

form·less

For·mo·sa

For·mo·san

for·mu·la

for·mu·late

for·mu·la·tion

for·mu·la·tor

for·ni·cate

for·ni·ca·tion

for·ni·ca·tor

for·sake
  for·sook
  for·sak·en
  for·sak·ing

for·sooth

for·swear
  or **fore·swear**
  for·swore
    or **fore·swore**
  for·sworn
    or **fore·sworn**
  for·swear·ing
    or **fore·swear·ing**

for·syth·ia

fort
  fortified place

forte
  special skill

for·te
  loudly

forth·com·ing

forth·right

forth·with

for·ti·eth

for·ti·fi·ca·tion

for·ti·fi·er

for·ti·fy

for·tis·si·mo
  pl **for·tis·si·mos** *or* **for·tis·si·mi**

for·ti·tude

Fort Lau·der·dale

fort·night·ly

for·tress

for·tu·itous

for·tu·ity

for·tu·nate

for·tune

for·tune-tell·er

for·tune-tell·ing

Fort Wayne

Fort Worth

for·ty

forty-five

for·ty-nin·er

fo·rum
  pl **fo·rums** *also* **fo·ra**

for·ward
  brash, toward the front (*see* **foreword**)

for·ward·er

for·ward·ing

fos·sil

fos·sil·ize

fos·ter

foul
  dirty (*see* **fowl**)

fou·lard

foul·ly

foul·mouthed

foul·ness

foun·da·tion

foun·der
  verb, collapse

found·er
  noun, establisher

found·ling

found·ry

foun·tain

foun·tain·head

four-flush·er

four·fold

four-foot·ed

four-hand·ed

four-in-hand

four-post·er

four•score
four•some
four•square
four•teen
four•teenth
fourth
four-wheel•er
fowl
bird (*see* foul)
fox
pl fox•es *or* fox
fox•glove
fox•hole
fox•hound
fox•i•ly
fox•i•ness
fox-trot
foxy
foy•er
fra•cas
frac•tion
frac•tion•al
frac•tion•al•ize
frac•tion•al•ly
frac•tious
frac•ture
frag•ile
fra•gil•i•ty
frag•ment
frag•men•tal•ly
frag•men•tary
frag•men•ta•tion
frag•men•tize
fra•grance
fra•grant

frail•ty
fram•er
frame-up
frame•work
franc
currency (*see* frank)
France
fran•chise
fran•chi•see
fran•gi•bil•i•ty
fran•gi•ble
frank
forthright (*see* franc)
Fran•ken•stein
Frank•fort
frank•furt•er
or frank•fort•er *or* frank•furt *or* frank•fort
frank•in•cense
fran•tic
fran•ti•cal•ly
frap•pé
or frappe
fra•ter•nal
fra•ter•nal•ly
fra•ter•ni•ty
frat•er•ni•za•tion
frat•er•nize
frat•ri•cide
fraud•u•lence
fraud•u•lent
fraught
fray•ing
fraz•zle
freak•ish

freck•le
free•bie
or free•bee
free•boo•ter
free•born
freed•man
free•dom
freed•wom•an
free-fall
free-for-all
free•hand
free•hold
free-lance
free•ly
free•man
Free•ma•son
free•stand•ing
free•stone
free•style
free•think•er
free•way
free•wheel
freeze
chill (*see* frieze)
froze
fro•zen
freez•ing
freeze-dry
freez•er
freight•age
freight•er
Fre•mont
French
French•man
French•wom•an

fre·net·ic
fre·net·i·cal·ly
fren·zied
fren·zy
fre·quen·cy
fre·quent
fres·co
pl fres·coes *or* fres·cos
fresh·en
fresh·et
fresh·ly
fresh·man
fresh·ness
fresh·wa·ter
Fres·no
fret
fret·ted
fret·ting
fret·ful
fret·ful·ly
fret·ful·ness
fret·work
fri·a·ble
fri·ar
monk (*see* fryer)
fric·as·see
fric·tion
fric·tion·al·ly
Fri·day
friend·less
friend·li·ness
friend·ly
friend·ship
fri·er
var of fryer
frieze
ornament (*see* freeze)
frig·ate
fright·en
fright·ful
fright·ful·ly
frig·id
fri·gid·i·ty
frilly
frip·pery
frisk·i·ly
frisk·i·ness
frisky
frit·ter
fri·vol·i·ty
friv·o·lous
frizz·i·ly
frizz·i·ness
friz·zle
friz·zly
frizzy
frog·man
frol·ic
frol·icked
frol·ick·ing
frol·ic·some
front·age
fron·tal
fron·tier
fron·tiers·man
fron·tis·piece
frost·bite
frost·ed
frost·i·ly
frost·i·ness
frost·ing
frosty
froth·i·ly
froth·i·ness
frothy
frou·frou
fro·ward
frown
frow·sy
also frow·zy
fro·zen
fruc·ti·fi·ca·tion
fruc·ti·fy
fruc·tose
fruc·tu·ous
fru·gal
fru·gal·i·ty
fru·gal·ly
fruit·cake
fruit·ful·ly
fru·ition
fruit·less
fruity
frump·ish
frumpy
frus·trate
frus·tra·tion
fry
fried
fry·ing

fry·er
or fri·er
one that fries (*see* friar)

fuch·sia

fud·dle

fudge

fu·el
  fu·eled
  or fu·elled
  fu·el·ing
  or fu·el·ling

fu·gi·tive

fugue

füh·rer
or fueh·rer

ful·crum
pl ful·crums *or* ful·cra

ful·fill
or ful·fil
  ful·filled
  ful·fill·ing

ful·fill·ment

full·back

full-blood·ed

full-blown

full-bod·ied

full·er
one that fulls cloth

ful·ler
blacksmith's hammer

full-fash·ioned

full-fledged

full-length

full·ness
also ful·ness

full-scale

ful·ly

ful·mi·nate

ful·mi·na·tion

ful·mi·na·tor

ful·some

fu·ma·role

fum·ble

fu·mi·gant

fu·mi·gate

fu·mi·ga·tion

fu·mi·ga·tor

func·tion

func·tion·al

func·tion·al·ism

func·tion·al·ly

func·tion·ary

func·tion·less

fun·da·men·tal

fun·da·men·tal·ism

fun·da·men·tal·ist

fun·da·men·tal·ly

fu·ner·al

fu·ner·ary

fu·ne·re·al

fun·gi·cid·al

fun·gi·cide

fun·gus
pl fun·gi *also* fun·gus·es

fu·nic·u·lar

funky

fun·nel
  fun·neled
  also fun·nelled
  fun·nel·ing
  also fun·nel·ling

fun·ni·ly

fun·ni·ness

fun·ny

fur
hair (*see* fir)

fur·be·low

fur·bish

fu·ri·ous

furl

fur·long

fur·lough

fur·nace

fur·nish

fur·nish·ings

fur·ni·ture

fu·ror
rage, vogue, uproar

fu·rore
vogue, uproar

fur·ri·er

fur·row

fur·ry

fur·ther

fur·ther·ance

fur·ther·more

fur·ther·most

fur·thest

fur·tive

fur·tive·ness

fu·ry

fu·se·lage
fus·ibil·i·ty
fus·ible
fu·sil·lade
fu·sion
fuss·bud·get
fuss·i·ly
fuss·i·ness
fussy
fus·tian
fus·ti·ly
fus·ti·ness
fus·ty
fu·tile
fu·til·i·ty
fu·ture
fu·tur·ism
fu·tur·ist
fu·tur·is·tic
fu·tu·ri·ty
fuzz·i·ly
fuzz·i·ness
fuzzy

G

gab
  gabbed
  gab·bing
gab·ar·dine
  or **gab·er·dine**
gab·ble
gab·by
gab·fest
ga·ble
ga·bled
Ga·bon
Gab·o·nese
gad
  gad·ded
  gad·ding
gad·about
gad·fly
gad·get
gad·get·ry
Gael·ic
gaff
  spear, hook
gaffe
  blunder
gaf·fer
gag
  gagged
  gag·ging
gage
  pledge (*see* gauge)
gag·gle
gag·man
gag·ster
gai·ety
  or **gay·ety**
gai·ly
  or **gay·ly**
gain·er
gain·ful
gain·ful·ly
gain·say
  gain·said
  gain·say·ing
gain·say·er
gait
  walk (*see* gate)
gai·ter
ga·la
ga·lac·tic
Gal·a·had
gal·axy
gal·lant
gal·lant·ry
gall·blad·der
gal·le·on
gal·ler·ied
gal·lery
gal·ley
Gal·lic
gall·ing
gal·li·vant
gal·lon
gal·lop
gal·lop·er
gal·lows
gall·stone
ga·lore
ga·losh
gal·van·ic
gal·va·nism
gal·va·ni·za·tion
gal·va·nize
gal·va·nom·e·ter
Gam·bia
Gam·bi·an
gam·bit
gam·ble
  wager (*see* gambol)

gam•bler

gam•bol
leap about (*see* gamble)

gam•boled
or gam•bolled

gam•bol•ing
or gam•bol•ling

gam•brel

game•cock

game•keep•er

game•ly

game•ster

ga•mete

gam•in

gam•i•ness

gam•ma glob•u•lin

gam•ut

gamy
or gam•ey

gan•der

gan•dy danc•er

gang•land

gan•gling

gan•gli•on
pl gan•glia *also* gan•gli•ons

gang•plank

gan•grene

gan•gre•nous

gang•ster

gang•way

gant•let

gan•try

ga•rage

ga•rage•man

gar•bage

gar•ble

gar•çon

gar•den

gar•den•er

Gar•den Grove

gar•de•nia

gar•gan•tuan

gar•gle

gar•goyle

gar•ish

gar•land

gar•lic

gar•licky

gar•ment

gar•ner

gar•net

gar•nish

gar•nish•ee

gar•nish•eed

gar•nish•ment

gar•ni•ture

gar•ret

gar•ri•son

gar•rote
or ga•rotte

gar•ru•li•ty

gar•ru•lous

gar•ru•lous•ness

gar•ter

Gary

gas•eous

gas•ket

gas•light

gas•o•line
also gas•o•lene

gas•ser

gas•si•ness

gas•sy

gas•tric

gas•tri•tis

gas•tro•en•ter•ol•o•gist

gas•tro•en•ter•ol•o•gy

gas•tro•in•tes•ti•nal

gas•tro•nom•ic

gas•tron•o•my

gas•works

gate
door (*see* gait)

gate-crash•er

gate•post

gate•way

gath•er

gath•er•er

gauche
crude (*see* gouache)

gau•che•rie

gau•cho
pl gau•chos

gaud•i•ly

gaud•i•ness

gaudy

gauge
measure (*see* gage)

gaunt

gaunt•let
or gant•let

gauze
gauzy
gav·el
ga·votte
gawk·ish
gawky
gay·ety
var of **gaiety**
gay·ly
var of **gai·ly**
ga·ze·bo
pl **ga·ze·bos**
ga·zelle
gaz·er
ga·zette
gaz·et·teer
gear·box
gear·ing
gear·shift
gee·zer
Gei·ger
gei·sha
pl **gei·sha** *or* **gei·shas**
gel
gelled
gel·ling
gel·a·tin
also **gel·a·tine**
ge·la·ti·ni·za·tion
ge·la·ti·nize
ge·lat·i·nous
geld·ing
gel·id
ge·lid·i·ty
gel·ig·nite
gem·i·nate
gem·i·na·tion
gem·stone
gen·darme
gen·dar·mer·ie
or **gen·dar·mery**
gen·der
ge·ne·a·log·i·cal
ge·ne·a·log·i·cal·ly
ge·ne·al·o·gist
ge·ne·al·o·gy
gen·er·a·ble
gen·er·al
gen·er·a·lis·si·mo
gen·er·al·i·ty
gen·er·al·iza·tion
gen·er·al·ize
gen·er·al·ly
gen·er·al·ship
gen·er·ate
gen·er·a·tion
gen·er·a·tive
gen·er·a·tor
ge·ner·ic
ge·ner·i·cal·ly
gen·er·os·i·ty
gen·er·ous
gen·e·sis
pl **gen·e·ses**
ge·net·ic
also **ge·net·i·cal**
ge·net·i·cal·ly
ge·net·ics
ge·nial
ge·nial·i·ty
ge·nial·ly
gen·ic
ge·nie
pl **ge·nies** *also* **ge·nii**
gen·i·tal
gen·i·ta·lia
gen·i·tals
gen·i·tive
gen·i·to·uri·nary
ge·nius
pl **ge·nius·es** *or* **ge·nii**
geno·cid·al
geno·cide
genre
gens
pl **gen·tes**
gen·teel
gen·tian
gen·tile
gen·til·i·ty
gen·tle
gen·tle·folk
also **gen·tle·folks**
gen·tle·man
gen·tle·man·ly
gen·tle·wom·an
gen·tly
gen·try
gen·u·flect
gen·u·flec·tion
gen·u·ine
gen·u·ine·ly
gen·u·ine·ness

ge·nus
pl gen·era

geo·cen·tric

geo·cen·tri·cal·ly

geo·chem·i·cal

geo·chem·i·cal·ly

geo·chem·is·try

geo·chro·no·log·i·cal

geo·chro·nol·o·gy

geo·de·sic

ge·od·e·sy

geo·det·ic

geo·det·i·cal·ly

geo·graph·ic
or geo·graph·i·cal

ge·o·graph·i·cal·ly

ge·og·ra·phy

geo·log·ic
or geo·log·i·cal

geo·log·i·cal·ly

ge·ol·o·gist

ge·ol·o·gy

geo·mag·net·ic

geo·mag·ne·tism

ge·o·met·ric
or ge·o·met·ri·cal

ge·o·met·ri·cal·ly

geo·me·tri·cian

ge·om·e·try

geo·phys·i·cal

geo·phys·i·cist

geo·phys·ics

geo·po·lit·i·cal

geo·po·lit·i·cal·ly

geo·pol·i·ti·cian

geo·pol·i·tics

Geor·gia

geo·ther·mal

ge·ra·ni·um

ger·i·at·ric

ger·i·at·rics

Ger·man

ger·mane

Ger·man·ic

Ger·ma·ny

ger·mi·cid·al

ger·mi·cide

ger·mi·nal

ger·mi·nate

ger·mi·na·tion

ger·on·tol·o·gist

ger·on·tol·o·gy

ger·ry·man·der

ger·und

ge·sta·po
pl ges·ta·pos

ges·tate

ges·ta·tion

ges·tic·u·late

ges·tic·u·la·tion

ges·ture

ge·sund·heit

get
got
got
or got·ten
get·ting

get·away

get-to·geth·er

get·up

gew·gaw

gey·ser

Gha·na

Gha·na·ian
or Gha·nian

ghast·li·ness

ghast·ly

gher·kin

ghet·to
pl ghet·tos *or* ghet·toes

ghet·to·iza·tion

ghet·to·ize

ghost·li·ness

ghost·ly

ghost·write

ghost-writ·er

ghoul·ish

gi·ant

gi·ant·ess

gi·ant·ism

gib

gib·ber

gib·ber·ish

gib·bet

gib·bon

gib·bos·i·ty

gib·bous

gibe
taunt (see jibe)

gib·er

gib·lets

Gib·son

gid·di·ly

gid·di·ness

gid·dy
gift·ed
gig
  gigged
  gig·ging
gi·gan·tic
gi·gan·ti·cal·ly
gig·gle
gig·gly
gig·o·lo
gild
  overlay with gold (*see* guild)
  gild·ed
  or gilt
  gild·ing
gilt
  gold (*see* guilt)
gilt-edged
  or gilt-edge
gim·crack
gim·let
gim·mick
gim·mick·ry
gim·micky
gimpy
gin
  ginned
  gin·ning
gin·ger
gin·ger·bread
gin·ger·ly
gin·ger·snap
ging·ham
gin·gi·vi·tis
gi·raffe
gird
  gird·ed
  or girt
  gird·ing
gird·er
gir·dle
girl·hood
girl·ish
girth
gist
give
  gave
  giv·en
  giv·ing
give-and-take
give·away
giv·en
giz·mo
  or gis·mo
giz·zard
gla·brous
gla·cé
gla·cial
gla·ci·ate
gla·ci·a·tion
gla·cier
gla·ci·ol·o·gist
gla·ci·ol·o·gy
glad·den
glad·i·a·tor
glad·i·a·to·ri·al
glad·i·o·la
glad·i·o·lus
  pl glad·i·o·li *or* glad·i·o·lus *or* glad·i·o·lus·es
glad·ly
glad·ness
glad·some
glad·stone
glam·or·ize
  also glam·our·ize
glam·or·ous
  also glam·our·ous
glam·our
  or glam·or
glanc·ing
glan·du·lar
glar·ing
glass·ful
glass·i·ly
glass·ine
glass·i·ness
glass·ware
glassy
glau·co·ma
gla·zier
glaz·ing
glean·able
glean·er
glean·ings
glee·ful
glee·ful·ly
Glen·dale
glib·ly
glib·ness
glid·er
glim·mer

glimpse
glis·ten
glit·ter
glit·tery
gloam·ing
gloat
glob·al
glob·al·ly
globe-trot·ter
glob·u·lar
glob·ule
glob·u·lin
glock·en·spiel
gloom·i·ly
gloom·i·ness
gloomy
glo·ri·fi·ca·tion
glo·ri·fy
glo·ri·ous
glo·ry
glos·sa·ry
gloss·i·ly
gloss·i·ness
glossy
glot·tal
glot·tis
pl **glot·tis·es** *or* **glot·ti·des**
glow·er
glow·worm
glu·cose
glue
glu·ey
glu·i·ly
glut
glut·ted
glut·ting
glu·ta·mate
glu·ten
glu·ten·ous
containing gluten (*see* **glutinous**)
glu·ti·nous
sticky (*see* **glutenous**)
glut·ton
glut·ton·ous
glut·tony
glyc·er·in
or **glyc·er·ine**
glyc·er·ol
gly·co·gen
G-man
gnarled
gnash
gnat
gnaw
gneiss
gnome
gnom·ish
Gnos·tic
gnos·ti·cism
gnu
go
went
gone
go·ing
goad
go-ahead
goal·ie
goal·keep·er
goal·post
goa·tee
goat·skin
gob·ble
gob·ble·dy·gook
or **gob·ble·de·gook**
gob·bler
go-be·tween
gob·let
gob·lin
god·child
god·daugh·ter
god·dess
god·fa·ther
god·less
god·like
god·li·ness
god·ly
god·moth·er
god·par·ent
god·send
god·son
go-get·ter
gog·gle
gog·gles
go-go
go·ings-on
goi·ter
also **goi·tre**
gold·brick
gold·en
gold·en·rod
gold·field
gold-filled

gold•finch
gold•fish
gold•smith
golf•er
go•nad
gon•do•la
gon•do•lier
gon•er
gon•fa•lon
gon•or•rhea
gon•or•rhe•al
good
  bet•ter
  best
good-bye
  or **good-by**
good-heart•ed
good-hu•mored
good-look•ing
good•ly
good-na•tured
good•ness
good-tem•pered
good•will
goody-goody
goof•i•ness
goofy
goose
  pl **geese**
goose•ber•ry
goose•flesh
goose•neck
go•pher
Gor•di•an knot
gorge
gor•geous
Gor•gon•zo•la
go•ril•la
gor•man•dize
gor•man•diz•er
gory
gos•hawk
gos•ling
gos•pel
gos•sa•mer
gos•sip
Goth•ic
gouache
  painting (*see* **gauche**)
Gou•da
gouge
gou•lash
gourd
  plant (*see* **gourde**)
gourde
  currency (*see* **gourd**)
gour•mand
gour•met
gout
gov•ern
gov•er•nance
gov•ern•ess
gov•ern•ment
gov•ern•men•tal
gov•er•nor
gov•er•nor-gen•er•al
  pl **gov•er•nors-gen•er•al** *or* **gov•er•nor-gen•er•als**
grab
  grabbed
  grab•bing
grace•ful
grace•ful•ly
grace•less
gra•cious
grack•le
gra•da•tion
grad•er
gra•di•ent
grad•u•al
grad•u•al•ism
grad•u•al•ly
grad•u•ate
grad•u•a•tion
graf•fi•to
  pl **graf•fi•ti**
graft•er
gra•ham
  crack•er
grain•field
grainy
gram
  or **gramme**
gram•mar
gram•mar•i•an
gram•mat•i•cal
gram•mat•i•cal•ly
gra•na•ry
gran•dam
  or **gran•dame**
grand•child
grand•daugh•ter

gran·dee
gran·deur
grand·fa·ther
gran·dil·o·quence
gran·dil·o·quent
gran·di·ose
grand·ly
grand·moth·er
grand·par·ent
Grand Rap·ids
grand·son
grand·stand
grange
gran·ite
gran·ite·ware
gran·ny
or gran·nie
grant·ee
grant-in-aid
pl grants-in-aid
grant·or
gran·u·lar
gran·u·late
gran·u·la·tion
gran·ule
grape·fruit
grape·shot
grape·vine
graph·ic
graph·i·cal·ly
graph·ics
graph·ite
grap·nel
grap·ple
grap·pling
grapy
grasp·er
grass·hop·per
grass·land
grassy
grate·ful
grate·ful·ly
grat·er
grat·i·fi·ca·tion
grat·i·fy
grat·ing
gra·tis
grat·i·tude
gra·tu·itous
gra·tu·ity
gra·va·men
pl gra·va·men *or* gra·vam·i·na
grave
graved
grav·en
or graved
grav·ing
grav·el
grav·eled
or grav·elled
grav·el·ing
or grav·el·ling
grav·el·ly
grave·ly
grave·stone
grave·yard
grav·i·tate
grav·i·ta·tion
grav·i·ty
gra·vy
gray·ish
grease·paint
greas·i·ness
greasy
Great Brit·ain
great·coat
great·ly
great·ness
Gre·cian
Greece
greed·i·ly
greed·i·ness
greedy
Greek
green·back
green·belt
green·ery
green·gro·cer
green·horn
green·house
green·ish
green·ness
green·room
Greens·boro
green·sward
greet·er
greet·ing
gre·gar·i·ous
grem·lin
Gre·na·da
gre·nade
gren·a·dier
gren·a·dine
grey·hound
grid·dle

grid·iron

griev·ance

griev·ous

grill
cooking (*see* grille)

gril·lage

grille
or grill
grating (*see* grill)

grill·work

gri·mace

grim·i·ness

grim·ly

grimy

grin
grinned
grin·ning

grind
ground
grind·ing

grind·er

grind·stone

grip
hold (*see* gripe, grippe)
gripped
grip·ping

gripe
complain (*see* grip, grippe)

grippe
influenza (*see* grip, gripe)

gris-gris
pl gris-gris

gris·li·ness

gris·ly

grist

gris·tle

gris·tli·ness

gris·tly

grist·mill

grit
grit·ted
grit·ting

grit·ti·ness

grit·ty

griz·zled

griz·zly

gro·cer

gro·cery

grog·gi·ly

grog·gi·ness

grog·gy

gro·gram

groin

grom·met

gro·schen
pl gro·schen

gros·grain

gross·ly

gross·ness

grosz
pl gro·szy

gro·tesque

gro·tesque·ly

gro·tes·que·rie

grot·to
pl grot·toes *also* grot·tos

grouch·i·ly

grouch·i·ness

grouchy

ground·er

ground·hog

ground·less

ground·wa·ter

ground·work

group·ing

grouse
pl grouse *or* grous·es

grov·el
grov·eled
or grov·elled
grov·el·ing
or grov·el·ling

grov·el·er

grow
grew
grown
grow·ing

grow·er

growl·er

growl·ing

grown-up

growth

grub
grubbed
grub·bing

grub·bi·ly

grub·bi·ness

grub·by

grub·stake

grudge

grudg·ing·ly

gru·el
gru·el·ing
or gru·el·ling
grue·some
gruff·ly
grum·ble
grum·bler
grump·i·ly
grump·i·ness
grumpy
Gru·yère
G-string
gua·no
gua·ra·ni
pl gua·ra·nis *or* gua·ra·nies
guar·an·tee
guar·an·tor
guar·an·ty
guard·house
guard·ian
guard·room
guards·man
Gua·te·ma·la
Gua·te·ma·lan
gua·va
gu·ber·na·to·ri·al
guern·sey
guer·ril·la
or gue·ril·la
guess·ti·mate
guess·work
guest
guf·faw
guid·able
guid·ance
guide·book
guide·line
gui·don
guild
association (*see* gild)
guil·der
guild·hall
guile
guile·ful
guile·ful·ly
guile·less
guil·lo·tine
guilt
blame (*see* gilt)
guilt·i·ly
guilt·i·ness
guilt·less
guilty
Guin·ea
Guin·ea-Bis·sau
Guin·ean
guise
gui·tar
gulch
gul·den
pl gul·dens *or* gul·den
gul·let
gull·ibil·i·ty
gull·ible
or gull·able
gull·ibly
gul·ly
gum
gummed
gum·ming
gum·bo
gum·boil
gum·drop
gum·mi·ness
gum·my
gump·tion
gum·shoe
gun
gunned
gun·ning
gun·boat
gun·cot·ton
gun·fight
gun·fire
gun·lock
gun·man
gun·met·al
gun·ner
gun·nery
gun·ny
gun·ny·sack
gun·point
gun·pow·der
gun·run·ner
gun·ship
gun·shot
gun-shy
gun·smith
gun·wale
or gun·nel
gup·py

gur·gle
gu·ru
gush·er
gushy
gus·set
gus·ta·to·ry
gust·i·ly
gust·i·ness
gus·to
pl gus·toes
gusty
gut
gut·ted
gut·ting
gut·less
gutsy
gut·ta-per·cha
gut·ter
gut·ter·snipe
gut·tur·al
gut·tur·al·ly
Guy·ana
Guy·a·nese
guy·ot
guz·zle
gym·na·si·um
pl gym·na·si·ums *or* gym·na·sia
gym·nast
gym·nas·tic
gym·no·sperm
gy·ne·co·log·i·cal
gy·ne·col·o·gist
gy·ne·col·o·gy
gyp
gypped
gyp·ping
gyp·sum
gyp·sy
gy·rate
gy·ra·tion
gy·ro·com·pass
gy·ro·scope
gy·ro·sta·bi·liz·er
gy·ro·stat

H

ha·ba·ne·ra
ha·be·as cor·pus
hab·er·dash·er
hab·er·dash·ery
ha·bil·i·ment
hab·it
hab·it·abil·i·ty
hab·it·able
hab·it·ably
ha·bi·tant
hab·i·tat
hab·i·ta·tion
hab·it-form·ing
ha·bit·u·al
ha·bit·u·al·ly
ha·bit·u·ate
ha·bit·u·a·tion
ha·bi·tué
ha·chure
ha·ci·en·da
hack·le
hack·man
hack·ney
hack·neyed
hack·saw
hack·work
had·dock
Ha·des
hag·gard
hag·gis
hag·gle
hag·gler
ha·gi·og·ra·pher
ha·gi·og·ra·phy
hail
ice, greet (*see* hale)
hail·stone
hail·storm
hair·breadth
or hairs·breadth
hair·brush
hair·cloth
hair·cut
hair·do
pl hair·dos
hair·dress·er
hair·i·ness
hair·less
hair·line
hair·piece
hair·pin
hair-rais·ing
hair·split·ter
hair·split·ting
hair·spring
hair·style

hair-trig·ger
hairy
Hai·ti
Hai·tian
ha·la·la
also ha·la·lah
pl ha·la·la *or* ha·la·las
ha·la·tion
hal·berd
or hal·bert
hal·cy·on
hale
healthy, haul (*see* hail)
ha·ler
half
pl halves
half·back
half-baked
half-breed
half-caste
half-cocked
half-dol·lar
half·heart·ed
half-length
half-life
half-light
half-mast
half-moon
half-slip
half-staff
half·tone
half-track
half-truth
half·way
half-wit
half-wit·ted
hal·i·but
ha·lide
Hal·i·fax
ha·lite
hal·i·to·sis
hal·le·lu·jah
hal·liard
var of halyard
hall·mark
hal·low
hal·lowed
Hal·low·een
hal·lu·ci·nate
hal·lu·ci·na·tion
hal·lu·ci·na·to·ry
hal·lu·ci·no·gen
hal·lu·ci·no·gen·ic
hall·way
ha·lo
pl ha·los *or* ha·loes
halo·gen
hal·ter
halt·ing
halve
hal·yard
or hal·liard
ham
hammed
ham·ming
ham·burg·er
or ham·burg
Ham·il·ton
ham·let
ham·mer
ham·mer·head
ham·mer·lock
ham·mock
Ham·mond
ham·my
ham·per
Hamp·ton
ham·ster
ham·string
hand·bag
hand·ball
hand·bar·row
hand·bill
hand·book
hand·car
hand·clasp
hand·cuff
hand·ful
pl hand·fuls *also* hands·ful
hand·gun
hand·i·cap
hand·i·capped
hand·i·cap·ping
hand·i·cap·per
hand·i·craft
hand·i·crafts·man
hand·i·ly
hand·i·ness
hand·i·work
hand·ker·chief
pl hand·ker·chiefs *also* hand·ker·chieves
han·dle

han·dle·bar
hand·made
hand·maid·en
or hand·maid
hand-me-down
hand·off
hand·out
hand·pick
hand·rail
hand·saw
hands-down
hand·set
hand·shake
hand·some
good looking (*see* hansom)
hand·spike
hand·spring
hand-to-hand
hand·wo·ven
hand·writ·ing
hand·writ·ten
handy
handy·man
hang
hung
also hanged
hang·ing
han·gar
airplanes (*see* hanger)
hang·dog
hang·er
one that hangs (*see* hangar)
hang·er-on
pl hangers-on

hang·ing
hang·man
hang·nail
hang·out
hang·over
han·ker
han·ky-pan·ky
han·som
cab (*see* handsome)
Ha·nuk·kah
or Cha·nu·kah
hao·le
hap·haz·ard
hap·less
hap·pen
hap·pen·ing
hap·pen·stance
hap·pi·ly
hap·pi·ness
hap·py
hap·py-go-lucky
hara-kiri
ha·rangue
ha·rangu·er
ha·rass
ha·rass·ment
har·bin·ger
har·bor
har·bor·age
hard-and-fast
hard·back
hard·ball
hard-bit·ten
hard-boiled
hard·edge

hard·en
hard·ened
hard·head·ed
hard·heart·ed
har·di·hood
har·di·ly
har·di·ness
hard·ly
hard-of-hear·ing
hard·pan
hard-shell
hard·ship
hard·stand
hard-sur·face
hard·tack
hard·top
hard·ware
hard·wood
hard·work·ing
har·dy
hare·brained
hare·lip
hare·lipped
har·em
har·le·quin
har·lot
harm·ful
harm·ful·ly
harm·less
har·mon·ic
har·mon·i·ca
har·mon·i·cal·ly
har·mon·ics
har·mo·ni·ous
har·mo·ni·um

har·mo·ni·za·tion
har·mo·nize
har·mo·ny
har·ness
harp·er
har·poon
harp·si·chord
har·py
har·ri·dan
har·ri·er
Har·ris·burg
har·row
har·ry
harsh·ness
Hart·ford
har·um-scar·um
har·vest
har·vest·er
has-been
hash·ish
has·sle
has·sock
haste
has·ten
hast·i·ly
hast·i·ness
hasty
hat·box
hatch
hatch·ery
hatch·et
hatch·ing
hatch·way
hate·ful
hate·ful·ly

ha·tred
hat·ter
haugh·ti·ly
haugh·ti·ness
haugh·ty
haul·age
haul·er
haunch
haunt
haunt·ing·ly
haute cou·ture
hau·teur
have
  had
  hav·ing
  has
ha·ven
have-not
hav·er·sack
hav·oc
Hawaii
Ha·wai·ian
hawk
hawk·er
hawk·ish
haw·ser
haw·thorn
hay·cock
hay·fork
hay·loft
hay·mow
hay·rack
hay·rick
hay·seed

hay·wire
haz·ard
haz·ard·ous
ha·zel
ha·zel·nut
haz·i·ly
haz·i·ness
hazy
head·ache
head·band
head·board
head·dress
head·ed
head·er
head·first
head·gear
head·hunt·er
head·i·ly
head·i·ness
head·ing
head·land
head·less
head·light
head·line
head·lin·er
head·lock
head·long
head·man
head·mas·ter
head·mis·tress
head·most
head·note
head-on
head·phone
head·piece

head·pin
head·quar·ters
head·rest
head·set
head·ship
heads·man
head·stall
head·stock
head·stone
head·strong
head·wait·er
head·wa·ter
head·way
head·word
head·work
heady
heal
  cure (*see* heel)
heal·er
health·ful
health·i·ly
health·i·ness
healthy
heap
hear
  heard
  hear·ing
hear·er
hear·ken
hear·say
hearse
heart·ache
heart·beat
heart·break
heart·bro·ken
heart·burn
heart·en
heart·felt
hearth
hearth·stone
heart·i·ly
heart·i·ness
heart·land
heart·less
heart·rend·ing
heart·sick
heart·sore
heart·string
heart·throb
heart-to-heart
hearty
heat·ed·ly
heat·er
heath
hea·then
heath·er
heat·stroke
heave
  heaved
    or hove
  heav·ing
heav·en
heav·en·ward
heav·i·ly
heavi·ness
heavy
heavy-du·ty
heavy-hand·ed
heavy·heart·ed
heavy·set
heavy·weight
He·bra·ic
He·brew
heck·le
heck·ler
hect·are
hec·tic
hec·ti·cal·ly
hedge
hedge·hog
hedge·hop
hedge·row
he·do·nism
he·do·nist
he·do·nis·tic
heed·ful
heed·ful·ly
heed·less
heel
  foot (*see* heal)
hefty
he·gem·o·ny
he·gi·ra
  also he·ji·ra
heif·er
height
height·en
hei·nous
heir
  inheritor (*see* air)
heir·ess
heir·loom
Hel·e·na
he·li·cal

he·li·coid
or **he·li·coi·dal**

he·li·cop·ter

he·lio·cen·tric

he·lio·trope

he·li·port

he·li·um

he·lix
pl **hel·i·ces** *also* **he·lix·es**

hell-bent

hell·cat

Hel·len·ic

Hel·le·nist

Hel·le·nis·tic

hel·lion

hell·ish

hel·lo
pl **hel·los**

helm

hel·met

helms·man

hel·ot

help·er

help·ful

help·ful·ly

help·less

help·mate

hel·ter-skel·ter

hem
hemmed
hem·ming

he·mal

he-man

he·ma·tite

he·ma·tol·o·gist

he·ma·tol·o·gy

hemi·sphere

hemi·spher·i·cal

hem·line

hem·lock

he·mo·glo·bin
also **hae·mo·glo·bin**

he·mo·ly·sis

he·mo·lyt·ic

he·mo·phil·ia

he·mo·phil·i·ac

hem·or·rhage

hem·or·rhag·ic

hem·or·rhoid

hem·stitch

hence·forth

hence·for·ward

hench·man

hen·na

hen·peck

he·pat·ic

hep·a·ti·tis

hep·ta·gon

hep·tam·e·ter

her·ald

he·ral·dic

her·ald·ry

her·ba·ceous

her·bar·i·um

her·bi·cid·al

her·bi·cide

her·bi·vore

her·biv·o·rous

her·cu·le·an

herd·er

herds·man

here·abouts
or **here·about**

here·af·ter

here·by

he·red·i·tary

he·red·i·ty

here·in

here·of

here·on

her·e·sy

her·e·tic

he·ret·i·cal

here·to

here·to·fore

here·un·der

here·un·to

here·upon

here·with

her·i·ta·ble

her·i·tage

her·met·ic
also **her·met·i·cal**

her·met·i·cal·ly

her·mit

her·mit·age

her·nia

her·ni·ate

he·ro
pl **he·roes**

he·ro·ic

he·ro·ical·ly

he·ro·ics

her·o·in
narcotic (*see* heroine)

her·o·ine
female hero (*see* heroin)

her·o·ism

her·on

her·pes

her·pe·tol·o·gist

her·pe·tol·o·gy

her·ring

her·ring·bone

her·self

hes·i·tance

hes·i·tan·cy

hes·i·tant

hes·i·tate

hes·i·ta·tion

het·ero·dox

het·ero·doxy

het·er·o·ge·ne·ity

het·er·o·ge·neous

het·ero·sex·u·al

het·ero·sex·u·al·i·ty

hew
cut (*see* hue)
hewed
hewed
or hewn
hew·ing

hexa·chlo·ro·phene

hexa·gon

hex·ag·o·nal

hexa·gram

hex·am·e·ter

hey·day

Hi·a·le·ah

hi·a·tus

hi·ba·chi

hi·ber·nate

hi·ber·na·tion

hi·ber·na·tor

hi·bis·cus

hic·cup
also hic·cough
hic·cuped
also hic·cupped
hic·cup·ing
also hic·cup·ping

hick·o·ry

hi·dal·go
pl hi·dal·gos

hide
hid
hid·den
or hid
hid·ing

hide·away

hide·bound

hid·eous

hide·out

hie
hied
hy·ing
or hie·ing

hi·er·ar·chi·cal
or hi·er·ar·chic

hi·er·ar·chi·cal·ly

hi·er·ar·chy

hi·ero·glyph·ic
or hi·ero·glyph·i·cal

hi-fi

hig·gle·dy-pig·gle·dy

high·ball

high·born

high·boy

high·bred

high·brow

high·er-up

high·fa·lu·tin

high-flown

high-fly·ing

high-hand·ed

high-hat

high·land

high·land·er

high-lev·el

high·light

high-mind·ed

high·ness

high-oc·tane

high-pres·sure

high-rise

high·road

high-sound·ing

high-spir·it·ed

high-strung

high·tail

high-ten·sion

high-test

high-toned

high-wa·ter

high·way

high·way·man

hi·jack
or high-jack

hi·jack·er

hik·er
hi·lar·i·ous
hi·lar·i·ty
hill·bil·ly
hill·ock
hill·side
hill·top
hilly
him·self
hin·der
hind·most
hind·quar·ter
hin·drance
hind·sight
Hin·du·ism
hin·ter·land
hip·bone
hip·pie
or hip·py

Hip·po·crat·ic
hip·po·drome
hip·po·pot·a·mus
pl hip·po·pot·a·mus·es *or* hip·po·pot·a·mi

hip·ster
hire·ling
hir·sute
His·pan·ic
his·ta·mine
his·to·gen
his·to·gen·e·sis
his·to·gram
his·tol·o·gist
his·tol·o·gy
his·to·ri·an
his·tor·ic
his·tor·i·cal
his·tor·i·cal·ly
his·to·ric·i·ty
his·to·ri·og·ra·pher
his·to·ri·og·ra·phy
his·to·ry
his·tri·on·ic
his·tri·on·i·cal·ly
his·tri·on·ics
hit
hit
hit·ting

hitch·hike
hitch·hik·er
hith·er·to
hit·ter
hive
bee house

hives
pl hives
allergic disorder

hoard
accumulate (*see* horde)

hoar·frost
hoar·i·ness
hoarse
harsh (*see* horse)

hoarse·ly
hoary
hoax
hob·ble
hob·by
hob·by·horse
hob·gob·lin
hob·nail
hob·nob
hob·nobbed
hob·nob·bing

ho·bo
pl ho·boes *also* ho·bos

hob·by·ist
hock·ey
ho·cus-po·cus
hodge·podge
ho·gan
hog·gish
hogs·head
hog-tie
hog·wash
hoi pol·loi
hoist
ho·kum
hold
held
hold·ing

hold·out
hold·over
hold·up
hol·i·day
ho·li·ness
Hol·land
(*see* Netherlands)

Hol·land·er
hol·low
hol·ly
hol·ly·hock
Hol·ly·wood
ho·lo·caust

ho·lo·gram
ho·lo·graph
ho·log·ra·phy
hol·stein
hol·ster
ho·ly
hom·age
hom·bre
hom·burg
home·body
home·bred
home·com·ing
home·grown
home·land
home·less
home·li·ness
home·ly
home·made
home·mak·er
ho·meo·path·ic
ho·me·op·a·thy
hom·er
home·room
home·sick
home·spun
home·stead
home·stead·er
home·stretch
home·ward
or **home·wards**
home·work
hom·ey
also **homy**
ho·mi·cid·al
ho·mi·cide
hom·i·let·ic
hom·i·let·ics
hom·i·ly
hom·i·nid
hom·i·noid
hom·i·ny
ho·mo·ge·ne·i·ty
ho·mo·ge·neous
ho·mog·e·ni·za·tion
ho·mog·e·nize
ho·mog·e·nous
ho·mo·graph
ho·mol·o·gous
hom·onym
ho·mo·phone
ho·mo sa·pi·ens
ho·mo·sex·u·al
ho·mo·sex·u·al·i·ty
Hon·du·ran
Hon·du·ras
hone
hon·est
hon·es·ty
hon·ey
hon·ey·bee
hon·ey·comb
hon·ey·dew
hon·ey·moon
hon·ey·suck·le
hon·ky-tonk
Ho·no·lu·lu
hon·or
hon·or·able
hon·or·ably
hon·o·rar·i·um
pl **hon·o·rar·ia** *also* **hon·o·rar·i·ums**
hon·or·ary
hon·or·if·ic
hood·ed
hood·lum
hoo·doo
pl **hoo·doos**
hood·wink
hoo·ey
hoof
pl **hooves** *or* **hoofs**
hoo·kah
hook·up
hook·worm
hoo·li·gan
hoop·la
hoo·te·nan·ny
hop
hopped
hop·ping
hope·ful
hope·ful·ly
hope·less
hop·per
hop·scotch
horde
throng (see **hoard**)
hore·hound
ho·ri·zon
hor·i·zon·tal
hor·i·zon·tal·ly
hor·mon·al
hor·mone

horn·book
hor·net
horn·pipe
horn·swog·gle
horny
hor·o·log·i·cal
ho·rol·o·gist
ho·rol·o·gy
horo·scope
hor·ren·dous
hor·ri·ble
hor·ri·bly
hor·rid
hor·ri·fy
hor·ror
hors d'oeuvre
horse
animal (*see* hoarse)
horse·back
horse·flesh
horse·fly
horse·hair
horse·hide
horse·laugh
horse·man
horse·play
horse·pow·er
horse·rad·ish
horse·shoe
horse·whip
horse·wom·an
hors·ey
or horsy
hor·ta·tive
hor·ta·to·ry

hor·ti·cul·tur·al
hor·ti·cul·ture
hor·ti·cul·tur·ist
ho·san·na
hose
pl hose *or* hos·es
ho·siery
hos·pice
hos·pi·ta·ble
hos·pi·ta·bly
hos·pi·tal
hos·pi·tal·i·ty
hos·pi·tal·iza·tion
hos·pi·tal·ize
hos·tage
hos·tel
hos·tel·er
hos·tel·ry
host·ess
hos·tile
hos·tile·ly
hos·til·i·ty
hos·tler
hot·bed
hot-blood·ed
hot·box
ho·tel
hot·foot
pl hot·foots
hot·head·ed
hot·house
hot-rod·der
hot·shot
hour·glass
hour·ly

house
pl hous·es
house·boat
house·boy
house·break·ing
house·bro·ken
house·clean
house·coat
house·fly
house·ful
house·hold
house·keep·er
house·lights
house·man
house·maid
house·moth·er
house·top
house·warm·ing
house·wife
house·work
hous·ing
Hous·ton
hov·el
hov·er
Hov·er·craft
how·be·it
how·dah
how·ev·er
how·it·zer
howl·er
how·so·ev·er
hoy·den
hua·ra·che
hub·bub
hu·bris

huck•le•ber•ry
huck•ster
hud•dle
hue
color (*see* hew)
huff•ish
huffy
hug
hugged
hug•ging
huge•ly
Hu•gue•not
hu•la
also hu•la-hu•la
hulk•ing
hul•la•ba•loo
pl hul•la•ba•loos
hum
hummed
hum•ming
hu•man
hu•mane
hu•mane•ly
hu•man•ism
hu•man•ist
hu•man•is•tic
hu•man•i•tar•i•an
hu•man•i•ty
hu•man•iza•tion
hu•man•ize
hu•man•kind
hu•man•ly
hum•ble
hum•bler
hum•bly
hum•bug
hum•ding•er
hum•drum
hu•mer•al
hu•mer•us
hu•mid
hu•mid•i•fi•ca•tion
hu•mid•i•fi•er
hu•mid•i•fy
hu•mid•i•ty
hu•mi•dor
hu•mil•i•ate
hu•mil•i•a•tion
hu•mil•i•ty
hum•ming•bird
hum•mock
hu•mor
hu•mor•ist
hu•mor•ous
hump•back
hu•mus
hunch•back
hun•dred
hun•dredth
hun•dred•weight
Hun•gar•i•an
Hun•ga•ry
hun•ger
hun•gri•ly
hun•gry
hun•ky-do•ry
hunt•er
Hun•ting•ton Beach
hunt•ress
hunts•man
Hunts•ville
hur•dle
obstacle (*see* hurtle)
hur•dy-gur•dy
hurl•er
hur•ly-bur•ly
hur•rah
hur•ri•cane
hur•ried•ly
hur•ried•ness
hur•ry
hurt
hurt
hurt•ing
hurt•ful
hur•tle
hurl (*see* hurdle)
hus•band
hus•band•man
hus•band•ry
hush-hush
husk•er
hus•ki•ly
hus•ki•ness
husk•ing
hus•ky
hus•sar
hus•sy
hus•tings
hus•tle
hus•tler
huz•zah
or huz•za
hy•a•cinth

hy·brid
hy·brid·iza·tion
hy·brid·ize
hy·dran·gea
hy·drant
hy·drate
hy·drau·lic
hy·drau·lics
hy·dride
hy·dro
pl hy·dros
hy·dro·car·bon
hy·dro·chlo·ric acid
hy·dro·elec·tric
hy·dro·foil
hy·dro·gen
hy·dro·ge·nate
hy·dro·ge·na·tion
hy·drog·e·nous
hy·dro·log·ic
hy·drol·o·gist
hy·drol·o·gy
hy·dro·ly·sis
hy·drom·e·ter
hy·dron·ic
hy·dro·pho·bia
hy·dro·plane
hy·dro·pon·ics
hy·dro·stat·ic
hy·dro·ther·a·py
hy·drous
hy·drox·ide
hy·e·na
hy·giene
hy·gien·ic
hy·gien·i·cal·ly
hy·gien·ist
hy·grom·e·ter
hy·gro·scop·ic
hy·men
hy·me·ne·al
hymn
hym·nal
hym·no·dy
hym·nol·o·gy
hy·per·acid·i·ty
hy·per·ac·tive
hy·per·bar·ic
hy·per·bo·la
curve
hy·per·bo·le
exaggeration
hy·per·bol·ic
hy·per·crit·i·cal
hy·per·crit·i·cal·ly
hy·per·gly·ce·mia
excess sugar (*see* hypoglycemia)
hy·per·sen·si·tive
hy·per·sen·si·tiv·i·ty
hy·per·son·ic
hy·per·ten·sion
hy·per·tro·phic
hy·per·tro·phy
hy·phen
hy·phen·ate
hy·phen·ation
hyp·no·sis
hyp·not·ic
hyp·not·i·cal·ly
hyp·no·tism
hyp·no·tist
hyp·no·tize
hy·po·chon·dria
hy·po·chon·dri·ac
hy·poc·ri·sy
hyp·o·crite
hyp·o·crit·i·cal
hyp·o·crit·i·cal·ly
hy·po·der·mic
hy·po·gly·ce·mia
decrease of sugar (*see* hyperglycemia)
hy·pot·e·nuse
hy·poth·e·cate
hy·poth·e·sis
hy·poth·e·size
hy·po·thet·i·cal
hy·po·thet·i·cal·ly
hys·ter·ec·to·my
hys·te·ria
hys·ter·ic
hys·ter·i·cal
hys·ter·i·cal·ly
hys·ter·ics

I

iam·bic
ibi·dem
ice·berg
ice·boat
ice·bound
ice·box

ice•break•er
ice-cold
ice•house
Ice•land
Ice•land•er
Ice•lan•dic
ice•man
ice-skate
ich•thy•ol•o•gist
ich•thy•ol•o•gy
ici•cle
ic•i•ly
ic•i•ness
ic•ing
icon
or ikon
icon•o•clasm
icon•o•clast
icy
Ida•ho
idea
ide•al
ide•al•ism
ide•al•ist
ide•al•is•tic
ide•al•is•ti•cal•ly
ide•al•iza•tion
ide•al•ize
ide•al•ly
ide•ate
ide•ation
idem
iden•ti•cal
iden•ti•cal•ly
iden•ti•fi•able
iden•ti•fi•ably
iden•ti•fi•ca•tion
iden•ti•fi•er
iden•ti•fy
iden•ti•ty
ideo•gram
ideo•graph
ideo•log•i•cal
also ideo•log•ic
ideo•log•i•cal•ly
ide•ol•o•gist
ide•ol•o•gy
id•i•o•cy
id•i•om
id•i•om•at•ic
id•i•om•at•i•cal•ly
id•io•syn•cra•sy
id•io•syn•crat•ic
id•io•syn•crat•i•cal•ly
id•i•ot
id•i•ot•ic
id•i•ot•i•cal•ly
idle
inactive (*see* idol, idyll)
idle•ness
idler
idly
idol
object of worship (*see* idle, idyll)
idol•a•ter
idol•a•trous
idol•a•try
idol•iza•tion
idol•ize
idyll
or idyl
poem (*see* idle, idol)
idyl•lic
if•fy
ig•loo
pl ig•loos
ig•ne•ous
ig•nit•able
also ig•nit•ible
ig•nite
ig•ni•tion
ig•no•ble
ig•no•bly
ig•no•min•i•ous
ig•no•mi•ny
ig•no•ra•mus
ig•no•rance
ig•no•rant
ig•nore
igua•na
ikon
var of icon
il•e•itis
il•e•um
pl il•ea
intestine (*see* ilium)
il•i•um
pl il•ia
bone (*see* ileum)
ill
worse
worst
ill-ad•vised
ill-be•ing

ill-bod•ing
ill-bred
il•le•gal
il•le•gal•i•ty
il•le•gal•ly
il•leg•i•bil•i•ty
il•leg•i•ble
il•leg•i•bly
il•le•git•i•ma•cy
il•le•git•i•mate
il•le•git•i•mate•ly
ill-fat•ed
ill-fa•vored
ill-got•ten
ill-hu•mored
il•lib•er•al
il•lic•it
unlawful (*see* elicit)
il•lim•it•able
il•lim•it•ably
Il•li•nois
il•lit•er•a•cy
il•lit•er•ate
ill-man•nered
ill-na•tured
ill•ness
il•log•i•cal
il•log•i•cal•ly
ill-sort•ed
ill-starred
ill-tem•pered
ill-treat
il•lu•mi•nate
il•lu•mi•na•tion
il•lu•mi•na•tor
il•lu•mine
ill-us•age
ill-use
il•lu•sion
mistaken idea (*see* allusion)
il•lu•sion•ist
il•lu•sive
deceptive (*see* allusive)
il•lu•so•ry
il•lus•trate
il•lus•tra•tion
il•lus•tra•tive
il•lus•tra•tor
il•lus•tri•ous
im•age
im•ag•ery
imag•in•able
imag•in•ably
imag•i•nary
imag•i•na•tion
imag•i•na•tive
imag•ine
im•ag•ism
im•ag•ist
im•bal•ance
im•be•cile
im•be•cil•i•ty
im•bed
var of embed
im•bibe
im•bib•er
im•bri•cate
im•bri•ca•tion
im•bro•glio
pl im•bro•glios
im•brue
im•bue
im•i•ta•ble
im•i•tate
im•i•ta•tion
im•i•ta•tive
im•i•ta•tor
im•mac•u•late
im•ma•nent
inherent (*see* eminent, imminent)
im•ma•te•ri•al
im•ma•ture
im•ma•tu•rity
im•mea•sur•able
im•mea•sur•ably
im•me•di•a•cy
im•me•di•ate
im•me•di•ate•ly
im•me•mo•ri•al
im•mense
im•mense•ly
im•men•si•ty
im•merse
im•mer•sion
im•mi•grant
im•mi•grate
come into a country (*see* emigrate)
im•mi•gra•tion
im•mi•nence

im·mi·nent
impending (*see* eminent, immanent)

im·mis·ci·ble

im·mit·i·ga·ble

im·mo·bile

im·mo·bil·i·ty

im·mo·bi·li·za·tion

im·mo·bi·lize

im·mod·er·a·cy

im·mod·er·ate

im·mod·est

im·mod·es·ty

im·mo·late

im·mo·la·tion

im·mor·al

im·mo·ral·i·ty

im·mor·al·ly

im·mor·tal

im·mor·tal·i·ty

im·mor·tal·ize

im·mor·tal·ly

im·mov·abil·i·ty

im·mov·able

im·mov·ably

im·mune

im·mu·ni·ty

im·mu·ni·za·tion

im·mu·nize

im·mu·nol·o·gist

im·mu·nol·o·gy

im·mure

im·mu·ta·bil·i·ty

im·mu·ta·ble

im·mu·ta·bly

im·pact

im·pact·ed

im·pair

im·pair·ment

im·pa·la

im·pale

im·pal·pa·bil·i·ty

im·pal·pa·ble

im·pal·pa·bly

im·pan·el

im·part

im·part·able
able to communicate (*see* impartible)

im·par·tial

im·par·tial·i·ty

im·par·tial·ly

im·par·ti·ble
not partible (*see* impartable)

im·pass·able
not passable (*see* impassible)

im·pass·ably

im·passe

im·pas·si·ble
unfeeling (*see* impassable)

im·pas·si·bly

im·pas·sioned

im·pas·sive

im·pas·siv·i·ty

im·pa·tience

im·pa·tient

im·peach

im·peach·ment

im·pec·ca·bil·i·ty

im·pec·ca·ble

im·pec·ca·bly

im·pe·cu·nious

im·ped·ance

im·pede

im·ped·i·ment

im·ped·i·men·ta

im·pel
im·pelled
im·pel·ling

im·pend

im·pen·e·tra·bil·i·ty

im·pen·e·tra·ble

im·pen·e·tra·bly

im·pen·i·tent

im·per·a·tive

im·per·ceiv·able

im·per·cep·ti·bil·i·ty

im·per·cep·ti·ble

im·per·cep·ti·bly

im·per·cep·tive

im·per·fect

im·per·fec·tion

im·per·fo·rate

im·pe·ri·al

im·pe·ri·al·ism

im·pe·ri·al·ist

im·pe·ri·al·is·tic

im·pe·ri·al·is·ti·cal·ly

im·pe·ri·al·ly

im·per·il
  im·per·iled
    or im·per·illed
  im·per·il·ing
    or im·per·il·ling
im·pe·ri·ous
im·per·ish·abil·i·ty
im·per·ish·able
im·per·ish·ably
im·per·ma·nence
im·per·ma·nen·cy
im·per·ma·nent
im·per·me·abil·i·ty
im·per·me·able
im·per·me·ably
im·per·mis·si·bil·i·ty
im·per·mis·si·ble
im·per·son·al
im·per·son·al·i·ty
im·per·son·al·ize
im·per·son·al·ly
im·per·son·ate
im·per·son·ation
im·per·son·ator
im·per·ti·nence
im·per·ti·nent
im·per·turb·abil·i·ty
im·per·turb·able
im·per·turb·ably
im·per·vi·ous
im·pe·ti·go
im·pet·u·os·i·ty
im·pet·u·ous
im·pe·tus
im·pi·ety
im·pinge
im·pinge·ment
im·pi·ous
imp·ish
im·pla·ca·ble
im·pla·ca·bly
im·plant
im·plan·ta·tion
im·plau·si·bil·i·ty
im·plau·si·ble
im·plau·si·bly
im·ple·ment
im·ple·men·ta·tion
im·pli·cate
im·pli·ca·tion
im·plic·it
im·plode
im·plore
im·plo·sion
im·plo·sive
im·ply
im·po·lite
im·pol·i·tic
im·pon·der·abil·i·ty
im·pon·der·a·ble
im·pon·der·a·bly
im·port
im·port·able
im·por·tance
im·por·tant
im·por·ta·tion
im·port·er
im·por·tu·nate
im·por·tune
im·por·tu·ni·ty
im·pose
im·pos·ing
im·po·si·tion
im·pos·si·bil·i·ty
im·pos·si·ble
im·pos·si·bly
im·post
im·pos·tor
  or im·pos·ter
im·pos·ture
im·po·tence
im·po·ten·cy
im·po·tent
im·pound
im·pov·er·ish
im·prac·ti·ca·bil·i·ty
im·prac·ti·ca·ble
im·prac·ti·ca·bly
im·prac·ti·cal
im·prac·ti·cal·i·ty
im·pre·cate
im·pre·ca·tion
im·pre·cise
im·pre·ci·sion
im·preg·na·bil·i·ty
im·preg·na·ble
im·preg·na·bly
im·preg·nate
im·preg·na·tion
im·pre·sa·rio
  pl im·pre·sa·ri·os
im·press
im·press·ible
im·pres·sion

im·pres·sion·abil·i·ty
im·pres·sion·able
im·pres·sion·ably
im·pres·sion·ism
im·pres·sion·ist
im·pres·sion·is·tic
im·pres·sive
im·pres·sive·ly
im·press·ment
im·pri·ma·tur
im·print
im·pris·on
im·pris·on·ment
im·prob·a·bil·i·ty
im·prob·a·ble
im·prob·a·bly
im·promp·tu
im·prop·er
im·pro·pri·ety
im·prov·abil·i·ty
im·prov·able
im·prove
im·prove·ment
im·prov·i·dence
im·prov·i·dent
im·pro·vi·sa·tion
im·pro·vise
im·pro·vis·er *or* im·pro·vi·sor
im·pru·dence
im·pru·dent
im·pu·dence
im·pu·dent
im·pugn
im·pulse
im·pul·sion
im·pul·sive
im·pul·sive·ly
im·pu·ni·ty
im·pure
im·pu·ri·ty
im·put·abil·i·ty
im·put·able
im·pu·ta·tion
im·pute
in·abil·i·ty
in ab·sen·tia
in·ac·ces·si·bil·i·ty
in·ac·ces·si·ble
in·ac·cu·ra·cy
in·ac·cu·rate
in·ac·tion
in·ac·ti·vate
in·ac·ti·va·tion
in·ac·tive
in·ac·tiv·i·ty
in·ad·e·qua·cy
in·ad·e·quate
in·ad·mis·si·bil·i·ty
in·ad·mis·si·ble
in·ad·ver·tence
in·ad·ver·ten·cy
in·ad·ver·tent
in·ad·vis·abil·i·ty
in·ad·vis·able
in·alien·abil·i·ty
in·alien·able
in·alien·ably
in·al·ter·abil·i·ty
in·al·ter·able
in·al·ter·ably
in·amo·ra·ta
inane
in·an·i·mate
inan·i·ty
in·ap·pli·ca·bil·i·ty
in·ap·pli·ca·ble
in·ap·pli·ca·bly
in·ap·pre·cia·ble
in·ap·pre·cia·bly
in·ap·pro·pri·ate
in·apt *not suitable (see* inept)
in·ap·ti·tude
in·ar·tic·u·late
in·as·much as
in·at·ten·tion
in·at·ten·tive
in·au·di·bil·i·ty
in·au·di·ble
in·au·di·bly
in·au·gu·ral
in·au·gu·rate
in·au·gu·ra·tion
in·aus·pi·cious
in·board
in·born
in·bound
in·bred
in·breed·ing
in·cal·cu·la·bil·i·ty
in·cal·cu·la·ble
in·cal·cu·la·bly

in•can•des•cence
in•can•des•cent
in•can•ta•tion
in•ca•pa•bil•i•ty
in•ca•pa•ble
in•ca•pac•i•tate
in•ca•pac•i•ta•tion
in•ca•pac•i•ty
in•car•cer•ate
in•car•cer•a•tion
in•car•nate
in•car•na•tion
in•cau•tious
in•cen•di•a•rism
in•cen•di•ary
in•cense
in•cen•tive
in•cep•tion
in•cep•tive
in•cer•ti•tude
in•ces•sant
in•cest
in•ces•tu•ous
in•cho•ate
in•ci•dence
in•ci•dent
in•ci•den•tal
in•ci•den•tal•ly
in•cin•er•ate
in•cin•er•a•tion
in•cin•er•a•tor
in•cip•i•en•cy
also in•cip•i•ence
in•cip•i•ent
in•cise
in•ci•sion
in•ci•sive
in•ci•sive•ly
in•ci•sor
in•ci•ta•tion
in•cite
in•cite•ment
in•ci•vil•i•ty
in•clem•en•cy
in•clem•ent
in•clin•able
in•cli•na•tion
in•cline
in•clin•ing
in•cli•nom•e•ter
in•clud•able
or in•clud•ible
in•clude
in•clu•sion
in•clu•sive
in•cog•ni•to
in•cog•ni•zant
in•co•her•ence
in•co•her•ent
in•com•bus•ti•ble
in•come
in•com•ing
in•com•men•su•ra•ble
in•com•men•su•ra•bly
in•com•men•su•rate
in•com•mode
in•com•mo•di•ous
in•com•mu•ni•ca•bil•i•ty
in•com•mu•ni•ca•ble
in•com•mu•ni•ca•bly
in•com•mu•ni•ca•do
in•com•mu•ni•ca•tive
in•com•mut•able
in•com•mut•ably
in•com•pa•ra•bil•i•ty
in•com•pa•ra•ble
in•com•pa•ra•bly
in•com•pat•i•bil•i•ty
in•com•pat•i•ble
in•com•pe•tence
in•com•pe•ten•cy
in•com•pe•tent
in•com•plete
in•com•pre•hen•si•ble
in•com•press•ible
in•con•ceiv•abil•i•ty
in•con•ceiv•able
in•con•ceiv•ably
in•con•clu•sive
in•con•gru•ent
in•con•gru•ity
in•con•gru•ous
in•con•se•quen•tial
in•con•se•quen•tial•ly
in•con•sid•er•able
in•con•sid•er•ate
in•con•sid•er•ate•ly

in·con·sis·ten·cy
also **in·con·sis·tence**
in·con·sis·tent
in·con·sol·able
in·con·sol·ably
in·con·spic·u·ous
in·con·stan·cy
in·con·stant
in·con·test·abil·i·ty
in·con·test·able
in·con·test·ably
in·con·ti·nence
in·con·ti·nent
in·con·trol·la·ble
in·con·tro·vert·ible
in·con·tro·vert·ibly
in·con·ve·nience
in·con·ve·nient
in·con·vert·ibil·i·ty
in·con·vert·ible
in·con·vert·ibly
in·cor·po·rate
in·cor·po·rat·ed
in·cor·po·ra·tion
in·cor·po·ra·tor
in·cor·po·re·al
in·cor·po·re·al·ly
in·cor·rect
in·cor·ri·gi·bil·i·ty
in·cor·ri·gi·ble
in·cor·ri·gi·bly
in·cor·rupt
in·cor·rupt·ibil·i·ty
in·cor·rupt·ible
in·cor·rupt·ibly
in·creas·able
in·crease
in·creas·ing·ly
in·cred·ibil·i·ty
in·cred·i·ble
in·cred·i·bly
in·cre·du·li·ty
in·cred·u·lous·ly
in·cre·ment
in·cre·men·tal
in·crim·i·nate
in·crim·i·na·tion
in·crim·i·na·to·ry
in·crust
var of **encrust**
in·crus·ta·tion
in·cu·bate
in·cu·ba·tion
in·cu·ba·tor
in·cu·bus
pl **in·cu·bi** *also* **in·cu·bus·es**
in·cul·cate
in·cul·ca·tion
in·cul·pa·ble
in·cul·pate
in·cul·pa·tion
in·cul·pa·to·ry
in·cum·ben·cy
in·cum·bent
in·cu·nab·u·lum
pl **in·cu·nab·u·la**
in·cur
in·curred
in·cur·ring
in·cur·abil·i·ty
in·cur·able
in·cur·ably
in·cu·ri·ous
in·cur·sion
in·debt·ed
in·de·cen·cy
in·de·cent
in·de·ci·pher·able
in·de·ci·sion
in·de·ci·sive
in·de·clin·able
in·de·co·rous
in·de·co·rum
in·deed
in·de·fa·ti·ga·bil·i·ty
in·de·fat·i·ga·ble
in·de·fat·i·ga·bly
in·de·fea·si·ble
in·de·fea·si·bly
in·de·fen·si·bil·i·ty
in·de·fen·si·ble
in·de·fen·si·bly
in·de·fin·able
in·def·i·nite
in·del·i·ble
in·del·i·bly
in·del·i·ca·cy
in·del·i·cate
in·dem·ni·fi·ca·tion
in·dem·ni·fy
in·dem·ni·ty
in·dent
in·den·ta·tion

in·den·tion
in·den·ture
in·de·pen·dence
in·de·pen·den·cy
in·de·pen·dent
in·de·scrib·able
in·de·scrib·ably
in·de·struc·ti·bil·i·ty
in·de·struc·ti·ble
in·de·struc·ti·bly
in·de·ter·min·able
in·de·ter·min·ably
in·de·ter·mi·na·cy
in·de·ter·mi·nate
in·de·ter·mi·nate·ly
in·de·ter·mi·na·tion
in·de·ter·min·ism
in·dex
pl in·dex·es *or* in·di·ces
in·dex·er
In·dia
In·di·an
In·di·ana
In·di·a·nap·o·lis
in·di·cate
in·di·ca·tion
in·dic·a·tive
in·di·ca·tor
in·di·cia
in·dict
charge (*see* indite)
in·dict·able
in·dict·ment
in·dif·fer·ence
in·dif·fer·ent
in·dif·fer·ent·ism
in·di·gence
in·di·gene
also in·di·gen
in·dig·e·nous
in·di·gent
in·di·gest·ibil·i·ty
in·di·gest·ible
in·di·ges·tion
in·dig·nant
in·dig·na·tion
in·dig·ni·ty
in·di·go
pl in·di·gos *or* in·di·goes
in·di·rect
in·di·rec·tion
in·dis·cern·ible
in·dis·creet
imprudent
in·dis·crete
not separated
in·dis·cre·tion
imprudence
in·dis·crim·i·nate
in·dis·pens·abil·i·ty
in·dis·pens·able
in·dis·pens·ably
in·dis·posed
in·dis·po·si·tion
in·dis·put·able
in·dis·put·ably
in·dis·sol·u·ble
in·dis·sol·u·bly
in·dis·tinct
in·dis·tin·guish·able
in·dis·tin·guish·ably
in·dite
compose (*see* indict)
in·di·vid·u·al
in·di·vid·u·al·ism
in·di·vid·u·al·ist
in·di·vid·u·al·is·tic
in·di·vid·u·al·is·ti·cal·ly
in·di·vid·u·al·i·ty
in·di·vid·u·al·iza·tion
in·di·vid·u·al·ize
in·di·vid·u·al·ly
in·di·vis·i·bil·i·ty
in·di·vis·i·ble
in·di·vis·i·bly
in·doc·tri·nate
in·doc·tri·na·tion
in·doc·tri·na·tor
in·do·lence
in·do·lent
in·dom·i·ta·bil·i·ty
in·dom·i·ta·ble
in·dom·i·ta·bly
In·do·ne·sia
In·do·ne·sian
in·door
in·doors
in·dorse
var of endorse
in·du·bi·ta·bil·i·ty

in·du·bi·ta·ble
in·du·bi·ta·bly
in·duce
in·duce·ment
in·duct
in·duc·tance
in·duct·ee
in·duc·tion
in·duc·tive
in·duc·tor
in·dulge
in·dul·gence
in·dul·gent
in·du·rate
in·du·ra·tion
in·dus·tri·al
in·dus·tri·al·ism
in·dus·tri·al·ist
in·dus·tri·al·iza·tion
in·dus·tri·al·ize
in·dus·tri·al·ly
in·dus·tri·ous
in·dus·try
ine·bri·ate
ine·bri·a·tion
in·ebri·ety
in·ed·i·ble
in·ed·it·ed
in·ed·u·ca·ble
in·ef·fa·bil·i·ty
in·ef·fa·ble
in·ef·fa·bly
in·ef·face·abil·i·ty
in·ef·face·able
in·ef·fec·tive
in·ef·fec·tu·al
in·ef·fec·tu·al·ly
in·ef·fi·ca·cious
in·ef·fi·ca·cy
in·ef·fi·cien·cy
in·ef·fi·cient
in·elas·tic
in·elas·tic·i·ty
in·el·e·gance
in·el·e·gant
in·el·i·gi·bil·i·ty
in·el·i·gi·ble
in·el·o·quent
in·eluc·ta·bil·i·ty
in·eluc·ta·ble
in·eluc·ta·bly
in·ept
unfit (*see* inapt)
in·ep·ti·tude
in·equal·i·ty
in·eq·ui·ta·ble
in·eq·ui·ty
injustice (*see* iniquity)
in·erad·i·ca·ble
in·erad·i·ca·bly
in·er·ran·cy
in·er·rant
in·ert
in·er·tia
in·er·tial
in·es·cap·able
in·es·cap·ably
in·es·sen·tial
in·es·ti·ma·ble
in·es·ti·ma·bly
in·ev·i·ta·bil·i·ty
in·ev·i·ta·ble
in·ev·i·ta·bly
in·ex·act
in·ex·cus·able
in·ex·cus·ably
in·ex·haust·ibil·i·ty
in·ex·haust·ible
in·ex·haust·ibly
in·ex·o·ra·ble
in·ex·o·ra·bly
in·ex·pe·di·en·cy
in·ex·pe·di·ent
in·ex·pen·sive
in·ex·pe·ri·ence
in·ex·pert
in·ex·pi·a·ble
in·ex·pli·ca·bil·i·ty
in·ex·pli·ca·ble
in·ex·pli·ca·bly
in·ex·press·ibil·i·ty
in·ex·press·ible
in·ex·press·ibly
in·ex·pres·sive
in·ex·pug·na·ble
in·ex·pug·na·bly
in ex·ten·so
in·ex·tin·guish·able
in·ex·tin·guish·ably
in ex·tre·mis
in·ex·tri·ca·bil·i·ty
in·ex·tri·ca·ble
in·ex·tri·ca·bly
in·fal·li·bil·i·ty

in·fal·li·ble
in·fal·li·bly
in·fa·mous
in·fa·my
in·fan·cy
in·fant
in·fan·ti·cide
in·fan·tile
in·fan·til·ism
in·fan·til·i·ty
in·fan·try
in·fan·try·man
in·fat·u·ate
in·fat·u·a·tion
in·fect
in·fec·tion
in·fec·tious
in·fec·tive
in·fec·tor
in·fe·lic·i·tous
in·fe·lic·i·ty
in·fer
  in·ferred
  in·fer·ring
in·fer·able
  or in·fer·ri·ble
in·fer·ence
in·fer·en·tial
in·fer·en·tial·ly
in·fe·ri·or
in·fe·ri·or·i·ty
in·fer·nal
in·fer·nal·ly
in·fer·no
in·fer·tile
in·fer·til·i·ty
in·fest
in·fes·ta·tion
in·fi·del
in·fi·del·i·ty
in·field
in·field·er
in·fight·ing
in·fil·trate
in·fil·tra·tion
in·fil·tra·tor
in·fi·nite
in·fi·nite·ly
in·fin·i·tes·i·mal
in·fin·i·tes·i·mal·ly
in·fin·i·tive
in·fin·i·tude
in·fin·i·ty
in·firm
in·fir·ma·ry
in·fir·mi·ty
in·flame
in·flam·ma·ble
in·flam·ma·tion
in·flam·ma·to·ry
in·flat·able
in·flate
in·fla·tion
in·fla·tion·ary
in·flect
in·flec·tion
in·flex·i·bil·i·ty
in·flex·i·ble
in·flex·i·bly
in·flict
in·flic·tion
in·flo·res·cence
in·flow
in·flu·ence
in·flu·en·tial
in·flu·en·za
in·flux
in·fold
in·form
in·for·mal
in·for·mal·i·ty
in·for·mal·ly
in·for·mant
in·for·ma·tion
in·for·ma·tive
in·formed
in·form·er
in·fra
in·frac·tion
in·fran·gi·bil·i·ty
in·fran·gi·ble
in·fran·gi·bly
in·fra·red
in·fra·son·ic
in·fre·quent
in·fringe
in·fringe·ment
in·fu·ri·ate
in·fu·ri·a·tion
in·fuse
in·fus·ible
in·fu·sion
in·gath·er·ing

in·ge·nious
clever (see ingenuous)

in·ge·nue
or in·gé·nue

in·ge·nu·ity

in·gen·u·ous
straightforward (see ingenious)

in·gest

in·gest·ible

in·ges·tion

in·glo·ri·ous

in·got

in·grain

in·grained

in·grate

in·gra·ti·ate

in·gra·ti·at·ing

in·grat·i·tude

in·gre·di·ent

in·gress

in-group

in·grow·ing

in·grown

in·hab·it

in·hab·it·able

in·hab·it·an·cy

in·hab·it·ant

in·hal·ant

in·ha·la·tion

in·ha·la·tor

in·hale

in·hal·er

in·har·mon·ic

in·har·mo·ni·ous

in·har·mo·ny

in·here

in·her·ence

in·her·ent

in·her·it

in·her·it·able

in·her·i·tance

in·her·i·tor

in·hib·it

in·hi·bi·tion

in·hib·i·tor
or in·hib·it·er

in·hib·i·to·ry

in·hos·pi·ta·ble

in·hos·pi·ta·bly

in-house

in·hu·man

in·hu·mane

in·hu·man·i·ty

in·hu·ma·tion

in·im·i·cal

in·im·i·cal·ly

in·im·i·ta·ble

in·im·i·ta·bly

in·iq·ui·tous

in·iq·ui·ty
wickedness (see inequity)

ini·tial

ini·tialed
or ini·tialled

ini·tial·ing
or ini·tial·ling

ini·tial·ly

ini·ti·ate

ini·ti·a·tion

ini·tia·tive

ini·ti·a·tor

ini·tia·to·ry

in·ject

in·jec·tion

in·jec·tor

in·ju·di·cious

in·junc·tion

in·jure

in·ju·ri·ous

in·ju·ry

in·jus·tice

ink·blot

in·kling

ink·stand

ink·well

inky

in·laid

in·land

in-law

in·lay

in·let

in·mate

in me·di·as res

in me·mo·ri·am

in·most

in·nards

in·nate

in·nate·ly

in·ner

in·ner-di·rect·ed

in·ner·most

in·ner·sole

in·ning

inn·keep·er

in•no•cence
in•no•cent
in•noc•u•ous
in•no•vate
in•no•va•tion
in•no•va•tive
in•no•va•tor
in•nu•en•do
pl **in•nu•en•dos** *or* **in•nu•en•does**
in•nu•mer•a•ble
in•nu•mer•a•bly
in•oc•u•late
in•oc•u•la•tion
in•of•fen•sive
in•op•er•a•ble
in•op•er•a•tive
in•op•por•tune
in•or•di•nate
in•or•gan•ic
in•pa•tient
in•put
in•quest
in•qui•etude
in•quire
in•quir•er
in•quir•ing•ly
in•qui•ry
in•qui•si•tion
in•quis•i•tive
in•quis•i•tor
in re
in rem
in•road
in•rush
in•sa•lu•bri•ous
in•sane
in•san•i•tary
in•san•i•ty
in•sa•tia•bil•i•ty
in•sa•tia•ble
in•sa•tia•bly
in•sa•tiate
in•scribe
in•scrip•tion
in•scru•ta•bil•i•ty
in•scru•ta•ble
in•scru•ta•bly
in•seam
in•sect
in•sec•ti•cide
in•se•cure
in•se•cu•ri•ty
in•sem•i•na•tion
in•sem•i•nate
in•sen•sate
in•sen•si•bil•i•ty
in•sen•si•ble
in•sen•si•bly
in•sen•si•tive
in•sen•si•tiv•i•ty
in•sen•tience
in•sen•tient
in•sep•a•ra•bil•i•ty
in•sep•a•ra•ble
in•sep•a•ra•bly
in•sert
in•ser•tion
in•set
in•set *or* **in•set•ted**
in•set•ting
in•shore
in•side
in•sid•er
in•sid•i•ous
in•sight
in•sig•nia
or **in•sig•ne**
pl **in•sig•nia** *or* **in•sig•ni•as**
in•sig•nif•i•cance
in•sig•nif•i•cant
in•sin•cere
in•sin•cere•ly
in•sin•cer•i•ty
in•sin•u•ate
in•sin•u•at•ing
in•sin•u•a•tion
in•sip•id
in•si•pid•i•ty
in•sist
in•sis•tence
in•sis•tent
in si•tu
in•so•far
in•sole
in•so•lence
in•so•lent
in•sol•u•bil•i•ty
in•sol•u•ble
in•sol•u•bly
in•solv•able
in•solv•ably

in·sol·ven·cy
in·sol·vent
in·som·nia
in·so·much
in·sou·ci·ance
in·sou·ci·ant
in·spect
in·spec·tion
in·spec·tor
in·spi·ra·tion
in·spire
in·spir·er
in·spir·it
in·sta·bil·i·ty
in·stall
or **in·stal**
in·stalled
in·stall·ing
in·stal·la·tion
in·stall·ment
or **in·stal·ment**
in·stance
in·stant
in·stan·ta·neous
in·stan·ter
in·state
in sta·tu quo
in·stead
in·step
in·sti·gate
in·sti·ga·tion
in·sti·ga·tor
in·still
also **in·stil**
in·stilled
in·still·ing
in·stinct
in·stinc·tive
in·stinc·tu·al
in·sti·tute
in·sti·tu·tion
in·sti·tu·tion·al·ize
in·sti·tu·tion·al·ly
in·struct
in·struc·tion
in·struc·tive
in·struc·tor
in·stru·ment
in·stru·men·tal
in·stru·men·tal·ist
in·stru·men·tal·i·ty
in·stru·men·tal·ly
in·stru·men·ta·tion
in·sub·or·di·nate
in·sub·or·di·na·tion
in·sub·stan·tial
in·sub·stan·ti·al·i·ty
in·suf·fer·able
in·suf·fer·ably
in·suf·fi·cien·cy
in·suf·fi·cient
in·su·lant
in·su·lar
in·su·lar·i·ty
in·su·late
in·su·la·tion
in·su·la·tor
in·su·lin
in·sult
in·su·per·a·ble
in·su·per·a·bly
in·sup·port·able
in·sup·port·ably
in·sup·press·ible
in·sup·press·ibly
in·sur·abil·i·ty
in·sur·able
in·sur·ance
in·sure
in·sured
in·sur·er
in·sur·gence
in·sur·gen·cy
in·sur·gent
in·sur·mount·able
in·sur·mount·ably
in·sur·rec·tion
in·sur·rec·tion·ary
in·sur·rec·tion·ist
in·sus·cep·ti·bil·i·ty
in·sus·cep·ti·ble
in·sus·cep·ti·bly
in·tact
in·ta·glio
in·take
in·tan·gi·bil·i·ty
in·tan·gi·ble
in·tan·gi·bly
in·te·ger
in·te·gral
in·te·grate
in·te·gra·tion

in·teg·ri·ty
in·teg·u·ment
in·tel·lect
in·tel·lec·tu·al
in·tel·lec·tu·al·ize
in·tel·lec·tu·al·ly
in·tel·li·gence
in·tel·li·gent
in·tel·li·gen·tsia
in·tel·li·gi·bil·i·ty
in·tel·li·gi·ble
in·tel·li·gi·bly
in·tem·per·ance
in·tem·per·ate
in·tend
in·ten·dant
in·tend·ed
in·tense
in·tense·ly
in·ten·si·fi·ca·tion
in·ten·si·fy
in·ten·si·ty
in·ten·sive
in·tent
in·ten·tion
in·ten·tion·al
in·ten·tion·al·ly
in·ter
  in·terred
  in·ter·ring
in·ter·act
in·ter·ac·tion
in·ter alia
in·ter·breed
in·ter·ca·late
in·ter·ca·la·tion
in·ter·cede
in·ter·cept
in·ter·cep·tion
in·ter·cep·tor
in·ter·ces·sion
in·ter·ces·sor
in·ter·ces·so·ry
in·ter·change
in·ter·change·able
in·ter·col·le·giate
in·ter·com
in·ter·com·mu·ni·ca·tion
in·ter·con·ti·nen·tal
in·ter·cos·tal
in·ter·course
in·ter·cul·tur·al
in·ter·de·nom·i·na·tion·al
in·ter·de·part·men·tal
in·ter·de·pen·dence
in·ter·de·pen·den·cy
in·ter·de·pen·dent
in·ter·dict
in·ter·dic·tion
in·ter·dis·ci·plin·ary
in·ter·est
in·ter·est·ing
in·ter·face
in·ter·faith
in·ter·fere
in·ter·fer·ence
in·ter·fer·on
in·ter·fuse
in·ter·im
in·te·ri·or
in·ter·ject
in·ter·jec·tion
in·ter·jec·tion·al·ly
in·ter·lace
in·ter·lard
in·ter·lay·er
in·ter·leaf
in·ter·leave
in·ter·line
in·ter·lin·ear
in·ter·lin·ing
in·ter·link
in·ter·lock
in·ter·lo·cu·tion
in·ter·loc·u·tor
in·ter·loc·u·to·ry
in·ter·lop·er
in·ter·lude
in·ter·lu·nar
in·ter·mar·riage
in·ter·mar·ry
in·ter·me·di·ary
in·ter·me·di·ate
in·ter·ment
in·ter·mez·zo
  pl in·ter·mez·zi *or* in·ter·mez·zos
in·ter·mi·na·ble
in·ter·mi·na·bly
in·ter·min·gle

in·ter·mis·sion
in·ter·mit·tent
in·ter·mix
in·tern
confine
in·tern
or in·terne
doctor
in·ter·nal
in·ter·nal·iza·tion
in·ter·nal·ize
in·ter·na·tion·al
in·ter·na·tion·al·iza·tion
in·ter·na·tion·al·ize
in·ter·na·tion·al·ly
in·ter·ne·cine
in·tern·ee
in·ter·nist
in·tern·ment
in·tern·ship
in·ter·nun·cio
in·ter·of·fice
in·ter·pen·e·trate
in·ter·pen·e·tra·tion
in·ter·per·son·al
in·ter·per·son·al·ly
in·ter·plan·e·tary
in·ter·play
in·ter·po·late
in·ter·po·la·tion
in·ter·pose
in·ter·po·si·tion
in·ter·pret
in·ter·pre·ta·tion
in·ter·pret·er
in·ter·pre·tive
in·ter·ra·cial
in·ter·reg·num
pl in·ter·reg·nums *or* in·ter·reg·na
in·ter·re·late
in·ter·re·la·tion
in·ter·ro·gate
in·ter·ro·ga·tion
in·ter·rog·a·tive
in·ter·ro·ga·tor
in·ter·rog·a·to·ry
in·ter·rupt
in·ter·rup·tion
in·ter·scho·las·tic
in·ter·sect
in·ter·sec·tion
in·ter·sperse
in·ter·sper·sion
in·ter·state
in·ter·stel·lar
in·ter·stice
in·ter·sti·tial
in·ter·tid·al
in·ter·twine
in·ter·twist
in·ter·ur·ban
in·ter·val
in·ter·vene
in·ter·ven·tion
in·ter·ven·tion·ism
in·ter·ven·tion·ist
in·ter·view
in·ter·view·er
in·ter·weave
in·ter·wove
also in·ter·weaved
in·ter·wo·ven
also in·ter·weaved
in·ter·weav·ing
in·tes·tate
in·tes·ti·nal
in·tes·tine
in·ti·ma·cy
in·ti·mate
in·ti·ma·tion
in·tim·i·date
in·tim·i·da·tion
in·to
in·tol·er·a·ble
in·tol·er·a·bly
in·tol·er·ance
in·tol·er·ant
in·to·na·tion
in·tone
in to·to
in·tox·i·cant
in·tox·i·cate
in·tox·i·ca·tion
in·trac·ta·bil·i·ty
in·trac·ta·ble
in·trac·ta·bly
in·tra·mu·ral
in·tra·mus·cu·lar
in·tran·si·gence
in·tran·si·gent
in·tran·si·tive
in·tra·state
in·tra·uter·ine

in·tra·ve·nous
in·trep·id
in·tre·pid·i·ty
in·tri·ca·cy
in·tri·cate
in·trigue
in·trin·sic
in·trin·si·cal·ly
in·tro·duce
in·tro·duc·tion
in·tro·duc·to·ry
in·tro·spec·tion
in·tro·spec·tive
in·tro·ver·sion
in·tro·vert
in·trude
in·trud·er
in·tru·sion
in·tru·sive
in·tu·ition
in·tu·itive
in·tu·mes·cence
in·tu·mes·cent
in·un·date
in·un·da·tion
in·ure
in vac·uo
in·vade
in·vad·er
in·val·id
not valid
in·va·lid
sickly
in·val·i·date
in·val·i·da·tion
in·valu·able
in·valu·ably
in·vari·able
in·vari·ably
in·va·sion
in·vec·tive
in·veigh
in·vei·gle
in·vent
in·ven·tion
in·ven·tive
in·ven·tor
in·ven·to·ry
in·ver·ness
in·verse
in·ver·sion
in·vert
in·ver·te·brate
in·vest
in·ves·ti·gate
in·ves·ti·ga·tion
in·ves·ti·ga·tor
in·ves·ti·ture
in·vest·ment
in·ves·tor
in·vet·er·ate
in·vid·i·ous
in·vig·o·rate
in·vig·o·ra·tion
in·vin·ci·bil·i·ty
in·vin·ci·ble
in·vin·ci·bly
in·vi·o·la·bil·i·ty
in·vi·o·la·ble
in·vi·o·la·bly
in·vi·o·late
in·vis·i·bil·i·ty
in·vis·i·ble
in·vis·i·bly
in·vi·ta·tion
in·vite
in·vit·ing
in·vo·ca·tion
in·voice
in·voke
in·vol·un·tari·ly
in·vol·un·tary
in·vo·lute
in·vo·lu·tion
in·volve
in·vul·ner·a·bil·i·ty
in·vul·ner·a·ble
in·vul·ner·a·bly
in·ward
or in·wards
in·ward·ly
in-wrought
io·dide
io·dine
io·dize
ion
ion·ic
ion·iza·tion
ion·ize
iono·sphere
io·ta
Io·wa
ip·so fac·to
Iran
Ira·ni·an

Iraq
Iraqi
iras•ci•bil•i•ty
iras•ci•ble
iras•ci•bly
irate
ire•ful
Ire•land
ir•i•des•cence
ir•i•des•cent
iris
pl iris•es *or* iri•des
Irish
Irish•man
irk•some
iron•bound
iron•clad
iron•ic
or iron•i•cal
iron•i•cal•ly
iron•ware
iron•work
iro•ny
ir•ra•di•ate
ir•ra•di•a•tion
ir•ra•tio•nal
ir•ra•tio•nal•i•ty
ir•ra•tio•nal•ly
ir•re•claim•able
ir•rec•on•cil•abil•i•ty
ir•rec•on•cil•able
ir•rec•on•cil•ably
ir•re•cov•er•able
ir•re•cov•er•ably
ir•re•deem•able
ir•re•deem•ably
ir•re•den•tism
ir•re•den•tist
ir•re•duc•ible
ir•re•fut•able
ir•re•fut•ably
ir•reg•u•lar
ir•reg•u•lar•i•ty
ir•rel•e•vance
ir•rel•e•van•cy
ir•rel•e•vant
ir•re•li•gious
ir•re•me•di•a•ble
ir•re•me•di•a•bly
ir•re•mov•able
ir•re•mov•ably
ir•rep•a•ra•ble
ir•rep•a•ra•bly
ir•re•place•able
ir•re•press•ible
ir•re•press•ibly
ir•re•proach•able
ir•re•proach•ably
ir•re•sist•ible
ir•re•sist•ibly
ir•res•o•lute
ir•res•o•lu•tion
ir•re•solv•able
ir•re•spec•tive of
ir•re•spon•si•bil•i•ty
ir•re•spon•si•ble
ir•re•spon•si•bly
ir•re•triev•able
ir•re•triev•ably
ir•rev•er•ence
ir•rev•er•ent
ir•re•vers•ible
ir•re•vers•ibly
ir•rev•o•ca•ble
ir•re•vo•ca•bly
ir•ri•gate
ir•ri•ga•tion
ir•ri•ta•bil•i•ty
ir•ri•ta•ble
ir•ri•ta•bly
ir•ri•tant
ir•ri•tate
ir•ri•ta•tion
ir•rupt
to rush in (*see* erupt)
ir•rup•tion
isin•glass
Is•lam
Is•lam•ic
is•land
isle
island (*see* aisle)
is•let
small island (*see* eyelet)
iso•bar
iso•late
iso•la•tion
iso•la•tion•ism
iso•la•tion•ist
iso•mer
iso•met•ric
iso•met•ri•cal•ly
iso•met•rics
isos•ce•les

iso·therm
iso·ther·mal
iso·tope
iso·to·pic
Is·ra·el
Is·rae·li
is·su·ance
is·sue
isth·mi·an
isth·mus
Ital·ian
ital·ic
ital·i·cize
It·a·ly
itch
itch·i·ness
itchy
item·iza·tion
item·ize
it·er·ate
it·er·a·tion
itin·er·ant
itin·er·ary
it·self
ivied
ivo·ry
Ivo·ry Coast
ivy

J

jab
  jabbed
  jab·bing
jab·ber
jab·ber·wocky
ja·bot
ja·cinth
jack·al
jack·a·napes
jack·ass
jack·boot
jack·daw
jack·et
jack·ham·mer
jack-in-the-box
  pl jack-in-the-box·es *or* jacks-in-the-box
jack-in-the-pul·pit
  pl jack-in-the-pul·pits *or* jacks-in-the-pul·pit
jack·knife
jack-of-all-trades
  pl jacks-of-all-trades
jack-o'-lan·tern
jack·pot
jack·rab·bit
jack·screw
Jack·son
Jack·son·ville
jack·straw
jac·o·net
jac·quard
jac·que·rie
jad·ed
jade·ite
jag
  jagged
  jag·ging
jag·ged
jag·uar
jai alai
jail·bird
jail·break
jail·er
  or jail·or
ja·lopy
jal·ou·sie
  window blind (see jealousy)
jam
  jammed
  jam·ming
Ja·mai·ca
Ja·mai·can
jam·ba·laya
jam·bo·ree
jan·gle
jan·i·tor
Jan·u·ary
Ja·pan
Jap·a·nese
jar
  jarred
  jar·ring
jar·di·niere
jar·gon
jas·mine
jas·per
ja·to unit
jaun·dice
jaun·diced
jaun·ti·ly
jaun·ti·ness

jaun•ty
jav•e•lin
jaw•bone
jaw•break•er
Jay•cee
jay•vee
jay•walk
jay•walk•er
jazz•i•ly
jazz•i•ness
jazzy
jeal•ous
jeal•ou•sy
suspicion (*see* **jalousie**)
jeans
Jef•fer•son City
je•hu
je•june
Jell-O
jel•ly
jel•ly•fish
jen•ny
jeop•ar•dize
jeop•ar•dy
jer•boa
jer•e•mi•ad
jerk•i•ly
jer•kin
jerk•i•ness
jerk•wa•ter
jerky
in fits and starts
jer•ky
meat
jer•o•bo•am
jer•ry-built
jer•sey
jes•sa•mine
jest•er
Je•su•it
je•su•it•ic
or **je•su•it•i•cal**
je•su•it•i•cal•ly
jet
jet•ted
jet•ting
je•té
jet•port
jet-pro•pelled
jet•sam
jet•ti•son
jet•ty
jeu d'es•prit
pl **jeux d'es•prit**
jew•el
jew•el•er
or **jew•el•ler**
jew•el•ry
Jew•ish
Jew•ry
jibe
agree (*see* **gibe**)
jif•fy
jig
jigged
jig•ging
jig•ger
jig•gle
jig•saw
jim-dan•dy
jim•my
jim•son•weed
jin•gle
jin•go•ism
jin•go•is•tic
jin•go•is•ti•cal•ly
jin•rik•i•sha
jinx
jit•ney
jit•ter•bug
jit•ter
jit•tery
jiu•jit•su
or **jiu•jut•su**
var of **jujitsu**
job
jobbed
job•bing
job•ber
job•hold•er
job•less•ness
jock•ey
jock•strap
jo•cose
jo•cos•i•ty
joc•u•lar
joc•u•lar•i•ty
jo•cund
jo•cun•di•ty
jodh•pur
jog
jogged
jog•ging
jog•ger

jog·gle
john·ny
joie de vi·vre
join·er
joint·ly
jok·er
jol·li·ty
jol·ly
jon·quil
Jor·dan
Jor·da·ni·an
jos·tle
jot
  jot·ted
  jot·ting
jour·nal
jour·nal·ese
jour·nal·ism
jour·nal·ist
jour·nal·is·tic
jour·ney
jour·ney·man
jo·vial
jo·vi·al·i·ty
jo·vial·ly
jowl
joy·ful
joy·ful·ly
joy·ous
joy·ride
joy·rid·er
ju·bi·lant
ju·bi·la·tion
ju·bi·lee

Ju·da·ic
Ju·da·ism
judg·ment
  or judge·ment
ju·di·ca·ture
ju·di·cial
ju·di·cial·ly
ju·di·cia·ry
ju·di·cious
ju·do
jug·ger·naut
jug·gle
jug·gler
jug·u·lar
juic·er
juic·i·ly
juic·i·ness
juicy
ju·jit·su
  or ju·jut·su *or* jiu·jit·su *or* jiu·jut·su
ju·jube
juke·box
ju·lep
ju·li·enne
Ju·ly
jum·ble
jum·bo
  pl jum·bos
jump·er
jump·i·ness
jumpy
jun

jun·co
  pl jun·cos *or* jun·coes
junc·tion
junc·ture
June
Ju·neau
jun·gle
ju·nior
ju·ni·per
jun·ker
jun·ket
junk·ie
  or junky
junk·yard
jun·ta
Ju·pi·ter
ju·rid·i·cal
  or ju·rid·ic
ju·rid·i·cal·ly
ju·ris·dic·tion
ju·ris·dic·tion·al
ju·ris·pru·dence
ju·ris·pru·den·tial·ly
ju·rist
ju·ris·tic
ju·ror
ju·ry
jus·tice
jus·ti·cia·ble
jus·ti·fi·able
jus·ti·fi·ably
jus·ti·fi·ca·tion
jus·ti·fy

just•ly

jut
  jut•ted
  jut•ting

jute

ju•ve•nile

ju•ve•nil•ia

jux•ta•pose

jux•ta•po•si•tion

K

ka•bob
  or ke•bab *or* ke•bob

Ka•bu•ki

kaf•fee•klatsch

kai•ser

ka•lei•do•scope

ka•lei•do•scop•ic

ka•ma•ai•na

ka•mi•ka•ze

kan•ga•roo

Kan•sas

ka•olin
  also ka•oline

ka•pok

ka•put
  also ka•putt

kar•a•kul

kar•at
  or car•at
  gold measure (see carat, caret, carrot)

ka•ra•te

kar•ma

ka•ty•did

kat•zen•jam•mer

kay•ak

kayo
  kay•oed
  kayo•ing

ka•zoo
  pl ka•zoos

ke•bab
  or ke•bob
  var of kabob

kedge

keel•boat

keel•haul

keel•son

keen•ly

keep
  kept
  keep•ing

keep•er

keep•sake

keg•ler

kel•vin

ken•nel

ke•no

Ken•tucky

Ke•nya

Ke•nyan

ke•pi

ker•a•tin

ker•chief

ker•nel
  seed, core (see colonel)

ker•o•sene
  or ker•o•sine

ker•sey

ker•sey•mere

ketch•up
  var of cat•sup

ke•tene

ke•tone

ket•tle

ket•tle•drum

key
  lock (see quay)

key•board

key•hole

key•note

key•not•er

key•stone

key•way

kha•ki

khe•dive

Khmer

kib•butz
  pl kib•but•zim

kib•itz•er

ki•bosh

kick•back

kick•off

kid
  kid•ded
  kid•ding

kid•nap
  kid•napped
    or kid•naped
  kid•nap•ping
    or kid•nap•ing

kid·nap·per
or kid·nap·er

kid·ney

kid·skin

kill·er

kill·ing

kill·joy

kiln

ki·lo
pl ki·los

kilo·cy·cle

ki·lo·gram

kilo·li·ter

ki·lo·me·ter

ki·lo·volt

kilo·watt

kilo·watt-hour

kil·ter

ki·mo·no
pl ki·mo·nos

kin·der·gar·ten

kind·heart·ed

kin·dle

kind·li·ness

kin·dling

kind·ly

kin·dred

ki·ne·mat·ic
or ki·ne·mat·i·cal

ki·ne·mat·ics

kin·e·scope

ki·ne·si·ol·o·gy

ki·net·ic

ki·net·ics

kin·folk
or kin·folks

king·bolt

king·dom

king·fish

king·fish·er

king·ly

king·mak·er

king·pin

king-size
or king-sized

kinky

kins·folk

kin·ship

kins·man

kins·wom·an

ki·osk

kip
pl kip *or* kips

kip·per

kir·tle

kis·met

kitch·en

kitch·en·ette

kitch·en·ware

kitsch

kit·ten

kit·ten·ish

kit·ty

kit·ty-cor·ner
or kit·ty-cor·nered
var of catercorner

klep·to·ma·nia

klep·to·ma·ni·ac

knap·sack

knave
rogue (*see* nave)

knav·ery

knav·ish

knead
massage (*see* need)

knee·cap

knee-deep

knee-high

knee·hole

kneel

knelt
or kneeled

kneel·ing

knick·ers

knick·knack

knife
pl knives

knife-edge

knight
rank (*see* night)

knight-er·rant

knight·hood

knit

knit
or knit·ted

knit·ting

knit·ter

knit·wear

knob·by

knock·about

knock·down

knock·er

knock-kneed

knock·out

knoll

knot

knot•ted

knot•ting

knot•hole

knot•ty

know

knew

known

know•ing

know•able

know-how

know-it-all

knowl•edge

knowl•edge•able

knowl•edge•ably

Knox•ville

knuck•le

knuck•le•bone

knurl

ko•ala

ko•bo

kohl•ra•bi

kooky
also kook•ie

ko•peck
also ko•pek

Ko•ran

Ko•rea

Ko•re•an

ko•ru•na
pl ko•ru•ny *or* ko•ru•nas

ko•sher

kow•tow

kro•na
pl kro•nur
Icelandic currency

kro•na
pl kro•nor
Swedish currency

kro•ne
pl kro•ner
Danish and Norwegian currency

kryp•ton

ku•do
pl ku•dos

ku•lak

kum•quat

ku•rus
pl ku•rus

Ku•wait
or Ku•weit *or* Ko•wait *or* Al Ku•wait

Ku•waiti

kwa•cha
pl kwa•cha

kwash•i•or•kor

kyat

L

la•bel

la•beled
or la•belled

la•bel•ing
or la•bel•ling

la•bi•al

la•bile

la•bor

lab•o•ra•to•ry

la•bored

la•bor•er

la•bo•ri•ous

la•bor•sav•ing

la•bur•num

lab•y•rinth

lab•y•rin•thine

lac•er•ate

lac•er•a•tion

la•ches
pl la•ches

lach•ry•mal
or lach•ri•mal

lach•ry•mose

lac•ing

lack•a•dai•si•cal

lack•a•dai•si•cal•ly

lack•ey

lack•lus•ter

la•con•ic

la•con•i•cal•ly

lac•quer

la•crosse

lac•tate

lac•ta•tion

lac•te•al

lac•tic

lac•tose

la•cu•na
pl la•cu•nae *or* la•cu•nas

la•cus•trine

lacy

lad•der

lad·der-back
lad·en
lad·ing
la·dle
la·dy
la·dy·bug
la·dy·fin·ger
la·dy-in-wait·ing
pl la·dies-in-wait·ing
la·dy·like
la·dy·love
la·dy·ship
lag
lagged
lag·ging
la·ger
lag·gard
la·gniappe
la·goon
lair
den (*see* layer)
lais·sez-faire
la·ity
lak·er
la·ma
monk (*see* llama)
lam·baste
or lam·bast
lam·bent
lam·bre·quin
lamb·skin
lame
disabled
la·mé
brocade

la·ment
la·men·ta·ble
la·men·ta·bly
lam·en·ta·tion
lam·i·na
pl lam·i·nae
or lam·i·nas
lam·i·nat·ed
lam·i·na·tion
lamp·black
lamp·light·er
lam·poon
lam·prey
la·nai
lanc·er
lan·cet
lan·dau
land·ed
land·fall
land·fill
land·form
land·hold·er
land·ing
land·la·dy
land·locked
land·lord
land·lub·ber
land·mark
land·mass
land·own·er
land·scape
land·slide
lands·man
land·ward
also land·wards

lan·guage
lan·guid
lan·guish
lan·guor
lan·guor·ous
lank·i·ness
lanky
lan·o·lin
Lan·sing
lan·tern
lan·yard
Laos
Lao·tian
lap
lapped
lap·ping
lap·board
lap·dog
la·pel
lap·i·dary
lap·in
la·pis la·zu·li
lap·pet
lapse
lar·ce·nous
lar·ce·ny
lar·der
large·ly
large-scale
lar·gess
or lar·gesse
lar·go
pl lar·gos
lar·i·at
lark·spur

lar·va
pl lar·vae *also* lar·vas

lar·val

la·ryn·geal

lar·yn·gi·tis

lar·ynx
pl la·ryn·ges *or* lar·ynx·es

las·car

las·civ·i·ous

la·ser

lash·ing

las·si·tude

las·so
pl las·sos *or* las·soes

Las·tex

last·ing

Las Ve·gas

lat·a·kia

latch

latch·key

latch·string

late·com·er

la·teen
also la·teen·er

late·ly

la·ten·cy

la·tent

lat·er·al

lat·er·al·ly

la·tex
pl la·ti·ces *or* la·tex·es

lath
strip of wood

lathe
machine

lath·er

Lat·in

lat·i·tude

lat·i·tu·di·nar·i·an

la·trine

lat·ter

lat·ter-day

lat·tice

lat·tice·work

Lat·via

Lat·vi·an

laud·able

laud·ably

lau·da·num

lau·da·to·ry

laugh·able

laugh·ing·stock

laugh·ter

launch·er

laun·der

laun·der·er

laun·dress

Laun·dro·mat

laun·dry

laun·dry·man

laun·dry·wom·an

lau·re·ate

lau·rel

la·va

la·va·bo

la·va·liere
or la·val·liere

lav·a·to·ry

lav·en·der

lav·ish

law-abid·ing

law·break·er

law·ful

law·ful·ly

law·giv·er

law·less

law·mak·er

law·suit

law·yer

lax·a·tive

lax·ity

lax·ness

lay
laid
lay·ing

lay·er
level (*see* lair)

lay·ette

lay·man

lay·off

lay·out

la·zi·ly

la·zi·ness

la·zy

la·zy·bones

leach
filter (*see* leech)

lead
led
lead·ing

lead·en

lead·er

lead·er·ship
lead-in
lead·ing
lead·off
lead-up
leaf
pl **leaves**
leaf·age
leaf·let
leafy
league
lea·guer
camp, siege
leagu·er
league member
leak
escape (*see* **leek**)
leak·age
leaky
lean
incline (*see* **lien**)
lean·ness
lean-to
leap
leaped
or **leapt**
leap·ing
leap·frog
learned
learn·er
learn·ing
lease·hold
least
least·wise
leath·er
leath·ery
leave
left
leav·ing
leav·en
leav·en·ing
leave-tak·ing
leav·ings
Leb·a·nese
Leb·a·non
lech·er
lech·er·ous
lech·ery
lec·tern
lec·tor
lec·ture
lec·tur·er
le·der·ho·sen
ledge
led·ger
leech
or **leach**
worm (*see* **leach**)
leek
plant (*see* **leak**)
leery
lee·ward
lee·way
left-hand·ed
left·ist
left·over
leg
legged
leg·ging
leg·a·cy
le·gal
le·gal·ism
le·gal·is·tic
le·gal·i·ty
le·gal·iza·tion
le·gal·ize
le·gal·ly
leg·ate
leg·a·tee
le·ga·tion
le·ga·to
le·ga·tor
leg·end
leg·end·ary
leg·er·de·main
leg·ging
or **leg·gin**
leg·gy
leg·horn
leg·i·bil·i·ty
leg·i·ble
leg·i·bly
le·gion
le·gion·ary
le·gion·naire
leg·is·late
leg·is·la·tion
leg·is·la·tive
leg·is·la·tor
leg·is·la·ture
le·gist
le·git·i·ma·cy
le·git·i·mate
le·git·i·mate·ly
le·git·i·mize

leg•man
le•gume
le•gu•mi•nous
lei
lei•sure
lei•sure•li•ness
lei•sure•ly
leit•mo•tiv
or leit•mo•tif
lek
lem•ming
lem•on
lem•on•ade
lem•pi•ra
le•mur
lend
lent
lend•ing
lend•er
lend-lease
length
length•en
length•wise
lengthy
le•nien•cy
le•nient
len•i•tive
len•i•ty
lens
also lense
Lent•en
len•til
le•one
le•o•nine
leop•ard
le•o•tard
lep•er
lep•re•chaun
lep•ro•sy
lep•rous
lep•ton
pl lep•ta
les•bi•an
le•sion
Le•so•tho
les•see
less•en
make less (*see* lesson)
less•er
smaller (*see* lessor)
les•son
instruction (*see* lessen)
les•sor
one who leases out (*see* lesser)
let
let
let•ting
let•down
le•thal
le•thal•ly
le•thar•gic
leth•ar•gy
let•ter
let•ter•er
let•ter•head
let•ter-per•fect
let•ter•press
let•tuce
let•up
leu
pl lei
leu•ke•mia
leu•ko•cyte
also leu•co•cyte
lev
pl le•va
lev•ee
embankment (*see* levy)
lev•el
lev•eled
or lev•elled
lev•el•ing
or lev•el•ling
lev•el•er
or lev•el•ler
lev•el•head•ed
lev•el•ly
lev•er
le•ver•age
le•vi•a•than
lev•i•tate
lev•i•ta•tion
lev•i•ty
levy
impose (*see* levee)
lewd
lewd•ness
lex•i•cog•ra•pher
lex•i•co•graph•ic
lex•i•cog•ra•phy
lex•i•con
Lex•ing•ton
li•a•bil•i•ty

li·a·ble
responsible (*see* libel)

li·ai·son

li·ar
one who lies (*see* lyre)

li·ba·tion

li·bel
malign (*see* liable)
li·beled
or **li·belled**
li·bel·ing
or **li·bel·ling**

li·bel·er
or **li·bel·ler**

li·bel·ous
or **li·bel·lous**

lib·er·al
lib·er·al·ism
lib·er·al·i·ty
lib·er·al·iza·tion
lib·er·al·ize
lib·er·al·ly
lib·er·ate
lib·er·a·tion
lib·er·a·tor
Li·be·ria
Li·be·ri·an
lib·er·tar·i·an
lib·er·tine
lib·er·ty
li·bid·i·nal
li·bid·i·nous
li·bi·do
li·brar·i·an
li·brary
li·bret·tist
li·bret·to
pl **li·bret·tos** *or* **li·bret·ti**

Lib·ya
Lib·y·an
li·cense
also **li·cence**

li·cens·ee
li·cen·ti·ate
li·cen·tious
li·chen
lic·it
lick·e·ty-split
lick·spit·tle
lic·o·rice
li·do
lie
rest, recline
lay
lain
ly·ing

lie
tell an untruth
lied
ly·ing

lie
untruth (*see* lye)

Liech·ten·stein
Liech·ten·stein·er
lied
pl **lie·der**
song

lien
claim (*see* lean)

lieu
lieu·ten·an·cy
lieu·ten·ant
life
pl **lives**

life·blood
life·boat
life·guard
life·less
life·like
life·line
life·long
life·sav·er
life·sav·ing
life-size
or **life-sized**

life·time
life·work
lift-off
lig·a·ment
lig·a·ture
light
light·ed
or **lit**
light·ing

light·en
ligh·ter
barge

light·er
one that lights

light·face
light-fin·gered
light-foot·ed
light-hand·ed
light-head·ed

light·heart·ed
light·house
light·ing
light·ly
light·ning
light·proof
light·ship
lights-out
light·weight
light-year
lig·ne·ous
lig·nite
lik·able
also **like·able**
like·li·hood
like·ly
like-mind·ed
lik·en
like·ness
like·wise
lik·ing
li·ku·ta
pl **ma·ku·ta**
li·lac
lil·li·pu·tian
lily
lily-white
limb
appendage (*see* **limn**)
lim·ber
lim·bo
pl **lim·bos**
lime·ade
lime·light
lim·er·ick
lime·stone
lim·it
lim·i·ta·tion
lim·it·ed
limn
draw (*see* **limb**)
lim·ou·sine
lim·pet
lim·pid
limp·ly
lin·age
lines (*see* **lineage**)
linch·pin
Lin·coln
lin·den
lin·eage
ancestry (*see* **linage**)
lin·eal
lin·ea·ment
outline (*see* **liniment**)
lin·ear
line·man
lin·en
lin·er
lines·man
line·up
lin·ger
lin·ger·ie
lin·go
pl **lin·goes**
lin·gua fran·ca
pl **lin·gua fran·cas** *or* **lin·guae fran·cae**
lin·gual
lin·guist
lin·guis·tic
lin·guis·tics
lin·i·ment
balm (*see* **lineament**)
lin·ing
link·age
link·up
li·no·leum
Li·no·type
lin·seed
lin·sey-wool·sey
lin·tel
li·on
li·on·ess
li·on·heart·ed
li·on·iza·tion
li·on·ize
lip·id
also **lip·ide**
lip·read·ing
lip·stick
liq·ue·fac·tion
liq·ue·fi·able
liq·ue·fi·er
liq·ue·fy
also **liq·ui·fy**
li·ques·cent
li·queur
liq·uid
liq·ui·date
liq·ui·da·tion
liq·ui·da·tor

li·quid·i·ty

li·quor

li·ra
pl li·re *also* li·ras

lisle

lis·some
also lis·som

lis·ten

lis·ten·er

list·ing

list·less

lit·a·ny

li·ter
or li·tre

lit·er·a·cy

lit·er·al
verbatim (see littoral)

lit·er·al·ly

lit·er·ary

lit·er·ate

li·te·ra·ti

lit·er·a·ture

lithe

lithe·some

litho·graph

li·tho·gra·pher

li·thog·ra·phy

Lith·u·a·nia

Lith·u·a·nian

lit·i·ga·ble

lit·i·gant

lit·i·gate

lit·i·ga·tion

li·ti·gious

lit·mus

li·tre
var of liter

lit·ter

lit·ter·a·teur

lit·ter·bug

lit·tle

Lit·tle Rock

lit·to·ral
shore (see literal)

li·tur·gi·cal

li·tur·gi·cal·ly

lit·ur·gist

lit·ur·gy

liv·able
also live·able

live·li·hood

live·li·ness

live·long

live·ly

liv·en

liv·er

liv·er·ied

liv·er·wort

liv·er·wurst

liv·ery

liv·ery·man

live·stock

liv·id

liv·ing

Li·vo·nia

liz·ard

lla·ma
animal (see lama)

lla·no
pl lla·nos

load
pack (see lode)

load·ed

load·stone

loaf
pl loaves

loaf·er

loamy

loan
lend (see lone)

loan·word

loath
also loathe
adj (see loathe)

loathe
verb (see loath)

loath·ing

loath·some

lob
lobbed
lob·bing

lo·bar

lob·by

lob·by·ist

lob·ster

lo·cal

lo·cale

lo·cal·i·ty

lo·cal·iza·tion

lo·cal·ize

lo·cal·ly

lo·cate

lo·ca·tion

lock·er
lock·et
lock·jaw
lock·out
lock·smith
lock·step
lock·up
lo·co·mo·tion
lo·co·mo·tive
lo·co·mo·tor
lo·cus
pl **lo·ci**
lo·cust
lo·cu·tion
lode
ore deposit (*see* load)
lode·star
lode·stone
lodge
contain (*see* loge)
lodg·er
lodg·ing
lodg·ment
or **lodge·ment**
loess
loft·i·ly
loft·i·ness
lofty
log
logged
log·ging
log·a·rithm
loge
theater section (*see* lodge)
log·ger
log·ger·head
log·gia
log·ic
log·i·cal
log·i·cal·ly
lo·gi·cian
lo·gis·tics
log·jam
logo·gram
logo·graph
logo·type
log·roll·ing
lo·gy
also **log·gy**
loin·cloth
loi·ter
loi·ter·er
lol·li·pop
or **lol·ly·pop**
Lon·don
lone
solitary (*see* loan)
lone·li·ness
lone·ly
lone·some
Long Beach
long·bow
long-dis·tance
lon·gev·i·ty
long·hair
long-haired
long·hand
long·ing
lon·gi·tude
lon·gi·tu·di·nal
lon·gi·tu·di·nal·ly
long-lived
long-play·ing
long-range
long·shore·man
long-suf·fer·ing
long-term
long-wind·ed
look·er-on
pl **look·ers-on**
look·out
loo·ny
or **loo·ney**
loop·hole
loose-joint·ed
loose·ly
loos·en
loose·ness
loot·er
lop
lopped
lop·ping
lop-eared
lop·sid·ed
lo·qua·cious
lo·quac·i·ty
lord·ly
lor·do·sis
lord·ship
lor·gnette
lor·ry
Los An·ge·les

lose
lost
los·ing
los·er
lo·tion
lot·tery
lo·tus
also **lo·tos**
loud·mouthed
loud·speak·er
Lou·i·si·ana
Lou·is·ville
louse
pl **lice**
lousy
lout·ish
lou·ver
or **lou·vre**
lov·able
also **love·able**
love·li·ness
love·ly
lov·er
love·sick
lov·ing
low·born
low·boy
low·bred
low·brow
low·down
low·er
low·er·case
low·er·most
low-key
also **low-keyed**
low·land
low-lev·el
low·li·ness
low·ly
low-pres·sure
low-rise
low-spir·it·ed
low-ten·sion
lox
pl **lox** *or* **lox·es**
loy·al
loy·al·ist
loy·al·ly
loy·al·ty
loz·enge
lu·au
lub·ber
Lub·bock
lu·bri·cant
lu·bri·cate
lu·bri·ca·tion
lu·bri·ca·tor
lu·bri·cious
or **lu·bri·cous**
lu·cent
lu·cid
lu·cid·i·ty
Lu·cite
luck·i·ly
lucky
lu·cra·tive
lu·cre
lu·cu·bra·tion
lu·di·crous
lug
lugged
lug·ging
lug·gage
lug·ger
lu·gu·bri·ous
lug·worm
luke·warm
lul·la·by
lum·ba·go
lum·ber
lum·ber·jack
lum·ber·yard
lu·men
pl **lu·mi·na** *or* **lu·mens**
lu·mi·nary
lu·mi·nos·i·ty
lu·mi·nous
lum·mox
lump·i·ly
lump·i·ness
lump·ish
lumpy
lu·na·cy
lu·nar
lu·na·tic
lun·cheon
lun·cheon·ette
lunch·room
lung·fish
lung·wort
lunk·head
lu·pine
lu·rid

lus•cious

lush•ness

lus•ter
or lus•tre

lus•ter•ware

lust•i•ly

lust•i•ness

lus•trous

lusty

Lu•ther•an

Lu•ther•an•ism

Lux•em•bourg
or Lux•em•burg

Lux•em•bourg•er
or Lux•em•burg•er

lux•u•ri•ance

lux•u•ri•ant

lux•u•ri•ate

lux•u•ri•ous

lux•u•ry

ly•ce•um

lye
corrosive (*see* lie)

ly•ing

ly•ing-in
pl ly•ings-in *or* ly•ing-ins

lymph

lym•phat•ic

lym•pho•cyte

lynch

lynx
pl lynx *or* lynx•es

lyre
harp (*see* liar)

lyr•ic

lyr•i•cal

lyr•i•cal•ly

lyr•i•cism

lyr•i•cist

M

ma•ca•bre

mac•ad•am

mac•ad•am•ize

ma•caque

mac•a•ro•ni
pl mac•a•ro•nis *or* mac•a•ro•nies

mac•a•roon

ma•caw

Mc•Coy

mac•er•ate

mac•er•a•tion

ma•chete

mach•i•nate

mach•i•na•tion

ma•chine

ma•chine•like

ma•chin•ery

ma•chin•ist

mack•er•el

mack•i•naw

mack•in•tosh
also mac•in•tosh

Ma•con

mac•ra•me

mac•ro
pl mac•ros

mac•ro•cosm

ma•cron

mac•ro•scop•ic

mac•ule

Mad•a•gas•can

Mad•a•gas•car

mad•am
pl mes•dames *or* mad•ams
form of address

ma•dame
pl mes•dames *or* ma•dames
title

mad•cap

mad•den

mad•der

Ma•dei•ra

ma•de•moi•selle
pl ma•de•moi•selles *or* mes•de•moi•selles

made-up

mad•house

Mad•i•son

mad•ly

mad•man

mad•ness

ma•dras

mad•ri•gal

mad•wom•an

mael•strom

mae•stro
pl mae•stros *or* mae•stri

Ma•fia

mag•a•zine

ma•gen•ta

mag·got
mag·goty
ma·gi
mag·ic
mag·i·cal
mag·i·cal·ly
ma·gi·cian
mag·is·te·ri·al
mag·is·tra·cy
ma·gis·tral
mag·is·trate
mag·ma
mag·na·nim·i·ty
mag·nan·i·mous
mag·nate
important person (*see* magnet)
mag·ne·sia
mag·ne·sium
mag·net
one that attracts (*see* magnate)
mag·net·ic
mag·ne·tism
mag·ne·ti·za·tion
mag·ne·tize
mag·ne·to
mag·ne·tom·e·ter
mag·ne·to·sphere
mag·ni·fi·ca·tion
mag·nif·i·cence
mag·nif·i·cent
mag·ni·fi·er
mag·ni·fy
mag·nil·o·quence
mag·nil·o·quent
mag·ni·tude
mag·no·lia
mag·num
mag·pie
ma·ha·ra·ja
or ma·ha·ra·jah
ma·ha·ra·ni
or ma·ha·ra·nee
ma·hat·ma
ma·hog·a·ny
maid·en
maid·en·hair
maid·en·hood
maid·en·ly
maid-in-wait·ing
pl maids-in-wait·ing
maid·ser·vant
mail·bag
mail·box
mail·er
mail·ing
mail·man
maim
Maine
main·land
main·ly
main·mast
main·sail
main·sheet
main·spring
main·stay
main·stream
main·tain
main·tain·able
main·te·nance
mai·son·ette
maî·tre d'hô·tel
pl maî·tres d'hô·tel
maize
grain (*see* maze)
ma·jes·tic
ma·jes·ti·cal·ly
maj·es·ty
ma·jol·i·ca
also ma·iol·i·ca
ma·jor
ma·jor·do·mo
ma·jor·i·ty
ma·jus·cule
mak·able
or make·able
make
made
mak·ing
make-be·lieve
make-do
mak·er
make·shift
make·up
ma·ku·ta
pl of likuta
mal·ad·ap·ta·tion
mal·adapt·ed
mal·ad·just·ed
mal·ad·min·is·ter
mal·ad·min·is·tra·tion
mal·adroit
mal·a·dy
mal·aise

mal·a·prop·ism
mal·ap·ro·pos
ma·lar·ia
ma·lar·i·al
Ma·la·wi
Ma·la·wi·an
Ma·lay·sia
Ma·lay·sian
mal·con·tent
mal de mer
Mal·dive
Mal·div·i·an
male·dic·tion
male·fac·tion
male·fac·tor
ma·lef·ic
ma·lef·i·cence
ma·lef·i·cent
male·ness
ma·lev·o·lence
ma·lev·o·lent
mal·fea·sance
mal·for·ma·tion
mal·formed
mal·func·tion
mal·ice
ma·li·cious
ma·lign
ma·lig·nan·cy
ma·lig·nant
ma·lig·ni·ty
ma·lin·ger
ma·lin·ger·er
Ma·li
Ma·li·an

mall
promenade (*see* maul)

mal·lard
mal·le·a·bil·i·ty
mal·lea·ble
mal·let
mal·low
malm·sey
mal·nour·ished
mal·nu·tri·tion
mal·oc·clu·sion
mal·odor·ous
mal·prac·tice
Mal·ta
Mal·tese
malt·ose
mal·treat
mam·bo
ma·ma
or **mam·ma**

mam·mal
mam·ma·li·an
mam·ma·ry
mam·mon
mam·moth
man
pl **men**

man
manned
man·ning

man-about-town
pl **men-about-town**

man·a·cle
man·age

man·age·abil·i·ty
man·age·able
man·age·ably
man·age·ment
man·ag·er
man·a·ge·ri·al
ma·ña·na
man-at-arms
pl **men-at-arms**

man·da·mus
man·da·rin
man·date
man·da·to·ry
man·di·ble
man·do·lin
also **man·do·line**

man·drake
man·drel
also **man·dril**
metal bar

man·drill
baboon

ma·nege
also **ma·nège**
horsemanship (*see* ménage)

ma·neu·ver
ma·neu·ver·abil·i·ty
ma·neu·ver·able
man·ful
man·ful·ly
man·ga·nese
mange
man·gel-wur·zel
man·ger
man·gle

man·gler

man·go
pl man·goes *or* man·gos

man·grove

mangy

man·han·dle

man·hat·tan

man·hole

man·hood

man-hour

man·hunt

ma·nia

ma·ni·ac

ma·ni·a·cal

ma·ni·a·cal·ly

man·ic

man·ic-de·pres·sive

man·i·cure

man·i·cur·ist

man·i·fest

man·i·fes·ta·tion

man·i·fes·to
pl man·i·fes·tos *or* man·i·fes·toes

man·i·fold

man·i·kin
or man·ni·kin

Ma·nila

ma·nip·u·late

ma·nip·u·la·tion

ma·nip·u·la·tive

ma·nip·u·la·tor

Man·i·to·ba

man·kind

man·li·ness

man·ly

man-made

man·na

manned

man·ne·quin

man·ner
mode (*see* manor)

man·nered

man·ner·ism

man·ner·ly

man·nish

man-of-war
pl men-of-war

man·or
estate (*see* manner)

ma·no·ri·al

man pow·er
or man·pow·er

man·qué

man·sard

man·ser·vant
pl men·ser·vants

man·sion

man-size
or man-sized

man·slaugh·ter

man·ta

man·teau

man·tel
fireplace shelf (*see* mantle)

man·telet

man·tel·piece

man·til·la

man·tis
pl man·tis·es *or* man·tes

man·tle
garment (*see* mantel)

man·u·al

man·u·al·ly

man·u·fac·to·ry

man·u·fac·ture

man·u·fac·tur·er

man·u·mis·sion

man·u·mit
man·u·mit·ted
man·u·mit·ting

ma·nure

manu·script

many
more
most

many·fold

many-sid·ed

map
mapped
map·ping

ma·ple

mar
marred
mar·ring

mar·a·bou
or mar·a·bout

ma·ra·ca

mar·a·schi·no

ma·ras·mus

mar·a·thon

ma•raud
ma•raud•er
mar•ble
mar•ble•ize
mar•bling
mar•cel
  mar•celled
  mar•cel•ling
March
march•er
mar•chio•ness
march-past
Mar•di Gras
mar•ga•rine
mar•ga•ri•ta
mar•gay
mar•gin
mar•gin•al
mar•gin•al•ly
mar•gi•na•lia
mar•grave
ma•ri•a•chi
mar•i•gold
mar•i•jua•na
  or **mar•i•hua•na**
ma•rim•ba
ma•ri•na
mar•i•nade
  noun
mar•i•nate
  or **mar•i•nade**
  verb
ma•rine
mar•i•ner
mar•i•o•nette
mar•i•tal
mar•i•time
mar•jo•ram
mark•down
marked
mark•ed•ly
mark•er
mar•ket
mar•ket•abil•i•ty
mar•ket•able
mar•ket•ing
mar•ket•place
mark•ing
mark•ka
  pl **mark•kaa** *or* **mark•kas**
marks•man
marks•man•ship
mark•up
mar•lin
  fish
mar•line
  also **mar•lin**
  rope
mar•line•spike
  also **mar•lin•spike**
mar•ma•lade
mar•mo•re•al
mar•mo•set
mar•mot
ma•roon
mar•quee
mar•quess
  or **marquis**
mar•que•try
mar•quise
mar•qui•sette
mar•riage
mar•riage•able
mar•ried
mar•row
mar•row•bone
mar•ry
Mars
mar•shal
  lead (*see* **martial**)
  mar•shaled
    or **mar•shalled**
  mar•shal•ing
    or **mar•shal•ling**
marsh•mal•low
marshy
mar•su•pi•al
mar•ten
  mammal (*see* **martin**)
mar•tial
  warlike (*see* **marshal**)
mar•tian
mar•tin
  bird (*see* **marten**)
mar•ti•net
mar•tin•gale
mar•ti•ni
mar•tyr
mar•tyr•dom
mar•vel
  mar•veled
    or **mar•velled**
  mar•vel•ing
    or **mar•vel•ling**

mar•vel•ous
or mar•vel•lous

Marx•ism

Marx•ist

Mary•land

mar•zi•pan

mas•cara

mas•con

mas•cot

mas•cu•line

mas•cu•lin•i•ty

ma•ser

mask
conceal (*see* masque)

mas•och•ism

mas•och•ist

mas•och•is•tic

ma•son

Ma•son•ic

ma•son•ry

masque
also mask
play (*see* mask)

mas•quer•ade

Mas•sa•chu•setts

mas•sa•cre

mas•sage

mas•seur

mas•seuse

mas•sif
mountain

mas•sive
huge

mass-pro•duce

mas•ter

master-at-arms
pl masters-at-arms

mas•ter•ful

mas•ter•ful•ly

mas•ter•ly

mas•ter•mind

mas•ter•piece

mas•ter•stroke

mas•ter•work

mas•tery

mast•head

mas•ti•cate

mas•ti•ca•tion

mas•tiff

mast•odon

mas•toid

mas•tur•bate

mas•tur•ba•tion

mat
mat•ted
mat•ting

mat•a•dor

match•book

match•less

match•lock

match•mak•er

match•wood

ma•te•ri•al
of matter (*see* matériel)

ma•te•ri•al•ism

ma•te•ri•al•ist

ma•te•ri•al•is•tic

ma•te•ri•al•is•ti•cal•ly

ma•te•ri•al•iza•tion

ma•te•ri•al•ize

ma•te•ri•al•ly

ma•te•ria med•i•ca

ma•té•ri•el
or ma•te•ri•el
equipment (*see* material)

ma•ter•nal

ma•ter•nal•ly

ma•ter•ni•ty

math•e•mat•i•cal
also math•e•matic

math•e•mat•i•cal•ly

math•e•ma•ti•cian

math•e•mat•ics

mat•i•nee
or mat•i•née

mat•ins

ma•tri•arch

ma•tri•ar•chal

ma•tri•ar•chy

ma•tri•cid•al

ma•tri•cide

ma•tric•u•lant

ma•tric•u•late

ma•tric•u•la•tion

ma•tri•lin•eal

ma•tri•lin•eal•ly

mat•ri•mo•nial

mat•ri•mo•nial•ly

mat•ri•mo•ny

ma•trix
pl ma•tri•ces *or* ma•trix•es

ma•tron

ma·tron·ly
mat·ro·nym·ic
mat·ter
mat·ter-of-fact
mat·ting
mat·tins
mat·tock
mat·tress
mat·u·rate
mat·u·ra·tion
ma·ture
ma·tu·ri·ty
mat·zo
pl **mat·zoth** *or* **mat·zos**
maud·lin
maul
mangle (*see* **mall**)
maun·der
Mau·ri·ta·nia
Mau·ri·ta·nian
Mau·ri·tian
Mau·ri·ti·us
mau·so·le·um
pl **mau·so·le·ums** *or* **mau·so·lea**
mauve
mav·er·ick
ma·vis
mawk·ish
max·il·la
pl **max·il·lae** *or* **max·il·las**
max·im
max·i·mal
max·i·mal·ly
max·i·mum
pl **max·i·ma** *or* **max·i·mums**
May
may·ap·ple
may·be
may·flow·er
may·hem
may·on·naise
may·or
may·or·al·ty
may·pole
maze
intricate network (*see* **maize**)
ma·zur·ka
also **ma·zour·ka**
mead·ow
mead·ow·lark
mea·ger
or **mea·gre**
mea·ger·ly
meal·time
mealy
mealy·mouthed
mean
intend (*see* **mien**)
meant
mean·ing
me·an·der
mean·ing
mean·ing·ful
mean·ing·less
mean·ly
mean·ness
mean·time
mean·while
mea·sles
mea·sly
mea·sur·abil·i·ty
mea·sur·able
mea·sur·ably
mea·sure
mea·sure·less
mea·sure·ment
mea·sur·er
meat
food (*see* **meet, mete**)
meat·ball
meat·i·ness
me·atus
pl **me·atus·es** *or* **me·atus**
meaty
mec·ca
me·chan·ic
me·chan·i·cal
me·chan·i·cal·ly
me·chan·ics
mech·a·nism
mech·a·nis·tic
mech·a·nis·ti·cal·ly
mech·a·ni·za·tion
mech·a·nize
med·al
award (*see* **meddle**)
med·al·ist
or **med·al·list**
me·dal·lion
med·dle
interfere (*see* **medal**)

med•dler
med•dle•some
me•dia
me•di•al
me•di•an
me•di•ate
me•di•a•tion
me•di•a•tor
med•ic
med•i•ca•ble
med•ic•aid
med•i•cal
med•i•cal•ly
medi•care
med•i•cate
med•i•ca•tion
me•dic•i•nal
me•dic•i•nal•ly
med•i•cine
med•i•co
pl med•i•cos
me•di•eval
or me•di•ae•val
me•di•eval•ist
me•di•o•cre
me•di•oc•ri•ty
med•i•tate
med•i•ta•tion
med•i•ta•tive
Med•i•ter•ra•nean
me•di•um
pl me•di•ums *or* me•dia
med•ley
me•dul•la
pl me•dul•las *or* me•dul•lae
me•dul•la ob•lon•ga•ta
meek•ly
meek•ness
meer•schaum
meet
come upon (see meat, mete)
met
meet•ing
meet•ing•house
mega•cy•cle
mega•death
mega•lith
meg•a•lo•ma•nia
meg•a•lo•ma•ni•ac
meg•a•lo•ma•ni•a•cal
meg•a•lop•o•lis
mega•phone
mega•ton
mei•o•sis
mel•a•mine
mel•an•cho•lia
mel•an•chol•ic
mel•an•choly
mé•lange
mel•a•nin
mel•ba toast
me•lee
me•lio•rate
me•lio•ra•tion
me•lio•ra•tive
mel•lif•lu•ous
mel•low
me•lo•de•on
me•lod•ic
me•lod•i•cal•ly
me•lo•di•ous
melo•dra•ma
melo•dra•mat•ic
melo•dra•mat•i•cal•ly
mel•o•dy
mel•on
melt
melt•ed
melt•ed
also mol•ten
melt•ing
mel•ton
melt•wa•ter
mem•ber
mem•ber•ship
mem•brane
mem•bra•nous
me•men•to
pl me•men•tos *or* me•men•toes
me•men•to mo•ri
memo
pl mem•os
mem•oir
mem•o•ra•bil•ia
mem•o•ra•ble
mem•o•ra•bly

mem·o·ran·dum
pl **mem·o·ran·dums** *or* **mem·o·ran·da**

me·mo·ri·al

me·mo·ri·al·ize

mem·o·ri·za·tion

mem·o·rize

mem·o·ry

Mem·phis

men·ace

men·ac·ing·ly

mé·nage
household (*see* **manege**)

me·nag·er·ie

men·da·cious

men·dac·i·ty

Men·de·lian

men·di·cant

men·folk
or **men·folks**

men·ha·den

me·nial

me·nial·ly

men·in·gi·tis

me·nis·cus
pl **me·nis·ci** *also* **me·nis·cus·es**

meno·paus·al

meno·pause

me·no·rah

men·ses

men·stru·al

men·stru·ate

men·stru·a·tion

men·su·ra·bil·i·ty

men·su·ra·ble

men·su·ra·tion

men·tal

men·tal·i·ty

men·tal·ly

men·thol

men·tho·lat·ed

men·tion

men·tion·able

men·tor

menu

me·phit·ic

mer·can·tile

mer·can·til·ism

mer·ce·nary

mer·cer·ize

mer·chan·dise

mer·chan·dis·er

mer·chant

mer·ci·ful

mer·ci·ful·ly

mer·ci·less

mer·cu·ri·al

mer·cu·ri·al·ly

mer·cu·ric

mer·cu·ry

mer·cy

mere·ly

mer·e·tri·cious

mer·gan·ser

merg·er

me·rid·i·an

me·ringue

me·ri·no
pl **me·ri·nos**

mer·it

mer·i·to·ri·ous

mer·maid

mer·ri·ly

mer·ri·ment

mer·ry

mer·ry-an·drew

mer·ry-go-round

mer·ry·mak·er

mer·ry·mak·ing

Mer·thi·o·late

me·sa

més·al·liance

mes·cal

mes·ca·line

mes·dames
pl of **madam, madame**

mes·de·moi·selles
pl of **mademoiselle**

mesh·work

mes·mer·ism

mes·mer·ize

me·son

mes·quite

mes·sage

mes·sen·ger

mes·si·ah

mes·si·an·ic

mes·sieurs
pl of **monsieur**

mess·i·ly

mess·i·ness

mess·mate

messy

mes·ti·zo
pl mes·ti·zos

met·a·bol·ic

me·tab·o·lism

me·tab·o·lize

met·al
chemical element (*see* mettle)
met·aled
or met·alled
met·al·ing
or met·al·ling

me·tal·lic

met·al·lur·gi·cal

met·al·lur·gist

met·al·lur·gy

met·al·ware

met·al·work

meta·mor·phic

meta·mor·phism

meta·mor·phose

meta·mor·pho·sis

met·a·phor

met·a·phor·i·cal

met·a·phor·i·cal·ly

meta·phys·ic

meta·phys·i·cal

meta·phys·i·cal·ly

meta·phys·ics

me·tas·ta·sis
pl me·tas·ta·ses

meta·tar·sal

meta·tar·sus

mete
allot (*see* meat, meet)

me·tem·psy·cho·sis

me·te·or

me·te·or·ic

me·te·or·i·cal·ly

me·te·or·ite

me·te·or·oid

me·te·o·ro·log·ic
or me·te·o·ro·log·i·cal

me·te·o·ro·log·i·cal·ly

me·te·o·rol·o·gist

me·te·o·rol·o·gy

me·ter

meth·a·done
or meth·a·don

meth·ane

meth·a·nol

meth·od

me·thod·i·cal
or me·thod·ic

me·thod·i·cal·ly

Meth·od·ist

meth·od·ize

meth·od·olog·i·cal

meth·od·olog·i·cal·ly

meth·od·ol·o·gy

me·tic·u·lous

mé·tier

me-too

met·ric

met·ri·cal

met·ri·cal·ly

met·ro
pl met·ros

met·ro·nome

me·trop·o·lis

met·ro·pol·i·tan

met·tle
spirit (*see* metal)

met·tle·some

Mex·i·can

Mex·i·co

mez·za·nine

mez·zo-so·pra·no

Mi·ami

mi·as·ma
pl mi·as·mas *or* mi·as·ma·ta

mi·ca

Mich·i·gan

mi·crobe

mi·cro·bi·al

mi·cro·cir·cuit

mi·cro·copy

mi·cro·cosm

mi·cro·fiche

mi·cro·film

mi·cro·form

mi·cro·groove

mi·crom·e·ter

mi·cron

mi·cro·or·gan·ism

mi·cro·phone

mi·cro·print

mi·cro·probe

mi·cro·read·er

mi·cro·scope

mi·cro·scop·ic

mi·cro·scop·i·cal·ly

mi•cros•co•py
mi•cro•wave
mid•day
mid•den
mid•dle
mid•dle-aged
mid•dle•brow
mid•dle•man
middle-of-the-road
middle-of-the-road•er
mid•dle•weight
mid•dling
mid•dy
midshipman, blouse (*see* midi)
midg•et
midi
skirt (*see* middy)
mid•land
mid•most
mid•night
mid•point
mid•riff
mid•sec•tion
mid•ship•man
mid•ships
midst
mid•stream
mid•sum•mer
mid•way
mid•week
mid•wife
mid•wife•ry
mid•win•ter
mid•year
mien
appearance (*see* mean)
might
strength (*see* mite)
might•i•ly
might•i•ness
mighty
mi•gnon•ette
mi•graine
mi•grant
mi•grate
mi•gra•tion
mi•gra•to•ry
mi•ka•do
pl mi•ka•dos
mil
thousandth, coin (*see* mill)
mil•dew
mild•ly
mild•ness
mile•age
mile•post
mil•er
mi•le•si•mo
mile•stone
mill
building (*see* mil)
mi•lieu
mil•i•tan•cy
mil•i•tant
mil•i•tari•ly
mil•i•ta•rism
mil•i•ta•ris•tic
mil•i•ta•ri•za•tion
mil•i•ta•rize
mil•i•tary
mil•i•tate
mi•li•tia
mi•li•tia•man
milk•er
milk•i•ness
milk•maid
milk•man
milk•sop
milk•weed
milk•wort
milky
mill•dam
mil•len•ni•al
mil•len•ni•um
pl mil•len•nia *or* mil•len•ni•ums
mill•er
mil•let
mil•li•ard
mil•li•bar
mil•lieme
mil•li•gram
mil•lime
mil•li•me•ter
mil•li•ner
mil•li•nery
mill•ing
mil•lion
mil•lion•aire
mil•lionth
mill•pond
mill•race

mill·stone
mill·stream
mill·wright
Mil·wau·kee
mim·eo·graph
mim·er
mi·me·sis
mi·met·ic
mim·ic
mim·icked
mim·ick·ing
mim·ic·ry
mi·mo·sa
min·a·ret
mi·na·to·ry
mince·meat
minc·ing
mind·ed
mind-ex·pand·ing
mind·ful
mind·ful·ly
mind·less
mine·lay·er
min·er
one that mines (*see* **minor**)
min·er·al
min·er·al·iza·tion
min·er·al·ize
min·er·al·og·i·cal
min·er·al·o·gist
min·er·al·o·gy
min·e·stro·ne
mine·sweep·er
min·gle
min·ia·ture
min·ia·tur·ist
min·ia·tur·iza·tion
min·ia·tur·ize
mini·bus
min·ié ball
min·im
min·i·mal
min·i·mal·ly
min·i·mi·za·tion
min·i·mize
min·i·mum
pl **min·i·ma** *or* **min·i·mums**
min·ing
min·ion
min·is·cule
mini·skirt
mini·state
min·is·ter
min·is·te·ri·al
min·is·trant
min·is·tra·tion
min·is·try
mini·track
min·i·ver
mink
pl **mink** *or* **minks**
Min·ne·ap·o·lis
min·ne·sing·er
Min·ne·so·ta
min·now
mi·nor
lesser (*see* **miner**)
mi·nor·i·ty
min·strel
min·strel·sy
mint·age
mint·er
minty
min·u·end
min·u·et
mi·nus
mi·nus·cule
min·ute
noun
mi·nute
adj
mi·nute·ly
min·ute·man
mi·nu·tia
pl **mi·nu·ti·ae**
minx
mir·a·cle
mi·rac·u·lous
mir·a·dor
mi·rage
mir·ror
mirth·ful
mirth·ful·ly
miry
mis·ad·ven·ture
mis·al·li·ance
mis·al·lo·ca·tion
mis·an·thrope
mis·an·throp·ic
mis·an·throp·i·cal·ly
mis·an·thro·py
mis·ap·pli·ca·tion
mis·ap·ply

mis·ap·pre·hend
mis·ap·pre·hen·sion
mis·ap·pro·pri·ate
mis·ap·pro·pri·a·tion
mis·be·got·ten
mis·be·have
mis·be·hav·ior
mis·be·lief
mis·be·liev·er
mis·brand
mis·cal·cu·late
mis·cal·cu·la·tion
mis·call
mis·car·riage
mis·car·ry
mis·cast
mis·ce·ge·na·tion
mis·cel·la·nea
mis·cel·la·ne·ous
mis·cel·la·ny
mis·chance
mis·chief
mis·chie·vous
mis·ci·bil·i·ty
mis·ci·ble
mis·con·ceive
mis·con·cep·tion
mis·con·duct
mis·con·struc·tion
mis·con·strue
mis·count
mis·cre·ant
mis·cue
mis·deal
mis·deed
mis·de·mean·ant
mis·de·mean·or
mis·di·rect
mis·di·rec·tion
mis·do·er
mis·do·ing
mise-en-scène
mi·ser
mis·er·a·ble
mis·er·a·bly
mi·ser·li·ness
mi·ser·ly
mis·ery
mis·es·ti·mate
mis·es·ti·ma·tion
mis·fea·sance
mis·file
mis·fire
mis·fit
mis·for·tune
mis·giv·ing
mis·gov·ern
mis·gov·ern·ment
mis·guid·ance
mis·guide
mis·han·dle
mis·hap
mish·mash
mis·in·form
mis·in·for·ma·tion
mis·in·ter·pret
mis·in·ter·pre·ta·tion
mis·judge
mis·judg·ment
mis·lay
mis·lead
mis·man·age
mis·man·age·ment
mis·match
mis·mate
mis·name
mis·no·mer
mi·sog·a·mist
mi·sog·a·my
mi·sog·y·nist
mi·sog·y·ny
mis·place
mis·play
mis·print
mis·pri·sion
mis·pro·nounce
mis·pro·nun·ci·a·tion
mis·quo·ta·tion
mis·quote
mis·read
mis·rep·re·sent
mis·rep·re·sen·ta·tion
mis·rule
mis·sal
book (*see* missile)
mis·send
mis·sent
mis·send·ing
mis·shape
mis·shap·en

mis•sile
weapon (*see* missal)

mis•sile•ry
also mis•sil•ry

miss•ing

mis•sion

mis•sion•ary

mis•sion•er

Mis•sis•sip•pi

mis•sive

Mis•sou•ri

mis•spell

mis•spend

mis•state

mis•state•ment

mis•step

mis•tak•able

mis•take
mis•took
mis•tak•en
mis•tak•ing

mis•ter

mist•i•ly

mis•time

mist•i•ness

mis•tle•toe

mis•tral

mis•treat

mis•treat•ment

mis•tress

mis•tri•al

mis•trust

misty

mis•un•der•stand

mis•us•age

mis•use

mis•val•ue

mis•ven•ture

mite
small thing (*see* might)

mi•ter
or mi•tre
mi•tered
or mi•tred
mi•ter•ing
or mi•tring

mit•i•gate

mit•i•ga•tion

mit•i•ga•tive

mit•i•ga•tor

mi•to•sis
pl mi•to•ses

mitt

mit•ten

mix•able

mix•er

mix•ture

mix-up

miz•zen
or miz•en

miz•zen•mast

mne•mon•ic

mne•mon•ics

moat
trench (*see* mote)

mob
mobbed
mob•bing

Mo•bile

mo•bile

mo•bil•i•ty

mo•bi•li•za•tion

mo•bi•lize

mob•oc•ra•cy

mob•ster

moc•ca•sin

mo•cha

mock•er

mock•ery

mock-he•ro•ic

mock•ing•bird

mock-up

mod•al

mod•el
mod•eled
or mod•elled
mod•el•ing
or mod•el•ling

mod•er•ate

mod•er•ate•ly

mod•er•a•tion

mod•er•a•to

mod•er•a•tor

mod•ern

mod•ern•ism

mod•ern•is•tic

mo•der•ni•ty

mod•ern•iza•tion

mod•ern•ize

mod•ern•iz•er

mod•est

mod•es•ty

mod•i•cum

mod•i•fi•ca•tion

mod•i•fi•er

mod·i·fy
mod·ish
mo·diste
mod·u·lar
mod·u·late
mod·u·la·tion
mod·u·la·tor
mod·ule
mo·dus ope·ran·di
pl mo·di ope·ran·di
mo·dus vi·ven·di
pl mo·di vi·ven·di
mo·gul
or Mo·ghul
mo·hair
moi·ety
moi·ré
or moire
moist·en
moist·ly
moist·ness
mois·ture
mo·lar
mo·las·ses
mold·board
mold·er
mold·i·ness
mold·ing
moldy
mo·lec·u·lar
mol·e·cule
mole·hill
mole·skin
mo·lest
mo·les·ta·tion
mo·lest·er
mol·li·fi·ca·tion
mol·li·fy
mol·lusk
or mol·lusc
mol·ly·cod·dle
molt
mol·ten
mol·to
mo·lyb·de·num
mo·ment
mo·men·tari·ly
mo·men·tary
mo·men·tous
mo·men·tum
pl mo·men·ta *or* mo·men·tums
Mo·na·can
Mo·na·co
mo·nad
mon·arch
mo·nar·chi·cal
or mo·nar·chic
mon·ar·chism
mon·ar·chist
mon·ar·chy
mon·as·te·ri·al
mon·as·tery
mo·nas·tic
mo·nas·ti·cal·ly
mo·nas·ti·cism
mon·au·ral
Mon·day
Mon·e·gasque
mon·e·tari·ly
mon·e·tary
mon·e·ti·za·tion
mon·e·tize
mon·ey
pl mon·eys *or* mon·ies
mon·ey·bags
mon·eyed
also mon·ied
mon·ey·lend·er
mon·ey-mak·er
mon·ey·wort
mon·ger
Mon·go·lia
Mon·go·lian
mon·gol·ism
Mon·gol·oid
mon·goose
pl mon·goos·es *also* mon·geese
mon·grel
mo·nism
mo·nist
mon·i·tor
mon·i·to·ry
mon·key
mon·key·shine
monk·ish
monks·hood
mono·chro·mat·ic
mono·chro·mat·i·cal·ly
mono·chrome
mon·o·cle
mon·oc·u·lar

mon•o•dy
mo•nog•a•mist
mo•nog•a•mous
mo•nog•a•my
mono•gram
mono•graph
mo•nog•y•ny
mono•lith
mono•logue
also **mono•log**
mono•logu•ist
or **mo•no•lo•gist**
mono•ma•nia
mono•ma•ni•ac
mono•nu•cle•o•sis
mono•pho•nic
mono•plane
mo•nop•o•list
mo•nop•o•lis•tic
mo•nop•o•lis•ti•cal•ly
mo•nop•o•li•za•tion
mo•nop•o•lize
mo•nop•o•ly
mono•rail
mono•syl•lab•ic
mono•syl•lab•i•cal•ly
mono•syl•la•ble
mono•the•ism
mono•the•ist
mono•tone
mo•not•o•nous
mo•not•o•ny
mono•type
mon•ox•ide
mon•sei•gneur
pl **mes•sei•gneurs**
mon•sieur
pl **mes•sieurs**
mon•si•gnor
pl **mon•si•gnors** *or* **mon•si•gno•ri**
mon•soon
mon•ster
mon•strance
mon•stros•i•ty
mon•strous
mon•tage
mon•ta•gnard
Mon•tana
mon•tane
Mon•tes•so•ri•an
Mont•gom•ery
month•ly
Mont•pe•lier
Mon•tre•al
mon•u•ment
mon•u•men•tal
mon•u•men•tal•ly
mood•i•ly
mood•i•ness
moody
moon•beam
moon-eyed
moon•light
moon•light•er
moon•lit
moon•scape
moon•shine
moon•stone
moon•struck
moor•age
moor•ing
moor•land
moose
pl **moose**
animal (*see* **mousse**)
mop
mopped
mop•ping
mop•board
mop•pet
mop-up
mo•raine
mor•al
mo•rale
mor•al•ist
mor•al•is•tic
mor•al•is•ti•cal•ly
mo•ral•i•ty
mor•al•iza•tion
mor•al•ize
mor•al•iz•er
mor•al•ly
mo•rass
mor•a•to•ri•um
pl **mor•a•to•ri•ums** *or* **mor•a•to•ria**
mor•bid
mor•bid•i•ty
mor•dant
caustic (*see* **mordent**)
mor•dent
music (*see* **mordant**)
more•over

mo·res
mor·ga·nat·ic
mor·ga·nat·i·cal·ly
morgue
mor·i·bund
mor·i·bun·di·ty
Mor·mon
Mor·mon·ism
morn·ing
day (*see* mourning)
Mo·roc·can
Mo·roc·co
mo·ron
mo·ron·ic
mo·ron·i·cal·ly
mo·rose
mor·pheme
mor·phe·mic
mor·phia
mor·phine
mor·pho·log·i·cal
mor·pho·log·i·cal·ly
mor·phol·o·gist
mor·phol·o·gy
mor·ris
mor·row
mor·sel
mor·tal
mor·tal·i·ty
mor·tal·ly
mor·tar
mor·tar·board
mort·gage
mort·gag·ee
mort·gag·or
mor·ti·cian
mor·ti·fi·ca·tion
mor·ti·fy
mor·tise
also mor·tice
mort·main
mor·tu·ary
mo·sa·ic
mo·sey
mosque
mos·qui·to
pl mos·qui·toes
also mos·qui·tos
moss·back
moss-grown
mossy
most·ly
mote
particle (*see* moat)
mo·tel
mo·tet
moth·ball
moth-eat·en
moth·er
moth·er·hood
moth·er·house
moth·er-in-law
pl moth·ers-in-law
moth·er·land
moth·er·less
moth·er·li·ness
moth·er·ly
moth·er-of-pearl
mo·tif
mo·tile
mo·til·i·ty
mo·tion
mo·ti·vate
mo·ti·va·tion
mo·tive
mo·tiv·i·ty
mot·ley
mo·tor
mo·tor·boat
mo·tor·cade
mo·tor·car
mo·tor·cy·cle
mo·tor·cy·clist
mo·tor·drome
mo·tor·ist
mo·tor·iza·tion
mo·tor·ize
mo·tor·man
mo·tor·truck
mot·tle
mot·to
pl mot·toes *also* mot·tos
mou·lage
mound
mount·able
moun·tain
moun·tain·eer
moun·tain·ous
moun·tain·side
moun·tain·top
moun·te·bank
Mount·ie
mount·ing
mourn·er

mourn·ful

mourn·ful·ly

mourn·ing
grief (*see* morning)

mouse
pl mice
rodent (*see* mousse)

mous·er

mousse
dessert (*see* moose, mouse)

mous·se·line

mous·se·line de soie
pl mous·se·lines de soie

mousy
or mous·ey

mouth·ful

mouth·part

mouth·piece

mouth·wash

mou·ton
sheepskin (*see* mutton)

mov·abil·i·ty

mov·able
or move·able

mov·ably

move·ment

mov·er

mov·ie

mov·ing

mow
mowed
mowed
or mown
mow·ing

mow·er

Mo·zam·bique

much
more
most

mu·ci·lage

mu·ci·lag·i·nous

muck·rak·er

mu·cous
adj

mu·cus
noun

mud·di·ly

mud·di·ness

mud·dle

mud·dle·head·ed

mud·dler

mud·dy

mud·guard

mud·sling·er

mu·ez·zin

muf·fin

muf·fle

muf·fler

muf·ti

mug
mugged
mug·ging

mug·ger

mug·gi·ness

mug·gy

mug·wump

muk·luk

mu·lat·to
pl mu·lat·toes *or* mu·lat·tos

mul·ber·ry

mulch

mulct

mul·ish

mul·lah

mul·let

mul·li·gan stew

mul·li·ga·taw·ny

mul·lion

mul·ti·col·ored

mul·ti·far·i·ous

mul·ti·form

mul·ti·lane

mul·ti·lat·er·al

mul·ti·lat·er·al·ly

mul·ti·lev·el

mul·ti·me·dia

mul·ti·mil·lion·aire

mul·ti·na·tion·al

mul·ti·par·tite

mul·ti·par·ty

mul·ti·ple

mul·ti·ple-choice

mul·ti·pli·cand

mul·ti·pli·ca·tion

mul·ti·plic·i·ty

mul·ti·pli·er

mul·ti·ply

mul·ti·tude

mul·ti·tu·di·nous

mul·ti·ver·si·ty

mul·ti·vi·ta·min

mum•ble
mum•bler
mum•ble•ty-peg
or **mum•ble-the-peg**
mum•bo jum•bo
mum•mer
mum•mery
mum•mi•fi•ca•tion
mum•mi•fy
mum•my
mun•dane
mung bean
mu•nic•i•pal
mu•nic•i•pal•i•ty
mu•nic•i•pal•ly
mu•nif•i•cence
mu•nif•i•cent
mu•ni•tion
mu•ral
mu•ral•ist
mur•der
mur•der•er
mur•der•ess
mur•der•ous
murk•i•ly
murk•i•ness
murky
mur•mur
mur•mur•er
mur•rain
mus•ca•dine
mus•ca•tel
mus•cle
body tissue (*see* **mussel**)

mus•cle-bound
mus•cu•lar
mus•cu•lar•i•ty
mus•cu•la•ture
mu•sette
mu•se•um
mush•i•ly
mush•i•ness
mush•room
mushy
mu•sic
mu•si•cal
of music (*see* **musicale**)
mu•si•cale
concert (*see* **musical**)
mu•si•cal•ly
mu•si•cian
mu•si•col•o•gist
mu•si•col•o•gy
mus•keg
mus•kel•lunge
mus•ket
mus•ke•teer
mus•ket•ry
musk•i•ness
musk•mel•on
musk•rat
musky
Mus•lim
mus•lin
mus•sel
shell fish (*see* **muscle**)
muss•i•ly
muss•i•ness

mussy
mus•tache
mus•tang
mus•tard
mus•ter
must•i•ly
must•i•ness
musty
mu•ta•bil•i•ty
mu•ta•ble
mu•ta•bly
mu•tant
mu•tate
mu•ta•tion
mu•ta•tis mu•tan•dis
mute•ly
mu•ti•late
mu•ti•la•tion
mu•ti•la•tor
mu•ti•neer
mu•ti•nous
mu•ti•ny
mut•ter
mut•ton
meat (*see* **mouton**)
mut•ton•chops
mu•tu•al
mu•tu•al•i•ty
mu•tu•al•ly
muu•muu
muz•zle
my•col•o•gist
my•col•o•gy
my•co•sis

my•elin

my•eli•tis

my•ia•sis

my•na
or **my•nah**

myo•gen•ic

my•o•pia

my•o•pic

my•o•pi•cal•ly

myr•i•ad

myr•mi•don

myrrh

myr•tle

my•self

mys•te•ri•ous

mys•tery

mys•tic

mys•ti•cal

mys•ti•cal•ly

mys•ti•cism

mys•ti•fi•ca•tion

mys•ti•fy

mys•tique

myth

myth•i•cal

myth•i•cal•ly

myth•o•log•i•cal

myth•o•log•i•cal•ly

my•thol•o•gist

my•thol•o•gy

N

nab
nabbed
nab•bing

na•bob

na•celle

na•cre

na•dir

nag
nagged
nag•ging

na•iad
pl **na•iads** *or* **na•ia•des**

nain•sook

na•ive
or **na•ïve**

na•ive•ly

na•ive•té
or **na•ïve•té**
or **na•ive•te**

na•ive•ty
also **na•ïve•ty**

na•ked

nam•by-pam•by

name•able
also **nam•able**

name•less

name•ly

name•plate

name•sake

nan•keen

nan•ny

nap
napped
nap•ping

na•palm

na•pery

naph•tha

naph•tha•lene

nap•kin

na•po•leon

nap•per

nap•py

nar•cis•sism

nar•cis•sist

nar•cis•sis•tic

nar•cis•sus
pl **nar•cis•sus** *or* **nar•cis•sus•es** *or* **nar•cis•si**

nar•co•lep•sy

nar•co•sis
pl **nar•co•ses**

nar•cot•ic

nar•co•tize

na•ris
pl **na•res**

nar•rate

nar•ra•tion

nar•ra•tive

nar•ra•tor

nar•row

nar•row-mind•ed

nar•whal
also **nar•wal** *or* **nar•whale**

na•sal

na•sal•i•ty

na•sal•iza•tion
na•sal•ize
na•sal•ly
na•scence
na•scent
Nash•ville
na•so•phar•ynx
nas•ti•ly
nas•ti•ness
nas•tur•tium
nas•ty
na•tal
na•tal•i•ty
na•tant
na•ta•to•ri•al
or na•ta•to•ry
na•ta•to•ri•um
na•tion
na•tion•al
na•tion•al•ism
na•tion•al•ist
na•tion•al•is•tic
na•tion•al•is•ti•cal•ly
na•tion•al•i•ty
na•tion•al•iza•tion
na•tion•al•ize
na•tion•al•ly
na•tion•hood
na•tion-state
na•tion•wide
na•tive
na•tiv•ism
na•tiv•ist
na•tiv•i•ty
nat•ti•ly
nat•ti•ness
nat•ty
nat•u•ral
nat•u•ral•ism
nat•u•ral•ist
nat•u•ral•is•tic
nat•u•ral•is•ti•cal•ly
nat•u•ral•iza•tion
nat•u•ral•ize
nat•u•ral•ly
na•ture
naught
naugh•ti•ly
naugh•ti•ness
naughty
Na•u•ru
nau•sea
nau•se•ate
nau•seous
nau•ti•cal
nau•ti•cal•ly
nau•ti•lus
pl nau•ti•lus•es *or* nau•ti•li
na•val
of a navy (*see* navel)
nave
center of a church (*see* knave)
na•vel
abdominal depression (*see* naval)
nav•i•ga•bil•i•ty
nav•i•ga•ble
nav•i•gate
nav•i•ga•tion
nav•i•ga•tor
na•vy
nay
no (*see* née, neigh)
na•ya pai•sa
pl na•ye pai•se
na•zi
Na•zism
or Na•zi•ism
Ne•an•der•thal
near•by
near•ly
near•ness
near•sight•ed
neat•ly
neat•ness
Ne•bras•ka
neb•u•la
pl neb•u•las *or* neb•u•lae
neb•u•lar
neb•u•lize
neb•u•los•i•ty
neb•u•lous
nec•es•sar•i•ly
nec•es•sary
ne•ces•si•tate
ne•ces•si•tous
ne•ces•si•ty
neck•er•chief
pl neck•er•chiefs *also* neck•er•chieves
neck•lace
neck•line

neck·tie

ne·crol·o·gist

ne·crol·o·gy

nec·ro·man·cer

nec·ro·man·cy

ne·crop·o·lis
pl **ne·crop·o·lis·es** *or* **ne·crop·o·les** *or* **ne·crop·o·leis** *or* **ne·crop·o·li**

nec·rop·sy

ne·cro·sis
pl **ne·cro·ses**

nec·tar

nec·tar·ine

née
or nee
born (*see* nay, neigh)

need
require (*see* knead)

need·ful

need·ful·ly

need·i·ness

nee·dle

nee·dle·like

nee·dle·point

nee·dler

need·less

nee·dle·work

nee·dling

needy

ne'er-do-well

ne·far·i·ous

ne·gate

ne·ga·tion

neg·a·tive

neg·a·tive·ly

neg·a·tiv·ism

neg·a·tiv·i·ty

ne·glect

ne·glect·ful

neg·li·gee
also **neg·li·gé**

neg·li·gence

neg·li·gent

neg·li·gi·bil·i·ty

neg·li·gi·ble

neg·li·gi·bly

ne·go·tia·bil·i·ty

ne·go·tia·ble

ne·go·tiant

ne·go·ti·ate

ne·go·ti·a·tion

ne·go·ti·a·tor

ne·gri·tude

Ne·gro
pl **Ne·groes**

Ne·groid

ne·gus

neigh
horse cry (*see* nay, née)

neigh·bor

neigh·bor·hood

neigh·bor·li·ness

neigh·bor·ly

nei·ther

nel·son

nem·a·tode

Nem·bu·tal

nem·e·sis
pl **nem·e·ses**

ne·moph·i·la

neo·clas·sic

neo·clas·si·cal

neo·clas·si·cism

neo·co·lo·nial

neo·co·lo·nial·ism

neo·lith·ic

ne·ol·o·gism

ne·ol·o·gy

neo·my·cin

ne·on

neo·phyte

neo·plasm

neo·prene

Ne·pal

Nep·a·lese

Ne·pali

ne·pen·the

neph·ew

ne·phri·tis

ne plus ul·tra

nep·o·tism

Nep·tune

nerve·less

nerve-rack·ing
or **nerve-wrack·ing**

ner·vous

nervy

nes·tle

nest·ling

net
net·ted
net·ting

neth·er

Neth·er·land·er

Neth·er·lands
or Hol·land
neth·er·most
neth·er·world
net·ting
net·tle
net·tle·some
net·work
neu·ral
neu·ral·gia
neu·ral·gic
neur·as·the·nia
neur·as·then·ic
neu·rit·ic
neu·ri·tis
neu·ro·log·i·cal
neu·rol·o·gist
neu·rol·o·gy
neu·ro·mus·cu·lar
neu·ron
also neu·rone
neu·ro·sis
pl neu·ro·ses
neu·rot·ic
neu·rot·i·cal·ly
neu·ter
neu·tral
neu·tral·ism
neu·tral·i·ty
neu·tral·iza·tion
neu·tral·ize
neu·tral·iz·er
neu·tri·no
neu·tron
Ne·va·da
nev·er
nev·er·more
nev·er-nev·er land
nev·er·the·less
ne·vus
pl ne·vi
New·ark
New Bed·ford
new·born
New Bruns·wick
new·com·er
new·el
new·fan·gled
new-fash·ioned
new·found
New·found·land
New Hamp·shire
New Ha·ven
new·ish
New Jer·sey
new·ly
new·ly·wed
New Mex·i·co
new·ness
New Or·leans
New·port News
news·boy
news·break
news·cast
news·cast·er
news·let·ter
news·man
news·mon·ger
news·pa·per
news·pa·per·man
news·print
news·reel
news·stand
news·wor·thy
New York
New Zea·land
New Zea·land·er
nex·us
pl nex·ux·es *or* nex·us
ngwee
pl ngwee
ni·a·cin
Ni·ag·a·ra
nib·ble
Nic·a·ra·gua
Nic·a·ra·guan
nice·ly
nice·ness
nice·ty
niche
nick
nick·el
nick·el·ode·on
nick·name
nic·o·tine
nic·o·tin·ic
niece
nif·ty
Ni·ger
Ni·ge·ria
Ni·ge·ri·an
nig·gard·li·ness
nig·gard·ly
nig·gling

night
dark (*see* knight)

night•cap

night•clothes

night•club

night•dress

night•fall

night•gown

night•hawk

night•in•gale

night•long

night•ly

night•mare

night•shade

night•shirt

night•stick

night•time

night•walk•er

ni•hil•ism

ni•hil•ist

ni•hil•is•tic

Ni•ke

nim•ble

nim•bly

nim•bus
pl nim•bi *or* nim•bus•es

Nim•rod

nin•com•poop

nine•pins

nine•teen

nine•teenth

nine•ti•eth

nine•ty

nin•ny

ni•non

ninth

nip
nipped
nip•ping

nip•per

nip•ple

nip•py

nip-up

nir•va•na

ni•sei
pl ni•sei *also* ni•seis

ni•ter
also ni•tre

nit-pick•ing

ni•trate

ni•tra•tion

ni•tric

ni•tro
pl ni•tros

ni•tro•gen

ni•trog•e•nous

ni•tro•glyc•er•in
or ni•tro•glyc•er•ine

nit•ty-grit•ty

nit•wit

no•bil•i•ty

no•ble

no•ble•man

no•blesse oblige

no•bly

no•body

noc•tur•nal

noc•tur•nal•ly

noc•turne

noc•u•ous

nod
nod•ded
nod•ding

nod•al

node

nod•u•lar

nod•ule

no•el

nog•gin

no-good

noise•less

noise•mak•er

nois•i•ly

nois•i•ness

noi•some

noisy

no•lo con•ten•de•re

no•mad

no•mad•ic

no-man's-land

nom de guerre
pl noms de guerre

nom de plume
pl noms de plume

no•men•cla•ture

nom•i•nal

nom•i•nal•ly

nom•i•nate

nom•i•na•tion

nom•i•na•tive

nom•i•na•tor

nom•i•nee

non•age

no•na•ge•nar•i•an

non·aligned
non·align·ment
non·book
non·can·di·date
nonce
non·cha·lance
non·cha·lant
non·com
non·com·ba·tant
non·com·mis·sioned
non·com·mit·tal
non com·pos men·tis
non·con·duc·tor
non·con·form·ist
non·con·for·mi·ty
non·co·op·er·a·tion
non·de·script
non·en·ti·ty
none·such
none·the·less
non·fic·tion
non·in·ter·ven·tion
non·met·al
non·me·tal·lic
non·pa·reil
non·par·ti·san
non·plus
  non·plussed
    also non·plused
  non·plus·sing
    also non·plus·ing
non·prof·it
non·res·i·dent
non·re·sis·tance
non·re·stric·tive
non·sched·uled
non·sense
non·sen·si·cal
non·sen·si·cal·ly
non se·qui·tur
non·sked
non·skid
non·stop
non·sup·port
non trop·po
non·union
non·vi·o·lence
noo·dle
noon·day
noon·time
no-par
  or no-par-val·ue
Nor·folk
nor·mal
nor·mal·cy
nor·mal·i·ty
nor·mal·iza·tion
nor·mal·ize
nor·mal·ly
nor·ma·tive
Norse
north·bound
North Car·o·li·na
North Da·ko·ta
north·east
north·east·er·ly
north·east·ern
north·er·ly
north·ern
north·ern·most
north·ward
north·wards
north·west
north·west·er·ly
north·west·ern
Nor·way
Nor·we·gian
nose·band
nose·bleed
nose·gay
nose·piece
no-show
nos·i·ly
nos·i·ness
nos·tal·gia
nos·tal·gic
nos·tal·gi·cal·ly
nos·tril
nos·trum
nosy
  or nos·ey
no·ta be·ne
no·ta·bil·i·ty
no·ta·ble
no·ta·bly
no·tar·i·al
no·ta·ri·za·tion
no·ta·rize
no·ta·ry pub·lic
  pl no·ta·ries pub·lic
    or no·ta·ry pub·lics
no·tate
no·ta·tion
no·ta·tion·al
notch

notch•back
note•book
note•case
not•ed
note•wor•thi•ly
note•wor•thi•ness
note•wor•thy
noth•ing
noth•ing•ness
no•tice
no•tice•able
no•tice•ably
no•ti•fi•ca•tion
no•ti•fi•er
no•ti•fy
no•tion
no•tion•al
no•to•ri•ety
no•to•ri•ous
no-trump
not•with•stand•ing
nou•gat
nought
nour•ish
nour•ish•ing
nour•ish•ment
nou•veau riche
pl nou•veaux riches
no•va
pl no•vas *or* no•vae
No•va Sco•tia
nov•el
nov•el•ette
nov•el•ist
nov•el•iza•tion
nov•el•ize
no•vel•la
pl no•vel•las *or* no•vel•le
nov•el•ty
No•vem•ber
no•ve•na
nov•ice
no•vi•tiate
now•a•days
no•way
or no•ways
no•where
no•wise
nox•ious
noz•zle
nth
nu•ance
nub•ble
nub•bly
nu•bile
nu•cle•ar
nu•cle•ate
nu•cle•ic acid
nu•cle•on
nu•cle•on•ics
nu•cle•us
pl nu•clei *also* nu•cle•us•es
nu•clide
nude
nudge
nud•ism
nud•ist
nu•di•ty
nu•ga•to•ry
nug•get
nui•sance
nul•li•fi•ca•tion
nul•li•fi•er
nul•li•fy
nul•li•ty
numb
num•ber
num•ber•less
numb•ly
numb•ness
nu•mer•a•ble
nu•mer•al
nu•mer•ate
nu•mer•a•tion
nu•mer•a•tor
nu•mer•ic
nu•mer•i•cal
nu•mer•i•cal•ly
nu•mer•ol•o•gy
nu•mer•ous
nu•mis•mat•ic
nu•mis•mat•ics
nu•mis•ma•tist
num•skull
nun•ci•a•ture
nun•cio
pl nun•ci•os
nun•nery
nup•tial
nurse•maid
nurs•ery
nurs•ery•man
nur•ture
nut•crack•er

nut·hatch
nut·meg
nut·pick
nu·tria
nu·tri·ent
nu·tri·ment
nu·tri·tion
nu·tri·tious
nu·tri·tive
nut·shell
nut·ty
nuz·zle
ny·lon
nym·pho·ma·nia
nym·pho·ma·ni·ac

O

oaf·ish
oak·en
Oak·land
oa·kum
oar
long pole (*see* ore)
oar·lock
oars·man
oa·sis
pl oa·ses
oat·cake
oat·en
oath
oat·meal
ob·bli·ga·to
pl ob·bli·ga·tos *also* ob·bli·ga·ti

ob·du·ra·cy
ob·du·rate
obe·di·ence
obe·di·ent
obei·sance
obei·sant
obe·lisk
obese
obe·si·ty
obey
ob·fus·cate
ob·fus·ca·tion
ob·fus·ca·to·ry
obi
obit
obi·ter dic·tum
pl obi·ter dic·ta
obit·u·ary
ob·ject
ob·jec·ti·fy
ob·jec·tion
ob·jec·tion·able
ob·jec·tion·ably
ob·jec·tive
ob·jec·tive·ly
ob·jec·tiv·i·ty
ob·jec·tor
ob·jet d'art
pl ob·jets d'art
ob·jur·gate
ob·jur·ga·tion
ob·late
ob·la·tion
ob·li·gate
ob·li·ga·tion

oblig·a·to·ry
oblige
oblig·ing
oblique
oblique·ly
obliq·ui·ty
oblit·er·ate
oblit·er·a·tion
obliv·i·on
obliv·i·ous
ob·long
ob·lo·quy
ob·nox·ious
oboe
obo·ist
ob·scene
ob·scene·ly
ob·scen·i·ty
ob·scu·ran·tism
ob·scu·ran·tist
ob·scure
ob·scure·ly
ob·scu·ri·ty
ob·se·qui·ous
ob·se·quy
ob·serv·able
ob·serv·ably
ob·ser·vance
ob·ser·vant
ob·ser·va·tion
ob·ser·va·to·ry
ob·serve
ob·serv·er
ob·sess
ob·ses·sion

ob•ses•sive
ob•sid•i•an
ob•so•lesce
ob•so•les•cence
ob•so•les•cent
ob•so•lete
ob•sta•cle
ob•stet•ric
or ob•stet•ri•cal
ob•ste•tri•cian
ob•stet•rics
ob•sti•na•cy
ob•sti•nate
ob•sti•nate•ly
ob•strep•er•ous
ob•struct
ob•struc•tion
ob•struc•tion•ism
ob•struc•tion•ist
ob•struc•tive
ob•struc•tor
ob•tain
ob•tain•able
ob•trude
ob•tru•sion
ob•tru•sive
ob•tuse
ob•verse
ob•vert
ob•vi•ate
ob•vi•a•tion
ob•vi•ous
oc•a•ri•na
oc•ca•sion
oc•ca•sion•al
oc•ca•sion•al•ly
oc•ci•den•tal
oc•clude
oc•clu•sion
oc•clu•sive
oc•cult
oc•cul•ta•tion
oc•cult•ism
oc•cu•pan•cy
oc•cu•pant
oc•cu•pa•tion
oc•cu•pa•tion•al
oc•cu•pa•tion•al•ly
oc•cu•pi•er
oc•cu•py
oc•cur
oc•cur•rence
ocean
ocean•go•ing
oce•an•ic
ocean•og•ra•pher
ocean•o•graph•ic
ocean•og•ra•phy
ocean•ol•o•gy
oce•lot
ocher
or ochre
o'•clock
oc•ta•gon
oc•tag•o•nal
oc•tag•o•nal•ly
oc•tane
oc•tave
oc•ta•vo
pl oc•ta•vos
oc•tet
Oc•to•ber
oc•to•ge•nar•i•an
oc•to•pod
oc•to•pus
oc•to•roon
oc•u•lar
oc•u•list
odd•ball
odd•i•ty
odd•ly
odd•ment
odds-on
odi•ous
odi•um
odom•e•ter
odor
odor•ant
odor•ous
od•ys•sey
oe•di•pal
Oe•di•pus
of•fal
waste (*see* awful)
off•beat
off-col•or
or off-col•ored
of•fend
of•fend•er
of•fense
or of•fence
of•fen•sive
of•fer
of•fer•ing
of•fer•to•ry

off·hand
off·hand·ed
of·fice
of·fice·hold·er
of·fi·cer
of·fi·cial
of·fi·cial·dom
of·fi·cial·ly
of·fi·ci·ant
of·fi·ci·ate
of·fi·ci·a·tion
of·fi·cious
off·ing
off·ish
off·print
off·set
off·shoot
off·shore
off·spring
  pl off·spring *also* off·springs
off·stage
off-the-rec·ord
off-white
of·ten
of·ten·times
  or oft·times
ogle
ogre
ogre·ish
Ohio
ohm
ohm·me·ter
oil·cloth
oil·er
oil·i·ly
oil·i·ness
oil·seed
oil·skin
oil·stone
oily
oint·ment
OK
  or okay
  OK'd
    or okayed
  OK'·ing
    or okay·ing
Okla·ho·ma
okra
old·en
old-fash·ioned
old·ish
old-line
old·ster
old-tim·er
old-world
ole·ag·i·nous
ole·an·der
oleo
  pl ole·os
oleo·mar·ga·rine
ol·fac·tion
ol·fac·to·ry
oli·garch
oli·gar·chic
  or oli·gar·chi·cal
oli·gar·chy
oli·gop·o·ly
ol·ive
Olym·pia
olym·pi·ad
Olym·pic
Oma·ha
Oman
om·buds·man
  pl om·buds·men
ome·ga
om·elet
  or om·elette
omen
om·i·nous
omis·si·ble
omis·sion
omit
  omit·ted
  omit·ting
om·ni·bus
om·ni·di·rec·tion·al
om·nip·o·tence
om·nip·o·tent
om·ni·pres·ence
om·ni·pres·ent
om·ni·range
om·ni·science
om·ni·scient
om·niv·o·rous
once-over
on·com·ing
one·ness
oner·ous
one·self
one-shot
one-sid·ed
one·time
one-to-one

one-track
one-up·man·ship
one-way
on·go·ing
on·ion
on·ion·skin
on-line
on·look·er
on·ly
on·o·mato·poe·ia
on·o·mato·poe·ic
or on·o·mato·po·et·ic
on·o·mato·poe·i·cal·ly
or on·o·mato·po·et·i·cal·ly
on·rush
on·set
on·shore
on·slaught
On·tar·io
on·to
onus
on·ward
also on·wards
on·yx
oo·dles
oozy
opac·i·ty
opal
opal·es·cence
opal·es·cent
opaque
opaque·ly
open-air
open-and-shut
open-end
open·er
open-eyed
open·hand·ed
open·heart·ed
open-hearth
open·ing
open-mind·ed
open·mouthed
open·ness
open·work
op·era
op·er·a·ble
op·er·a·bly
op·er·ate
op·er·at·ic
op·er·at·i·cal·ly
op·er·a·tion
op·er·a·tion·al
op·er·a·tive
op·er·a·tor
op·er·et·ta
oph·thal·mic
oph·thal·mol·o·gist
oph·thal·mol·o·gy
opi·ate
opin·ion
opin·ion·at·ed
opi·um
opos·sum
pl opos·sums *also* opos·sum
op·po·nent
op·por·tune
op·por·tune·ly
op·por·tun·ism
op·por·tun·ist
op·por·tu·nis·tic
op·por·tu·ni·ty
op·pose
op·po·site
op·po·si·tion
op·press
op·pres·sion
op·pres·sive
op·pres·sive·ly
op·pres·sor
op·pro·bri·ous
op·pro·bri·um
op·tic
op·ti·cal
op·ti·cal·ly
op·ti·cian
op·tics
op·ti·mal
op·ti·mal·ly
op·ti·mism
op·ti·mist
op·ti·mis·tic
op·ti·mis·ti·cal·ly
op·ti·mize
op·ti·mum
pl op·ti·ma *also* op·ti·mums
op·tion
op·tion·al
op·tion·al·ly
op·to·met·ric
op·tom·e·trist

op•tom•e•try
op•u•lence
op•u•lent
opus
pl opera *also* opus•es
or•a•cle
prophesier (*see* auricle)
orac•u•lar
oral
spoken (*see* aural)
oral•ly
or•ange
or•ange•ade
orang•utan
or orang•ou•tan
orate
ora•tion
or•a•tor
or•a•tor•i•cal
or•a•tor•i•cal•ly
or•a•to•rio
pl or•a•to•ri•os
or•a•to•ry
or•bic•u•lar
or•bit
or•bit•al
or•chard
or•ches•tra
or•ches•tral
or•ches•trate
or•ches•tra•tion
or•chid
or•dain
or•deal
or•der
or•dered
or•der•li•ness
or•der•ly
or•di•nal
or•di•nance
law (*see* ordnance)
or•di•nari•ly
or•di•nary
or•di•nate
or•di•na•tion
ord•nance
military supplies (*see* ordinance)
or•dure
ore
mineral (*see* oar)
öre
pl öre
oreg•a•no
Or•e•gon
or•gan
or•gan•dy
also or•gan•die
or•gan•ic
or•gan•i•cal•ly
or•gan•ism
or•gan•ist
or•gan•iz•able
or•ga•ni•za•tion
or•ga•ni•za•tion•al
or•ga•nize
or•ga•niz•er
or•gan•za
or•gasm
or•gi•as•tic
or•gi•as•ti•cal•ly
or•gu•lous
or•gy
ori•el
ori•ent
Ori•en•tal
ori•en•tate
ori•en•ta•tion
or•i•fice
ori•flamme
ori•ga•mi
or•i•gin
orig•i•nal
orig•i•nal•i•ty
orig•i•nal•ly
orig•i•nate
orig•i•na•tion
orig•i•na•tor
ori•ole
or•i•son
or•mo•lu
or•na•ment
or•na•men•tal
or•na•men•ta•tion
or•nate
or•nate•ly
or•nery
or•ni•thol•o•gist
or•ni•thol•o•gy
orog•e•ny
oro•tund
or•phan
or•phan•age
or•ris
orth•odon•tics
orth•odon•tist

or·tho·dox
or·tho·doxy
or·tho·graph·ic
or·thog·ra·phy
or·tho·pe·dic
also or·tho·pae·dic
or·tho·pe·dics
also or·tho·pae·dics
or·tho·pe·dist
os·cil·late
os·cil·la·tion
os·cil·la·tor
os·cil·la·to·ry
os·cil·lo·scope
os·cu·late
os·cu·la·tion
osier
os·mo·sis
os·mot·ic
os·prey
os·si·fi·ca·tion
os·si·fy
os·su·ary
os·ten·si·ble
os·ten·si·bly
os·ten·ta·tion
os·ten·ta·tious
os·teo·path
os·teo·path·ic
os·te·op·a·thy
os·tra·cism
os·tra·cize
os·trich
oth·er
oth·er·wise
oth·er·world
oti·ose
Ot·ta·wa
ot·ter
ot·to·man
ought
should (*see* aught)
our·selves
oust·er
out·age
out-and-out
out·bid
out·board
out·bound
out·break
out·build·ing
out·burst
out·cast
out·class
out·come
out·crop
out·cry
out·dat·ed
out·dis·tance
out·do
out·door
also out·doors
adj
out·doors
adverb, noun
out·draw
out·er
out·er·most
out·face
out·field
out·field·er
out·fight
out·fit
out·fit·ted
out·fit·ting
out·fit·ter
out·flank
out·flow
out·fox
out·gen·er·al
out·go
out·go·ing
out·grow
out·growth
out·guess
out·house
out·ing
out·land·ish
out·last
out·law
out·law·ry
out·lay
out·let
out·li·er
out·line
out·live
out·look
out·ly·ing
out·ma·neu·ver
out·match
out·mod·ed
out·most
out·num·ber
out-of-bounds

out-of-date
out-of-door
or out-of-doors
out-of-the-way
out•pa•tient
out•play
out•point
out•post
out•pour
out•put
out•rage
out•ra•geous
out•rank
ou•tré
out•reach
out•ride
out•rid•er
out•rig•ger
out•right
out•run
out•sell
out•set
out•shine
out•side
out•sid•er
out•sit
out•size
out•skirt
out•smart
out•spo•ken
out•spread
out•stand•ing
out•sta•tion
out•stay
out•stretch
out•strip
out•ward
out•ward•ly
out•wear
out•weigh
out•wit
out•work
out•worn
oval
oval•ly
ovar•i•an
ova•ry
ova•tion
ov•en
oven•bird
over•abun•dance
over•abun•dant
over•act
over•ac•tive
over•age
over•all
over•arm
over•awe
over•bal•ance
over•bear•ing
over•bid
over•blown
over•board
over•build
over•bur•den
over•call
over•cap•i•tal•ize
over•cast
over•charge
over•cloud
over•coat
over•come
over•con•fi•dence
over•crowd
over•do
over•dose
over•draft
over•draw
over•dress
over•drive
over•due
over•em•pha•size
over•es•ti•mate
over•ex•pose
over•ex•po•sure
over•ex•tend
over•flight
over•flow
over•grow
over•hand
over•hang
over•haul
over•head
over•hear
over•heat
over•in•dulge
over•in•dul•gence
over•joy
over•kill
over•land
over•lap
over•lay
over•leap
over•lie
over•load

over•long
over•look
over•lord
over•ly
over•match
over•much
over•night
over•pass
over•play
over•pow•er
over•price
over•print
over•pro•tect
over•rate
over•reach
over•ride
over•rode
over•rid•den
over•rid•ing
over•ripe
over•rule
over•run
over•ran
over•run•ning
over•seas
over•see
over•saw
over•seen
over•see•ing
over•seer
over•sell
over•sold
over•sell•ing
over•sen•si•tive
over•set
over•sexed
over•shad•ow
over•shoe
over•shoot
over•shot
over•shoot•ing
over•sight
over•sim•pli•fi•ca•tion
over•sim•pli•fy
over•size
or over•sized
over•sleep
over•spend
over•spent
over•spend•ing
over•spread
over•state
over•state•ment
over•stay
over•step
over•strung
over•stuff
over•sub•scribe
over•sup•ply
overt
over•take
over•took
over•tak•en
over•tak•ing
over•tax
over-the-count•er
over•throw
over•threw
over•thrown
over•throw•ing
over•time
over•tone
over•train
over•trick
over•trump
over•ture
over•turn
over•use
over•ween•ing
over•weigh
over•weight
over•whelm
over•wind
over•wound
also over•wind•ed
over•wind•ing
over•work
over•write
over•wrote
over•writ•ten
over•writ•ing
over•wrought
ovip•a•rous
ovoid
or ovoi•dal
ovu•late
ovu•la•tion
ovu•la•to•ry
ovule
ovum
pl ova

owe
owl·ish
own·er
ox
pl ox·en
ox·blood
ox·bow
ox·ford
ox·i·da·tion
ox·ide
ox·i·dize
oxy·acet·y·lene
ox·y·gen
ox·y·gen·ate
ox·y·gen·ation
oxy·mo·ron
pl oxy·mo·ra
oys·ter
ozone

P

pa·'an·ga
pab·u·lum
pace·mak·er
pac·er
pachy·derm
pach·ys·an·dra
pa·cif·ic
pac·i·fi·ca·tion
pac·i·fi·er
pac·i·fism
pac·i·fist
pac·i·fy
pack·age
pack·ag·er
pack·er
pack·et
pack·ing
pack·ing·house
pack·sack
pack·sad·dle
pack·thread
pact
pad
pad·ded
pad·ding
pad·dle
pad·dle·ball
pad·dock
pad·dy
pad·lock
pa·dre
pae·an
song (*see* peon)
pa·gan
pag·eant
pag·eant·ry
page boy
or page·boy
pag·i·nate
pag·i·na·tion
pa·go·da
pail
bucket (*see* pale)
pail·ful
pain
hurt (*see* pane)
pain·ful
pain·ful·ly
pain·less
pains·tak·ing
paint·brush
paint·er
paint·ing
pair
two (*see* pare, pear)
pai·sa
pl pai·se *or* pai·sa
or pai·sas
pais·ley
pa·ja·mas
Pa·ki·stan
Pa·ki·stani
pal·ace
pal·a·din
pa·lan·quin
pal·at·able
pal·at·ably
pal·a·tal
pal·a·tal·iza·tion
pal·ate
roof of the mouth
(*see* palette, pallet)
pa·la·tial
pal·a·tine
pa·la·ver
pale
light (*see* pail)
pale·face
pa·le·og·ra·pher
pa·le·og·ra·phy
Pa·leo·lith·ic
pa·le·on·to·lo·gist
pa·le·on·tol·o·gy

pal•ette
painter's tablet (*see* palate, pallet)

pa•limp•sest

pal•in•drome

pal•ing

pal•i•sade

pal•la•di•um

pall•bear•er

pal•let
bed (*see* palate, palette)

pal•li•ate

pal•lia•tive

pal•lid

pal•lor

pal•mate
also pal•mat•ed

pal•met•to
pl pal•met•tos *or* pal•met•toes

palm•ist•ry

pal•o•mi•no

pal•pa•ble

pal•pa•bly

pal•pate

pal•pi•tate

pal•pi•ta•tion

pal•sied

pal•sy

pal•tri•ness

pal•try

pam•pa
pl pam•pas

pam•per

pam•phlet

pam•phle•teer

pan
panned
pan•ning

pan•a•cea

pa•nache

Pan•a•ma

Pan•a•ma•ni•an

Pan-Amer•i•can

pan•a•tela

pan•cake

pan•chro•mat•ic

pan•cre•as

pan•cre•at•ic

pan•da

pan•dem•ic

pan•de•mo•ni•um

pan•der

pan•der•er

pan•dow•dy

pane
glass (*see* pain)

pan•e•gy•ric

pan•e•gy•rist

pan•el
pan•eled
or pan•elled
pan•el•ing
or pan•el•ling

pan•el•ing
noun

pan•el•ist

pan•fish

pan•han•dle

pan•han•dler

pan•ic
pan•icked
pan•ick•ing

pan•icky

pan•i•cle

pan•ic-strick•en

pan•jan•drum

pan•nier
or pan•ier

pan•o•plied

pan•o•ply

pan•ora•ma

pan•oram•ic

pan•sy

pan•ta•loons

pan•the•ism

pan•the•ist

pan•the•is•tic

pan•the•on

pan•ther

pant•ie
or panty

pan•to•mime

pan•to•mim•ic

pan•try

pant•suit

panty hose

pa•pa•cy

pa•pal

pa•paw

pa•pa•ya

pa•per

pa•per•back

pa•per•hang•er

pa•per•weight

pa·pery
pa·pier-mâ·ché
pa·pil·la
pl pa·pil·lae
pap·il·lary
pap·il·lo·ma
pl pap·il·lo·mas *or* pap·il·lo·ma·ta
pa·pil·lote
pa·poose
pa·pri·ka
Pa·pua New Guin·ea
pap·ule
pa·py·rus
pl pa·py·rus·es *or* pa·py·ri
pa·ra
pl pa·ras *or* pa·ra
par·a·ble
pa·rab·o·la
par·a·bol·ic
para·chute
para·chut·ist
pa·rade
par·a·digm
par·a·dise
par·a·di·si·a·cal
par·a·di·si·a·cal·ly
par·a·dox
par·a·dox·i·cal
par·a·dox·i·cal·ly
par·af·fin
par·a·gon
para·graph
Par·a·guay
Par·a·guay·an
par·a·keet
or par·ra·keet
par·al·lax
par·al·lel
par·al·lel·ism
par·al·lel·o·gram
pa·ral·y·sis
pl pa·ral·y·ses
par·a·lyt·ic
par·a·ly·za·tion
par·a·lyze
par·a·me·cium
pl par·a·me·cia *also* par·a·me·ciums
pa·ram·e·ter
factor (*see* perimeter)
par·a·mount
par·a·mount·cy
par·amour
para·noia
para·noi·ac
para·noid
par·a·pet
par·a·pher·na·lia
para·phrase
para·ple·gia
para·ple·gic
para·psy·chol·o·gy
par·a·site
par·a·sit·ic
also par·a·sit·i·cal
par·a·sit·i·cal·ly
par·a·sit·ism
par·a·si·tol·o·gist
par·a·si·tol·o·gy
para·sol
para·thy·roid
para·troop·er
para·troops
para·ty·phoid
par·boil
par·buck·le
par·cel
par·celed
or par·celled
par·cel·ing
or par·cel·ling
parch·ment
par·don
par·don·able
par·don·ably
pare
trim (*see* pair, pear)
par·e·go·ric
par·ent
par·ent·age
pa·ren·tal
pa·ren·the·sis
pl pa·ren·the·ses
pa·ren·the·size
par·en·thet·ic
or par·en·thet·i·cal
par·en·thet·i·cal·ly
par·ent·hood
pa·re·sis
pl pa·re·ses
par ex·cel·lence
par·fait
pa·ri·ah
pa·ri·etal

pari-mu•tu•el
par•ing
pa•ri pas•su
par•ish
pa•rish•io•ner
par•i•ty
par•ka
park•way
par•lance
par•lay
bets
par•ley
discussion
par•lia•ment
par•lia•men•tar•i•an
par•lia•men•ta•ry
par•lor
Par•ma
Par•me•san
pa•ro•chi•al
pa•ro•chi•al•ly
par•o•dist
par•o•dy
pa•role
pa•rol•ee
par•ox•ysm
par•ox•ys•mal
par•quet
par•que•try
par•ra•keet
var of parakeet
par•ri•cide
par•rot
par•ry
parse

par•sec
par•si•mo•ni•ous
par•si•mo•ny
pars•ley
pars•nip
par•son
par•son•age
par•take
par•took
par•tak•en
par•tak•ing
par•tak•er
par•terre
par•the•no•gen•e•sis
par•tial
par•tial•i•ty
par•tial•ly
par•ti•ble
par•tic•i•pant
par•tic•i•pate
par•tic•i•pa•tion
par•tic•i•pa•tor
par•tic•i•pa•to•ry
par•ti•cip•i•al
par•ti•cip•i•al•ly
par•ti•ci•ple
par•ti•cle
par•ti-col•ored
par•tic•u•lar
par•tic•u•lar•i•ty
par•tic•u•lar•iza•tion
par•tic•u•lar•ize
par•tic•u•lar•ly
par•tic•u•late

part•ing
par•ti•san
or par•ti•zan
par•ti•san•ship
par•tite
par•ti•tion
par•ti•tive
part•ly
part•ner
part•ner•ship
par•tridge
part-song
part-time
par•tu•ri•ent
par•tu•ri•tion
par•ty
par•ve•nu
Pas•a•de•na
pa•sha
pass
go by (*see* past)
passed
pass•ing
pass•able
pass•ably
pas•sage
pas•sage•way
pass•book
pas•sé
pas•sel
pas•sen•ger
passe-par•tout
pass•er
pas•ser•by
pl pas•sers•by

pas·ser·ine
pas·si·ble
pas·sim
pass·ing
pas·sion
pas·sion·ate
pas·sion·ate·ly
pas·sive
pas·sive·ly
pas·siv·i·ty
pass·key
Pass·over
pass·port
pass·word
past
  ago, beyond (*see* pass)
pas·ta
paste
paste·board
pas·tel
pas·tern
pas·teur·iza·tion
pas·teur·ize
pas·teur·iz·er
pas·tiche
pas·tille
  also pas·til
pas·time
past·i·ness
pas·tor
pas·to·ral
pas·tor·ate
pas·tra·mi
  also pas·tro·mi
past·ry

pas·tur·age
pas·ture
pasty
pat
  pat·ted
  pat·ting
patch
patch·board
patch·work
pa·tel·la
  pl pa·tel·lae *or* pa·tel·las
pat·en
  plate (*see* patten)
pa·tent
pat·ent·able
pat·en·tee
pa·ter·fa·mil·i·as
  pl pa·tres·fa·mil·i·as
pa·ter·nal
pa·ter·nal·ism
pa·ter·nal·is·tic
pa·ter·nal·ly
pa·ter·ni·ty
Pat·er·son
pa·thet·ic
pa·thet·i·cal·ly
path·find·er
patho·gen
patho·gen·ic
patho·ge·nic·i·ty
patho·log·i·cal
  or patho·log·ic
patho·log·i·cal·ly
pa·thol·o·gist

pa·thol·o·gy
pa·thos
path·way
pa·tience
pa·tient
pa·ti·na
  pl pa·ti·nas *or* pa·ti·nae
pa·tio
  pl pa·ti·os
pa·tois
  pl pa·tois
pa·tri·arch
pa·tri·ar·chal
pa·tri·arch·ate
pa·tri·ar·chy
pa·tri·cian
pat·ri·cide
pat·ri·lin·eal
pat·ri·mo·ny
pa·tri·ot
pa·tri·ot·ic
pa·tri·ot·i·cal·ly
pa·tri·o·tism
pa·tris·tic
pa·trol
  pa·trolled
  pa·trol·ling
pa·trol·man
pa·tron
pat·ron·age
pa·tron·ess
pa·tron·ize
pat·ro·nym·ic
pa·troon

pat·sy
pat·ten
shoe (*see* paten)
pat·ter
pat·tern
pat·ty
also pat·tie
pau·ci·ty
paunch·i·ness
paunchy
pau·per
pau·per·ize
pa·vane
also pa·van
pave·ment
pa·vil·ion
pav·ing
pawn·bro·ker
pawn·shop
pay
paid
also payed
pay·ing
pay·able
pay·check
pay·ee
pay·er
also pay·or
pay·load
pay·mas·ter
pay·ment
pay·off
pay·roll
pea
pl peas *also* pease

peace
tranquillity (*see* piece)
peace·able
peace·ably
peace·ful
peace·ful·ly
peace·mak·er
peace·time
peach
pea·cock
pea·fowl
pea·hen
peak
mountain (*see* peek, pique)
peal
resound (*see* peel)
pea·nut
pear
fruit (*see* pair, pare)
pearl
gem (*see* purl)
pearly
pear-shaped
peas·ant
peas·ant·ry
pea·shoot·er
peb·ble
peb·bly
pe·can
pec·ca·dil·lo
pl pec·ca·dil·loes *or* pec·ca·dil·los
pec·ca·ry
pec·tate

pec·tin
pec·to·ral
pec·u·late
pec·u·la·tion
pe·cu·liar
pe·cu·liar·i·ty
pe·cu·liar·ly
pe·cu·ni·ary
ped·a·gog·ic
ped·a·gog·i·cal·ly
ped·a·gogue
also ped·a·gog
ped·a·go·gy
ped·al
ped·aled
also ped·alled
ped·al·ing
also ped·al·ling
ped·ant
pe·dan·tic
pe·dan·ti·cal·ly
ped·ant·ry
ped·dle
ped·dler
or ped·lar
ped·er·ast
ped·er·as·ty
ped·es·tal
pe·des·tri·an
pe·di·at·ric
pe·di·a·tri·cian
or pe·di·a·trist
pe·di·at·rics
pedi·cab
ped·i·cure

ped·i·gree
ped·i·greed
ped·i·ment
pe·dol·o·gist
pe·dol·o·gy
pe·dom·e·ter
pe·dun·cle
peek
look (*see* peak, pique)
peel
skin (*see* peal)
peel·ing
peen
or pein
peep·hole
peer
equal, look (*see* pier)
peer·age
peer·less
peeve
pee·vish
pee·wee
peg
pegged
peg·ging
pei·gnoir
pe·jo·ra·tive
Pe·king·ese
or Pe·kin·ese
pe·koe
pel·age
pe·lag·ic
pel·i·can
pel·la·gra
pel·let
pell-mell
pel·lu·cid
pel·vic
pel·vis
pl pel·vis·es *or* pel·ves
pem·mi·can
also pem·i·can
pen
penned
pen·ning
pe·nal
pe·nal·iza·tion
pe·nal·ize
pen·al·ty
pen·ance
pen·chant
pen·cil
pen·ciled
or pen·cilled
pen·cil·ing
or pen·cil·ling
pen·dant
also pen·dent
noun
pen·dent
or pen·dant
adj
pend·ing
pen·du·lous
pen·du·lum
pe·ne·plain
also pe·ne·plane
pen·e·tra·bil·i·ty
pen·e·tra·ble
pen·e·tra·bly
pen·e·trate
pen·e·trat·ing
pen·e·tra·tion
pen·e·tra·tive
pen·guin
pen·hold·er
pen·i·cil·lin
pen·in·su·la
pen·in·su·lar
pe·nis
pl pe·nes *or* pe·nis·es
pen·i·tence
pen·i·tent
pen·i·ten·tial
pen·i·ten·tial·ly
pen·i·ten·tia·ry
pen·knife
pen·man·ship
pen·nant
pen·ni
pl pen·nia *or* pen·nis
pen·ni·less
pen·non
Penn·syl·va·nia
pen·ny
pl pen·nies *or* pence
pen·ny-pinch
pen·ny·weight
pen·ny-wise
pen·ny·wort
pe·no·log·i·cal
pe·nol·o·gist
pe·nol·o·gy
pen·sion

pen·sion·er
pen·sive
pen·sive·ly
pen·ta·cle
pen·ta·gon
pen·tag·o·nal
pen·tam·e·ter
pen·ta·ton·ic
  scale
Pen·te·cost
Pen·te·cos·tal
pent·house
pen·tom·ic
pe·nu·che
pen·ul·ti·mate
pen·um·bra
  pl pen·um·brae *or* pen·um·bras
pe·nu·ri·ous
pen·u·ry
pe·on
  laborer (*see* paean)
pe·on·age
pe·o·ny
peo·ple
  pl peo·ple
Pe·o·ria
pep
  pepped
  pep·ping
pep·lum
pep·per
pep·per·box
pep·per·corn
pep·per·mint
pep·pery
pep·pi·ness
pep·py
pep·sin
pep·tic
pep·tone
per·am·bu·late
per·am·bu·la·tion
per·am·bu·la·tor
per an·num
per·cale
per cap·i·ta
per·ceiv·able
per·ceiv·ably
per·ceive
per·cent
  pl per·cent *or* per·cents
per·cent·age
per·cen·tile
per·cept
per·cep·ti·bil·i·ty
per·cep·ti·ble
per·cep·ti·bly
per·cep·tion
per·cep·tive
per·cep·tu·al
per·cep·tu·al·ly
per·chance
Per·che·ron
per·cip·i·ence
per·cip·i·ent
per·co·late
per·co·la·tion
per·co·la·tor
per·cus·sion
per·cus·sive
per di·em
per·di·tion
per·du·ra·bil·i·ty
per·du·ra·ble
per·du·ra·bly
per·e·gri·na·tion
pe·remp·to·ri·ly
pe·remp·to·ri·ness
pe·remp·to·ry
pe·ren·ni·al
pe·ren·ni·al·ly
per·fect
per·fect·ibil·i·ty
per·fect·ible
per·fec·tion
per·fec·tion·ist
per·fec·to
per·fid·i·ous
per·fi·dy
per·fo·rate
per·fo·ra·tion
per·fo·ra·tor
per·force
per·form
per·form·able
per·for·mance
per·fume
per·fum·ery
per·func·to·ri·ly
per·func·to·ri·ness
per·func·to·ry
per·go·la
per·haps

peri·cyn·thi·on
per·i·gee
peri·he·lion
per·il
  per·iled
    also **per·illed**
  per·il·ing
    also **per·il·ling**
per·il·ous
peri·lune
pe·rim·e·ter
  boundary (*see* parameter)
pe·ri·od
pe·ri·od·ic
pe·ri·od·i·cal
pe·ri·od·i·cal·ly
pe·ri·od·ic·i·ty
peri·odon·tal
peri·pa·tet·ic
pe·riph·er·al
pe·riph·er·al·ly
pe·riph·ery
pe·riph·ra·sis
  pl **pe·riph·ra·ses**
peri·phras·tic
pe·rique
peri·scope
peri·scop·ic
per·ish
per·ish·abil·i·ty
per·ish·able
peri·stal·sis
peri·stal·tic
peri·style
peri·to·ni·tis
peri·wig
per·i·win·kle
per·jure
per·jur·er
per·ju·ri·ous
per·ju·ry
perk·i·ly
perk·i·ness
perky
per·ma·frost
per·ma·nence
per·ma·nen·cy
per·ma·nent
per·man·ga·nate
per·me·abil·i·ty
per·me·able
per·me·ably
per·me·ance
per·me·ate
per·me·ation
per·mis·si·bil·i·ty
per·mis·si·ble
per·mis·si·bly
per·mis·sion
per·mis·sive
per·mit
  per·mit·ted
  per·mit·ting
per·mu·ta·tion
per·mute
per·ni·cious
per·orate
per·ora·tion
per·ox·ide
per·pen·dic·u·lar
per·pe·trate
per·pe·tra·tion
per·pe·tra·tor
per·pet·u·al
per·pet·u·al·ly
per·pet·u·ate
per·pet·u·a·tion
per·pet·u·a·tor
per·pe·tu·ity
per·plex
per·plexed
per·plexed·ly
per·plex·i·ty
per·qui·site
  privilege (*see* prerequisite)
per se
per·se·cute
per·se·cu·tion
per·se·cu·tor
per·se·ver·ance
per·se·vere
Per·sian
per·si·flage
per·sim·mon
per·sist
per·sis·tence
per·sis·ten·cy
per·sis·tent
per·snick·e·ty
per·son
per·son·able
per·son·age

per·son·al
private (see personnel)

per·son·al·i·ty
character (see personalty)

per·son·al·ize

per·son·al·ly

per·son·al·ty
property (see personality)

per·so·na non gra·ta

per·so·nate
adj

per·son·ate
verb

per·son·i·fi·ca·tion

per·son·i·fi·er

per·son·i·fy

per·son·nel
employees (see personal)

per·spec·tive

per·spi·ca·cious

per·spi·cac·i·ty

per·spi·cu·i·ty

per·spic·u·ous

per·spi·ra·tion

per·spi·ra·to·ry

per·spire

per·suad·able

per·suade

per·sua·si·ble

per·sua·sion

per·sua·sive

per·tain

per·ti·na·cious

per·ti·nac·i·ty

per·ti·nence

per·ti·nen·cy

per·ti·nent

pert·ly

pert·ness

per·turb

per·tur·ba·tion

Pe·ru

pe·rus·al

pe·ruse

Pe·ru·vi·an

per·vade

per·va·sive

per·verse

per·verse·ly

per·ver·sion

per·ver·si·ty

per·ver·sive

per·vert

per·vi·ous

pe·se·ta

pe·se·wa

pes·ky

pe·so
pl **pe·sos**

pes·si·mism

pes·si·mist

pes·si·mis·tic

pes·si·mis·ti·cal·ly

pes·ter

pest·hole

pes·ti·cide

pes·tif·er·ous

pes·ti·lence

pes·ti·lent

pes·ti·len·tial

pes·tle

pet
pet·ted
pet·ting

pet·al

pe·tard

pe·ter

pet·i·ole

pet·it

pe·tite

pe·tit four
pl **petits fours** *or* **petit fours**

pe·ti·tion

pe·ti·tion·er

pet·rel

pet·ri·fac·tion

pet·ri·fy

pet·ro·chem·i·cal

pe·trog·ra·phy

pet·rol

pet·ro·la·tum

pe·tro·leum

pet·ro·log·ic

pe·trol·o·gist

pe·trol·o·gy

pet·ti·coat

pet·ti·fog
pet·ti·fogged
pet·ti·fog·ging

pet·ti·fog·ger

pet·ti·ly

pet·ti·ness

pet·tish
pet·ty
pet·u·lance
pet·u·lant
pe·tu·nia
pew·ter
pey·o·te
or pey·otl
pfen·nig
pha·eton
phago·cyte
pha·lanx
pl pha·lanx·es *or* pha·lan·ges
phal·a·rope
phal·lic
phal·lus
pl phal·li *or* phal·lus·es
phan·tasm
phan·tas·ma·go·ria
phan·tas·ma·go·ric
phan·tom
pha·raoh
phar·i·sa·ic
phar·i·sa·ical
phar·i·sa·ical·ly
phar·i·see
phar·ma·ceu·ti·cal
also phar·ma·ceu·tic
phar·ma·ceu·tics
phar·ma·cist
phar·ma·cog·no·sy
phar·ma·co·log·i·cal
phar·ma·co·log·i·cal·ly
phar·ma·col·o·gist
phar·ma·col·o·gy
phar·ma·co·poe·ia
phar·ma·cy
phar·os
pha·ryn·geal
phar·ynx
pl pha·ryn·ges *also* phar·ynx·es
phase
aspect (*see* faze)
phase·out
pheas·ant
phe·no·bar·bi·tal
phe·nol
phe·no·lic
phe·nom·e·nal
phe·nom·e·non
pl phe·nom·e·na *or* phe·nom·e·nons
phi·al
Phil·a·del·phia
phi·lan·der
phi·lan·der·er
phil·an·throp·ic
phil·an·thro·pist
phi·lan·thro·py
phil·a·tel·ic
phi·lat·e·list
phi·lat·e·ly
phil·har·mon·ic
phi·lip·pic
Phil·ip·pine
Phil·ip·pines
phi·lis·tine
phil·o·den·dron
pl phil·o·den·drons *or* phil·o·den·dra
phil·o·log·i·cal
phi·lol·o·gist
phi·lol·o·gy
phi·los·o·pher
philo·soph·ic
philo·soph·i·cal·ly
phi·los·o·phize
phi·los·o·phy
phil·ter
or phil·tre
potion (*see* filter)
phle·bi·tis
phlegm
phleg·mat·ic
phleg·mat·i·cal·ly
phlox
pl phlox *or* phlox·es
pho·bia
pho·bic
phoe·be
Phoe·nix
pho·neme
pho·ne·mic
pho·ne·mi·cal·ly
pho·ne·mics
pho·net·ic
pho·net·i·cal·ly
pho·ne·ti·cian
pho·net·ics
phon·ic
pho·ni·cal·ly
phon·ics

pho•ni•ly
pho•ni•ness
pho•no•graph
pho•no•graph•ic
pho•no•log•i•cal
pho•no•log•i•cal•ly
pho•nol•o•gist
pho•nol•o•gy
pho•ny
or pho•ney
phos•phate
phos•phat•ic
phos•pho•res•cence
phos•pho•res•cent
phos•phor•ic
phos•pho•rus
pho•to
pl pho•tos
pho•to•cell
pho•to•chro•mic
pho•to•com•po•si•tion
pho•to•copy
pho•to•elec•tric
pho•to•elec•tron
pho•to•emis•sive
pho•to•en•grave
pho•to•en•grav•ing
pho•to•flash
pho•to•flood
pho•to•ge•nic
pho•to•graph
pho•tog•ra•pher
pho•to•graph•ic
pho•to•graph•i•cal•ly
pho•tog•ra•phy
pho•to•gra•vure
pho•to•litho•graph
pho•to•li•thog•ra•phy
pho•to•map
pho•tom•e•ter
pho•to•met•ric
pho•tom•e•try
pho•to•mi•cro•graph
pho•to•mu•ral
pho•ton
pho•to•off•set
pho•to•sen•si•tive
pho•to•sen•si•ti•za•tion
pho•to•stat
pho•to•syn•the•sis
phra•se•ol•o•gy
phras•ing
phre•net•ic
phre•nol•o•gy
phy•lac•tery
phy•log•e•ny
phy•lum
pl phy•la
phys•ic
phys•i•cal
phys•i•cal•ly
phy•si•cian
phys•i•cist
phys•ics
phys•i•og•no•my
phys•io•graph•ic
phys•i•og•ra•phy
phys•i•o•log•i•cal
or phys•i•o•log•ic
phys•i•o•log•i•cal•ly
phys•i•ol•o•gist
phys•i•ol•o•gy
phys•io•ther•a•py
phy•sique
phy•to•gen•ic
pi
mathematics (*see* pie)
pi
also pie
jumble type (*see* pie)
pied
pi•ing
pi•a•nis•si•mo
pi•an•ist
pi•ano
also pi•ano•forte
pi•as•ter
or pi•as•tre
pi•az•za
pi•ca
pi•ca•resque
pic•a•yune
pic•ca•lil•li
pic•co•lo
pl pic•co•los
pice
pl pice
pick•ax
pick•er•el
pick•et
pick•ings
pick•le
pick•pock•et

pick·up

picky

pic·nic
  pic·nicked
  pic·nick·ing

pic·nick·er

pi·cot

pic·to·graph

pic·to·ri·al

pic·to·ri·al·ly

pic·ture

pic·tur·esque

pid·dle

pid·dling

pid·gin
  language (*see* pigeon)

pie
  pastry (*see* pi)

pie·bald

piece
  fragment (*see* peace)

pièce de ré·sis·tance

piece-dye

piece·meal

piece·work

piece·work·er

pied-à-terre

pied·mont

pier
  landing (*see* peer)

pierce

Pierre

pi·etism

pi·ety

pi·geon
  bird (*see* pidgin)

pi·geon·hole

pi·geon-toed

pig·gish

pig·gy·back

pig·head·ed

pig·ment

pig·men·ta·tion

pig·pen

pig·skin

pig·sty

pig·tail

pik·er

pi·las·ter

pil·chard

pil·fer

pil·fer·age

pil·fer·er

pil·grim

pil·grim·age

pil·ing

pil·lage

pil·lar

pill·box

pil·lion

pil·lo·ry

pil·low

pil·low·case

pi·lot

pi·lot·age

pi·lot·house

pil·sner
  also pil·sen·er

pi·ma

pi·men·to

pim·per·nel

pim·ple

pim·pled

pim·ply

pin
  pinned
  pin·ning

pin·afore

pi·ña·ta
  or pi·na·ta

pin·ball

pince-nez

pin·cer
  instrument (*see* pincher)

pinch·cock

pinch·er
  one that pinches (*see* pincer)

pinch-hit

pin·cush·ion

pine·ap·ple

pine·wood

pin·feath·er

pin·fish

Ping-Pong

pin·head

pin·hole

pin·ion

pink·eye

pin·kie
  or pin·ky

pin·nace

pin·na·cle

pin·nate

pi·noch·le

pi·ñon
or **pin·yon**
pl **pi·ñons** *or* **pin·yons**
or **pi·ño·nes**

pin·point

pin·prick

pin·set·ter

pin·stripe

pin·striped

pin·to
pl **pin·tos** *also* **pin·toes**

pint-size
or **pint-sized**

pin·up

pin·wale

pin·wheel

pin·work

pin·worm

pi·o·neer

pi·ous

pipe·ful

pipe·line

pip·er

pi·pette
or **pi·pet**

pip·ing

pip·pin

pip·squeak

pi·quan·cy

pi·quant

pique
resentment (*see* peak, peek)

pi·qué
or **pi·que**
fabric

pi·ra·cy

pi·rate

pi·rat·i·cal

pi·rat·i·cal·ly

pir·ou·ette

pis·ca·to·ri·al

pis·mire

pis·tach·io

pis·til
flower part (*see* pistol)

pis·til·late

pis·tol
handgun (*see* pistil)

pis·tol-whip

pis·ton

pit
pit·ted
pit·ting

pit-a-pat

pitch

pitch-black

pitch·blende

pitch-dark

pitch·er

pitch·fork

pitch·man

pitch·out

pit·e·ous

pit·fall

pit·head

pith·ec·an·thro·pus

pith·i·ly

pith·i·ness

pithy

piti·able

piti·ably

piti·ful

piti·ful·ly

piti·less

pi·ton

pit·tance

pit·ted

pit·ter-pat·ter

Pitts·burg
Calif., Kans.

Pitts·burgh
Penna.

pi·tu·itary

pity

pity·ing

piv·ot

piv·ot·al

pix·ie
or **pixy**

pix·ie·ish

piz·za

piz·ze·ri·a

piz·zi·ca·to

pla·ca·bil·i·ty

pla·ca·ble

pla·ca·bly

plac·ard

pla·cate

pla·ce·bo
pl **pla·ce·bos**

place·ment

pla•cen•ta
pl pla•cen•tas *or* pla•cen•tae

pla•cen•tal

plac•er

plac•id

pla•cid•i•ty

plack•et

pla•gia•rism

pla•gia•rist

pla•gia•rize

plague

plain
clear (*see* plane)

plain•clothes•man

plain•ly

plain•ness

plain•spo•ken

plaint

plain•tiff

plain•tive

plain•tive•ly

plait
pleat (*see* plate)

plan
planned
plan•ning

plane
level (*see* plain)

plan•et

plan•e•tar•i•um

plan•e•tary

plan•e•tes•i•mal

plan•e•toid

plan•e•tol•o•gy

plan•gen•cy

plan•gent

plank•ing

plank•ton

plan•tain

plan•ta•tion

plant•er

plaque

plas•ma

plas•ter

plas•ter•board

plas•ter•er

plas•tic

plas•ti•cal•ly

plas•tic•i•ty

plas•ti•cize

plat
plat•ted
plat•ting

plate
dish (*see* plait)

pla•teau
pl pla•teaus *or* pla•teaux

plate•ful

plat•en

plat•form

plat•ing

plat•i•num

plat•i•tude

plat•i•tu•di•nous

pla•ton•ic

pla•ton•i•cal•ly

pla•toon

plat•ter

platy•pus
pl platy•pus•es *also* platy•pi

plau•dit

plau•si•bil•i•ty

plau•si•ble

plau•si•bly

pla•ya

play•able

play•act

play•back

play•bill

play•book

play•boy

play-by-play

play•er

play•ful

play•ful•ly

play•ful•ness

play•go•er

play•ground

play•house

play•land

play•mate

play-off

play•pen

play•room

play•suit

play•thing

play•wear

play•wright

pla•za

plea

plead
plead·ed
or pled
plead·ing
plead·er
pleas·ant
pleas·ant·ry
please
pleas·ing
plea·sur·able
plea·sur·ably
plea·sure
ple·be·ian
pleb·i·scite
plec·trum
pl plec·tra
pledge
ple·na·ry
pleni·po·ten·tia·ry
plen·i·tude
plen·te·ous
plen·ti·ful
plen·ti·ful·ly
plent·i·tude
plen·ty
ple·num
pl ple·nums *or* ple·na
pleth·o·ra
pleu·ri·sy
plex·us
pli·abil·i·ty
pli·able
pli·ably
pli·an·cy
pli·ant
pli·ers
plight
plis·sé
or plis·se
plod
plod·ded
plod·ding
plod·der
plop
plopped
plop·ping
plot
plot·ted
plot·ting
plot·ter
plov·er
pl plov·er *or* plov·ers
plow
or plough
plow·boy
plow·share
pluck·i·ly
pluck·i·ness
plucky
plug
plugged
plug·ging
plum
fruit (*see* plumb)
plum·age
plumb
weight (*see* plum)
plumb·er
plumb·ing
plum·met
plump·ish
plump·ness
plun·der
plun·der·er
plunge
plung·er
plu·per·fect
plu·ral
plu·ral·ism
plu·ral·is·tic
plu·ral·i·ty
plu·ral·iza·tion
plu·ral·ize
plus
pl plus·es *also* plus·ses
plush·ly
plushy
plu·toc·ra·cy
plu·to·crat
plu·to·crat·ic
plu·to·crat·i·cal·ly
plu·to·ni·um
plu·vi·al
ply
plied
ply·ing
ply·wood
pneu·mat·ic
pneu·mo·nia
poach·er
po·chard
pock·et

pock•et•book
pock•et•ful
pock•et•knife
pock•et-size
or pock•et-sized
pock•mark
po•co•sin
po•di•a•trist
po•di•a•try
po•di•um
pl po•di•ums *or* po•dia
po•em
po•esy
po•et
po•et•ess
po•et•ic
or po•et•i•cal
po•et•i•cal•ly
po•et•ry
po•grom
poi•gnan•cy
poi•gnant
poin•ci•ana
poin•set•tia
point-blank
point•ed
point•ed•ly
point•er
poin•til•lism
poin•til•list
also poin•til•liste
point•less
poi•son
poi•son•ous

pok•er
poky
or pok•ey
Po•land
po•lar
Po•lar•is
po•lar•i•ty
po•lar•iza•tion
po•lar•ize
Po•lar•oid
pol•der
pole
staff (*see* poll)
pole•ax
pole•cat
po•lem•ic
or po•lem•i•cal
po•lem•i•cal•ly
po•lem•i•cist
pole•star
po•lice
po•lice•man
po•lice•wom•an
pol•i•cy
pol•i•cy•hold•er
po•lio
po•lio•my•eli•tis
Pol•ish
pol•ish
po•lite
po•lite•ly
po•lite•ness
po•li•tesse
pol•i•tic
po•lit•i•cal

po•lit•i•cal•ly
pol•i•ti•cian
pol•i•tick
po•lit•i•co
pl po•lit•i•cos *also* po•lit•i•coes
pol•i•tics
pol•i•ty
pol•ka
poll
survey (*see* pole)
pol•lack
or pol•lock
pol•len
pol•li•nate
pol•li•na•tion
pol•li•na•tor
pol•li•nize
pol•li•wog
or pol•ly•wog
poll•ster
pol•lut•ant
pol•lute
pol•lut•er
pol•lu•tion
po•lo
po•lo•naise
pol•ter•geist
pol•troon
poly•an•drous
poly•an•dry
poly•clin•ic
poly•es•ter
poly•eth•yl•ene
po•lyg•a•mous

po·lyg·a·my
poly·glot
poly·gon
po·lyg·o·nal
poly·graph
poly·mer
poly·mer·ic
po·ly·mer·iza·tion
Poly·ne·sian
poly·no·mi·al
pol·yp
poly·phon·ic
or poly·phon·ous
po·lyph·o·ny
poly·sty·rene
poly·syl·lab·ic
poly·syl·la·ble
poly·tech·nic
poly·the·ism
poly·the·is·tic
poly·un·sat·u·rat·ed
po·made
pome·gran·ate
pom·mel
pom·meled
or pom·melled
pom·mel·ing
or pom·mel·ling
pom·pa·dour
pom·pa·no
pl pom·pa·no *or* pom·pa·nos
pom-pom
pom·pon
pom·pos·i·ty
pomp·ous
Pon·ce
pon·cho
pl pon·chos
pon·der
pon·der·a·ble
pon·der·ous
pon·gee
pon·iard
pon·tiff
pon·tif·i·cal
pon·tif·i·cal·ly
pon·tif·i·cate
pon·toon
po·ny
po·ny·tail
poo·dle
pooh-pooh
also pooh
pool·room
poor·house
poor·ly
pop
popped
pop·ping
pop·corn
pop-eyed
pop·gun
pop·in·jay
pop·lar
pop·lin
pop-off
pop·over
pop·py
pop·py·cock
pop·u·lace
masses (see populous)
pop·u·lar
pop·u·lar·i·ty
pop·u·lar·i·za·tion
pop·u·lar·ize
pop·u·lar·iz·er
pop·u·lar·ly
pop·u·late
pop·u·la·tion
pop·u·lous
crowded (see populace)
pop-up
por·ce·lain
por·ce·lain·ize
por·cine
por·cu·pine
pore
ponder (see pour)
pork·er
por·nog·ra·pher
por·no·graph·ic
por·nog·ra·phy
po·ros·i·ty
po·rous
por·phy·ry
por·poise
por·ridge
por·rin·ger
por·ta·bil·i·ty
por·ta·ble
por·ta·bly
por·tage
por·tal

por·tal-to-por·tal
port·cul·lis
porte co·chere
por·tend
por·tent
por·ten·tous
por·ter
por·ter·house
port·fo·lio
pl port·fo·lios
port·hole
por·ti·co
pl por·ti·coes *or* por·ti·cos
por·tiere
por·tion
Port·land
port·li·ness
port·ly
port·man·teau
pl port·man·teaus *or* port·man·teaux
por·trait
por·trait·ist
por·trai·ture
por·tray
por·tray·al
Ports·mouth
Por·tu·gal
Por·tu·guese
pl Por·tu·guese
pos·er
one who poses
po·seur
affected person
pos·it

po·si·tion
pos·i·tive
pos·i·tive·ly
pos·i·tiv·ism
pos·i·tron
pos·se
pos·sess
pos·sessed
pos·ses·sion
pos·ses·sive
pos·sess·or
pos·si·bil·i·ty
pos·si·ble
pos·si·bly
pos·sum
post·age
post·al
post·box
post·card
post·clas·si·cal
post·con·so·nan·tal
post·date
post·di·lu·vi·an
post·doc·tor·al
post·er
pos·te·ri·or
pos·ter·i·ty
post·grad·u·ate
post·haste
post·hole
post·hu·mous
post·hyp·not·ic
pos·til·ion
or pos·til·lion
post·lude

post·man
post·mark
post·mas·ter
post me·ri·di·em
post·mis·tress
post·mor·tem
post·na·sal
post·na·tal
post·op·er·a·tive
post·paid
post·par·tum
post·pone
post·pone·ment
post·script
pos·tu·lant
pos·tu·late
pos·tu·la·tion
pos·tu·la·tor
pos·ture
post·war
po·sy
pot
pot·ted
pot·ting
po·ta·ble
po·tage
pot·ash
po·ta·tion
po·ta·to
pl po·ta·toes
pot·bel·lied
pot·bel·ly
pot·boil·er
po·ten·cy
po·tent

po•ten•tate
po•ten•tial
po•ten•ti•al•i•ty
po•ten•tial•ly
pot•ful
poth•er
pot•herb
pot•hole
pot•hook
po•tion
pot•latch
pot•luck
pot•pie
pot•pour•ri
pot•sherd
pot•shot
pot•tage
pot•ter
pot•tery
pouchy
poul•tice
poul•try
poul•try•man
pounce
pound-fool•ish
pour
flow (*see* **pore**)
pour•par•ler
pout
pov•er•ty
pov•er•ty-strick•en
pow•der
pow•dery
pow•er
pow•er•ful
pow•er•ful•ly
pow•er•house
pow•er•less
pow•wow
pox
prac•ti•ca•bil•i•ty
prac•ti•ca•ble
prac•ti•ca•bly
prac•ti•cal
prac•ti•cal•i•ty
prac•ti•cal•ly
prac•tice
or **prac•tise**
prac•ticed
or **prac•tised**
prac•tic•er
prac•ti•tio•ner
prae•to•ri•an
prag•mat•ic
also **prag•mat•i•cal**
prag•mat•i•cal•ly
prag•ma•tism
prag•ma•tist
prai•rie
praise•wor•thy
pra•line
prance
pranc•er
prank•ster
prat•fall
pra•tique
prat•tle
pray
entreat (*see* **prey**)
prayer
request
pray•er
one that prays
prayer•ful
prayer•ful•ly
preach•er
preach•ment
pre•ad•o•les•cence
pre•ad•o•les•cent
pre•am•ble
pre•ar•range
pre•ar•range•ment
pre•as•signed
pre•can•cel
pre•can•cel•la•tion
pre•car•i•ous
pre•cau•tion
pre•cau•tion•ary
pre•cede
pre•ce•dence
pre•ce•dent
prior
prec•e•dent
example
pre•ced•ing
pre•cept
pre•cep•tor
pre•cinct
pre•ci•os•i•ty
pre•cious
prec•i•pice
pre•cip•i•tan•cy
pre•cip•i•tate
pre•cip•i•tate•ly

pre·cip·i·ta·tion
pre·cip·i·tous
pré·cis
pl **pré·cis**
summary
pre·cise
exact
pre·cise·ly
pre·ci·sion
pre·clude
pre·clu·sive
pre·co·cious
pre·coc·i·ty
pre·con·ceive
pre·con·cep·tion
pre·con·di·tion
pre·cook
pre·cur·sor
pre·da·ceous
or **pre·da·cious**
pre·dac·i·ty
pre·date
pred·a·tor
pred·a·to·ri·ly
pred·a·to·ry
pre·de·cease
pre·de·ces·sor
pre·des·ig·nate
pre·des·ig·na·tion
pre·des·ti·na·tion
pre·des·tine
pre·de·ter·mine
pred·i·ca·ble
pre·dic·a·ment
pred·i·cate
pred·i·ca·tion
pre·dict
pre·dict·abil·i·ty
pre·dict·able
pre·dict·ably
pre·dic·tion
pre·di·gest
pre·di·ges·tion
pre·di·lec·tion
pre·dis·pose
pre·dis·po·si·tion
pre·dom·i·nance
pre·dom·i·nant
pre·dom·i·nate
pre·em·i·nence
pre·em·i·nent
pre·empt
pre·emp·tion
pre·emp·tive
pre·emp·tor
pre·ex·ist
pre·ex·is·tence
pre·ex·is·tent
pre·fab
pre·fab·ri·cate
pre·fab·ri·ca·tion
pref·ace
pref·a·to·ry
pre·fect
pre·fec·ture
pre·fer
pre·ferred
pre·fer·ring
pref·er·a·bil·i·ty
pref·er·a·ble
pref·er·a·bly
pref·er·ence
pref·er·en·tial
pre·fer·ment
pre·fig·u·ra·tion
pre·fig·u·ra·tive
pre·fig·ure
pre·fix
pre·flight
pre·form
preg·nan·cy
preg·nant
pre·heat
pre·hen·sile
pre·his·tor·ic
pre·judge
prej·u·dice
prej·u·di·cial
prel·a·cy
prel·ate
pre·lim·i·nary
pre·lude
pre·ma·ture
pre·ma·ture·ly
pre·med
pre·med·i·cal
pre·med·i·tate
pre·med·i·ta·tion
pre·mier
chief
pre·miere
first performance
prem·ise
pre·mi·um

pre·mix
pre·mo·ni·tion
pre·mon·i·to·ry
pre·na·tal
pre·oc·cu·pan·cy
pre·oc·cu·pa·tion
pre·oc·cu·pied
pre·oc·cu·py
pre·op·er·a·tive
pre·or·dain
prep·a·ra·tion
pre·pa·ra·to·ry
pre·pare
pre·pared·ness
pre·pay
pre·pon·der·ance
pre·pon·der·ant
pre·pon·der·ate
prep·o·si·tion
prep·o·si·tion·al
pre·pos·sess
pre·pos·sess·ing
pre·pos·ses·sion
pre·pos·ter·ous
pre·puce
pre·re·cord
pre·req·ui·site
required beforehand (*see* perquisite)
pre·rog·a·tive
pres·age
noun
pre·sage
verb
pres·by·ter
Pres·by·te·ri·an
pres·by·tery
pre·school
pre·science
pre·scient
pre·scribe
direct (*see* proscribe)
pre·scrip·tion
pre·scrip·tive
pre·sell
pres·ence
pres·ent
noun
pre·sent
verb
pre·sent·abil·i·ty
pre·sent·able
pre·sent·ably
pre·sen·ta·tion
pres·ent-day
pre·sen·ti·ment
premonition (*see* presentment)
pres·ent·ly
pre·sent·ment
presentation (*see* presentiment)
pre·serv·able
pres·er·va·tion
pre·ser·va·tive
pre·serve
pre·serv·er
pre·set
pre·shrunk
pre·side
pres·i·den·cy
pres·i·dent
pres·i·den·tial
pre·si·dio
pl **pre·si·di·os**
pre·sid·i·um
pl **pre·sid·ia** *or* **pre·sid·i·ums**
pre·sig·ni·fy
pre·soak
press·board
press·er
press·ing
press·man
press·room
press·run
pres·sure
pres·sur·iza·tion
pres·sur·ize
press·work
pres·ti·dig·i·ta·tion
pres·ti·dig·i·ta·tor
pres·tige
pres·ti·gious
pres·tis·si·mo
pres·to
pl **pres·tos**
pre·stress
pre·sum·able
pre·sum·ably
pre·sume
pre·sump·tion
pre·sump·tive
pre·sump·tu·ous
pre·sup·pose
pre·sup·po·si·tion

pre·teen

pre·tend

pre·tend·er

pre·tense
or **pre·tence**

pre·ten·sion

pre·ten·tious

pre·ten·tious·ness

pret·er·it
or **pret·er·ite**

pre·ter·nat·u·ral

pre·ter·nat·u·ral·ly

pre·test

pre·text

pret·ti·fy

pret·ti·ly

pret·ti·ness

pret·ty

pret·zel

pre·vail

pre·vail·ing

prev·a·lence

prev·a·lent

pre·var·i·cate

pre·var·i·ca·tion

pre·var·i·ca·tor

pre·vent

pre·vent·abil·i·ty

pre·vent·able

pre·ven·ta·tive

pre·ven·tion

pre·ven·tive

pre·view

pre·vi·ous

pre·vi·sion

pre·war

prey
victim (*see* pray)

price-cut·ter

price·less

prick·le

prick·li·ness

prick·ly

pride·ful

pride·ful·ly

prie-dieu
pl **prie-dieux**

priest·ess

priest·hood

priest·ly

prig·gish

pri·ma·cy

pri·ma don·na

pri·ma fa·cie

pri·mal

pri·mar·i·ly

pri·ma·ry

pri·mate

prim·er

pri·me·val

prim·i·tive

pri·mo·gen·i·tor

pri·mo·gen·i·ture

pri·mor·di·al

prim·rose

Prince Ed·ward Is·land

prince·ly

prin·cess
noun

prin·cess
or **prin·cesse**
adj

prin·ci·pal
chief (*see* principle)

prin·ci·pal·i·ty

prin·ci·pal·ly

prin·ci·ple
fundamental law (*see* principal)

prin·ci·pled

print·able

print·er

print·ing

print·out

pri·or

pri·or·ess

pri·or·i·ty

pri·o·ry

prism

pris·mat·ic

pris·on

pris·on·er

pris·si·ness

pris·sy

pris·tine

pri·va·cy

pri·vate

pri·va·teer

pri·vate·ly

pri·va·tion

priv·et

priv·i·lege

priv·i·leged

privy

prize·fight

prize·win·ner
prob·a·bil·i·ty
prob·a·ble
prob·a·bly
pro·bate
pro·ba·tion
pro·ba·tion·ary
pro·ba·tion·er
pro·ba·tive
pro·ba·to·ry
pro·bi·ty
prob·lem
prob·lem·at·ic
or prob·lem·at·i·cal
prob·lem·at·i·cal·ly
pro·bos·cis
pl pro·bos·cises *also* pro·bos·ci·des
pro·ca·the·dral
pro·ce·dur·al
pro·ce·dur·al·ly
pro·ce·dure
pro·ceed
pro·ceed·ing
pro·ceeds
pro·cess
pro·ces·sion
pro·ces·sion·al
pro·cès-ver·bal
pl pro·cès-ver·baux
pro·claim
proc·la·ma·tion
pro·cliv·i·ty
pro·con·sul
pro·cras·ti·nate
pro·cras·ti·na·tion
pro·cras·ti·na·tor
pro·cre·ant
pro·cre·ate
pro·cre·ation
pro·cre·ative
pro·cre·ator
pro·crus·te·an
proc·tol·o·gist
proc·tol·o·gy
proc·tor
proc·to·ri·al
pro·cur·able
proc·u·ra·tor
pro·cure
pro·cure·ment
pro·cur·er
prod
prod·ded
prod·ding
prod·i·gal
prod·i·gal·i·ty
prod·i·gal·ly
pro·di·gious
prod·i·gy
pro·duce
pro·duc·er
prod·uct
pro·duc·tion
pro·duc·tive
pro·duc·tiv·i·ty
pro·fa·na·tion
pro·fa·na·to·ry
pro·fane
pro·fane·ly
pro·fan·i·ty
pro·fess
pro·fessed
pro·fessed·ly
pro·fes·sion
pro·fes·sion·al
pro·fes·sion·al·ism
pro·fes·sion·al·ize
pro·fes·sion·al·ly
pro·fes·sor
pro·fes·so·ri·al
pro·fes·sor·ship
prof·fer
pro·fi·cien·cy
pro·fi·cient
pro·file
prof·it
gain (*see* prophet)
prof·it·abil·i·ty
prof·it·able
prof·it·ably
prof·i·teer
prof·li·ga·cy
prof·li·gate
pro for·ma
pro·found
pro·fun·di·ty
pro·fuse
pro·fuse·ly
pro·fu·sion
pro·gen·i·tor
prog·e·ny
prog·na·thous

prog·no·sis
pl **prog·no·ses**

prog·nos·tic

prog·nos·ti·cate

prog·nos·ti·ca·tion

prog·nos·ti·ca·tor

pro·gram
also **pro·gramme**
pro·grammed
or **pro·gramed**
pro·gram·ming
or **pro·gram·ing**

pro·gram·ma·ble

pro·gram·mat·ic

pro·grammed
or **pro·gramed**

pro·gram·mer
also **pro·gram·er**

pro·gram·ming
or **pro·gram·ing**

prog·ress
noun

pro·gress
verb

pro·gres·sion

pro·gres·sive

pro·gres·sive·ly

pro·hib·it

pro·hi·bi·tion

pro·hi·bi·tion·ist

pro·hib·i·tive

pro·hib·i·to·ry

proj·ect
noun

pro·ject
verb

pro·ject·able

pro·jec·tile

pro·jec·tion

pro·jec·tion·ist

pro·jec·tive

pro·jec·tor

pro·le·gom·e·non
pl **pro·le·gom·e·na**

pro·le·tar·i·an

pro·le·tar·i·an·iza·tion

pro·le·tar·i·an·ize

pro·le·tar·i·at

pro·lif·er·ate

pro·lif·er·a·tion

pro·lif·ic

pro·lif·i·cal·ly

pro·lix

pro·lix·i·ty

pro·loc·u·tor

pro·logue

pro·long

pro·lon·gate

pro·lon·ga·tion

prom·e·nade

prom·i·nence

prom·i·nent

pro·mis·cu·ity

pro·mis·cu·ous

prom·ise

prom·is·ing

prom·is·so·ry

prom·on·to·ry

pro·mote

pro·mot·er

pro·mo·tion

pro·mo·tion·al

prompt·book

prompt·er

promp·ti·tude

prompt·ly

pro·mul·gate

pro·mul·ga·tion

prone·ness

pro·noun

pro·nounce

pro·nounce·able

pro·nounced

pro·nounce·ment

pron·to

pro·nun·ci·a·men·to
pl **pro·nun·ci·a·men·tos** *or* **pro·nun·ci·a·men·toes**

pro·nun·ci·a·tion

proof·read

proof·read·er

prop
propped
prop·ping

pro·pa·gan·da

pro·pa·gan·dist

pro·pa·gan·dize

prop·a·gate

prop·a·ga·tion

pro·pane

pro·pel
pro·pelled
pro·pel·ling

pro·pel·lant
or pro·pel·lent

pro·pel·ler

pro·pen·si·ty

prop·er

prop·er·tied

prop·er·ty

proph·e·cy
noun, prediction (*see* prophesy)

proph·e·si·er

proph·e·sy
verb, to predict

proph·et
predictor (*see* profit)

proph·et·ess

pro·phet·ic
or pro·phet·i·cal

pro·phet·i·cal·ly

pro·phy·lac·tic

pro·phy·lax·is
pl pro·phy·lax·es

pro·pin·qui·ty

pro·pi·ti·able

pro·pi·ti·ate

pro·pi·ti·a·tion

pro·pi·tia·to·ry

pro·pi·tious

prop·jet en·gine

prop·man

pro·po·nent

pro·por·tion

pro·por·tion·able

pro·por·tion·ably

pro·por·tion·al

pro·por·tion·al·ly

pro·por·tion·ate

pro·por·tion·ate·ly

pro·pos·al

pro·pose

pro·pos·er

prop·o·si·tion

pro·pound

pro·pri·etary

pro·pri·etor

pro·pri·etress

pro·pri·ety

pro·pul·sion

pro·pul·sive

pro ra·ta

pro·rate

pro·ro·ga·tion

pro·rogue

pro·sa·ic

pro·sa·i·cal·ly

pro·sce·ni·um

pro·scribe
prohibit (*see* prescribe)

pro·scrib·er

pro·scrip·tion

pro·scrip·tive

pros·e·cut·able

pros·e·cute

pros·e·cu·tion

pros·e·cu·tor

pros·e·lyte

pros·e·ly·tism

pros·e·ly·tize

pro·sem·i·nar

pros·o·dy

pros·pect

pro·spec·tive

pro·spec·tive·ly

pros·pec·tor

pro·spec·tus

pros·per

pros·per·i·ty

pros·per·ous

pros·tate
gland (*see* prostrate)

pros·the·sis
pl pros·the·ses

pros·thet·ic

pros·ti·tute

pros·ti·tu·tion

pros·trate
helpless (*see* prostate)

pros·tra·tion

prosy

pro·tag·o·nist

pro·te·an

pro·tect

pro·tec·tion

pro·tec·tion·ism

pro·tec·tion·ist

pro·tec·tive

pro·tec·tor

pro·tec·tor·ate

pro·tec·tress

pro·té·gé
masc.

pro·té·gée
fem.

pro·tein

pro tem

pro tem•po•re
pro•test
prot•es•tant
Prot•es•tant•ism
pro•tes•ta•tion
pro•tho•no•tar•i•al
pro•tho•no•ta•ry
or pro•to•no•ta•ry
pro•tho•rax
pro•to•col
pro•to•his•to•ry
pro•ton
pro•to•plasm
pro•to•type
pro•to•zo•an
pro•tract
pro•trac•tion
pro•trac•tor
pro•trude
pro•tru•sion
pro•tu•ber•ance
pro•tu•ber•ant
proud•ly
prov•able
prov•ably
prove
proved
proved
or prov•en
prov•ing
prov•e•nance
prov•en•der
pro•ve•nience
prov•erb
pro•ver•bi•al
pro•ver•bi•al•ly
pro•vide
pro•vid•ed
Prov•i•dence
prov•i•dence
prov•i•dent
prov•i•den•tial
prov•i•den•tial•ly
pro•vid•er
pro•vid•ing
prov•ince
pro•vin•cial
pro•vin•cial•ism
pro•vin•cial•ly
pro•vi•sion
pro•vi•sion•al
pro•vi•sion•al•ly
pro•vi•so
pl pro•vi•sos *or* pro•vi•soes
pro•vi•so•ry
prov•o•ca•tion
pro•voc•a•tive
pro•voke
pro•vok•ing
pro•vost
pro•vost mar•shal
prow•ess
prowl
prowl•er
prox•i•mal
prox•i•mal•ly
prox•i•mate
prox•im•i•ty
prox•i•mo
proxy
pru•dence
pru•dent
pru•den•tial
pru•dent•ly
prud•ery
prud•ish
pru•nel•la
also pru•nelle
pru•ri•ence
pru•ri•ent
pry
pried
pry•ing
psalm
psalm•book
psalm•ist
psalm•o•dy
Psal•ter
psal•tery
also psal•try
pseu•do
pseud•onym
pseud•on•y•mous
pseu•do•sci•en•tif•ic
psit•ta•co•sis
pso•ri•a•sis
psy•che
psy•che•del•ic
psy•che•del•i•cal•ly
psy•chi•at•ric
psy•chi•at•ri•cal•ly
psy•chi•a•trist
psy•chi•a•try

psy·chic
also **psy·chi·cal**
psy·chi·cal·ly
psy·cho
psy·cho·anal·y·sis
psy·cho·an·a·lyst
psy·cho·an·a·lyt·ic
psy·cho·an·a·lyt·i·cal·ly
psy·cho·an·a·lyze
psy·cho·bi·o·log·i·cal
psy·cho·bi·ol·o·gy
psy·cho·chem·i·cal
psy·cho·dra·ma
psy·cho·dy·nam·ic
psy·cho·dy·nam·i·cal·ly
psy·cho·dy·nam·ics
psy·cho·gen·e·sis
psy·cho·ge·net·ic
psy·cho·log·i·cal
also **psy·cho·log·ic**
psy·cho·log·i·cal·ly
psy·chol·o·gist
psy·chol·o·gize
psy·chol·o·gy
psy·cho·met·ric
psy·cho·met·ri·cal·ly
psy·cho·met·rics
psy·cho·mo·tor
psy·cho·neu·ro·sis
psy·cho·neu·rot·ic
psy·cho·path
psy·cho·path·ic
psy·cho·path·i·cal·ly
psy·cho·patho·log·i·cal
psy·cho·phar·ma·ceu·ti·cal
psy·cho·sis
psy·cho·so·mat·ic
psy·cho·so·mat·i·cal·ly
psy·cho·ther·a·pist
psy·chot·ic
psy·chot·i·cal·ly
pto·maine
pu·ber·ty
pu·bes
pu·bic
pub·lic
pub·li·ca·tion
pub·li·cist
pub·lic·i·ty
pub·li·cize
pub·lic·ly
pub·lic-spir·it·ed
pub·lish
pub·lish·er
puck·er
puck·ish
pud·ding
pud·dle
pud·dling
pudg·i·ness
pudgy
pueb·lo
pu·er·ile
pu·er·il·i·ty
pu·er·per·al
Puer·to Ri·can
Puer·to Ri·co
puff·ball
puff·ery
puffy
pu·gi·lism
pu·gi·list
pu·gi·lis·tic
pug·na·cious
pug·nac·i·ty
puk·ka
pul
pl **puls** *or* **pu·li**
pul·chri·tude
pul·chri·tu·di·nous
pull·back
pul·let
pul·ley
Pull·man
pull·out
pull·over
pul·mo·nary
pul·mo·tor
pulp·i·ness
pul·pit
pulp·wood
pulpy
pul·sar
pul·sate
pul·sa·tion
pul·sa·tor
pulse

pul·ver·i·za·tion
pul·ver·ize
pu·ma
pum·ice
pum·mel
  pum·meled
    or **pum·melled**
  pum·mel·ing
    or **pum·mel·ling**
pum·per·nick·el
pump·kin
pun
  punned
  pun·ning
punch·board
punch-drunk
pun·cheon
punch·er
punc·til·io
punc·til·i·ous
punc·tu·al
punc·tu·al·i·ty
punc·tu·al·ly
punc·tu·ate
punc·tu·a·tion
punc·tu·a·tor
punc·ture
pun·dit
pun·gen·cy
pun·gent
pu·ni·ly
pu·ni·ness
pun·ish
pun·ish·able
pun·ish·ment
pu·ni·tive
pun·ster
punt·er
pu·ny
pu·pa
  pl **pu·pae** *or* **pu·pas**
pu·pil
pup·pet
pup·pe·teer
pup·pet·ry
pup·py
pur·blind
pur·chas·able
pur·chase
pur·chas·er
pur·dah
pure·bred
pu·ree
pure·ly
pur·ga·tion
pur·ga·tive
pur·ga·to·ry
purge
pu·ri·fi·ca·tion
pu·ri·fi·ca·to·ry
pu·ri·fi·er
pu·ri·fy
pur·ism
pur·ist
pu·ri·tan
pu·ri·tan·i·cal
pu·ri·tan·i·cal·ly
pu·ri·ty
purl
  knit (*see* **pearl**)
pur·lieu
pur·loin
pur·ple
pur·plish
pur·port
pur·pose
pur·pose·ful
pur·pose·ful·ly
pur·pose·less
pur·pose·ly
purs·er
purs·lane
pur·su·ance
pur·su·ant
pur·sue
pur·su·er
pur·suit
pu·ru·lence
pu·ru·lent
pur·vey
pur·vey·ance
pur·vey·or
pur·view
push-but·ton
push·cart
push·er
push·over
push·pin
pushy
pu·sil·la·nim·i·ty
pu·sil·lan·i·mous
pussy·foot
pus·tu·lant
pus·tule

put
place (*see* putt)
put
put·ting

pu·ta·tive

put-on

put·out

pu·tre·fac·tion

pu·tre·fy

pu·tres·cence

pu·tres·cent

pu·trid

putsch

putt
golf stroke (*see* put)

put·tee

put·ter
one that puts

putt·er
golf club

put·ty

puz·zle

puz·zle·ment

puz·zler

pya

pyg·my

py·lon

py·or·rhea

pyr·a·mid

py·ra·mi·dal

pyre

py·re·thrum

Py·rex

py·rol·y·sis

py·ro·ma·nia

py·ro·ma·ni·ac

py·rom·e·ter

py·ro·tech·nics

py·rox·y·lin

pyr·rhic

py·thon

Q

Qa·tar
or Ka·tar

qin·tar

quack·ery

quack·ish

quad·ran·gle

qua·dran·gu·lar

quad·rant

qua·drat·ic

qua·drat·ics

qua·dren·ni·al

qua·dren·ni·al·ly

qua·dren·ni·um
pl qua·dren·ni·ums
or qua·dren·nia

quad·ri·lat·er·al

qua·drille

qua·dril·lion

quad·ri·par·tite

qua·droon

quad·ru·ped

qua·dru·ple

qua·dru·plet

qua·dru·pli·cate

quaff

quag·mire

qua·hog
also qua·haug

quail

quaint·ly

Quak·er

qual·i·fi·ca·tion

qual·i·fied

qual·i·fi·er

qual·i·fy

qual·i·ta·tive

qual·i·ty

qualm

quan·da·ry

quan·ti·fi·able

quan·ti·fi·ca·tion

quan·ti·fi·er

quan·ti·fy

quan·ti·ta·tive

quan·ti·ty

quan·tum
pl quan·ta

quar·an·tin·able

quar·an·tine

quark

quar·rel
quar·reled
or quar·relled
quar·rel·ing
or quar·rel·ling

quar·rel·some

quar·ry

quart

quar·ter

quar·ter·back

quar·ter·deck

quar·ter·fi·nal
quar·ter·ly
quar·ter·mas·ter
quar·ter·sawed
also quar·ter·sawn

quar·tet
also quar·tette

quar·to
pl quar·tos

quartz
qua·sar
quash
qua·si
qua·si-ju·di·cial
qua·si-pub·lic
qua·ter·na·ry
qua·train
qua·ver
quay
wharf (*see* key)

queas·i·ly
queas·i·ness
quea·sy
also quea·zy

Que·bec
que·bra·cho
queer·ly
quell
quench·able
quer·u·lous
que·ry
quest
ques·tion
ques·tion·able
ques·tion·ably
ques·tion·naire
quet·zal
pl quet·zals *or* quet·za·les

queue
line (*see* cue)

quib·ble
quick·en
quick-freeze
quick·ie
quick·ly
quick·sand
quick·sil·ver
quick·step
quick-tem·pered
quick-wit·ted
quid pro quo
qui·es·cence
qui·es·cent
qui·et·ly
qui·etude
qui·etus
quince
qui·nine
quin·quen·ni·al
quin·quen·ni·al·ly
quin·sy
quin·tal
quin·tes·sence
quint·es·sen·tial
quin·tet
also quin·tette

quin·til·lion
quin·tu·ple
quin·tup·let
quin·tu·pli·cate
quip
quipped
quip·ping

quire
paper (*see* choir)

quirk
quis·ling
quit
quit
also quit·ted
quit·ting

quit·claim
quit·tance
quit·ter
quiv·er
quix·ot·ic
quix·ot·i·cal·ly
quiz
pl quiz·zes

quiz
quizzed
quiz·zing

quiz·zi·cal
quoit
quon·dam
Quon·set
quo·rum
quo·ta
quot·able
quo·ta·tion
quote
quo·tid·i·an
quo·tient

qursh

R

rab·bet
groove (*see* rabbit)

rab·bi

rab·bin·ate

rab·bin·ic
or rab·bin·i·cal

rab·bit
animal (*see* rabbet)

rab·ble

rab·ble-rous·er

ra·bid

ra·bies

rac·coon

race·course

race·horse

ra·ceme

rac·er

race·track

race·way

ra·cial

ra·cial·ism

ra·cial·ly

rac·i·ly

rac·i·ness

rac·ing

rac·ism

rac·ist

rack·et

rack·e·teer

ra·con·teur

racy

ra·dar

ra·dar·scope

ra·di·al

ra·di·al·ly

ra·di·ance

ra·di·an·cy

ra·di·ant

ra·di·ate

ra·di·a·tion

ra·di·a·tor

rad·i·cal

rad·i·cal·ism

rad·i·cal·ly

ra·dio
pl ra·di·os

ra·dio·ac·tive

ra·dio·ac·tiv·i·ty

ra·dio·car·bon

ra·dio·gen·ic

ra·dio·gram

ra·dio·graph

ra·di·og·ra·phy

ra·dio·iso·tope

ra·di·ol·o·gist

ra·di·ol·o·gy

ra·di·om·e·ter

ra·dio·pho·to

ra·di·os·co·py

ra·dio·sonde

ra·dio·tel·e·graph

ra·dio·te·leg·ra·phy

ra·dio·tele·phone

ra·dio·ther·a·pist

ra·dio·ther·a·py

rad·ish

ra·di·um

ra·di·us
pl ra·dii *also* ra·di·us·es

ra·dix
pl ra·di·ces *or* ra·dix·es

ra·don

raf·fia

raff·ish

raf·fle

raf·ter

rag·a·muf·fin

rag·ged

rag·ing

rag·lan

ra·gout

rag·pick·er

rag·time

rag·weed

rail·ing

rail·lery

rail·road

rail·way

rai·ment

rain
shower (*see* reign, rein)

rain·bow

rain·coat

rain·drop

rain·fall

rain·mak·ing

rain·proof

rain·storm

rain·wa·ter

rain·wear

rainy

raise
lift (*see* **raze**)

rai·sin

rai·son d'être

ra·ja
or **ra·jah**

rake-off

rak·ish

Ra·leigh

ral·ly

ram
rammed
ram·ming

ram·ble

ram·bler

ram·bunc·tious

ra·mie

ram·i·fi·ca·tion

ram·i·fy

ram·jet en·gine

ram·page

ram·pa·geous

ram·pan·cy

ram·pant

ram·part

ram·rod

ram·shack·le

ranch·er

ran·cid

ran·cid·i·ty

ran·cor

ran·cor·ous

rand

ran·dom

ran·dom·iza·tion

ran·dom·ize

rang·er

rang·i·ness

rangy

ra·ni
or **ra·nee**

rank·ing

ran·kle

ran·sack

ran·som

rant·er

rap
knock (*see* **wrap**)
rapped
rap·ping

ra·pa·cious

ra·pac·i·ty

rape

rape·seed

rap·id

rap·id-fire

ra·pid·i·ty

rap·id·ly

ra·pi·er

rap·ine

rap·ist

rap·pen
pl **rap·pen**

rap·port

rap·proche·ment

rap·scal·lion

rapt

rapt·ly

rap·ture

rap·tur·ous

ra·ra avis

rare·bit

rar·efac·tion

rar·efy
also **rar·i·fy**

rare·ly

rar·i·ty

ras·cal

ras·cal·i·ty

ras·cal·ly

rash·er

rash·ly

rash·ness

rasp·ber·ry

rat
rat·ted
rat·ting

ratch·et

rath·er

rat·i·fi·ca·tion

rat·i·fy

ra·ti·né
or **ra·tine**

rat·ing

ra·tio
pl **ra·tios**

ra·ti·o·ci·nate

ra·ti·o·ci·na·tion

ra·tion

ra·tio·nal

ra·tio·nale

ra·tio·nal·ism

ra·tio·nal·ist
or **ra·tio·nal·is·tic**

ra·tio·nal·i·ty

ra·tio·nal·iza·tion

ra·tio·nal·ize

ra·tio·nal·ly

rat·line

rat·tan

rat·teen

rat·tle

rat·tle·brain

rat·tler

rat·tle·snake

rat·tle·trap

rat·tling

rat·trap

rat·ty

rau·cous

raun·chy

rav·age

rav·ag·er

rav·el

rav·eled
or **rav·elled**

ra·vel·ing
or **rav·el·ling**

ra·ven

rav·en·ous

ra·vine

rav·i·o·li

rav·ish

raw·boned

raw·hide

ray·on

raze
demolish (*see* raise)

ra·zor

ra·zor-backed
or **ra·zor·back**

ra·zor·bill

raz·zle-daz·zle

razz·ma·tazz

reach·able

re·act

re·ac·tion

re·ac·tion·ary

re·ac·ti·vate

re·ac·ti·va·tion

re·ac·tive

re·ac·tiv·i·ty

re·ac·tor

read·abil·i·ty

read·able

read·ably

read·er

readi·ly

readi·ness

read·ing

read·out

ready

ready-made

ready-to-wear

re·agent

re·al
actual (*see* reel)

re·al·ism

re·al·ist

re·al·is·tic

re·al·is·ti·cal·ly

re·al·i·ty
real (*see* realty)

re·al·iz·able

re·al·iza·tion

re·al·ize

re·al·ly

realm

Re·al·tor

re·al·ty
real estate (*see* reality)

ream·er

reap·er

re·arm

re·ar·ma·ment

rear·most

rear·ward

rea·son

rea·son·abil·i·ty

rea·son·able

rea·son·ably

rea·son·ing

re·as·sur·ance

re·as·sure

re·bate

reb·el
noun

re·bel
verb

re·belled

re·bel·ling

re·bel·lion

re·bel·lious

re·birth

re·born

re·bound

re·broad·cast

re•buff
re•build
re•buke
re•bus
re•but
re•but•ted
re•but•ting
re•but•tal
re•cal•ci•trance
re•cal•ci•trant
re•cal•cu•late
re•cal•cu•la•tion
re•call
re•call•able
re•cant
re•can•ta•tion
re•cap
re•capped
re•cap•ping
re•ca•pit•u•late
re•ca•pit•u•la•tion
re•cap•pa•ble
re•cap•ture
re•cast
re•cede
re•ceipt
re•ceiv•able
re•ceive
re•ceiv•er
re•ceiv•er•ship
re•cen•cy
re•cen•sion
re•cent
re•cep•ta•cle
re•cep•tion
re•cep•tion•ist
re•cep•tive
re•cep•tiv•i•ty
re•cep•tor
re•cess
re•ces•sion
re•ces•sion•al
re•ces•sive
re•cher•ché
re•cid•i•vism
re•cid•i•vist
rec•i•pe
re•cip•i•ent
re•cip•ro•cal
re•cip•ro•cal•ly
re•cip•ro•cate
re•cip•ro•ca•tion
rec•i•proc•i•ty
re•ci•sion
re•cit•al
rec•i•ta•tion
rec•i•ta•tive
re•cite
reck•less
reck•on
reck•on•ing
re•claim
re•claim•able
rec•la•ma•tion
re•cline
re•cluse
rec•og•ni•tion
rec•og•niz•abil•i•ty
rec•og•niz•able
rec•og•niz•ably
re•cog•ni•zance
rec•og•nize
re•coil
re•coil•less
rec•ol•lect
rec•ol•lec•tion
re•com•bi•na•tion
rec•om•mend
rec•om•mend•able
rec•om•men•da•tion
re•com•mit
re•com•mit•tal
rec•om•pense
rec•on•cil•abil•i•ty
rec•on•cil•able
rec•on•cile
rec•on•cil•er
rec•on•cil•i•a•tion
re•con•dite
re•con•di•tion
re•con•firm
re•con•fir•ma•tion
re•con•nais•sance
re•con•noi•ter
re•con•sid•er
re•con•sid•er•a•tion
re•con•sti•tute
re•con•struct
re•con•struc•tion
re•con•ver•sion
re•con•vert
re•cord
verb

rec•ord
noun

re•cord•er

re•cord•ist

re•count

re•coup

re•course

re•cov•er
regain

re-cov•er
cover again

re•cov•er•able

re•cov•ery

rec•re•ant

rec•re•ate
refresh

re•cre•ate
create again

rec•re•ation
play

re•cre•ation
renewal

rec•re•ation•al

rec•re•ative
refreshing

re•cre•ative
able to create again

re•crim•i•nate

re•crim•i•na•tion

re•crim•i•na•to•ry

re•cruit

rec•tal

rect•an•gle

rect•an•gu•lar

rec•ti•fi•able

rec•ti•fi•ca•tion

rec•ti•fi•er

rec•ti•fy

rec•ti•lin•ear

rec•ti•tude

rec•to
pl **rec•tos**

rec•tor

rec•to•ry

rec•tum
pl **rec•tums** *or* **rec•ta**

re•cum•ben•cy

re•cum•bent

re•cu•per•ate

re•cu•per•a•tion

re•cu•per•a•tive

re•cur
re•curred
re•cur•ring

re•cur•rence

re•cur•rent

re•cy•cle

re•dact

re•dac•tion

re•dac•tor

red-blood•ed

red•cap

red-car•pet

red•coat

red•den

red•dish

re•dec•o•rate

re•dec•o•ra•tion

re•deem

re•deem•able

re•deem•er

re•demp•tion

re•demp•tive

re•demp•to•ry

re•de•sign

re•de•vel•op•ment

red-hand•ed

red•head

red-hot

re•di•rect

re•di•rec•tion

re•dis•trib•ute

re•dis•tri•bu•tion

re•dis•trict

red-let•ter

red•o•lence

red•o•lent

re•dou•ble

re•doubt

re•doubt•able

re•doubt•ably

re•dound

red-pen•cil

re•dress

red•skin

red•top

re•duce

re•duc•ible

re•duc•tion

re•dun•dan•cy

re•dun•dant

re•du•pli•cate

re•du•pli•ca•tion

red•wood

re•echo

re·ed·u·cate
re·ed·u·ca·tion
reedy
reek
smell (*see* wreak)
reel
spool (*see* real)
re·elect
re·em·ploy
re·en·act
re·en·try
re·fash·ion
re·fec·tion
re·fec·to·ry
re·fer
re·ferred
re·fer·ring
re·fer·able
ref·er·ee
ref·er·ence
ref·er·en·dum
pl **ref·er·en·da** *or* **ref·er·en·dums**
ref·er·ent
ref·er·en·tial
re·fer·ral
re·fill
re·fill·able
re·fi·nance
re·fine
re·fined
re·fine·ment
re·fin·er
re·fin·ery
re·fin·ish
re·fit
re·flect
re·flec·tion
re·flec·tive
re·flec·tor
re·flex
re·flex·ive
re·for·est
re·for·es·ta·tion
re·form
improve
re-form
form again
ref·or·ma·tion
re·for·ma·to·ry
re·form·er
re·fract
re·frac·tion
re·frac·tive
re·frac·tor
re·frac·to·ry
re·frain
re·fran·gi·ble
re·fresh
re·fresh·ment
re·frig·er·ant
re·frig·er·ate
re·frig·er·a·tion
re·frig·er·a·tor
ref·uge
ref·u·gee
re·ful·gence
re·ful·gent
re·fund
re·fund·able
re·fur·bish
re·fus·al
re·fuse
verb
ref·use
noun
re·fut·able
re·fut·ably
ref·u·ta·tion
re·fute
re·gain
re·gal
royal
re·gale
entertain
re·ga·lia
re·gal·ly
re·gard
re·gard·ing
re·gard·less
re·gat·ta
re·gen·cy
re·gen·er·a·cy
re·gen·er·ate
re·gen·er·a·tion
re·gen·er·a·tive
re·gen·er·a·tor
re·gent
reg·i·cide
re·gime
also **ré·gime**
reg·i·men
reg·i·ment
reg·i·men·tal
reg·i·men·ta·tion

Re·gi·na
re·gion
re·gion·al
re·gion·al·ly
reg·is·ter
reg·is·trant
reg·is·trar
reg·is·tra·tion
reg·is·try
re·gress
re·gres·sion
re·gres·sive
re·gret
re·gret·ted
re·gret·ting
re·gret·ful
re·gret·ful·ly
re·gret·ta·ble
re·gret·ta·bly
re·group
reg·u·lar
reg·u·lar·i·ty
reg·u·lar·ize
reg·u·lar·ly
reg·u·late
reg·u·la·tion
reg·u·la·tive
reg·u·la·tor
reg·u·la·to·ry
re·gur·gi·tate
re·gur·gi·ta·tion
re·ha·bil·i·tate
re·ha·bil·i·ta·tion
re·ha·bil·i·ta·tive

re·hash
re·hear·ing
re·hears·al
re·hearse
reign
rule (*see* rain, rein)
re·im·burs·able
re·im·burse
re·im·burse·ment
rein
restrain (*see* rain, reign)
re·in·car·nate
re·in·car·na·tion
rein·deer
re·in·fec·tion
re·in·force
re·in·force·ment
re·in·state
re·in·state·ment
re·in·sur·ance
re·in·sure
re·in·ter·pret
re·in·ter·pre·ta·tion
re·is·sue
re·it·er·ate
re·it·er·a·tion
re·ject
re·jec·tion
re·joice
re·join
re·join·der
re·ju·ve·nate
re·ju·ve·na·tion
re·lapse

re·lat·able
re·late
re·lat·ed
re·la·tion
re·la·tion·ship
rel·a·tive
rel·a·tive·ly
rel·a·tiv·is·tic
rel·a·tiv·i·ty
re·la·tor
re·lax
re·lax·ant
re·lax·ation
re·lay
re·lease
rel·e·gate
rel·e·ga·tion
re·lent
re·lent·less
rel·e·vance
rel·e·van·cy
rel·e·vant
re·lia·bil·i·ty
re·li·able
re·li·ably
re·li·ance
re·li·ant
rel·ic
re·lief
re·liev·able
re·lieve
re·liev·er
re·li·gion
re·li·gi·os·i·ty
re·li·gious

re•line
re•lin•quish
rel•i•quary
rel•ish
re•luc•tance
re•luc•tant
re•ly
re•main
re•main•der
re•mains
re•make
re•mand
re•mark
re•mark•able
re•mark•ably
re•me•di•a•ble
re•me•di•al
re•me•di•al•ly
rem•e•dy
re•mem•ber
re•mem•brance
re•mind
rem•i•nisce
rem•i•nis•cence
rem•i•nis•cent
re•miss
re•mis•si•ble
re•mis•sion
re•mit
  re•mit•ted
  re•mit•ting
re•mit•tal
re•mit•tance
rem•nant

re•mod•el
re•mon•strance
re•mon•strant
re•mon•strate
re•mon•stra•tion
re•mon•stra•tive
re•mon•stra•tor
re•morse
re•morse•ful
re•mote
re•mote•ly
re•mote•ness
re•mount
re•mov•able
re•mov•al
re•move
re•mu•ner•ate
re•mu•ner•a•tion
re•mu•ner•a•tive
re•mu•ner•a•tor
re•nais•sance
re•nal
re•nas•cence
rend
  rent
  rend•ing
ren•der
ren•dez•vous
  ren•dez•voused
  ren•dez•vous•ing
  ren•dez•vouses
ren•di•tion
ren•e•gade
re•nege

re•new
re•new•able
re•new•al
ren•net
ren•nin
re•nom•i•nate
re•nounce
ren•o•vate
ren•o•va•tion
ren•o•va•tor
re•nown
re•nowned
rent•al
re•num•ber
re•nun•ci•a•tion
re•open
re•or•der
re•or•ga•ni•za•tion
re•or•ga•nize
re•pack•age
re•pair
re•pair•able
re•pair•man
rep•a•ra•ble
rep•a•ra•tion
re•par•a•tive
rep•ar•tee
re•past
re•pa•tri•ate
re•pa•tri•a•tion
re•pay
re•pay•able
re•pay•ment
re•peal
re•peat

re·peat·ed
re·pel
 re·pelled
 re·pel·ling
re·pel·lent
 also re·pel·lant
re·pent
re·pen·tance
re·pen·tant
re·per·cus·sion
rep·er·toire
rep·er·tory
rep·e·ti·tion
rep·e·ti·tious
re·pet·i·tive
re·pet·i·tive·ly
re·place
re·place·able
re·place·ment
re·plen·ish
re·plete
re·plete·ness
re·ple·tion
rep·li·ca
rep·li·cate
rep·li·ca·tion
re·ply
 re·plied
 re·ply·ing
re·port
re·port·able
re·port·age
re·port·ed·ly
re·port·er
rep·or·to·ri·al
re·pose
re·pos·i·to·ry
re·pos·sess
re·pos·ses·sion
re·pous·sé
rep·re·hend
rep·re·hen·si·ble
rep·re·hen·si·bly
rep·re·hen·sion
rep·re·sent
rep·re·sen·ta·tion
rep·re·sen·ta·tive
re·press
re·pres·sion
re·pres·sive
re·prieve
rep·ri·mand
re·print
re·pri·sal
re·prise
re·pro
 pl re·pros
re·proach
re·proach·able
re·proach·ful
re·proach·ful·ly
rep·ro·bate
rep·ro·ba·tion
re·pro·duce
re·pro·duc·ible
re·pro·duc·tion
re·pro·duc·tive
re·proof
re·prove
re·prov·ing·ly
rep·tile
rep·til·i·an
re·pub·lic
re·pub·li·can
re·pub·li·ca·tion
re·pub·lish
re·pu·di·ate
re·pu·di·a·tion
re·pug·nance
re·pug·nant
re·pulse
re·pul·sion
re·pul·sive
re·pul·sive·ly
rep·u·ta·bil·i·ty
rep·u·ta·ble
rep·u·ta·bly
rep·u·ta·tion
re·pute
re·put·ed
re·quest
re·qui·em
re·quire
re·quire·ment
req·ui·site
req·ui·si·tion
re·quit·al
re·quite
rer·e·dos
re·run
 re·ran
 re·run
 re·run·ning

re•sal•able
re•sale
re•scale
re•scind
re•scis•sion
re•script
res•cue
res•cu•er
re•search
re•sec•tion
re•sem•blance
re•sem•ble
re•sent
re•sent•ful
re•sent•ful•ly
re•sent•ment
re•ser•pine
res•er•va•tion
re•serve
re•served
re•serv•ist
res•er•voir
res ges•tae
re•shape
re•ship
re•shuf•fle
re•side
res•i•dence
res•i•den•cy
res•i•dent
res•i•den•tial
res•i•den•tial•ly
re•sid•u•al
re•sid•u•al•ly
re•sid•u•ary
res•i•due
re•sid•u•um
pl re•sid•ua
re•sign
res•ig•na•tion
re•sign•ed•ly
re•sil•ience
re•sil•ien•cy
re•sil•ient
res•in
res•in•ate
res•in•ous
re•sist
re•sis•tance
re•sis•tant
re•sist•er
one who resists (see resistor)
re•sist•ible
or re•sist•able
re•sis•tor
electrical device (see resister)
res•o•lute
res•o•lute•ly
res•o•lu•tion
re•solv•able
re•solve
res•o•nance
res•o•nant
res•o•nate
res•o•na•tor
re•sorb
re•sorp•tion
re•sort
re•sound
re•sound•ing
re•source
re•source•ful
re•spect
re•spect•abil•i•ty
re•spect•able
re•spect•ably
re•spect•ful
re•spect•ful•ly
re•spect•ing
re•spec•tive
re•spec•tive•ly
res•pi•ra•tion
res•pi•ra•tor
re•spi•ra•to•ry
re•spire
re•spite
re•splen•dence
re•splen•dent
re•spond
re•spon•dent
re•sponse
re•spon•si•bil•i•ty
re•spon•si•ble
re•spon•si•bly
re•spon•sive
re•start
re•state
res•tau•rant
res•tau•ra•teur
rest•ful
rest•ful•ly
res•ti•tu•tion
res•tive
res•tive•ly

rest·less
re·stor·able
res·to·ra·tion
re·stor·ative
re·store
re·strain
re·strain·able
re·strained
re·straint
re·strict
re·stric·tion
re·stric·tive
re·sult
re·sul·tant
re·sume
ré·su·mé
or re·su·me *or* re·su·mé
re·sump·tion
re·su·pi·nate
re·sur·gence
re·sur·gent
res·ur·rect
res·ur·rec·tion
re·sus·ci·tate
re·sus·ci·ta·tion
re·sus·ci·ta·tor
ret
ret·ted
ret·ting
re·tail
re·tail·er
re·tain
re·tain·er
re·take
re·took
re·tak·en
re·tak·ing
re·tal·i·ate
re·tal·i·a·tion
re·tal·ia·to·ry
re·tard
re·tar·da·tion
re·tard·ed
retch
vomit (see wretch)
re·tell
re·told
re·tell·ing
re·ten·tion
re·ten·tive
re·ten·tiv·i·ty
re·test
ret·i·cence
ret·i·cent
ret·i·cle
re·tic·u·lar
re·tic·u·late
ret·i·na
pl ret·i·nas *or* ret·i·nae
ret·i·nue
re·tire
re·tire·ment
re·tir·ing
re·tool
re·tort
re·touch
re·trace
re·tract
re·tract·able
re·trac·tile
re·trac·tion
re·trac·tor
re·tread
re·treat
re·trench
re·trench·ment
re·tri·al
re·tri·bu·tion
re·trib·u·tive
re·trib·u·to·ry
re·triev·able
re·triev·al
re·trieve
re·triev·er
ret·ro·ac·tive
ret·ro·cede
ret·ro·ces·sion
ret·ro·fire
ret·ro·grade
ret·ro·gress
ret·ro·gres·sion
ret·ro-rock·et
ret·ro·spect
ret·ro·spec·tion
ret·ro·spec·tive
re·turn
re·turn·able
re·turn·ee
re·uni·fi·ca·tion
re·uni·fy
re·union
re·unite

re·us·able
re·use
rev
revved
rev·ving
re·val·u·ate
re·val·u·a·tion
re·val·ue
re·vamp
re·vanche
re·vanch·ist
re·veal
rev·eil·le
rev·el
rev·eled
or **rev·elled**
rev·el·ing
or **rev·el·ling**
rev·e·la·tion
rev·el·er
or **rev·el·ler**
rev·el·ry
re·venge
re·venge·ful
re·veng·er
rev·e·nue
rev·e·nu·er
re·ver·ber·ate
re·ver·ber·a·tion
re·vere
rev·er·ence
rev·er·end
rev·er·ent
rev·er·en·tial
rev·er·ie
or **rev·ery**
re·vers
lapel (*see* **reverse**)
re·ver·sal
re·verse
opposite (*see* **revers**)
re·vers·ibil·i·ty
re·vers·ible
re·vers·ibly
re·ver·sion
re·ver·sion·ary
re·vert
re·vert·ible
re·view
re·view·er
re·vile
re·vil·er
re·vis·able
re·vise
re·vis·er
or **re·vi·sor**
re·vi·sion
re·vi·sion·ism
re·vi·so·ry
re·vi·tal·iza·tion
re·vi·tal·ize
re·viv·al
re·viv·al·ist
re·vive
re·viv·i·fy
re·vo·ca·ble
re·vo·ca·tion
re·voke
re·vok·er
re·volt
re·volt·ing
rev·o·lu·tion
rev·o·lu·tion·ary
rev·o·lu·tion·ist
rev·o·lu·tion·ize
re·volv·able
re·volve
re·volv·er
re·volv·ing
re·vue
re·vul·sion
re·wake
re·wak·en
re·ward
re·wind
re·wound
re·wind·ing
re·work
re·write
re·wrote
re·writ·ten
re·writ·ing
re·zone
rhap·sod·ic
rhap·sod·i·cal·ly
rhap·so·dize
rhap·so·dy
rheo·stat
rhe·sus mon·key
rhet·o·ric
rhe·tor·i·cal
rhe·tor·i·cal·ly
rhet·o·ri·cian

rheu·mat·ic
rheu·mat·i·cal·ly
rheu·ma·tism
rheu·ma·toid
rheumy
Rh factor
rhine·stone
rhi·noc·er·os
rhi·zome
Rhode Is·land
rho·di·um
rho·do·den·dron
rhom·boid
or **rhom·boi·dal**
rhom·bus
rhu·barb
rhyme
rhy·o·lite
rhythm
rhyth·mic
or **rhyth·mi·cal**
rhyth·mi·cal·ly
ri·al
ri·al·to
rib
ribbed
rib·bing
rib·ald
rib·ald·ry
rib·bon
ri·bo·fla·vin
rich·es
rich·ly
Rich·mond
rich·ness
rick·ets
rick·ett·sia
pl **rick·ett·si·as** *or* **rick·ett·si·ae**
rick·ety
rick·ey
rick·sha
or **rick·shaw**
ric·o·chet
ric·o·cheted
or **ric·o·chet·ted**
ric·o·chet·ing
or **ric·o·chet·ting**
ric·tus
rid
rid
also **rid·ded**
rid·ding
rid·able
or **ride·able**
rid·dance
rid·dle
ride
rode
rid·den
rid·ing
rid·er
ridge
ridge·pole
rid·i·cule
ri·dic·u·lous
ri·ding
ri·el
rif·fle
riff·raff
ri·fle
ri·fling
rig
rigged
rig·ging
rig·ger
one that rigs (*see* **rigor**)
right
correct (*see* **rite**)
right-an·gled
or **right-an·gle**
righ·teous
right·ful
right·ful·ly
right-hand
right-hand·ed
right·ist
right·ly
right-of-way
right-wing·er
rig·id
ri·gid·i·ty
rig·ma·role
rig·or
severity (*see* **rigger**)
rig·or·ous
rim
rimmed
rim·ming
rin·der·pest
ring
encircle
ringed
ring·ing

ring
sound
rang
rung
ring·ing

ring·er
ring·lead·er
ring·let
ring·mas·ter
ring·side
ring·worm
rink
rins·ing
ri·ot
ri·ot·er
ri·ot·ous
rip
ripped
rip·ping
ri·par·i·an
ripe·ly
rip·en
ripe·ness
ri·poste
rip·per
rip·ple
rip·saw
rip·tide
rise
rose
ris·en
ris·ing
ris·er
ris·i·bil·i·ty

ris·i·ble
risk·i·ness
risky
ris·qué
rite
ceremony (*see* right)
rit·u·al
rit·u·al·ism
rit·u·al·is·tic
rit·u·al·is·ti·cal·ly
rit·u·al·ly
ri·val
ri·valed
or ri·valled
ri·val·ing
or ri·val·ling
ri·val·ry
rive
rived
riv·en
also rived
riv·ing
riv·er
riv·er·bed
ri·ver·boat
riv·er·side
riv·et
riv·et·er
riv·u·let
ri·yal
roach
road·abil·i·ty
road·bed
road·block
road·house

road·run·ner
road·side
road·ster
road·way
road·work
roam·er
roan
roar·ing
roast·er
rob
robbed
rob·bing
rob·ber
rob·bery
rob·in
ro·bot
ro·bust
Roch·es·ter
rock·bound
rock·er
rock·et
rock·et·ry
rock·fish
Rock·ford
rock-ribbed
rocky
ro·co·co
ro·dent
ro·deo
pl ro·de·os
roe
deer, fish eggs (*see* row)
roe·buck
roent·gen

ro·ga·tion
rog·er
rogue
rogu·ery
rogu·ish
roil
rile (*see* royal)
rois·ter
rois·ter·er
role
also rôle
part (*see* roll)
roll
list, bread, move (*see* role)
roll·back
roll·er
roll·er-skate
verb
rol·lick
ro·ly-po·ly
ro·maine
ro·man à clef
pl ro·mans à clef
ro·mance
ro·man·tic
ro·man·ti·cal·ly
ro·man·ti·cism
ro·man·ti·cist
ro·man·ti·ci·za·tion
ro·man·ti·cize
romp·er
ron·do
pl ron·dos
roof·ing
roof·top
rook·ery
rook·ie
room·er
lodger (*see* rumor)
room·ette
room·ful
room·i·ness
room·mate
roomy
roost·er
root
plant part (*see* route)
root·er
root·less
root·let
root·stock
rop·er
rope·way
ro·sa·ry
ro·sé
ro·se·ate
rose-col·ored
rose·mary
ro·se·o·la
ro·sette
rose·wood
Rosh Ha·sha·nah
ros·i·ly
ros·in
ros·i·ness
ros·in·ous
ros·ter
ros·trum
pl ros·trums *or* ros·tra
rosy
rot
rot·ted
rot·ting
Ro·tar·i·an
ro·ta·ry
ro·tat·able
ro·tate
ro·ta·tion
ro·ta·tor
ro·ti·fer
ro·tis·ser·ie
ro·to·gra·vure
ro·tor
rot·ten
rot·ten·ness
ro·tund
ro·tun·da
ro·tun·di·ty
roué
rouge
rough
uneven (*see* ruff)
rough·age
rough-and-ready
rough-and-tum·ble
rough·cast
rough-dry
rough·en
rough-hew
rough·house
rough·ish
rough·neck
rough·shod
rou·lade

rou·lette
round·about
round·ed
roun·de·lay
round·er
round·house
round·ish
round·ly
round-shoul·dered
round·up
round·worm
rous·ing
roust·about
rout
mob, rummage, defeat (*see* route)
route
way (*see* root, rout)
route·man
rou·tine
row
propel, quarrel, line (*see* roe)
row·boat
row·di·ly
row·di·ness
row·dy
row·dy·ish
row·dy·ism
row·el
roy·al
kingly (*see* roil)
roy·al·ist
roy·al·ly
roy·al·ty
rub
rubbed
rub·bing
rub·ber
rub·ber·ize
rub·ber-stamp
verb
rub·bery
rub·bing
rub·bish
rub·ble
waste (*see* ruble)
rub·down
ru·bel·la
ru·be·o·la
ru·ble
currency (*see* rubble)
ru·bric
ru·by
ruck·sack
ruck·us
rud·der
rud·di·ness
rud·dy
rude·ly
rude·ness
ru·di·ment
ru·di·men·ta·ry
rue
rue·ful
rue·ful·ly
ruff
collar (*see* rough)
ruf·fi·an
ruf·fle
rug·ged
ru·in
ru·in·ation
ru·in·ous
rul·er
rul·ing
Ru·ma·nia
or Ro·ma·nia
or Rou·ma·nia
rum·ba
rum·ble
ru·mi·nant
ru·mi·nate
ru·mi·na·tion
rum·mage
rum·my
ru·mor
hearsay (*see* roomer)
ru·mor·mon·ger
rum·ple
rum·pus
run
ran
run
run·ning
run·about
run·around
run·away
run·down
summary
run-down
dilapidated
rung
crosspiece (*see* wrung)
run-in

run•ner
run•ner-up
pl run•ners-up *also* run•ner-ups
run•ning
run•ny
run•off
run-on
run•way
ru•pee
ru•pi•ah
pl ru•pi•ah *or* ru•pi•ahs
rup•ture
ru•ral
rush•er
rus•set
Rus•sia
Rus•sian
rus•tic
rus•ti•cal•ly
rus•ti•cate
rus•ti•ca•tion
rust•i•ly
rust•i•ness
rus•tle
rus•tler
rust•proof
rusty
rut
rut•ted
rut•ting
ru•ta•ba•ga
ruth•less
Rwan•da
Rwan•dan
rye
grain (*see* wry)

S

Sab•bath
sab•bat•i•cal
sa•ber
or sa•bre
sa•ble
sa•ble•fish
sa•bot
sab•o•tage
sab•o•teur
sac
pouch of animal or plant (*see* sack)
sac•cha•rin
noun
sac•cha•rine
adj
sac•er•do•tal
sac•er•do•tal•ly
sa•chem
sa•chet
small bag (*see* sashay)
sack
bag, fire (*see* sac)
sack•cloth
sack•ful
pl sack•fuls *or* sacks•ful
sack•ing
sac•ra•ment
sac•ra•men•tal
sac•ra•men•tal•ly
Sac•ra•men•to
sa•cred
sac•ri•fice
sac•ri•fi•cial
sac•ri•fi•cial•ly
sac•ri•lege
sac•ri•le•gious
sac•ris•tan
sac•ris•ty
sa•cro•il•i•ac
sac•ro•sanct
sa•crum
pl sa•cra
sad•den
sad•dle
sad•dle•bag
sad•dle•bow
sad•dle•cloth
sad•iron
sa•dism
sa•dist
sa•dis•tic
sa•dis•ti•cal•ly
sa•fa•ri
safe-con•duct
safe-de•pos•it
safe•guard
safe•keep•ing
safe•light
safe•ty
saf•flow•er
saf•fron

sag
sagged
sag·ging

sa·ga

sa·ga·cious

sa·gac·i·ty

sage·brush

sage·ly

sa·go

sail·boat

sail·cloth

sail·er
ship (*see* sailor)

sail·fish

sail·ing

sail·or
one who sails (*see* sailer)

saint·hood

saint·li·ness

Saint Lou·is

saint·ly

Saint Paul

Saint Pe·ters·burg

sake
purpose

sa·ke
or **sa·ki**
rice wine

sa·laam

sal·abil·i·ty

sal·able
or **sale·able**

sa·la·cious

sal·ad

sal·a·man·der

sa·la·mi

sal·a·ried

sal·a·ry

Sa·lem

sal·era·tus

sales·clerk

sales·girl

sales·la·dy

sales·man

sales·man·ship

sales·peo·ple

sales·room

sales·wom·an

sa·lience

sa·lient

sa·line

sa·lin·i·ty

sa·li·va

sal·i·vary

sal·i·vate

sal·i·va·tion

sal·low

sal·ly

salm·on
pl **salm·on** *also* **salm·ons**

sal·mo·nel·la
pl **sal·mo·nel·lae** *or* **sal·mo·nel·las** *or* **sal·mo·nel·la**

sa·lon

sa·loon

salt·box

salt·cel·lar

salt·er

sal·tine

salt·i·ness

Salt Lake City

salt·pe·ter

salt·shak·er

salt·wa·ter

salt·wort

salty

sa·lu·bri·ous

sal·u·tary

sal·u·ta·tion

sa·lu·ta·to·ri·an

sa·lu·ta·to·ry

sa·lute

salv·able

Sal·va·dor

Sal·va·do·ran

sal·vage

sal·vage·able

sal·va·tion

sal·ver

sal·vo
pl **sal·vos** *or* **sal·voes**

sa·ma·ra

Sa·mar·i·tan

sam·ba

same·ness

sam·o·var

sam·pan

sam·ple

sam·pler

sam·pling

San An·to·nio

san·a·tar·i·um
pl **san·a·tar·i·ums** *or* **san·a·tar·ia**

san•a•to•ri•um
pl san•a•to•ri•ums *or* san•a•to•ria

San Ber•nar•di•no

sanc•ti•fi•ca•tion

sanc•ti•fy

sanc•ti•mo•nious

sanc•ti•mo•ny

sanc•tion

sanc•ti•ty

sanc•tu•ary

sanc•tum
pl sanc•tums *also* sanc•ta

san•dal

san•dal•wood

sand•bag

sand•bank

sand•bar

sand•blast

sand•box

sand•er

San Di•ego

sand•hog

sand•i•ness

sand•lot

sand•man

sand•pa•per

sand•pip•er

sand•soap

sand•stone

sand•storm

sand•wich

sandy

sane•ly

San Fran•cis•co

sang•froid

san•gría

san•gui•nary

san•guine

san•i•tar•i•ly

san•i•tar•i•um

san•i•tary

san•i•ta•tion

san•i•tize

san•i•ty

San Jo•se

San Juan

San Ma•ri•no

San•ta Ana

San•ta Fe

São To•mé and Prín•ci•pe

sap
sapped
sap•ping

sa•pi•ence

sa•pi•ent

sap•ling

sap•phire

sap•py

sap•suck•er

sap•wood

sa•ran

sa•ra•pe
var of serape

sar•casm

sar•cas•tic

sar•cas•ti•cal•ly

sar•co•ma
pl sar•co•mas *or* sar•co•ma•ta

sar•coph•a•gus
pl sar•coph•a•gi *also* sar•coph•a•gus•es

sar•dine

sar•don•ic

sar•don•i•cal•ly

sa•ri
or sa•ree
garment (*see* sorry)

sa•rong

sar•sa•pa•ril•la

sar•to•ri•al

Sas•katch•e•wan

sa•shay
walk (*see* sachet)

Sas•ka•toon

sas•sa•fras

sassy

sa•tang

sa•tan•ic

sa•tan•i•cal•ly

satch•el

sa•teen

sat•el•lite

sa•tia•ble

sa•tiate
adj

sa•ti•ate
verb

sa•ti•ety

sat•in

sat•in•wood

sat•iny

sat·ire
sa·tir·ic
or sa·tir·i·cal
sa·tir·i·cal·ly
sat·i·rist
sat·i·rize
sat·is·fac·tion
sat·is·fac·to·ri·ly
sat·is·fac·to·ry
sat·is·fi·able
sat·is·fy
sa·trap
sat·u·rant
sat·u·rate
sat·u·ra·tion
Sat·ur·day
sat·ur·nine
sa·tyr
sa·ty·ri·a·sis
sauce·pan
sau·cer
sauc·i·ly
sauc·i·ness
saucy
Sau·di
Sau·di Ara·bia
Sau·di Ara·bi·an
sau·er·kraut
sau·na
saun·ter
sau·sage
sau·té
sau·téed
or sau·téd
sau·té·ing

sau·terne
sav·age
sav·age·ly
sav·age·ry
Sa·van·nah
sa·vant
sav·able
or save·able
sav·er
one that saves (*see* savor)
sav·ing
sav·ior
or sav·iour
sa·voir faire
sa·vor
also sa·vour
flavor (*see* saver)
sa·vor·i·ly
sa·vor·i·ness
sa·vory
appetizing
sa·vo·ry
also sa·voury
herb
saw
sawed
sawed
or sawn
saw·ing
saw·dust
sawed-off
saw·horse
saw·mill
saw-toothed
sax·o·phone

sax·o·phon·ist
say
said
say·ing
say·able
say·ing
say-so
scab
scabbed
scab·bing
scab·bard
scab·by
sca·bies
scab·rous
scaf·fold
scaf·fold·ing
scal·able
scal·age
scal·a·wag
scald·ing
scaled
scale-down
scale·less
scale-up
scal·i·ness
scal·lion
scal·lop
scal·pel
scalp·er
scaly
scam·per
scam·pi

scan
scanned
scan·ning
scan·dal
scan·dal·ize
scan·dal·mon·ger
scan·dal·ous
scan·ner
scant·i·ly
scant·i·ness
scant·ling
scanty
scape·goat
scape·grace
scap·u·la
pl scap·u·lae *or* scap·u·las
scap·u·lar
scar
scarred
scar·ring
scar·ab
scarce·ly
scar·ci·ty
scare·crow
scarf
pl scarves *or* scarfs
scar·i·fi·ca·tion
scar·i·fy
scar·let
scary
also scar·ey
scat
scat·ted
scat·ting
scath·ing
scat·o·log·i·cal
scat·ter
scat·ter·brained
scat·ter·ing
scav·enge
scav·en·ger
sce·nar·io
sce·nar·ist
scene
stage setting (*see* see)
sce·nery
sce·nic
sce·ni·cal·ly
scent
smell (*see* sent)
scep·ter
sched·ule
sche·ma
pl sche·ma·ta
sche·mat·ic
sche·mat·i·cal·ly
scheme
schem·er
schem·ing
scher·zo
pl scher·zos *or* scher·zi
schil·ling
schism
schis·mat·ic
schis·to·so·mi·a·sis
schiz·oid
schizo·phre·nia
schizo·phren·ic
schol·ar
schol·ar·ly
schol·ar·ship
scho·las·tic
scho·las·ti·cal·ly
scho·las·ti·cism
school·bag
school·boy
school·child
pl school·chil·dren
school·girl
school·house
school·ing
school·marm
school·mate
school·room
school·teach·er
school·work
schoo·ner
sci·at·i·ca
sci·ence
sci·en·tif·ic
sci·en·tif·i·cal·ly
sci·en·tist
scim·i·tar
scin·til·la
scin·til·late
scin·til·la·tion
sci·on
scis·sors
scle·ro·sis
scoff·er
scoff·law
scold·ing
scone

scoop•ful
scoot•er
scorch•er
scorch•ing
score
pl scores *or* score
scor•er
score•board
score•card
score•keep•er
score•less
scorn•er
scorn•ful
scorn•ful•ly
scor•pi•on
scot-free
scoun•drel
scour
scourge
scout•ing
scout•mas•ter
scowl
scrab•ble
scrag•gly
scrag•gy
scram•ble
Scran•ton
scrap
scrapped
scrap•ping
scrap•book
scrap•er
scrap•per
scrap•ple
scrap•py
scratch
scratch•i•ness
scratchy
scrawl
scraw•ni•ness
scraw•ny
scream•er
screech
screen•able
screen•ing
screen•play
screen•writ•er
screw•ball
screw•driv•er
screw•worm
scrib•ble
scrib•bler
scrim•mage
scrim•mag•er
scrimpy
scrim•shaw
scrip
certificate (*see* script)
script
writing (*see* scrip)
scrip•tur•al
scrip•tur•al•ly
scrip•ture
script•writ•er
scriv•en•er
scroll•work
scro•tum
pl scro•ta *or* scro•tums
scroung•er
scroung•ing
scrub
scrubbed
scrub•bing
scrub•by
scruffy
scrump•tious
scru•ple
scru•pu•lous
scru•ta•ble
scru•ti•nize
scru•ti•ny
scu•ba
scuf•fle
scull
boat (*see* skull)
scul•lery
scul•lion
scul•pin
pl scul•pins *also* scul•pin
sculp•tor
sculp•tur•al
sculp•tur•al•ly
sculp•ture
scum•my
scup•per
scup•per•nong
scur•ril•i•ty
scur•ri•lous
scur•ry
scur•vy
scutch•eon
scut•tle
scut•tle•butt

sea·bag
sea·bed
sea·bird
sea·board
sea·borne
sea·coast
sea·far·er
sea·far·ing
sea·food
sea·go·ing
sea-lane
seal·ant
seal·skin
sea·man
sea·man·ship
seam·i·ness
seam·less
sea·mount
seam·stress
seamy
sé·ance
sea·plane
sea·port
sear
burn (*see* seer)
search·er
search·light
sea·scape
sea·shell
sea·shore
sea·sick
sea·side
sea·son
sea·son·able
sea·son·ably
sea·son·al
sea·son·ing
seat·ing
Se·at·tle
sea·wall
sea·ward
also sea·wards
sea·wa·ter
sea·way
sea·weed
sea·wor·thy
se·ba·ceous
se·cant
se·cede
se·ces·sion
se·ces·sion·ist
se·clude
se·clu·sion
sec·ond
sec·ond·ari·ly
sec·ond·ary
sec·ond-best
sec·ond-class
sec·ond-guess
sec·ond·hand
sec·ond·ly
sec·ond-rate
se·cre·cy
se·cret
sec·re·tari·al
sec·re·tar·i·at
sec·re·tary
se·crete
se·cre·tion
se·cre·tive
se·cre·to·ry
sect
sec·tar·i·an
sec·tion
sec·tion·al
sec·tion·al·ly
sec·tion·al·ism
sec·tor
sec·u·lar
sec·u·lar·ism
sec·u·lar·iza·tion
sec·u·lar·ize
se·cure
se·cure·ly
se·cu·ri·ty
se·dan
se·date
se·date·ly
se·da·tion
sed·a·tive
sed·en·tary
sed·i·ment
sed·i·men·ta·ry
sed·i·men·ta·tion
se·di·tion
se·di·tious
se·duce
se·duc·er
se·duc·tion
se·duc·tive
se·duc·tress
se·du·li·ty
sed·u·lous

see
perceive (*see* scene)
saw
seen
see·ing

see·able

seed
pl seed *or* seeds

seed·er

seed·i·ly

seed·i·ness

seed·ling

seed·time

seek
sought
seek·ing

seek·er

seem·ing

seem·li·ness

seem·ly

seep·age

seer
prophet (*see* sear)

seer·suck·er

see·saw

seethe

seeth·ing

seg·ment

seg·men·tal

seg·men·tal·ly

seg·men·tary

seg·men·ta·tion

seg·re·gate

seg·re·gat·ed

seg·re·ga·tion

seg·re·ga·tion·ist

seis·mic

seis·mo·graph

seis·mog·ra·pher

seis·mo·graph·ic

seis·mog·ra·phy

seis·mol·o·gist

seis·mol·o·gy

seize

sei·zure

sel·dom

se·lect

se·lect·ee

se·lec·tion

se·lec·tive

se·lec·tiv·i·ty

se·lect·man

se·lec·tor

self
pl selves

self-ab·ne·ga·tion

self-ac·cu·sa·tion

self-act·ing

self-ad·dressed

self-ad·just·ing

self-anal·y·sis

self-ap·point·ed

self-as·sert·ing

self-as·ser·tion

self-as·sur·ance

self-as·sured

self-cen·tered

self-com·mand

self-con·fi·dence

self-con·scious

self-con·tained

self-con·trol

self-con·trolled

self-crit·i·cism

self-de·feat·ing

self-de·fense

self-de·ter·mi·na·tion

self-dis·ci·pline

self-ed·u·cat·ed

self-ef·fac·ing

self-em·ployed

self-ev·i·dent

self-ex·plan·a·to·ry

self-ex·pres·sion

self-gov·erned

self-gov·ern·ing

self-im·age

self-im·por·tance

self-im·posed

self-im·prove·ment

self-in·crim·i·na·tion

self-in·dul·gence

self-in·flict·ed

self-in·ter·est

self·ish

self·less

self-liq·ui·dat·ing

self-load·ing

self-lock·ing

self-made

self-mail·ing

self-op·er·at·ing

self-per·pet·u·at·ing

self-per·pet·u·a·tion
self-pity
self-pity·ing
self-por·trait
self-pos·sessed
self-pres·er·va·tion
self-pro·claimed
self-pro·pelled
self-pro·tec·tion
self-reg·u·lat·ing
self-re·li·ance
self-re·spect
self-righ·teous
self-ris·ing
self-rule
self-sac·ri·fice
self-same
self-sat·is·fac·tion
self-sat·is·fied
self-seal·ing
self-seek·ing
self-ser·vice
self-start·ing
self-styled
self-suf·fi·cien·cy
self-suf·fi·cient
self-sus·tain·ing
self-taught
self-wind·ing
sell
  sold
  sell·ing
sell·er
sel·vage
  or sel·vedge
selves
se·man·tic
  also se·man·ti·cal
se·man·tics
sem·a·phore
sem·blance
se·men
se·mes·ter
semi·an·nu·al
semi·an·nu·al·ly
semi·ar·id
semi·au·to·mat·ic
semi·cir·cle
semi·cir·cu·lar
semi·co·lon
semi·con·duc·tor
semi·con·scious
semi·fi·nal
semi·flu·id
semi·for·mal
semi·lu·nar
semi·month·ly
sem·i·nal
sem·i·nar
sem·i·nar·i·an
sem·i·nary
semi·of·fi·cial
se·mi·ot·ic
  or se·mi·ot·ics
semi·per·me·able
semi·pre·cious
semi·pri·vate
semi·pro·fes·sion·al
semi·pub·lic
semi·rig·id
semi·skilled
semi·soft
semi·sol·id
semi·sweet
Sem·ite
Se·mit·ic
semi·trail·er
semi·trop·i·cal
  also semi·trop·ic
semi·week·ly
semi·works
semi·year·ly
sen
  pl sen
sen·ate
sen·a·tor
sen·a·to·ri·al
send
  sent
  send·ing
se·ne
Sen·e·gal
Sen·e·ga·lese
se·nes·cence
sen·gi
  pl sen·gi
se·nile
se·nil·i·ty
se·nior
se·nior·i·ty
sen·i·ti
  pl sen·i·ti
sen·na
sen·sa·tion
sen·sa·tion·al

sen•sa•tion•al•ly
sense•less
sen•si•bil•i•ty
sen•si•ble
sen•si•bly
sen•si•tive
sen•si•tiv•i•ty
sen•si•ti•za•tion
sen•si•tize
sen•so•ry
sen•su•al
sen•su•al•i•ty
sen•su•al•ly
sen•su•ous
sen•tence
sen•ten•tious
sen•ti
pl sen•ti
sen•tient
sen•ti•ment
sen•ti•men•tal
sen•ti•men•tal•i•ty
sen•ti•men•tal•ize
sen•ti•men•tal•ly
sen•ti•mo
sen•ti•nel
sen•try
se•pal
sep•a•ra•ble
sep•a•rate
sep•a•rate•ly
sep•a•ra•tion
sep•a•rat•ist
sep•a•ra•tive
sep•a•ra•tor

se•pia
sep•sis
pl sep•ses
Sep•tem•ber
sep•tic
sep•ti•ce•mia
sep•tu•a•ge•nar•i•an
sep•ul•cher
or sep•ul•chre
se•pul•chral
se•quel
se•quence
se•quen•tial
se•ques•ter
se•ques•trate
se•ques•tra•tion
se•quin
se•quoia
se•ra•glio
ser•a•pe
or sa•ra•pe
ser•aph
also ser•a•phim
pl ser•a•phim *or* ser•aphs
se•raph•ic
ser•e•nade
ser•en•dip•i•ty
se•rene
se•rene•ly
se•ren•i•ty
serf
peasant (*see* surf)
serf•dom
serge
cloth (*see* surge)

ser•geant
se•ri•al
of a series (*see* cereal)
se•ri•al•iza•tion
se•ri•al•ize
se•ri•al•ly
se•ries
pl se•ries
seri•graph
se•ri•ous
ser•mon
se•rous
ser•pent
ser•pen•tine
ser•rate
se•rum
pl se•rums *or* se•ra
ser•vant
ser•vice
ser•vice•abil•i•ty
ser•vice•able
ser•vice•man
ser•vile
ser•vil•i•ty
serv•ing
ser•vi•tor
ser•vi•tude
ser•vo•mech•a•nism
ses•a•me
ses•qui•cen•ten•ni•al
ses•sion
meeting (*see* cession)
set
set
set•ting

set·back
set·screw
set·tee
set·ter
set·ting
set·tle
set·tle·ment
set·tler
set·to
pl set·tos
set-up
sev·en
sev·en·teen
sev·en·ti·eth
sev·en·ty
sev·er
sev·er·al
sev·er·al·ly
sev·er·ance
se·vere
se·vere·ly
se·ver·i·ty
sew
stitch (*see* sow)
sewed
sewn
or sewed
sew·ing
sew·age
sew·er
sew·er·age
sex·a·ge·nar·i·an
sex·i·ness
sex·less
sex-linked
sex·tant
sex·tet
sex·ton
sex·u·al
sex·u·al·i·ty
sex·u·al·ly
Sey·chelles
shab·bi·ly
shab·bi·ness
shab·by
shack·le
shad·i·ly
shad·i·ness
shad·ing
shad·ow
shad·ow·box
shad·owy
shady
shag
shagged
shag·ging
shag·gi·ly
shag·gi·ness
shag·gy
shak·able
or shake·able
shake
shook
shak·en
shak·ing
shake·down
shak·er
shake-up
shak·i·ly
shak·i·ness
sha·ko
pl sha·kos *or* sha·koes
shaky
shal·lop
shal·low
sham
shammed
sham·ming
sha·man
sham·ble
sham·bles
shame·faced
shame·faced·ly
shame·ful
shame·ful·ly
shame·less
sham·mer
sham·my
var of chamois
sham·poo
sham·rock
shang·hai
shan·tung
shan·ty
shan·ty·town
shap·able
or shape·able
shape·less
shape·li·ness
shape·ly
share·crop·per
share·hold·er
shar·er

shark•skin

sharp•en

sharp-eyed

sharp•shoot•er

sharp-tongued

shat•ter

shave
  shaved
  shaved
    or shav•en
  shav•ing

shawl

sheaf
  pl sheaves

shear
  clip (*see* sheer)
  sheared
  sheared
    or shorn
  shear•ing

shears

sheath
  noun

sheathe
  verb
  also sheath

sheathed

sheath•ing

she•bang

shed
  shed
  shed•ding

sheen

sheep•fold

sheep•ish

sheep•skin

sheer
  thin, swerve (*see* shear)

sheet•ing

Sheet•rock

sheikh
  or sheik

shelf
  pl shelves

shel•lac
  shel•lacked
  shel•lack•ing

shell•fish

shell•proof

shell•work

shel•ter

shel•ter•belt

shelv•ing

she•nan•i•gan

shep•herd

shep•herd•ess

sher•bet
  or sher•bert

sher•iff

sher•ry

shib•bo•leth

shield

shift•i•ly

shift•i•ness

shift•less

shifty

shi•lingi
  pl shi•lingi

shil•le•lagh
  also shil•la•lah

shil•ling

shilly-shally

shim•mer

shim•mery

shim•my

shin
  shinned
  shin•ning

shin•bone

shin•dig

shine
  shone
    or shined
  shin•ing

shin•er

shin•gle

shin•gles

shin•i•ness

shiny

ship
  shipped
  ship•ping

ship•board

ship•build•ing

ship•mate

ship•ment

ship•per

ship•ping

ship•shape

ship•worm

ship•wreck

ship•wright

ship•yard

shirk•er

shirr
shirr·ing
shirt·ing
shirt·tail
shirt·waist
shiv·er
shoal
shock·er
shock·ing
shod·di·ly
shod·di·ness
shod·dy
shoe
  shod
    also shoed
  shoe·ing
shoe·horn
shoe·lace
shoe·mak·er
shoe·string
shoo·fly
shoo-in
shoot
  let fly (*see* chute)
  shot
  shoot·ing
shoot·er
shop
  shopped
  shop·ping
shop·keep·er
shop·lift·er
shop·per
shop·talk
shop·worn
sho·ran
shore·bird
shor·ing
short·age
short·bread
short·cake
short·change
short-cir·cuit
short·com·ing
short·cut
short·en
short·en·ing
short·hand
short·hand·ed
short·horn
short-lived
short·ly
short·sight·ed
short·stop
short-tem·pered
short-term
short·wave
short-wind·ed
shot·gun
should
shoul·der
shov·el
  shov·eled
    or shov·elled
  shov·el·ing
    or shov·el·ling
shov·el·ful
  pl shov·el·fuls
    also shov·els·ful
show
  showed
  shown
    or showed
  show·ing
show·boat
show·case
show·down
show·er
show·ery
show·i·ly
show·i·ness
show·man
show·piece
show·place
show·room
showy
shrap·nel
shred
  shred·ded
  shred·ding
Shreve·port
shrew
shrewd
shrew·ish
shriek
shrift
shrike
shrill·ness
shril·ly
shrine

shrink
  shrank
    also shrunk
  shrunk
    or shrunk•en

shrink•able

shrink•age

shrive
  shrived
    or shrove
  shriv•en
    or shrived
  shriv•ing

shriv•el
  shriv•eled
    or shriv•elled
  shriv•el•ing
    or shriv•el•ling

shrub•bery

shrug
  shrugged
  shrug•ging

shuck

shud•der

shuf•fle

shuf•fle•board

shun
  shunned
  shun•ning

shunt

shut
  shut
  shut•ting

shut•down

shut-in

shut•off

shut•out

shut•ter

shut•tle

shut•tle•cock

shy
  shied
  shy•ing

shy
  shi•er
    or shy•er
  shi•est
    or shy•est

shy•ly

shy•ness

shy•ster

Si•a•mese
  pl Si•a•mese

sib•i•lant

sib•ling

sib•yl

sib•yl•line

sick•bed

sick•en

sick•le

sick•li•ness

sick•ly

sick•ness

sick•room

side•arm

side•board

side•burns

side•car

side-glance

side•kick

side•light

side•line

side•long

side•man

side•piece

si•de•re•al

side•sad•dle

side•show

side•slip

side•spin

side•split•ting

side•step

side•stroke

side•swipe

side•track

side•walk

side•ways

sid•ing

si•dle

siege

si•er•ra

Si•er•ra Le•one

si•es•ta

sieve

sift•er

sigh

sight
  view (*see* cite, site)

sight•ed

sight•less

sight•ly

sight-read

sight-see•ing

sight•seer

sign
mark (*see* sine)

sig·nal
sig·naled
or **sig·nalled**
sig·nal·ing
or **sig·nal·ling**

sig·nal·ize
sig·nal·ly
sig·na·to·ry
sig·na·ture
sign·board
sign·er
sig·net
sig·nif·i·cance
sig·nif·i·cant
sig·ni·fi·ca·tion
sig·ni·fy
sign·post
si·lage
si·lence
si·lenc·er
si·lent
sil·hou·ette
sil·i·ca
sil·i·cate
si·li·ceous
or **si·li·cious**

sil·i·cone
sil·i·co·sis
silk·en
silk·i·ly
silk·i·ness
silk-screen
silk·weed
silk·worm
silky
sil·li·ness
sil·ly
si·lo
pl **si·los**

sil·ver
sil·ver·fish
sil·ver·smith
sil·ver-tongued
sil·ver·ware
sil·very
sil·vi·cul·ture
sim·i·an
sim·i·lar
sim·i·lar·i·ty
sim·i·lar·ly
sim·i·le
si·mil·i·tude
sim·mer
si·mo·nize
si·mo·ny
sim·per
sim·ple
sim·ple·mind·ed
sim·ple·ton
sim·plic·i·ty
sim·pli·fi·ca·tion
sim·pli·fi·er
sim·pli·fy
sim·ply
sim·u·late
sim·u·la·tion
sim·u·la·tor
si·mul·ta·ne·ous
sin
sinned
sin·ning

sin·cere
sin·cere·ly
sin·cer·i·ty
sine
math (*see* sign)

si·ne·cure
si·ne die
si·ne qua non
sin·ew
sin·ewy
sin·ful
sin·ful·ly
sing
sang
or **sung**
sung
sing·ing

Sin·ga·pore
singe
singed
singe·ing

sing·er
sin·gle
sin·gle-breast·ed
sin·gle-hand·ed
sin·gle-mind·ed
sin·gle-space
sin·gle·ton
sin·gle-track
sin·gly
sing·song

sin·gu·lar

sin·gu·lar·i·ty

sin·is·ter

sink
  sank
    or **sunk**
  sunk
  sink·ing

sink·able

sink·age

sink·er

sink·hole

sin·ner

sin·u·os·i·ty

sin·u·ous

si·nus

si·nus·itis

sip
  sipped
  sip·ping

si·phon

si·ren

sir·loin

si·roc·co
  pl **si·roc·cos**

si·sal

sis·ter

sis·ter·hood

sis·ter-in-law
  pl **sis·ters-in-law**

sis·ter·ly

sit
  sat
  sit·ting

si·tar

sit-down

site
  location (*see* **cite, sight**)

sit-in

sit·ter

sit·ting

sit·u·ate

sit·u·at·ed

sit·u·a·tion

six-pack

six·pence

six·pen·ny

six·teen

six·ti·eth

six·ty

siz·able
  or **size·able**

siz·ably

siz·ing

siz·zle

skate·board

skat·er

skein

skel·e·tal

skel·e·ton

skep·tic

skep·ti·cal

skep·ti·cal·ly

skep·ti·cism

sketch·book

sketch·i·ly

sketch·i·ness

sketchy

skew·er

ski
  pl **skis**

skid
  skid·ded
  skid·ding

ski·er

skiff

ski·ing

skil·let

skill·ful
  or **skil·ful**

skill·ful·ly

skim
  skimmed
  skim·ming

skim·mer

skimp·i·ly

skimp·i·ness

skimpy

skin
  skinned
  skin·ning

skin-deep

skin·flint

skin·ful

skin·ni·ness

skin·ny

skin·tight

skip
  skipped
  skip·ping

skip·jack

skip·per

skir·mish
skit·ter
skit·tish
ski·wear
skul·dug·gery
or skull·dug·gery
skulk·er
skull
skeleton of the head (*see* scull)
skull·cap
sky·borne
sky·diving
sky-high
sky·jack·er
sky·lark
sky·light
sky·line
sky·lounge
sky·rock·et
sky·scrap·er
sky·ward
sky·way
sky·writ·ing
slack·en
slack·er
slack·ly
sla·lom
slam
slammed
slam·ming
slam-bang
slan·der
slan·der·ous
slang·i·ness
slangy
slant·ways
slant·wise
slap
slapped
slap·ping
slap·dash
slap·hap·py
slap·stick
slash·ing
slat
slat·ted
slat·ting
slat·tern
slat·tern·li·ness
slaugh·ter
slaugh·ter·house
sla·ver
drool
slav·er
slave ship
slav·ery
slav·ish
slay
kill (*see* sleigh)
slew
slain
slay·ing
slay·er
slea·zi·ly
slea·zi·ness
slea·zy
sled
sled·ded
sled·ding
sledge·ham·mer
sleek·ly
sleep
slept
sleep·ing
sleep·er
sleep·i·ly
sleep·i·ness
sleep·less
sleep·walk
sleepy
sleeve·less
sleigh
snow vehicle (*see* slay)
sleight
dexterity (*see* slight)
slen·der
slen·der·ize
sleuth
slic·er
slick·er
slick·ly
slide
slid
slid·ing
slid·er
slight
frail (*see* sleight)
slim
slimmed
slim·ming

slim·i·ly
slim·i·ness
slim·ness
slimy
sling
  slung
  sling·ing
sling·shot
slink
  slunk
    also slinked
  slink·ing
slinky
slip
  slipped
  slip·ping
slip·case
slip·cov·er
slip·knot
slip-on
slip·over
slip·page
slip·per
slip·peri·ness
slip·pery
slip·shod
slip·stick
slip·stream
slip·up
slit
  slit
  slit·ting
slith·er
slith·ery
sliv·er
slob·ber
sloe
  fruit (*see* slow)
sloe-eyed
slog
  slogged
  slog·ging
slo·gan
sloop
slop
  slopped
  slop·ping
slop·pi·ly
slop·pi·ness
slop·py
slop·work
slosh
slot
  slot·ted
  slot·ting
sloth·ful
sloth·ful·ly
slouch·er
slouchy
slough
  or sluff
slov·en·li·ness
slov·en·ly
slow
  sluggish (*see* sloe)
slow·down
slow·poke
slow-wit·ted
sludge
sludgy
slug
  slugged
  slug·ging
slug·gard
slug·gish
sluice
sluice·way
slum
  slummed
  slum·ming
slum·ber
slum·ber·ous
  or slum·brous
slum·lord
slump
slur
  slurred
  slur·ring
slush·i·ness
slushy
slut·tish
sly
  sli·er
    also sly·er
  sli·est
    also sly·est
sly·ly
small·ish
small·pox
small-scale
small-time
smart·ly

smash·ing
smash·up
smat·ter
smat·ter·ing
smeary
smell
smelled
or smelt
smell·ing
smelly
smelt
pl smelts *or* smelt
smelt·er
smid·gen
or smid·geon *or* smid·gin
smi·lax
smil·ing·ly
smirch
smirk
smite
smote
smit·ten
or smote
smit·ing
smith·er·eens
smithy
smock·ing
smog·gy
smok·able
or smoke·able
smoke-filled
smoke·less
smoke·stack
smok·i·ly
smok·i·ness
smoky
also smok·ey
smol·der
or smoul·der
smooth·bore
smooth·en
smooth·ly
smooth-tongued
smor·gas·bord
smoth·er
smudge
smudg·i·ly
smudg·i·ness
smudgy
smug·gle
smug·gler
smug·ly
smut·ti·ly
smut·ti·ness
smut·ty
snaf·fle
sna·fu
snag
snagged
snag·ging
snail-paced
snake·bite
snake·like
snake·skin
snak·i·ly
snaky
snap
snapped
snap·ping
snap·back
snap-brim
snap·drag·on
snap·per
snap·pish
snap·py
snap·shot
snar·er
snarly
snatch
snaz·zy
sneak·er
sneak·i·ly
sneak·i·ness
sneak·ing
sneaky
sneer·er
snick·er
snif·fle
snif·ter
snig·ger
snip
snipped
snip·ping
snip·er·scope
snip·pet
snip·py
sniv·el
sniv·eled
or sniv·elled
sniv·el·ing
or sniv·el·ling
snob·bery
snob·bish
snoop·er

snoop·er·scope
snoopy
snor·kel
snout
snow·ball
snow-blind
or snow-blind·ed
snow·bound
snow·cap
snow·drift
snow·drop
snow·fall
snow·flake
snow·man
snow·mo·bile
snow·mo·bil·ing
snow·plow
snow·shoe
snow·storm
snow·suit
snowy
snub
snubbed
snub·bing
snub-nosed
snuff·er
snuf·fle
snug·gle
snug·ly
soak·age
so-and-so
pl so-and-sos
also so-and-so's
soap·box
soap·stone
soap·suds
soapy
soar
fly (*see* sore)
sob
sobbed
sob·bing
so·ber
so·bri·ety
so·bri·quet
so-called
soc·cer
so·cia·bil·i·ty
so·cia·ble
so·cia·bly
so·cial
so·cial·ism
so·cial·is·tic
so·cial·ite
so·cial·iza·tion
so·cial·ize
so·cial·ly
so·ci·etal
so·ci·etal·ly
so·ci·ety
so·cio·eco·nom·ic
so·cio·log·i·cal
so·cio·log·i·cal·ly
so·ci·ol·o·gist
so·ci·ol·o·gy
so·ci·om·e·try
so·cio·po·lit·i·cal
so·cio·re·li·gious
sock·et
sock·eye
sod
sod·ded
sod·ding
so·da
so·dal·i·ty
sod·den
so·di·um
sod·omy
so·ev·er
so·fa
soft·ball
soft-boiled
soft·bound
soft·en
soft·heart·ed
soft-ped·al
soft-shell
or soft-shelled
soft-soap
soft-spo·ken
soft·ware
soft·wood
sog·gi·ly
sog·gi·ness
sog·gy
soi·gné
or soi·gnée
soil·borne
soi·ree
or soi·rée
so·journ
sol
also so
musical note

sol
pl so•les
coin

so•lace

so•lar

so•lar•i•um
pl so•lar•ia *also* so•lar•i•ums

so•lar plex•us

sol•der

sol•dier

sole
undersurface, fish, only (*see* soul)

so•le•cism

sole•ly

sol•emn

so•lem•ni•fy

so•lem•ni•ty

sol•em•ni•za•tion

sol•em•nize

so•le•noid

so•le•noi•dal

sole•print

sol-fa

sol•fège

so•lic•it

so•lic•i•ta•tion

so•lic•i•tor

so•lic•i•tous

so•lic•i•tude

sol•id

sol•i•dar•i•ty

so•lid•i•fi•ca•tion

so•lid•i•fy

so•lid•i•ty

sol•id-state

so•lil•o•quize

so•lil•o•quy

so•lip•sism

sol•i•taire

sol•i•tary

sol•i•tude

so•lo
pl so•los

so•lo•ist

so•lon

sol•stice

sol•u•bil•i•ty

sol•u•ble

sol•u•bly

so•lu•tion

solv•abil•i•ty

solv•able

solve

sol•ven•cy

sol•vent

so•ma

So•ma•li
pl So•ma•li *or* So•ma•lis

So•ma•lia

So•ma•lian

so•mat•ic

so•ma•tol•o•gy

som•ber
or som•bre

som•bre•ro

some•body

some•day

some•how

some•one

some•place

som•er•sault

some•thing

some•time

some•times

some•what

some•where

som•me•lier

som•nam•bu•late

som•nam•bu•lism

som•nam•bu•list

som•no•lence

som•no•lent

so•nar

so•na•ta

son•a•ti•na

sonde

song•bird

song•book

song•ster

song•stress

song•writ•er

son•ic

son-in-law
pl sons-in-law

son•net

so•nor•i•ty

so•no•rous

soon•er

soothe

sooth•er

sooth•ing•ly

sooth•say•er

soot•i•ly

soot·i·ness
sooty
sop
  sopped
  sop·ping
soph·ism
soph·ist
so·phis·tic
  or so·phis·ti·cal
so·phis·ti·cat·ed
so·phis·ti·ca·tion
soph·ist·ry
soph·o·more
soph·o·mor·ic
so·po·rif·er·ous
sop·o·rif·ic
so·prano
  pl so·pra·nos
sor·bic acid
sor·cer·er
sor·cer·ess
  female wizard
sor·cer·ous
  magical
sor·cery
sor·did
sore
  painful (*see* soar)
sore·ly
sor·ghum
So·rop·ti·mist
so·ror·i·ty
sor·rel
sor·ri·ly
sor·ri·ness
sor·row
sor·row·ful
sor·row·ful·ly
sor·ry
  sad (*see* sari)
sor·tie
so-so
sot·to vo·ce
sou·brette
souf·flé
soul
  spirit (*see* sole)
soul·ful
soul·ful·ly
soul-search·ing
sound·board
sound·ing
sound·ly
sound·proof
soup·çon
soupy
sour·dough
sour·ish
sou·sa·phone
sou·tane
South Af·ri·ca
South Af·ri·can
South Bend
south·bound
South Car·o·li·na
South Da·ko·ta
south·east
south·east·er·ly
south·east·ern
south·east·ward
south·er·ly
south·ern
south·ern·most
south·ward
south·west
south·west·er·ly
south·west·ern
south·west·ward
sou·ve·nir
sov·er·eign
  also sov·ran
sov·er·eign·ty
  also sov·ran·ty
so·vi·et
sow
  plant, scatter (*see* sew)
  sowed
  sown
    or sowed
  sow·ing
sow·er
soy·bean
space·craft
space·flight
space·man
space·port
space·ship
space-time
spac·ing
spa·cious
spack·le
spade·ful
spade·work
spa·ghet·ti
Spain

span
  spanned
  span•ning

span•drel
  or span•dril

span•gle
Span•iard
span•iel
Span•ish
spank•ing
span•ner
spar
  sparred
  spar•ring

spare•ribs
spar•ing•ly
spar•kle
spark•ler
spar•row
sparse•ly
Spar•tan
spasm
spas•mod•ic
spas•mod•i•cal•ly
spas•tic
spat
  spat•ted
  spat•ting

spa•tial
spa•tial•ly
spat•ter
spat•u•la
spav•in
spav•ined

speak
  spoke
  spo•ken
  speak•ing

speak•easy
speak•er
spear•fish
spear•head
spear•mint
spear•wort
spe•cial
spe•cial•ist
spe•cial•iza•tion
spe•cial•ize
spe•cial•ly
spe•cial•ty
spe•cie
  money

spe•cies
  pl spe•cies
  kind

spec•i•fi•able
spe•cif•ic
spe•cif•i•cal•ly
spec•i•fi•ca•tion
spec•i•fi•er
spec•i•fy
spec•i•men
spe•cious
speck•le
spec•ta•cle
spec•ta•cled
spec•tac•u•lar
spec•ta•tor

spec•ter
  or spec•tre

spec•tral
spec•trom•e•ter
spec•tro•scope
spec•tro•scop•ic
spec•tro•scop•i•cal•ly
spec•tros•co•pist
spec•tros•co•py
spec•trum
  pl spec•tra *or* spec•trums

spec•u•late
spec•u•la•tion
spec•u•la•tive
spec•u•la•tive•ly
spec•u•la•tor
speech•less
speed
  sped
    or speed•ed
  speed•ing

speed•boat
speed•i•ly
speed•i•ness
speed•om•e•ter
speed•up
speed•way
speed•well
speedy
spe•le•ol•o•gist
spe•le•ol•o•gy
spell•bind•er
spell•bound
spell•er

spe·lunk·er

spend
  spent
  spend·ing

spend·able

spend·thrift

sperm
  pl sperm *or* sperms

sper·ma·ce·ti

sper·ma·to·zo·on
  pl sper·ma·to·zoa

spew

sphere

spher·i·cal

spher·i·cal·ly

spher·oid

sphinc·ter

sphinx
  pl sphinx·es *or* sphin·ges

spic·i·ly

spic·i·ness

spick-and-span
  or spic-and-span

spicy

spi·der

spi·dery

spig·ot

spill
  spilled
    also spilt
  spill·ing

spill·age

spill·way

spin
  spun
  spin·ning

spin·ach

spi·nal

spi·nal·ly

spin·dle

spin·dling

spin·dly

spin·drift

spine·less

spin·et

spin·ner

spin-off

spin·ster

spiny

spi·ral
  spi·raled
    or spi·ralled
  spi·ral·ing
    or spi·ral·ling

spi·ral·ly

spir·it

spir·it·ed

spir·it·less

spir·i·tu·al

spir·i·tu·al·ism

spir·i·tu·al·i·ty

spir·i·tu·al·ly

spir·i·tu·ous

spi·ro·chete
  or spi·ro·chaete

spit
  impale
  spit·ted
  spit·ting

spit
  eject saliva
  spit
    or spat
  spit·ting

spite·ful

spite·ful·ly

spit·fire

spit·tle

spit·toon

splash·board

splash·down

splat·ter

splay·foot

spleen·ful

splen·did

splen·dor

sple·net·ic

splen·ic

splic·er

splin·ter

split
  split
  split·ting

split-lev·el

splotch

splurge

splut·ter

spoil
spoiled
or spoilt
spoil·ing
spoil·able
spoil·age
spoil·er
spoil·sport
Spo·kane
spo·ken
spoke·shave
spokes·man
spokes·wom·an
spo·li·a·tion
sponge
spong·er
spong·i·ness
spongy
spon·sor
spon·ta·ne·ity
spon·ta·ne·ous
spoo·ner·ism
spoon-feed
spoon-fed
spoon-feed·ing
spoon·ful
pl spoon·fuls *or* spoons·ful
spo·rad·ic
spo·rad·i·cal·ly
sport·i·ly
sport·i·ness
sport·ing
sport·ive
sports·cast
sports·man
sports·wear
sports·writ·er
sporty
spot
spot·ted
spot·ting
spot-check
spot·less
spot·light
spot·ter
spot·ti·ly
spot·ti·ness
spot·ty
sprach·ge·fuhl
sprawl
spray·er
spread
spread
spread·ing
spread-ea·gle
spread·er
spright·li·ness
spright·ly
spring
sprang
or sprung
sprung
spring·ing
spring·board
spring-clean·ing
Spring·field
spring·house
spring·i·ly
spring·i·ness
spring·time
springy
sprin·kle
sprin·kler
sprin·kling
sprint·er
sprock·et
spruce·ly
spry
spri·er
or spry·er
spri·est
or spry·est
spunk·i·ly
spunk·i·ness
spunky
spur
spurred
spur·ring
spu·ri·ous
sput·nik
sput·ter
spu·tum
pl spu·ta
spy
spied
spy·ing
spy·glass
squab·ble
squad·ron
squal·id
squall
squa·lor
squan·der

square·ly
square-rigged
square-shoul·dered
squash·i·ly
squash·i·ness
squashy
squat
  squat·ted
  squat·ting
squat·ter
squawk
squeak·er
squeaky
squeal·er
squea·mish
squee·gee
squeez·er
squelch
squig·gle
squinty
squirmy
squir·rel
squishy
Sri Lan·ka
stab
  stabbed
  stab·bing
sta·bile
sta·bil·i·ty
sta·bi·li·za·tion
sta·bi·lize
sta·bi·liz·er
sta·ble
stac·ca·to
sta·di·um
  pl sta·dia *or* sta·di·ums
staff
  pl staffs *or* staves
stage·coach
stage·craft
stage·hand
stage-man·age
stage·struck
stag·ger
stag·i·ly
stag·i·ness
stag·ing
stag·nan·cy
stag·nant
stag·nate
stag·na·tion
stagy
  or stag·ey
staid
stain·able
stain·less
stair·case
stair·way
stair·well
stake
  post, bet (*see* steak)
stake·hold·er
sta·lac·tite
sta·lag·mite
stale·ly
stale·mate
stale·ness
stalk·ing-horse
stal·lion
stal·wart
sta·men
  plant part (*see* stamina)
  pl sta·mens *or* sta·mi·na
Stam·ford
stam·i·na
  endurance (*see* stamen)
stam·mer
stam·pede
stamp·er
stance
stanch
stan·chion
stand
  stood
  stand·ing
stan·dard
stan·dard-bear·er
stan·dard·iza·tion
stan·dard·ize
stand·by
stand·ee
stand-in
stand·ing
stand·off
stand·out
stand·pat
stand·pipe
stand·point
stand·still
stand-up
stan·za

staph·y·lo·coc·cus
pl staph·y·lo·coc·ci

sta·ple

sta·pler

star
starred
star·ring

star·board

star-cham·ber

starch·i·ness

starchy

star-crossed

star·dom

star·dust

sta·re de·ci·sis

star·fish

star·gaze

stark·ly

star·less

star·light

star·like

star·ling

star·lit

star·ry

star·ry-eyed

star-span·gled

start·er

star·tle

star·tling

star·va·tion

starve·ling

stat·able
or state·able

state·craft

state·hood

state·house

state·less

state·li·ness

state·ly

state·ment

state·room

state·side

states·man

stat·ic

stat·i·cal·ly

sta·tion

sta·tion·ary
fixed (*see* stationery)

sta·tio·ner

sta·tio·nery
writing materials (*see* stationary)

sta·tion·mas·ter

stat·ism

sta·tis·tic

sta·tis·ti·cal

sta·tis·ti·cal·ly

stat·is·ti·cian

sta·tis·tics

stat·u·ary

stat·ue

stat·u·esque

stat·u·ette

stat·ure

sta·tus

sta·tus quo

stat·ute

stat·u·to·ry

staunch

stave
staved
or stove
stav·ing

stay
stayed
or staid
stay·ing

stay-at-home

stead·fast

stead·i·ly

stead·i·ness

steady

steak
meat (*see* stake)

steal
take (*see* steel)
stole
sto·len
steal·ing

stealth·i·ly

stealth·i·ness

stealthy

steam·boat

steam·er

steam·i·ly

steam·i·ness

steam·roll·er

steam·ship

steamy

steel
metal (*see* steal)

steel·i·ness

steel·work

steely

steel·yard
stee·ple
stee·ple·chase
stee·ple·jack
steep·ly
steer·able
steer·age
steer·er
steers·man
stein
stel·lar
stem
stemmed
stem·ming
stem·less
stem·ware
sten·cil
sten·ciled
or sten·cilled
sten·cil·ing
or sten·cil·ling
ste·nog·ra·pher
steno·graph·ic
steno·graph·i·cal·ly
ste·nog·ra·phy
steno·type
steno·typ·ist
sten·to·ri·an
step
walk (*see* steppe)
stepped
step·ping
step·broth·er
step-by-step
step·child
step·daugh·ter
step-down
step·fa·ther
step-in
step·lad·der
step·moth·er
step·par·ent
steppe
plain (*see* step)
step·ping-stone
step·sis·ter
step·son
step-up
ster·eo
pl ste·re·os
ste·reo·phon·ic
ste·reo·scope
ste·reo·scop·ic
ste·re·os·co·py
ste·reo·type
ste·reo·typed
ster·ile
ste·ril·i·ty
ster·il·iza·tion
ster·il·ize
ster·il·iz·er
ster·ling
stern·ly
ster·num
pl ster·nums *or* ster·na
stet
stet·ted
stet·ting
stetho·scope
ste·ve·dore
stew·ard
stew·ard·ess
stick
stuck
stick·ing
stick·er
stick·i·ly
stick·i·ness
stick-in-the-mud
stick·ler
stick-to-it·ive·ness
sticky
stiff·en
stiff-necked
sti·fle
stig·ma
pl stig·ma·ta *or* stig·mas
stig·mat·ic
stig·ma·tism
stig·ma·tize
stile
steps (*see* style)
sti·let·to
pl sti·let·tos *or* sti·let·toes
still·birth
still·born
stilt·ed
Stil·ton
stim·u·lant
stim·u·late
stim·u·la·tion
stim·u·la·tive

stim·u·la·tor
stim·u·lus
pl stim·u·li
sting
stung
sting·ing
sting·er
stin·gi·ly
stin·gi·ness
sting·ray
stin·gy
stink
stank
or stunk
stunk
stink·ing
sti·pend
stip·ple
stip·u·late
stip·u·la·tion
stip·u·la·tor
stir
stirred
stir·ring
stir·ring
stir·rup
stitch
sto·chas·tic
stock·ade
stock·bro·ker
stock·hold·er
stock·i·nette
or stock·i·net
stock·ing
stock-in-trade
stock·man
stock·pile
stock·room
Stock·ton
stocky
stock·yard
stodg·i·ly
stodg·i·ness
stodgy
sto·gie
or sto·gy
sto·ic
or sto·i·cal
sto·ical·ly
sto·icism
stoke·hole
stok·er
stol·id
sto·lid·i·ty
stom·ach
stom·ach·ache
stone-blind
stone-broke
stone·cut·ter
stone-deaf
stone·ma·son
stone·ware
stone·work
ston·i·ly
ston·i·ness
stony
stop
stopped
stop·ping
stop·cock
stop·gap
stop·light
stop·over
stop·page
stop·per
stop·watch
stor·able
stor·age
store·house
store·keep·er
store·room
store·wide
sto·ried
or sto·reyed
storm·bound
storm·i·ly
storm·i·ness
stormy
sto·ry
sto·ry·book
sto·ry·tell·er
sto·tin·ka
pl sto·tin·ki
stout·heart·ed
stout·ly
stove·pipe
stow·age
stow·away
stra·bis·mus
strad·dle
strafe
strag·gle
strag·gler
strag·gly

straight
not crooked (see strait)

straight-arm

straight·away

straight·edge

straight·en
make straight (see straiten)

straight-faced

straight·for·ward
also straight·for·wards

strain·er

strait
channel (see straight)

strait·en
confine (see straighten)

strait·jack·et
or straight·jack·et

strait·laced
or straight·laced

strange·ly

strang·er

stran·gle

stran·gle·hold

stran·gler

stran·gu·late

stran·gu·la·tion

strap
strapped
strap·ping

strap·hang·er

strap·less

strap·ping

strat·a·gem

stra·te·gic

stra·te·gi·cal·ly

strat·e·gist

strat·e·gy

strat·i·fi·ca·tion

strat·i·fy

stra·tig·ra·phy

stra·to·cu·mu·lus

strato·sphere

stra·tum
pl stra·ta

stra·tus
pl stra·ti

straw·ber·ry

straw·flow·er

straw·worm

streak·i·ness

streaky

stream·er

stream·line

stream·lined

street·car

strength·en

stren·u·ous

strep·to·coc·cus
pl strep·to·coc·ci

strep·to·my·cin

stretch·abil·i·ty

stretch·able

stretch·er

stretch·er-bear·er

strew
strewed
strewed
or strewn
strew·ing

stri·at·ed

stri·a·tion

strick·en

strict·ly

stric·ture

stride
strode
strid·den
strid·ing

stri·den·cy

stri·dent

strife

strike
struck
struck
also strick·en
strik·ing

strike·bound

strike·break·er

strike·out

strike·over

strik·er

strik·ing

string
strung
string·ing

strin·gen·cy

strin·gent

string·er

string·i·ness
string·ing
stringy
strip
  stripped
    also **stript**
  strip·ping
strip-crop·ping
strip·ling
strip·per
strip·tease
strive
  strove
    also **strived**
  striv·en
    or **strived**
  striv·ing
stro·bo·scope
stro·bo·scop·ic
stroll·er
strong-arm
strong·box
strong·hold
strong-mind·ed
stron·tium
strop
  stropped
  strop·ping
stro·phe
stro·phic
struc·tur·al
struc·tur·al·ly
struc·ture
strug·gle
strum
  strummed
  strum·ming
strum·pet
strut
  strut·ted
  strut·ting
strych·nine
Stu·art
stub
  stubbed
  stub·bing
stub·ble
stub·bly
stub·born
stub·born·ness
stub·by
stuc·co
  pl **stuc·cos** *or* **stuc·coes**
stud
  stud·ded
  stud·ding
stud·book
stud·ding
stu·dent
stud·horse
stud·ied
stu·dio
  pl **stu·dios**
stu·di·ous
stuff·i·ly
stuff·i·ness
stuff·ing
stuffy
stul·ti·fi·ca·tion
stul·ti·fy
stum·ble
stun
  stunned
  stun·ning
stu·pe·fac·tion
stu·pe·fy
stu·pen·dous
stu·pid
stu·pid·i·ty
stu·por
stur·di·ly
stur·dy
stur·geon
stut·ter
sty
  pl **sties** *or* **styes**
  pig pen
sty
  or **stye**
  pl **sties** *or* **styes**
  eyelid swelling
style
  fashion (*see* **stile**)
style·book
styl·ish
styl·ist
sty·lis·ti·cal·ly
sty·lis·tics
styl·i·za·tion
styl·ize
sty·lus
  pl **sty·li** *also* **sty·lus·es**

sty·mie
  sty·mied
  sty·mie·ing
styp·tic
sty·rene
su·able
sua·sion
sua·sive
suave·ly
sua·vi·ty
sub
  subbed
  sub·bing
sub·agen·cy
sub·ar·ea
sub·as·sem·bly
sub·atom·ic
sub·av·er·age
sub·base·ment
sub·bing
sub·class
sub·com·mit·tee
sub·con·scious
sub·con·ti·nent
sub·con·tract
sub·con·trac·tor
sub·cul·ture
sub·cu·ta·ne·ous
sub·dis·ci·pline
sub·di·vide
sub·di·vi·sion
sub·due
sub·en·try
sub·fam·i·ly
sub·freez·ing
sub·group
sub·hu·man
sub·ject
sub·jec·tion
sub·jec·tive
sub·jec·tiv·i·ty
sub·join
sub ju·di·ce
sub·ju·gate
sub·ju·ga·tion
sub·junc·tive
sub·lease
sub·let
sub·li·mate
sub·li·ma·tion
sub·lime
sub·lim·i·nal
sub·lim·i·nal·ly
sub·lim·i·ty
sub·lu·na·ry
  also sub·lu·nar
sub·mar·gin·al
sub·mar·gin·al·ly
sub·ma·rine
sub·merge
sub·mer·gence
sub·mers·ible
sub·mer·sion
sub·mis·sion
sub·mis·sive
sub·mit
  sub·mit·ted
  sub·mit·ting
sub·nor·mal
sub·nor·mal·i·ty
sub·or·bit·al
sub·or·der
sub·or·di·nate
sub·or·di·na·tion
sub·orn
sub·or·na·tion
sub·plot
sub·poe·na
sub·re·gion
sub ro·sa
sub·scribe
sub·scrib·er
sub·scrip·tion
sub·se·quent
sub·ser·vi·ence
sub·ser·vi·ent
sub·side
sub·si·dence
sub·sid·iary
sub·si·di·za·tion
sub·si·dize
sub·si·dy
sub·sist
sub·sis·tence
sub·soil
sub·son·ic
sub·spe·cies
sub·stance
sub·stan·dard
sub·stan·tial
sub·stan·tial·ly
sub·stan·ti·ate
sub·stan·ti·a·tion
sub·stan·tive

sub·sta·tion
sub·sti·tut·able
sub·sti·tute
sub·sti·tu·tion
sub·stra·tum
pl **sub·stra·ta**
sub·struc·ture
sub·sume
sub·sur·face
sub·ter·fuge
sub·ter·ra·nean
sub·ti·tle
sub·tle
sub·tle·ty
sub·tly
sub·tract
sub·trac·tion
sub·tra·hend
sub·trop·i·cal
sub·urb
sub·ur·ban
sub·ur·ban·ite
sub·ur·bia
sub·ven·tion
sub·ver·sion
sub·ver·sive
sub·vert
sub·way
suc·ceed
suc·cess
suc·cess·ful
suc·cess·ful·ly
suc·ces·sion
suc·ces·sive
suc·ces·sive·ly
suc·ces·sor
suc·cinct
suc·cor
help (*see* sucker)
suc·co·tash
suc·cu·lence
suc·cu·lent
suc·cumb
such·like
suck·er
one that sucks (*see* succor)
suck·le
suck·ling
su·cre
su·crose
suc·tion
Su·dan
Su·da·nese
sud·den
sud·den·ness
su·do·rif·ic
sudsy
suede
or **suède**
su·et
suf·fer
suf·fer·able
suf·fer·ably
suf·fer·ance
suf·fer·ing
suf·fice
suf·fi·cien·cy
suf·fi·cient
suf·fix
suf·fo·cate
suf·fo·ca·tion
suf·fra·gan
suf·frage
suf·frag·ette
suf·frag·ist
suf·fuse
suf·fu·sion
sug·ar
sug·ar·cane
sug·ar·coat
sug·ar·plum
sug·ary
sug·gest
sug·gest·ibil·i·ty
sug·gest·ible
sug·ges·tion
sug·ges·tive
sui·cid·al
sui·cide
sui ge·ner·is
sui ju·ris
suit
legal action, clothes, cards, befit (*see* suite)
suit·abil·i·ty
suit·able
suit·ably
suit·case
suite
apartment, music (*see* suit, sweet)
suit·ing
suit·or
sul·fa

sul·fa·nil·amide
sul·fate
or sul·phate
sul·fide
or sul·phide
sul·fur
or sul·phur
sul·fu·ric
sul·fu·rous
sulk·i·ly
sulk·i·ness
sulky
sul·len
sul·len·ness
sul·ly
sul·tan
sul·ta·na
sul·tan·ate
sul·tri·ness
sul·try
sum
summed
sum·ming
su·mac
or su·mach
sum·mari·ly
sum·ma·ri·za·tion
sum·ma·rize
sum·ma·ry
concise (*see* summery)
sum·ma·tion
sum·mer
sum·mer·house
sum·mer·time
sum·mery
like summer (*see* summary)
sum·mit
sum·mon
sum·mons
pl sum·mons·es
sump·tu·ous
sun
sunned
sun·ning
sun·baked
sun·bathe
sun·beam
sun·bon·net
sun·burn
sun·burned
or sun·burnt
sun·burn·ing
sun·burst
sun·dae
Sun·day
sun·der
sun·di·al
sun·down
sun·dries
sun·dry
sun·fish
sun·flow·er
sun·glass·es
sunk·en
sun·lamp
sun·light
sun·lit
sun·ny
sun·rise
sun·set
sun·shade
sun·shine
sun·spot
sun·stroke
sun·suit
sun·tan
sun·up
sup
supped
sup·ping
su·per
su·per·abun·dance
su·per·abun·dant
su·per·an·nu·ate
su·per·an·nu·at·ed
su·perb
su·per·car·go
su·per·cil·ious
su·per·con·duc·tiv·i·ty
su·per·con·duc·tor
su·per·ego
su·per·fi·cial
su·per·fi·ci·al·i·ty
su·per·fi·cial·ly
su·per·flu·ity
su·per·flu·ous
su·per·high·way
su·per·hu·man
su·per·im·pose
su·per·in·duce
su·per·in·duc·tion

su·per·in·tend
su·per·in·ten·dence
su·per·in·ten·den·cy
su·per·in·ten·dent
su·pe·ri·or
su·pe·ri·or·i·ty
su·per·la·tive
su·per·lin·er
su·per·man
su·per·mar·ket
su·per·nal
su·per·nat·u·ral
su·per·nat·u·ral·ly
su·per·nu·mer·ary
su·per·pow·er
su·per·scribe
su·per·script
su·per·scrip·tion
su·per·sede
su·per·se·dure
su·per·sen·si·tive
su·per·son·ic
su·per·son·i·cal·ly
su·per·sti·tion
su·per·sti·tious
su·per·struc·ture
su·per·tank·er
su·per·vene
su·per·ven·tion
su·per·vise
su·per·vi·sion
su·per·vi·sor
su·per·vi·so·ry
su·pine
sup·per

sup·plant
sup·ple
sup·ple·ment
sup·ple·men·tal
sup·ple·men·ta·ry
sup·pli·ant
sup·pli·cant
sup·pli·cate
sup·pli·ca·tion
sup·pli·er
sup·ply
sup·port
sup·port·able
sup·port·ive
sup·pose
  sup·posed
  sup·pos·ing
sup·pos·ed·ly
sup·po·si·tion
sup·pos·i·to·ry
sup·press
sup·pres·sant
sup·press·ible
sup·pres·sion
sup·pres·sor
sup·pu·rate
sup·pu·ra·tion
su·pra
su·prem·a·cist
su·prem·a·cy
su·preme
sur·cease
sur·charge
sur·cin·gle

sure·fire
sure·foot·ed
sure·ly
sure·ty
surf
  sea swell (*see* **serf**)
sur·face
surf·board
surf·boat
sur·feit
surf·er
surf·ing
surge
  sweep (*see* **serge**)
sur·geon
sur·gery
sur·gi·cal
sur·gi·cal·ly
Su·ri·nam
  or **Su·ri·na·me**
sur·li·ness
sur·ly
sur·mise
sur·mount
sur·name
sur·pass
sur·plice
  vestment
sur·plus
  excess
sur·prise
  also **sur·prize**
sur·pris·ing
sur·re·al·ism
sur·re·al·ist

sur·re·al·is·ti·cal·ly
sur·ren·der
sur·rep·ti·tious
sur·rey
sur·ro·gate
sur·round
sur·round·ings
sur·tax
sur·veil·lance
sur·vey
sur·vey·ing
sur·vey·or
sur·viv·al
sur·vive
sur·vi·vor
sus·cep·ti·bil·i·ty
sus·cep·ti·ble
sus·cep·ti·bly
sus·pect
sus·pend
sus·pend·er
sus·pense
sus·pen·sion
sus·pen·so·ry
sus·pi·cion
sus·pi·cious
sus·tain
sus·tain·able
sus·te·nance
su·ture
su·zer·ain
su·zer·ain·ty
svelte

swab
  swabbed
  swab·bing
swad·dle
swad·dling
swag·ger
swal·low
swal·low·tail
swal·low-tailed
swampy
swank
  or **swanky**
swans·down
swap
  swapped
  swap·ping
swarth·i·ness
swar·thy
swash·buck·ler
swas·ti·ka
swat
  swat·ted
  swat·ting
swatch
swath
  or **swathe**
  sweep of a scythe
swathe
  to wrap
swathe
  or **swath**
  swathing band
sway·back
Swa·zi
  pl **Swa·zi** *or* **Swa·zis**

Swa·zi·land
swear
  swore
  sworn
  swear·ing
sweat
  sweat
  or **sweat·ed**
  sweat·ing
sweat·band
sweat·box
sweat·er
sweat·i·ly
sweat·i·ness
sweat·shop
sweaty
Swe·den
Swed·ish
sweep
  swept
  sweep·ing
sweep·back
sweep·er
sweep-sec·ond
sweep·stakes
  also **sweep·stake**
sweet
  pleasing, candy (see suite)
sweet·bread
sweet·bri·er
sweet·en
sweet·heart
sweet·meat
sweet-talk

swell
swelled
swelled
or swol·len
swell·ing
swel·ter
swept-back
swerve
swift·ly
swig
swigged
swig·ging
swill
swim
swam
swum
swim·ming
swim·mer
swim·suit
swin·dle
swin·dler
swine
pl swine
swing
swung
swing·ing
swin·ish
Swiss
pl Swiss
switch
switch·back
switch·board
switch-hit·ter
switch·man
switch·yard
Swit·zer·land
swiv·el
swiv·eled
or swiv·elled
swiv·el·ing
or swiv·el·ling
sword·fish
sword·play
swords·man
sword·tail
Syb·a·rite
Syb·a·rit·ic
syc·a·more
syc·o·phant
syc·o·phan·tic
syl·lab·ic
syl·lab·i·ca·tion
syl·lab·i·fi·ca·tion
syl·lab·i·fy
syl·la·ble
syl·la·bus
pl syl·la·bi *or* syl·la·bus·es
syl·lo·gism
syl·lo·gis·tic
sylph
syl·van
sym·bi·o·sis
pl sym·bi·o·ses
sym·bi·ot·ic
sym·bol
sign (*see* cymbal)
sym·bol·ic
or sym·bol·i·cal
sym·bol·i·cal·ly
sym·bol·ism
sym·bol·iza·tion
sym·bol·ize
sym·met·ri·cal
or sym·met·ric
sym·met·ri·cal·ly
sym·me·try
sym·pa·thet·ic
sym·pa·thet·i·cal·ly
sym·pa·thize
sym·pa·thiz·er
sym·pa·thy
sym·phon·ic
sym·pho·ny
sym·po·sium
pl sym·po·sia *or* sym·po·siums
symp·tom
symp·tom·at·ic
syn·a·gogue
or syn·a·gog
syn·apse
syn·chro·mesh
syn·chron·ic
syn·chro·nism
syn·chro·ni·za·tion
syn·chro·nize
syn·chro·nous
syn·chro·tron
syn·co·pate
syn·co·pa·tion
syn·co·pe
syn·cret·ic
syn·cre·tism
syn·di·cal·ism

syn·di·cate
syn·di·ca·tion
syn·drome
syn·ec·do·che
syn·ecol·o·gy
syn·er·gism
syn·er·gist
syn·er·gis·ti·cal·ly
syn·od
syn·od·i·cal
or syn·od·ic
syn·onym
syn·on·y·mous
syn·on·y·my
syn·op·sis
pl syn·op·ses
syn·op·size
syn·op·tic
also syn·op·ti·cal
syn·tac·tic
or syn·tac·ti·cal
syn·tac·ti·cal·ly
syn·tax
syn·the·sis
pl syn·the·ses
syn·the·size
syn·thet·ic
also syn·thet·i·cal
syn·thet·i·cal·ly
syph·i·lis
syph·i·lit·ic
Syr·a·cuse
Syr·ia
Syr·i·an
sy·ringe
syr·up
syr·upy
sys·tem
sys·tem·at·ic
also sys·tem·at·i·cal
sys·tem·at·i·cal·ly
sys·tem·ati·za·tion
sys·tem·atize
sys·tem·ic
sys·tem·iza·tion
sys·tem·ize

T

tab
tabbed
tab·bing
Ta·bas·co
tab·by
tab·er·na·cle
ta·ble
tab·leau
pl tab·leaux *also* tab·leaus
ta·ble·cloth
ta·ble d'hôte
ta·ble-hop
ta·ble·land
ta·ble·spoon
ta·ble·spoon·ful
pl ta·ble·spoon·fuls *or* ta·ble·spoons·ful
tab·let
ta·ble·top
ta·ble·ware
tab·loid
ta·boo
also ta·bu
ta·bor
also ta·bour
tab·o·ret
or tab·ou·ret
tab·u·lar
tab·u·late
tab·u·la·tion
tab·u·la·tor
ta·chom·e·ter
tac·it
tac·i·turn
tac·i·tur·ni·ty
tacki·ness
tack·le
tacky
ta·co
pl ta·cos
Ta·co·ma
tact·ful
tact·ful·ly
tac·tic
tac·ti·cal
tac·ti·cian
tac·tics
tac·tile
tact·less
tad·pole
taf·fe·ta
taff·rail
taf·fy

tag
tagged
tag·ging
tai·ga
tail·board
tail·coat
tail·gate
tail·light
tai·lor
tai·lor-made
tail·piece
tail·spin
ta·ka
take
took
tak·en
tak·ing
take·off
take·out
take-over
tak·er
tak·ing
ta·la
talc
tal·cum pow·der
tal·ent
tales·man
juror
tal·is·man
charm
pl **tal·is·mans**
talk·ative
talk·er
talk·ing-to
talky
Tal·la·has·see
tal·low
tal·ly
tal·ly·ho
pl **tal·ly·hos**
Tal·mud
tal·mu·dic
tal·on
tam·able
or **tame·able**
ta·ma·le
tam·a·rack
tam·a·rind
tam·ba·la
tam·bour
tam·bou·rine
tame·ly
tam·er
tam-o'-shan·ter
Tam·pa
tam·per
tam·pon
tan
tanned
tan·ning
tan·a·ger
tan·bark
tan·dem
tan·ge·lo
tan·gent
tan·gen·tial
tan·ger·ine
tan·gi·bil·i·ty
tan·gi·ble
tan·gi·bly
tan·gle
tan·go
pl **tan·gos**
tangy
tank·age
tan·kard
tank·er
tan·ner
tan·nery
tan·nic
tan·nin
tan·ta·lize
tan·ta·mount
tan·trum
Tan·za·nia
Tan·za·ni·an
tap
tapped
tap·ping
ta·per
candle, diminish
(*see* **tapir**)
tape-re·cord
tap·es·tried
tap·es·try
tape·worm
tap·hole
tap·i·o·ca
ta·pir
animal (*see* **taper**)
tap·pet
tap·room
tap·root

tar
tarred
tar·ring

tar·an·tel·la

ta·ran·tu·la

tar·di·ly

tar·di·ness

tar·dy

tare
weed, weight allowance (*see* tear)

tar·get

tar·iff

tar·nish

ta·ro
pl ta·ros

tar·pau·lin

tar·pon

tar·ra·gon

tar·ry

tar·tan

tar·tar

tar·tar·ic acid

tart·ly

task·mas·ter

tas·sel
tas·seled
or tas·selled
tas·sel·ing
or tas·sel·ling

taste·ful

taste·ful·ly

taste·less

tast·er

tast·i·ly

tast·i·ness

tasty

tat
tat·ted
tat·ting

tat·ter

tat·ter·de·ma·lion

tat·tered

tat·ter·sall

tat·ting

tat·tle

tat·tle·tale

tat·too
pl tat·toos

taught
past of teach (*see* taut)

taunt·er

taupe

taut
tense (*see* taught)

tau·to·log·i·cal

tau·to·log·i·cal·ly

tau·tol·o·gy

tav·ern

taw·dri·ly

taw·dri·ness

taw·dry

taw·ny

tax·abil·i·ty

tax·able

tax·a·tion

tax-ex·empt

taxi
pl tax·is *also* tax·ies

taxi
tax·ied
taxi·ing
or taxy·ing

taxi·cab

taxi·der·mist

taxi·der·my

taxi·me·ter

tax·ing

tax·o·nom·ic

tax·on·o·my

tax·pay·er

T-bar lift

T-bone

tea
beverage (*see* tee)

teach
taught
teach·ing

teach·abil·i·ty

teach·able

teach·er

teach-in

tea·cup

tea·cup·ful
pl tea·cup·fuls *or* tea·cups·ful

tea·house

tea·ket·tle

teak·wood

team
group (*see* teem)

team·mate

team·ster

team·work

tea·pot

tear
rip (*see* tare)
tore
torn
tear·ing

tear
cry (*see* tier)

tear·drop

tear·ful

tear·ful·ly

tea·room

tear·stained

tea·sel

teas·er

tea·spoon

tea·spoon·ful
pl tea·spoon·fuls *also* tea·spoons·ful

teat

tea·time

tech·nic

tech·ni·cal

tech·ni·cal·i·ty

tech·ni·cal·ly

tech·ni·cian

tech·nique

tech·noc·ra·cy

tech·no·crat

tech·no·log·i·cal
or tech·no·log·ic

tech·no·log·i·cal·ly

tech·nol·o·gist

tech·nol·o·gy

tec·ton·ic

tec·ton·ics

te·dious

te·di·um

tee
golf (*see* tea)
teed
tee·ing

teem
abound (*see* team)

teen·age
or teen·aged

teen·ag·er

tee·ter

tee·to·tal·er
or tee·to·tal·ler

tee·to·tal·ism

tele·cast
tele·cast
also tele·cast·ed
tele·cast·ing

tele·cast·er

tele·com·mu·ni·ca·tion

tele·course

tele·film

tele·ge·nic

tele·gram

tele·graph

te·leg·ra·pher

tele·graph·ic

tele·graph·i·cal·ly

te·leg·ra·phy

tele·ki·ne·sis

tele·me·ter

te·lem·e·try

te·le·o·log·i·cal
also te·le·o·log·ic

te·le·ol·o·gy

tele·path·ic

tele·path·i·cal·ly

te·lep·a·thy

tele·phone

tele·phon·ic

tele·phon·i·cal·ly

te·le·pho·ny

tele·pho·to

tele·pho·tog·ra·phy

tele·play

tele·print·er

Tele·Promp·Ter

tele·ran

tele·scope

tele·scop·ic

tele·thon

Tele·type

tele·type·writ·er

tele·view·er

tele·vise

tele·vi·sion

tel·ex

tell
told
tell·ing

tell·er

tell·tale

tel·pher

tem·blor

te·mer·i·ty

tem·per

tem·pera

tem·per·a·ment
tem·per·a·men·tal
tem·per·a·men·tal·ly
tem·per·ance
tem·per·ate
tem·per·a·ture
tem·pest
tem·pes·tu·ous
tem·plate
or tem·plet
tem·ple
tem·po
pl tem·pi *or* tem·pos
tem·po·ral
tem·po·rar·i·ly
tem·po·rary
tem·po·ri·za·tion
tem·po·rize
temp·ta·tion
tempt·er
tempt·ress
ten·a·bil·i·ty
ten·a·ble
te·na·cious
te·nac·i·ty
ten·an·cy
ten·ant
ten·ant·ry
ten·den·cy
ten·den·tious
also ten·den·cious
ten·der
soft, offer
tend·er
one that tends
ten·der·foot
pl ten·der·feet *also* ten·der·foots
ten·der·heart·ed
ten·der·ize
ten·der·loin
ten·der·ly
ten·der·ness
ten·don
ten·dril
te·neb·ri·ous
ten·e·brous
ten·e·ment
ten·et
ten·fold
Ten·nes·see
ten·nis
ten·on
ten·or
ten·pin
tense·ly
tense·ness
ten·sile
ten·sion
ten·si·ty
ten·sor
ten·ta·cle
ten·ta·tive
ten·ta·tive·ly
ten·ter
ten·ter·hook
tenth
tenth-rate
te·nu·i·ty
ten·u·ous
ten·ure
ten·ured
te·pee
tep·id
te·qui·la
ter·cen·te·na·ry
ter·gi·ver·sate
ter·i·ya·ki
ter·ma·gant
ter·mi·na·ble
ter·mi·na·bly
ter·mi·nal
ter·mi·nal·ly
ter·mi·nate
ter·mi·na·tion
ter·mi·na·tor
ter·mi·nol·o·gy
ter·mi·nus
pl ter·mi·ni *or* ter·mi·nus·es
ter·mite
ter·na·ry
terp·sich·o·re·an
ter·race
ter·ra-cot·ta
ter·ra fir·ma
ter·rain
Ter·ra·my·cin
ter·ra·pin
ter·rar·i·um
pl ter·rar·ia *or* ter·rar·i·ums
ter·raz·zo
ter·res·tri·al

ter·ri·ble
ter·ri·bly
ter·ri·er
ter·rif·ic
ter·rif·i·cal·ly
ter·ri·fy
ter·ri·fy·ing
ter·ri·to·ri·al
ter·ri·to·ri·al·i·ty
ter·ri·to·ry
ter·ror
ter·ror·ism
ter·ror·ist
ter·ror·iza·tion
ter·ror·ize
ter·ry
terse·ly
ter·tia·ry
tes·sel·late
tes·sel·lat·ed
tes·sel·la·tion
tes·ta·ment
tes·ta·men·ta·ry
tes·tate
tes·ta·tor
tes·ta·trix
tes·ti·cle
tes·ti·fi·er
tes·ti·fy
tes·ti·ly
tes·ti·mo·ni·al
tes·ti·mo·ny
tes·ti·ness
tes·tos·ter·one
tes·ty

tet·a·nus
tête-à-tête
teth·er
tet·ra·cy·cline
tet·ra·eth·yl
te·tral·o·gy
te·tram·e·ter
Tex·as
text·book
tex·tile
tex·tu·al
tex·tu·al·ly
tex·tur·al
tex·ture
Thai
Thai·land
tha·lid·o·mide
thank·ful
thank·ful·ly
thank·less
thanks·giv·ing
that
pl those

thatch
thaw
the·ater
or the·atre

the·ater·go·er
the·at·ri·cal
the·at·rics
theft
the·ism
the·ist
the·is·tic
the·mat·ic

the·mat·i·cal·ly
theme
them·selves
thence·forth
thence·for·ward
also
thence·for·wards

the·oc·ra·cy
theo·crat·ic
also theo·crat·i·cal

the·od·o·lite
theo·lo·gian
theo·log·i·cal
also theo·log·ic

the·ol·o·gy
the·o·rem
the·o·ret·i·cal
also the·o·ret·ic

the·o·ret·i·cal·ly
the·o·re·ti·cian
the·o·rize
the·o·ry
the·os·o·phist
the·os·o·phy
ther·a·peu·tic
ther·a·peu·ti·cal·ly
ther·a·peu·tics
ther·a·pist
ther·a·py
there·abouts
or there·about

there·af·ter
there·at
there·by
there·for
in return for

there•fore
for that reason

there•from

there•in

there•of

there•on

there•to

there•upon

there•with

ther•mal

therm•ion

ther•mo•dy•nam•i•cal•ly

ther•mo•dy•nam•ics

ther•mo•form

ther•mom•e•ter

ther•mo•nu•cle•ar

ther•mo•plas•tic

ther•mos

ther•mo•set•ting

ther•mo•sphere

ther•mo•stat

ther•mo•stat•i•cal•ly

the•sau•rus
pl **the•sau•ri** *or* **the•sau•rus•es**

the•sis
pl **the•ses**

thes•pi•an

thi•a•mine
also **thi•a•min**

thick•en

thick•et

thick•head•ed

thick•ly

thick•ness

thick•set

thick-skinned

thief
pl **thieves**

thieve

thiev•ery

thigh•bone

thim•ble

thim•ble•ful

thin
thinned
thin•ning

think
thought
think•ing

think•able

think•er

thin•ly

thin•ner

thin•ness

thin-skinned

third-class

third-rate

thirst•i•ly

thirst•i•ness

thirsty

thir•teen

thir•teenth

thir•ti•eth

thir•ty

this
pl **these**

this•tle

this•tle•down

thith•er

thith•er•ward

thole

thong

tho•rac•ic

tho•rax
pl **tho•rax•es** *or* **tho•ra•ces**

thorny

thor•ough

thor•ough•bred

thor•ough•fare

thor•ough•go•ing

thor•ough•ness

though

thought

thought•ful

thought•ful•ly

thought•less

thou•sand
pl **thou•sands** *or* **thou•sand**

thou•sandth

thrall•dom
or **thral•dom**

thrash•er

thread•bare

thread•i•ness

thready

threat•en

3-D

three-deck•er

three-di•men•sion•al

three•fold

three-hand•ed

three-legged
three-piece
three-quar·ter
three·score
three·some
thren·o·dy
thresh·er
thresh·old
thrice
thrift·i·ly
thrift·less
thrifty
thril·ler
thrive
  throve
    or thrived
  thriv·en
    also thrived
  thriv·ing

throat·i·ly
throat·i·ness
throaty
throb
  throbbed
  throb·bing

throe
  pang (*see* throw)

throm·bo·sis
  pl throm·bo·ses

throne
throng
throt·tle
through
  by way of, finished (*see* throw)

through·out
through·way
  or thruway

throw
  hurl (*see* throe, through)
  threw
  thrown
  throw·ing

throw·away
throw·back
thrum
  thrummed
  thrum·ming

thrust
  thrust
  thrust·ing

thrust·er
  also thrust·or

thru·way
  var of throughway

thud
  thud·ded
  thud·ding

thumb·hole
thumb·nail
thumb·print
thumb·screw
thumb·tack
thump
thun·der
thun·der·bird
thun·der·bolt
thun·der·clap
thun·der·cloud
thun·der·head
thun·der·ous
thun·der·show·er
thun·der·storm
thun·der·struck
Thurs·day
thwack
thwart
thyme
  herb (*see* time)

thy·mus
thy·roid
  or thy·roi·dal

ti·ara
tib·ia
  pl tib·i·ae *also* tib·i·as

tic
  twitch (*see* tick)

tick
  beat, insect (*see* tic)

tick·er
tick·et
tick·ing
tick·le
tick·ler
tick·lish
tick·tack·toe
  also tic-tac-toe

tid·al
tid·bit
tid·dle·dy·winks
  or tid·dly·winks

tide·land
tide·mark
tide·wa·ter

tide•way
ti•di•ly
ti•di•ness
tid•ing
ti•dy
tie
tied
ty•ing
or tie•ing
tie•back
tie-in
tie•pin
tier
row (*see* tear)
tie-up
tif•fa•ny
ti•ger
ti•ger•eye
or ti•ger's-eye
ti•ger•ish
tight•en
tight•fist•ed
tight-lipped
tight-mouthed
tight•ness
tight•rope
tights
tight•wad
ti•glon
ti•gress
til•ing
till•able
till•age
till•er
one that tills
til•ler
steering lever, sprout
tim•bal
drum
tim•bale
food
tim•ber
wood (*see* timbre)
tim•ber•land
tim•ber•line
tim•bre
also tim•ber
sound (*see* timber)
tim•brel
time
period (*see* thyme)
time-con•sum•ing
time-hon•ored
time•keep•er
time-lapse
time•less
time•li•ness
time•ly
time-out
time•piece
tim•er
time-sav•er
time•sav•ing
time•serv•er
time-shar•ing
time•ta•ble
time•worn
tim•id
ti•mid•i•ty
tim•id•ly
tim•ing
tim•o•rous
tim•o•thy
tim•pa•ni
tim•pa•nist
tin
tinned
tin•ning
tinc•ture
tin•der
tin•der•box
tin•foil
tinge
tinged
tinge•ing
or ting•ing
tin•gle
tin•horn
ti•ni•ly
ti•ni•ness
tin•ker
tin•ker•er
tin•kle
tin•kly
tin•ni•ly
tin•ni•ness
tin•ny
tin•plate
tin•sel
tin•seled
or tin•selled
tin•sel•ing
or tin•sel•ling
tin•smith
tint•ing
tin•tin•nab•u•la•tion

tin·type
tin·ware
tin·work
ti·ny
tip
  tipped
  tip·ping
tip-off
tip·pet
tip·ple
tip·pler
tip·si·ly
tip·si·ness
tip·ster
tip·sy
tip·toe
tip-top
ti·rade
tired
tire·less
tire·some
tis·sue
ti·tan
ti·tan·ic
tithe
tith·ing
ti·tian
tit·il·late
tit·il·la·tion
ti·tle
ti·tled
ti·tle·hold·er
tit·mouse
  pl tit·mice
ti·tra·tion
tit·ter
tit·tle-tat·tle
tit·u·lar
tiz·zy
toad·stool
toady
to-and-fro
toast·er
toast·mas·ter
to·bac·co
to·bac·co·nist
to·bog·gan
toc·ca·ta
toc·sin
  alarm (*see* toxin)
to·day
tod·dle
tod·dler
tod·dy
to-do
  pl to-dos
toe
  toed
  toe·ing
toe-dance
toe·hold
toe-in
toe·less
toe·nail
toe·piece
tof·fee
  or tof·fy
tog
  togged
  tog·ging
to·ga
to·geth·er
tog·gle
To·go
  or To·go·land
To·go·lese
toi·let
toi·let·ry
toil·some
toil·worn
to·ken
to·ken·ism
tole
  metal (*see* toll)
To·le·do
tol·er·a·ble
tol·er·a·bly
tol·er·ance
tol·er·ant
tol·er·ate
tol·er·a·tion
toll
  tax, sound (*see* tole)
toll·booth
toll·gate
toll·house
toll·man
tom·a·hawk
to·ma·to
  pl to·ma·toes
tom·boy
tomb·stone
tom·cat
tom·fool·ery
to·mor·row

tom-tom
ton
pl tons *also* ton *weight* (*see* tun)
ton·al
to·nal·i·ty
tone-deaf
tone·less
Ton·ga
tongs
tongue
tongued
tongu·ing
tongue-lash·ing
tongue-tied
ton·ic
to·night
ton·nage
ton·neau
ton·sil
ton·sil·lec·to·my
ton·sil·li·tis
ton·so·ri·al
ton·sure
ton·tine
tool·box
tool·head
tool·hold·er
tool·mak·er
tool·room
tooth
pl teeth
tooth·ache
tooth·brush
tooth·less
tooth·paste
tooth·pick
tooth·some
tooth·wort
toothy
top
topped
top·ping
to·paz
top·coat
to·pee
or to·pi
To·pe·ka
top·er
top-flight
top-heavy
top·ic
top·i·cal
top·i·cal·i·ty
top·i·cal·ly
top·knot
top·less
top·mast
top·most
top-notch
to·pog·ra·pher
top·o·graph·ic
top·o·graph·i·cal
top·o·graph·i·cal·ly
to·pog·ra·phy
to·po·log·i·cal
to·po·log·i·cal·ly
to·pol·o·gist
to·pol·o·gy
to·pos
pl to·poi
top·ping
top·ple
top·sail
top·side
top·soil
top·stitch
top·sy-tur·vy
toque
To·rah
torch·bear·er
torch·light
to·re·ador
tor·ment
tor·men·tor
also tor·ment·er
tor·na·do
pl tor·na·does *or* tor·na·dos
To·ron·to
tor·pe·do
pl tor·pe·does
tor·pid
tor·pid·i·ty
tor·por
torque
Tor·rance
tor·rent
tor·ren·tial
tor·ren·tial·ly
tor·rid
tor·sion
tor·so
pl tor·sos *or* tor·si

tort
wrongful act

torte
pl tor•ten *or* tortes
cake

tor•til•la

tor•toise

tor•toise•shell

tor•tu•ous
winding (*see* tortuous)

tor•ture

tor•tur•er

tor•tur•ous
painful (*see* tortuous)

toss-up

tot
tot•ted
tot•ting

to•tal
to•taled *or* to•talled
to•tal•ing *or* to•tal•ling

to•tal•i•tar•i•an

to•tal•i•ty

to•tal•iza•tor
or to•tal•isa•tor

to•tal•ly

to•tem

tot•ter

tou•can

touch•able

touch•back

touch•down

tou•ché

touch•i•ly

touch•i•ness

touch•ing

touch•mark

touch•stone

touch-type

touchy

tough•en

tough-mind•ed

tough•ness

tou•pee

tour de force
pl tours de force

tour•ism

tour•ist

tour•ma•line

tour•na•ment

tour•ney

tour•ni•quet

tou•sle

tow•age

to•ward
or to•wards

tow•boat

tow•el
tow•eled *or* tow•elled
tow•el•ing *or* tow•el•ling

tow•er

tow•er•ing

tow•head

tow•head•ed

tow•line

towns•folk

town•ship

towns•man

towns•peo•ple

tow•path

tow•rope

tox•e•mia

tox•ic

tox•i•cant

tox•ic•i•ty

tox•i•co•log•ic

tox•i•co•log•i•cal•ly

tox•i•col•o•gist

tox•i•col•o•gy

tox•in
poison (*see* tocsin)

tox•in-an•ti•tox•in

trace•able

trac•er

trac•ery

tra•chea
pl tra•che•ae

tra•cho•ma

trac•ing

track
route, follow (*see* tract)

track•age

track-and-field

track•less

track•walk•er

tract
pamphlet, land (*see* track)

trac•ta•bil•i•ty

trac•ta•ble

trac·ta·bly
trac·tion
trac·tor
trade-in
trade-last
trade·mark
trad·er
trades·man
trades·peo·ple
tra·di·tion
tra·di·tion·al
tra·di·tion·al·ly
tra·duce
tra·duc·er
traf·fic
  traf·ficked
  traf·fick·ing
traf·fick·er
tra·ge·di·an
tra·ge·di·enne
trag·e·dy
trag·ic
  also trag·i·cal
trag·i·cal·ly
tragi·com·e·dy
tragi·com·ic
  also tragi·com·i·cal
trail·blaz·er
trail·er
train·able
train·ee
train·er
train·ing
train·load
train·man
trait
trai·tor
trai·tor·ous
trai·tress
  or trai·tor·ess
tra·jec·to·ry
tram·mel
  tram·meled
    or tram·melled
  tram·mel·ing
    or tram·mel·ling
tram·ple
tram·po·line
tran·quil
tran·quil·ize
  or tran·quil·lize
tran·quil·iz·er
  also tran·quil·liz·er
tran·quil·li·ty
  or tran·quil·i·ty
tran·quil·ly
trans·act
trans·ac·tion
trans·ac·tion·al
trans·ac·tor
trans·at·lan·tic
trans·ceiv·er
tran·scend
tran·scen·dence
tran·scen·dent
tran·scen·den·tal
tran·scen·den·tal·ism
trans·con·ti·nen·tal
tran·scribe
tran·script
tran·scrip·tion
trans·duce
trans·duc·er
tran·sect
tran·sec·tion
tran·sept
trans·fer
  trans·ferred
  trans·fer·ring
trans·fer·able
trans·fer·al
trans·fer·ence
trans·fig·u·ra·tion
trans·fig·ure
trans·fix
trans·fix·ion
trans·form
trans·form·able
trans·for·ma·tion
trans·form·er
trans·fuse
trans·fus·ible
  or trans·fus·able
trans·fu·sion
trans·gress
trans·gres·sion
trans·gres·sor
tran·sience
tran·sient
tran·sis·tor
tran·sis·tor·ize
tran·sit
tran·si·tion
tran·si·tion·al

tran·si·tion·al·ly
tran·si·tive
tran·si·tive·ly
tran·si·to·ry
trans·lat·able
trans·late
trans·la·tion
trans·la·tor
trans·lit·er·ate
trans·lit·er·a·tion
trans·lu·cence
trans·lu·cent
trans·ma·rine
trans·mi·grate
trans·mi·gra·tion
trans·mi·gra·to·ry
trans·mis·si·ble
trans·mis·sion
trans·mit
  trans·mit·ted
  trans·mit·ting
trans·mit·ta·ble
trans·mit·tal
trans·mit·tance
trans·mit·ter
trans·mog·ri·fi·ca·tion
trans·mog·ri·fy
trans·mut·able
trans·mu·ta·tion
trans·mute
trans·oce·an·ic
tran·som
tran·son·ic
  also trans·son·ic
trans·pa·cif·ic
trans·par·en·cy
trans·par·ent
tran·spi·ra·tion
tran·spire
trans·plant
trans·plant·able
trans·po·lar
tran·spon·der
trans·port
trans·por·ta·tion
trans·port·er
trans·pos·able
trans·pose
trans·po·si·tion
trans·ship
  trans·shipped
  trans·ship·ping
trans·ship·ment
tran·sub·stan·ti·a·tion
trans·val·u·a·tion
trans·val·ue
trans·ver·sal
trans·verse
trans·verse·ly
trap
  trapped
  trap·ping
trap·door
tra·peze
tra·pe·zi·um
trap·e·zoid
trap·per
trap·pings
trap·shoot·ing
tra·pun·to
  pl tra·pun·tos
trash·i·ness
trashy
trau·ma
  pl trau·ma·ta *or* trau·mas
trau·mat·ic
trau·mat·i·cal·ly
trau·ma·tize
tra·vail
trav·el
  trav·eled
    or trav·elled
  trav·el·ing
    or trav·el·ling
trav·el·er
  or trav·el·ler
trav·el·ogue
  also trav·el·og
tra·vers·able
tra·verse
trav·er·tine
trav·es·ty
trawl·er
treach·er·ous
treach·ery
trea·cle
tread
  trod
    also tread·ed
  trod·den
    or trod
  tread·ing

trea•dle
tread•mill
trea•son
trea•son•able
trea•son•ous
trea•sur•able
trea•sure
trea•sur•er
trea•sury
treat•able
trea•tise
treat•ment
trea•ty
tre•ble
tre•bly
tree
  treed
  tree•ing
tree•less
tree•nail
  also **tre•nail**
tree•top
tre•foil
treil•lage
trek
  trekked
  trek•king
trel•lis
trel•lis•work
trem•ble
trem•bly
tre•men•dous
trem•o•lo
  pl **trem•o•los**
trem•or
trem•u•lous
tren•chant
tren•cher
Tren•ton
tre•pan
  tre•panned
  tre•pan•ning
trep•i•da•tion
tres•pass
tres•pass•er
tres•tle
  also **tres•sel**
tres•tle•work
tri•able
tri•ad
tri•al
tri•an•gle
tri•an•gu•lar
tri•an•gu•late
tri•an•gu•la•tion
trib•al
trib•al•ism
trib•al•ly
tribes•man
trib•u•la•tion
tri•bu•nal
trib•une
trib•u•tary
trib•ute
trice
tri•ceps
  pl **tri•ceps•es** *also* **tri•ceps**
tri•chi•na
  pl **tri•chi•nae** *also* **tri•chi•nas**
trich•i•no•sis
tri•chot•o•mous
tri•chot•o•my
tri•chro•mat•ic
trick•ery
trick•i•ly
trick•i•ness
trick•le
trick•ster
tricky
tri•col•or
tri•cor•nered
tri•cot
tri•cus•pid
tri•cy•cle
tri•dent
tri•di•men•sion•al
tri•en•ni•al
tri•er
tri•fle
tri•fler
tri•fling
tri•fo•cal
tri•fur•cate
trig•ger
trig•o•no•met•ric
  also **trig•o•no•met•ri•cal**
trig•o•nom•e•try
tri•lat•er•al
tri•lin•gual
tril•lion
tril•lionth

tril·o·gy
trim
  trimmed
  trim·ming
tri·ma·ran
tri·mes·ter
trim·e·ter
trim·mer
tri·month·ly
Trin·i·dad
Trin·i·dad and
  To·ba·go
Trin·i·da·di·an
Trin·i·ty
trin·ket
tri·no·mi·al
trio
  pl tri·os
tri·ode
trip
  tripped
  trip·ping
tri·par·tite
trip-ham·mer
triph·thong
tri·ple
tri·ple-space
trip·let
tri·plex
trip·li·cate
tri·ply
tri·pod
trip·tych
tri·sect
trite
trit·u·rate
tri·umph
tri·um·phal
tri·um·phant
tri·um·vir
tri·um·vi·rate
triv·et
triv·ia
triv·i·al
triv·i·al·i·ty
triv·i·al·ly
tri·week·ly
tro·cha·ic
tro·che
  lozenge
tro·chee
  poetic meter
trof·fer
trog·lo·dyte
troi·ka
troll
trol·ley
  or trol·ly
trol·lop
trom·bone
trom·bon·ist
troop
  soldiers (*see* troupe)
troop·er
troop·ship
tro·phy
trop·ic
trop·i·cal
tro·pism
tro·po·sphere
trot
  trot·ted
  trot·ting
trot·line
trot·ter
trou·ba·dour
trou·ble
trou·ble·mak·er
trou·ble·shoot·er
trou·ble·some
trough
trounce
troupe
  stage company (*see* troop)
troup·er
trou·sers
trous·seau
  pl trous·seaux *or* trous·seaus
trout
  pl trout *also* trouts
tro·ver
trow·el
  trow·eled
    or trow·elled
  trow·el·ing
    or trow·el·ling
tru·an·cy
tru·ant
truck·age
truck·er
truck·ing
truck·le
truck·line

truck·load

truc·u·lence

truc·u·lent

trudge

true

trued

true·ing
also tru·ing

true-blue

true·heart·ed

true-life

true·love

true·ness

truf·fle

tru·ism

tru·ly

trumped-up

trum·pery

trum·pet

trum·pet·er

trun·cate

trun·ca·tion

trun·cheon

trun·dle

truss

truss·ing

trust·ee
guardian (*see* trusty)

trust·ee·ship

trust·ful

trust·ful·ly

trust·ful·ness

trust·i·ness

trust·wor·thi·ly

trust·wor·thi·ness

trust·wor·thy

trusty
dependable (*see* trustee)

truth·ful

truth·ful·ly

truth·ful·ness

try

tried

try·ing

try·out

tryst

T-shirt

tsar
var of czar

tsu·na·mi

tub

tubbed

tub·bing

tu·ba

tub·by

tube·less

tu·ber

tu·ber·cle

tu·ber·cu·lar

tu·ber·cu·late
or tu·ber·cu·lat·ed

tu·ber·cu·lin

tu·ber·cu·lo·sis

tu·ber·cu·lous

tube·rose

tu·ber·ous

tub·ing

tu·bu·lar

tu·bule

tuck·er

Tuc·son

Tues·day

tu·fa

tug

tugged

tug·ging

tug·boat

tug-of-war
pl tugs-of-war

tu·ition

tu·la·re·mia

tu·lip

tulle

Tul·sa

tum·ble

tum·ble·down

tum·bler

tum·ble·weed

tum·bling

tum·brel
or tum·bril

tu·mes·cence

tu·mes·cent

tu·mid

tu·mid·i·ty

tu·mor

tu·mor·i·gen·ic

tu·mor·ous

tu·mult

tu·mul·tu·ous

tun
cask, measure (*see* ton)

tu•na
pl tu•na *or* tu•nas

tun•able
also tune•able

tun•dra

tune•ful

tune•ful•ly

tune•less

tun•er

tune-up

tung•sten

tu•nic

Tu•ni•sia

Tu•ni•sian

tun•nel

tun•neled
or tun•nelled

tun•nel•ing
or tun•nel•ling

tun•ny
pl tun•nies *also* tun•ny

tu•pe•lo
pl tu•pe•los

tuque

tur•ban

tur•bid

tur•bine

tur•bo
pl tur•bos

tur•bo•fan

tur•bo•jet

tur•bo•prop

tur•bot
pl tur•bot *also* tur•bots

tur•bu•lence

tur•bu•lent

tu•reen

turf
pl turfs *or* turves

tur•gid

tur•gid•i•ty

Tur•key

tur•key

Turk•ish

tur•mer•ic

tur•moil

turn•about

turn•around

turn•buck•le

turn•coat

turn•down

turn•er

turn-in

turn•ing

tur•nip

turn•key

turn•off

turn•out

turn•over

turn•pike

turn•spit

turn•stile

turn•ta•ble

tur•pen•tine

tur•pi•tude

tur•quoise
also tur•quois

tur•ret

tur•tle

tur•tle•back
or tur•tle-backed

tur•tle•dove

tur•tle•neck

tusk•er

tus•sle

tus•sock

tu•te•lage

tu•te•lary

tu•tor

tu•to•ri•al

tu•tu

Tu•va•lu

tux•e•do
pl tux•e•dos *or* tux•e•does

TV

twad•dle

twain

twang

tweak

tweed•i•ness

tweedy

tweet•er

tweez•ers

twelfth

twelve

twelve•month

twen•ti•eth

twen•ty

twice-told

twid•dle

twig•gy

twi•light

twi•lit

twill
twin
twinned
twin•ning
twinge
twi-night
twin•kle
twin•kler
twin•kling
twirl•er
twist•er
twit
twit•ted
twit•ting
twitch
twit•ter
two-bit
two-by-four
two-di•men•sion•al
two-faced
two-fist•ed
two•fold
two-hand•ed
two-ply
two-sid•ed
two•some
two-step
two-time
two-way
ty•coon
tyke
tym•pan•ic
tym•pa•num
pl tym•pa•na *also* tym•pa•nums

type•able
type•cast
type•face
type•found•ry
type•script
type•set
type•set
type•set•ting
type•set•ter
type•write
type•wrote
type•writ•ten
type•writ•ing
type•writ•er
ty•phoid
ty•phoon
ty•phus
typ•i•cal
typ•i•cal•ly
typ•i•fy
typ•ist
ty•po
pl ty•pos
ty•pog•ra•pher
ty•po•graph•ic
ty•po•graph•i•cal
ty•po•graph•i•cal•ly
ty•pog•ra•phy
ty•po•log•i•cal
ty•po•log•i•cal•ly
ty•pol•o•gy
ty•ran•ni•cal
also ty•ran•nic
ty•ran•ni•cal•ly

tyr•an•nize
tyr•an•niz•er
tyr•an•nous
tyr•an•ny
ty•rant
ty•ro
pl ty•ros
tzar
var of czar

U

ubiq•ui•tous
ubiq•ui•ty
U-boat
ud•der
Ugan•da
Ugan•dan
ug•li•ness
ug•ly
ukase
Ukraine
Ukrai•ni•an
uku•le•le
ul•cer
ul•cer•ate
ul•cer•ation
ul•cer•ous
ul•lage
ul•ster
ul•te•ri•or
ul•ti•mate
ul•ti•mate•ly
ul•ti•ma•tum
pl ul•ti•ma•tums *or* ul•ti•ma•ta

ul·ti·mo
ul·tra
ul·tra·cen·tri·fuge
ul·tra·con·ser·va·
tive
ul·tra·fash·ion·able
ul·tra·high
ul·tra·ism
ul·tra·ma·rine
ul·tra·mi·cro
ul·tra·mi·cro·scope
ul·tra·min·ia·ture
ul·tra·mod·ern
ul·tra·mon·tane
ul·tra·na·tion·al·
ism
ul·tra·pure
ul·tra·short
ul·tra·son·ic
ul·tra·sound
ul·tra·vi·o·let
ul·tra vi·res
ul·u·late
ul·u·la·tion
um·bel
um·bel·late
um·ber
um·bil·i·cal
um·bi·li·cus
pl um·bi·li·ci *or*
um·bi·li·cus·es
um·bra
pl um·bras *or*
um·brae
um·brage
um·bra·geous

um·brel·la
umi·ak
um·laut
um·pire
ump·teen
un·abashed
un·abat·ed
un·able
un·abridged
un·ac·com·pa·nied
un·ac·count·able
un·ac·count·ably
un·ac·count·ed
un·ac·cus·tomed
un·adorned
un·adul·ter·at·ed
un·ad·vised
un·af·fect·ed
un·aligned
un·al·loyed
un·al·ter·able
un·al·ter·ably
un-Amer·i·can
una·nim·i·ty
unan·i·mous
un·an·swer·able
un·ap·peal·ing
un·armed
un·asked
un·as·sail·able
un·as·sail·ably
un·as·sum·ing
un·at·tached
un·avail·ing
un·avoid·able

un·avoid·ably
un·aware
un·awares
un·bal·anced
un·bar
un·bear·able
un·bear·ably
un·beat·able
un·beat·en
un·be·com·ing
un·be·known
or un·be·knownst
un·be·lief
un·be·liev·able
un·be·liev·ably
un·be·liev·er
un·be·liev·ing
un·bend
un·bent
un·bend·ing
un·bi·ased
un·bid·den
also un·bid
un·bind
un·blush·ing
un·bod·ied
un·bolt
un·born
un·bo·som
un·bound·ed
un·bowed
un·braid
un·bri·dled
un·bro·ken
un·buck·le

un•bur•den
un•but•ton
un•cage
un•called-for
un•can•ni•ly
un•can•ny
un•cap
un•ceas•ing
un•cer•e•mo•ni•ous
un•cer•tain
un•cer•tain•ty
un•chain
un•change•able
un•change•ably
un•char•i•ta•ble
un•char•i•ta•bly
un•chart•ed
un•chris•tian
un•churched
un•cial
un•civ•il
un•civ•i•lized
un•clasp
un•clas•si•fied
un•cle
un•clean
un•clean•li•ness
un•clench
Un•cle Sam
un•cloak
un•clothe
un•coil
un•com•fort•able
un•com•fort•ably
un•com•mit•ted
un•com•mon
un•com•mu•ni•ca•
tive
un•com•pro•mis•ing
un•con•cern
un•con•cerned
un•con•di•tion•al
un•con•di•tion•al•ly
un•con•for•mi•ty
un•con•quer•able
un•con•scio•na•ble
un•con•scio•na•bly
un•con•scious
un•con•sti•tu•tion•al
un•con•sti•tu•tion•al•
i•ty
un•con•sti•tu•tion•al•
ly
un•con•trol•la•ble
un•con•trol•la•bly
un•con•ven•tion•al
un•con•ven•tion•al•i•
ty
un•con•ven•tion•al•
ly
un•cork
un•count•ed
un•cou•ple
un•couth
un•cov•er
un•crit•i•cal
un•crit•i•cal•ly
un•cross
unc•tion
unc•tu•ous
un•curl
un•cut
un•daunt•ed
un•de•mon•stra•tive
un•de•ni•able
un•de•ni•ably
un•der
un•der•achiev•er
un•der•act
un•der•age
un•der•arm
un•der•bel•ly
un•der•bid
un•der•brush
un•der•car•riage
un•der•charge
un•der•class•man
un•der•clothes
un•der•cloth•ing
un•der•coat
un•der•coat•ing
un•der•cov•er
un•der•cur•rent
un•der•cut
un•der•de•vel•oped
un•der•dog
un•der•done
un•der•es•ti•mate
un•der•es•ti•ma•tion
un•der•ex•pose
un•der•ex•po•sure
un•der•foot
un•der•gar•ment
un•der•gird
un•der•glaze

un·der·go
un·der·went
un·der·gone
un·der·go·ing
un·der·grad·u·ate
un·der·ground
un·der·growth
un·der·hand
un·der·hand·ed
un·der·hung
un·der·lay
un·der·laid
un·der·lay·ing
un·der·lie
un·der·lay
un·der·lain
un·der·ly·ing
un·der·line
un·der·ling
un·der·lip
un·der·ly·ing
un·der·mine
un·der·most
un·der·neath
un·der·nour·ished
un·der·paid
un·der·pants
un·der·part
un·der·pass
un·der·pin·ning
un·der·play
un·der·priv·i·leged
un·der·pro·duc·tion
un·der·rate
un·der·score
un·der·sea
un·der·sec·re·tary
un·der·sell
un·der·sold
un·der·sell·ing
un·der·sexed
un·der·shirt
un·der·shoot
un·der·shot
un·der·shoot·ing
un·der·shorts
un·der·side
un·der·signed
pl un·der·signed
un·der·sized
also un·der·size
un·der·skirt
un·der·slung
un·der·stand
un·der·stood
un·der·stand·ing
un·der·stand·able
un·der·stand·ably
un·der·stand·ing
un·der·state
un·der·state·ment
un·der·stood
un·der·study
un·der·sur·face
un·der·take
un·der·took
un·der·tak·en
un·der·tak·ing
un·der·tak·er
un·der·tak·ing
un·der-the-count·er
un·der·tone
un·der·tow
un·der·trick
un·der·val·u·a·tion
un·der·val·ue
un·der·wa·ter
un·der·way
un·der·wear
un·der·weight
un·der·world
un·der·write
un·der·wrote
un·der·writ·ten
un·der·writ·ing
un·der·writ·er
un·de·sir·able
un·de·sir·ably
un·de·vi·at·ing
un·dies
un·do
un·did
un·done
un·do·ing
un·doubt·ed
un·drape
un·dress
un·due
un·du·lant
un·du·late
un·du·la·tion
un·du·ly

un·dy·ing
un·earned
un·earth
un·eas·i·ly
un·eas·i·ness
un·easy
un·em·ploy·able
un·em·ployed
un·em·ploy·ment
un·end·ing
un·equal
un·equaled
un·equal·ly
un·equiv·o·cal
un·e·quiv·o·cal·ly
un·err·ing
un·es·sen·tial
un·even
un·event·ful
un·ex·am·pled
un·ex·cep·tion·able
un·ex·pect·ed
un·fail·ing
un·fair
un·faith·ful
un·faith·ful·ly
un·fa·mil·iar
un·fa·mil·iar·i·ty
un·fas·ten
un·fa·vor·able
un·fa·vor·ably
un·feel·ing
un·feigned
un·fet·ter
un·fit
un·flap·pa·ble
un·flinch·ing
un·fold
un·for·get·ta·ble
un·for·get·ta·bly
un·formed
un·for·tu·nate
un·found·ed
un·fre·quent·ed
un·friend·li·ness
un·friend·ly
un·frock
un·fruit·ful
un·furl
un·gain·li·ness
un·gain·ly
un·gen·er·ous
un·gird
un·god·li·ness
un·god·ly
un·gov·ern·able
un·grace·ful
un·grace·ful·ly
un·gra·cious
un·grate·ful
un·grate·ful·ly
un·guard·ed
un·guent
un·gu·late
un·hand
un·hap·pi·ly
un·hap·pi·ness
un·hap·py
un·healthy
un·heard
un·heard-of
un·hinge
un·hitch
un·hook
un·horse
un·hur·ried
uni·cam·er·al
uni·cel·lu·lar
uni·corn
uni·cy·cle
uni·di·rec·tion·al
uni·fi·able
uni·fi·ca·tion
uni·fi·er
uni·form
uni·for·mi·ty
uni·fy
uni·lat·er·al
uni·lat·er·al·ly
un·im·peach·able
un·im·peach·ably
un·in·hib·it·ed
un·in·tel·li·gent
un·in·tel·li·gi·ble
un·in·tel·li·gi·bly
un·in·ten·tion·al
un·in·ten·tion·al·ly
un·in·ter·rupt·ed
union
union·ism
union·iza·tion
union·ize
Union of So·vi·et So·cial·ist Re·pub·lics

unique
uni•sex
uni•son
unit
uni•tar•i•an
uni•tary
unite
unit•ed
Unit•ed Ar•ab Emir•ates
Unit•ed King•dom
Unit•ed Na•tions
Unit•ed States of Amer•i•ca
uni•ty
uni•ver•sal
Uni•ver•sal•ist
uni•ver•sal•i•ty
uni•ver•sal•ize
uni•ver•sal•ly
uni•verse
uni•ver•si•ty
un•just
un•kempt
un•kind
un•know•ing
un•known
un•lace
un•lade
un•latch
un•law•ful
un•law•ful•ly
un•learn
un•learned
un•leash
un•less
un•let•tered
un•like
un•like•li•hood
un•like•li•ness
un•like•ly
un•lim•ber
un•lim•it•ed
un•list•ed
un•load
un•lock
un•looked-for
un•loose
un•loos•en
un•love•ly
un•luck•i•ly
un•luck•i•ness
un•lucky
un•make
  un•made
  un•mak•ing
un•man
un•man•ly
un•man•ner•ly
un•mask
un•men•tion•able
un•mer•ci•ful
un•mer•ci•ful•ly
un•mind•ful
un•mis•tak•able
un•mis•tak•ably
un•mit•i•gat•ed
un•moor
un•muf•fle
un•muz•zle
un•nail
un•nat•u•ral
un•nat•u•ral•ly
un•nec•es•sar•i•ly
un•nec•es•sary
un•nerve
un•num•bered
un•ob•tru•sive
un•oc•cu•pied
un•or•ga•nized
un•or•tho•dox
un•pack
un•par•al•leled
un•peg
un•per•son
un•pile
un•pin
un•pleas•ant
un•plumbed
un•pop•u•lar
un•pop•u•lar•i•ty
un•prec•e•dent•ed
un•pre•dict•abil•i•ty
un•pre•dict•able
un•pre•dict•ably
un•prej•u•diced
un•pre•ten•tious
un•prin•ci•pled
un•print•able
un•prof•it•able
un•prof•it•ably
un•prom•is•ing
un•qual•i•fied
un•ques•tion•able

un•ques•tion•ably
un•ques•tion•ing
un•quote
un•rav•el
un•read
un•read•i•ness
un•ready
un•re•al
un•re•al•is•tic
un•re•al•is•ti•cal•ly
un•re•al•i•ty
un•rea•son•able
un•rea•son•ably
un•rea•son•ing
un•re•con•struct•ed
un•reel
un•re•gen•er•ate
un•re•lent•ing
un•re•mit•ting
un•re•served
un•rest
un•re•strained
un•rid•dle
un•righ•teous
un•ripe
un•ri•valed
or un•ri•valled
un•robe
un•roll
un•ruf•fled
un•rul•i•ness
un•ruly
un•sad•dle
un•sat•u•rat•ed
un•sa•vory
un•scathed
un•schooled
un•sci•en•tif•ic
un•sci•en•tif•i•cal•ly
un•scram•ble
un•screw
un•scru•pu•lous
un•seal
un•search•able
un•sea•son•able
un•sea•son•ably
un•seat
un•seem•ly
un•seen
un•seg•re•gat•ed
un•self•ish
un•set•tle
un•set•tled
un•shack•le
un•shaped
un•sheathe
un•shod
un•sight•ly
un•skilled
un•skill•ful
un•sling
un•slung
un•sling•ing
un•snap
un•snarl
un•so•phis•ti•cat•ed
un•sought
un•sound
un•spar•ing
un•speak•able
un•speak•ably
un•spot•ted
un•sta•ble
un•stead•i•ly
un•stead•i•ness
un•steady
un•stop
un•strap
un•stressed
un•string
un•strung
un•string•ing
un•stud•ied
un•sub•stan•tial
un•suc•cess•ful
un•suc•cess•ful•ly
un•suit•able
un•suit•ably
un•sung
un•tan•gle
un•taught
un•think•able
un•think•ing
un•thought
un•ti•dy
un•tie
un•tied
un•ty•ing
or un•tie•ing
un•til
un•time•li•ness
un•time•ly
un•ti•tled
un•to

un·told
un·touch·abil·i·ty
un·touch·able
un·to·ward
un·tried
un·true
un·truth
un·truth·ful
un·truth·ful·ly
un·tu·tored
un·twist
un·used
un·usu·al
un·usu·al·ly
un·ut·ter·able
un·ut·ter·ably
un·var·nished
un·veil
un·voiced
un·war·rant·able
un·wary
un·washed
un·weave
  un·wove
    or un·weaved
  un·wo·ven
    or un·weaved
  un·weav·ing
un·well
un·whole·some
un·wield·i·ness
un·wieldy
un·will·ing
un·wind
  un·wound
  un·wind·ing
un·wise
un·wit·ting
un·world·li·ness
un·world·ly
un·wor·thi·ly
un·wor·thi·ness
un·wor·thy
un·wrap
un·writ·ten
un·yield·ing
un·yoke
un·zip
up-and-down
up·beat
up·braid
up·bring·ing
up·com·ing
up-coun·try
up·date
up·draft
up·end
up·grade
up·growth
up·heav·al
up·hill
up·hold
  up·held
  up·hold·ing
up·hol·ster
up·hol·ster·er
up·hol·stery
up·keep
up·land
up·lift
up·most
up·on
up·per
up·per·case
up·per-class
up·per·class·man
up·per·cut
up·per·most
Up·per Vol·ta
Up·per Vol·tan
up·pish
up·pi·ty
up·right
up·ris·ing
up·roar
up·roar·i·ous
up·root
up·set
  up·set
  up·set·ting
up·shot
up·side down
up·stage
up·stairs
up·stand·ing
up·start
up·state
up·stream
up·stroke
up·surge
up·swept

up•swing
up•take
up-tem•po
up•thrust
up•tight
up-to-date
up•town
up•trend
up•turn
up•ward
or up•wards
up•wind
ura•ni•um
ur•ban
of the city
ur•bane
polished
ur•ban•ism
ur•ban•ite
ur•ban•i•ty
ur•ban•iza•tion
ur•ban•ize
ur•chin
urea
ure•mia
ure•ter
ure•thra
pl ure•thras *or* ure•thrae
urge
ur•gen•cy
ur•gent
uric
uri•nal
uri•nal•y•sis
uri•nary
uri•nate
uri•na•tion
urine
urn
uro•log•ic
or uro•log•i•cal
urol•o•gist
urol•o•gy
ur•sine
Ur•u•guay
Uru•guay•an
us•abil•i•ty
us•able
also use•able
us•age
use
used
us•ing
use•ful
use•ful•ly
use•less
us•er
ush•er
usu•al
usu•al•ly
usu•fruct
usu•rer
usu•ri•ous
usurp
usur•pa•tion
usurp•er
usu•ry
Utah
uten•sil
uter•ine
uter•us
pl uteri *also* uter•us•es
utile
util•i•tar•i•an
util•i•tar•i•an•ism
util•i•ty
uti•liz•able
uti•li•za•tion
uti•lize
ut•most
uto•pia
uto•pi•an
ut•ter
ut•ter•ance
ut•ter•most
uvu•la
pl uvu•las *or* uvu•lae
ux•o•ri•ous

V

va•can•cy
va•cant
va•cate
va•ca•tion
va•ca•tion•er
vac•ci•nate
vac•ci•na•tion
vac•cine
vac•il•late
vac•il•la•tion
vac•il•la•tor
va•cu•ity

vac•u•ole
vac•u•ous
vac•u•um
pl vac•u•ums *or* vac•ua
vac•u•um-packed
va•de me•cum
pl va•de me•cums
vag•a•bond
vag•a•bond•age
va•ga•ry
va•gi•na
pl va•gi•nae *or* va•gi•nas
va•gran•cy
va•grant
vague
vague•ly
vail
let fall (*see* vale, veil)
vain
futile, conceited (*see* vane, vein)
vain•glo•ri•ous
vain•glo•ry
va•lance
drapery (*see* valence)
vale
valley (*see* vail, veil)
vale•dic•tion
vale•dic•to•ri•an
vale•dic•to•ry
va•lence
chem (*see* valance)
Va•len•ci•ennes
val•en•tine

va•let
val•e•tu•di•nar•i•an
Val•hal•la
val•iant
val•id
val•i•date
val•i•da•tion
va•lid•i•ty
va•lise
val•ley
pl val•leys
val•or
val•o•ri•za•tion
val•o•rize
val•or•ous
val•u•able
val•u•ably
val•u•a•tion
val•ue
val•ued
val•ue•less
va•lu•ta
valve
val•vu•lar
vam•pire
Van•cou•ver
van•dal
van•dal•ism
van•dal•ize
Van•dyke
vane
wind indicator (*see* vain, vein)
van•guard
va•nil•la

van•ish
van•i•ty
van•quish
van•quish•able
van•tage
va•pid
va•pid•i•ty
va•por
va•por•iza•tion
va•por•ize
va•por•iz•er
va•por•ous
va•que•ro
vari•abil•i•ty
vari•able
vari•ably
vari•ance
vari•ant
vari•a•tion
vari•col•ored
var•i•cose
var•i•cos•i•ty
var•ied
var•ie•gate
var•ie•ga•tion
va•ri•etal
va•ri•etal•ly
va•ri•ety
var•i•o•rum
var•i•ous
var•mint
var•nish
var•si•ty
vary
vas•cu•lar

vas def·er·ens
pl va·sa def·er·en·tia

va·sec·to·my

Vas·e·line

vaso·mo·tor

vas·sal

vas·sal·age

vast·ness

vat-dyed

Vat·i·can

vaude·ville

vaude·vil·lian

vault·ed

vault·ing

vaunt

V-day

vec·tor

veer

veg·e·ta·ble

veg·e·tal

veg·e·tar·i·an

veg·e·tate

veg·e·ta·tion

veg·e·ta·tive

ve·he·mence

ve·he·ment

ve·hi·cle

ve·hic·u·lar

V-8

veil
screen (*see* vale, vail)

veil·ing

vein
blood vessel, mood (*see* vain, vane)

vel·lum

ve·loc·i·pede

ve·loc·i·ty

ve·lour
or ve·lours
pl ve·lours

vel·vet

vel·ve·teen

vel·vety

ve·nal
mercenary (*see* venial)

ve·nal·i·ty

ve·nal·ly

vend·ee

ven·det·ta

vend·ible
or vend·able

ven·dor

ve·neer

ven·er·a·ble

ven·er·ate

ven·er·a·tion

ve·ne·re·al

ven·ery

Ven·e·zu·e·la

Ven·e·zu·e·lan

ven·geance

venge·ful

venge·ful·ly

ve·nial
excusable (*see* venal)

ve·ni·re

ve·ni·re·man

ven·i·son

ven·om

ven·om·ous

ve·nous

ven·ti·late

ven·ti·la·tion

ven·ti·la·tor

ven·tral

ven·tral·ly

ven·tri·cle

ven·tril·o·quism

ven·tril·o·quist

ven·ture

ven·ture·some

ven·tur·ous

ven·ue

ve·ra·cious
truthful (*see* voracious)

ve·rac·i·ty

ve·ran·da
or ve·ran·dah

ver·bal

ver·bal·iza·tion

ver·bal·ize

ver·bal·ly

ver·ba·tim

ver·be·na

ver·biage

ver·bose

ver·bos·i·ty

ver·bo·ten

ver·dant

ver·dict

ver·di·gris

ver·dure

verge
ver•i•fi•able
ver•i•fi•ca•tion
ver•i•fi•er
ver•i•fy
ver•i•ly
veri•si•mil•i•tude
ver•i•ta•ble
ver•i•ta•bly
ver•i•ty
ver•meil
ver•mi•cel•li
ver•mi•form
ver•mi•fuge
ver•mil•ion
or ver•mil•lion
ver•min
pl ver•min
Ver•mont
ver•mouth
ver•nac•u•lar
ver•nal
ver•ni•er
ver•sa•tile
ver•sa•til•i•ty
ver•si•cle
ver•si•fi•ca•tion
ver•si•fy
ver•sion
ver•so
pl ver•sos
ver•sus
ver•te•bra
pl ver•te•brae *or* ver•te•bras
ver•te•bral
ver•te•brate
ver•tex
pl ver•ti•ces *also* ver•tex•es
ver•ti•cal
ver•ti•cal•ly
ver•ti•cil•late
ver•tig•i•nous
ver•ti•go
pl ver•ti•goes
ver•vain
verve
very
ves•i•cant
ves•i•cle
ve•sic•u•lar
ves•per
ves•pers
ves•sel
ves•tal
ves•ti•bule
ves•tige
ves•ti•gial
ves•ti•gial•ly
vest•ment
vest-pock•et
ves•try
ves•try•man
ves•ture
vetch
vet•er•an
vet•er•i•nar•i•an
vet•er•i•nary
ve•to
pl ve•toes
ve•to•er
vex
vexed
also vext
vex•ing
vex•a•tion
vex•a•tious
vi•a•bil•i•ty
vi•a•ble
vi•a•bly
vi•a•duct
vi•al
small bottle (*see* vile, viol)
vi•and
vi•bran•cy
vi•brant
vi•bra•phone
vi•brate
vi•bra•tion
vi•bra•to
pl vi•bra•tos
vi•bra•tor
vi•bra•to•ry
vi•bur•num
vic•ar
vic•ar•age
vi•car•i•al
vi•car•i•ate
vi•car•i•ous
vice
depravity (*see* vise)
vice-chan•cel•lor
vice-con•sul
vice-pres•i•den•cy

vice-pres·i·dent
vice·roy
vice ver·sa
vi·chys·soise
vi·chy
vi·cin·i·ty
vi·cious
vi·cis·si·tude
vic·tim
vic·tim·iza·tion
vic·tim·ize
vic·tim·iz·er
vic·tor
Vic·to·ria
Vic·to·ri·an
vic·to·ri·ous
vic·to·ry
vict·ual
vi·cu·ña
or vi·cu·na

vi·de
vid·eo
vid·eo·tape
vie
vied
vy·ing

vi·er
Viet·nam
Viet·nam·ese
pl Viet·nam·ese

view·er
view·point
vig·il
vig·i·lance
vig·i·lant
vig·i·lan·te
vig·i·lan·tism
vi·gnette
vig·or
vig·or·ous
vile
repulsive (*see* vial, viol)

vile·ly
vil·i·fi·ca·tion
vil·i·fi·er
vil·i·fy
vil·la
vil·lage
vil·lag·er
vil·lain
vil·lain·ous
vil·lainy
vil·lous
covered with villi

vil·lus
pl vil·li
hairlike projection

vin·ai·grette
vin·ci·ble
vin·di·ca·ble
vin·di·cate
vin·di·ca·tion
vin·di·ca·tor
vin·di·ca·to·ry
vin·dic·tive
vin·dic·tive·ly
vin·e·gar
vin·e·gary
vine·yard
vi·ni·cul·ture
vi·nous
vin·tage
vint·ner
vi·nyl
vi·ol
musical instrument (*see* vial, vile)

vi·o·la
vi·o·la·ble
vi·o·late
vi·o·la·tion
vi·o·la·tor
vi·o·lence
vi·o·lent
vi·o·let
vi·o·lin
vi·o·lin·ist
vi·o·list
vi·o·lon·cel·list
vi·o·lon·cel·lo
vi·os·ter·ol
VIP
vi·per
vi·per·ous
vi·ra·go
pl vi·ra·goes *or* vi·ra·gos

vi·ral
vir·eo
pl vir·e·os

vir·gin
vir·gin·al
vir·gin·al·ly
Vir·gin·ia
Vir·gin·ia Beach
vir·gin·i·ty

vir·gule

vir·ile

vi·ril·i·ty

vi·rol·o·gist

vi·rol·o·gy

vir·tu
objets d'art (*see* virtue)

vir·tu·al

vir·tu·al·ly

vir·tue
goodness (*see* virtu)

vir·tu·os·i·ty

vir·tu·o·so
pl vir·tu·o·sos *or* vir·tu·o·si

vir·tu·ous

vir·u·lence
or vir·u·len·cy

vir·u·lent

vi·rus

vi·sa

vi·saed

vi·sa·ing

vis·age

vis-à-vis
pl vis-à-vis

vis·cer·al

vis·cer·al·ly

vis·cid

vis·cid·i·ty

vis·co·elas·tic

vis·cose

vis·cos·i·ty

vis·cous
thick

vis·cus
pl vis·cera
body organ

vise
clamp (*see* vice)

vis·i·bil·i·ty

vis·i·ble

vis·i·bly

vi·sion

vi·sion·ary

vis·it

vis·i·tant

vis·i·ta·tion

vis·i·tor

vi·sor

vis·ta

vi·su·al

vi·su·al·iza·tion

vi·su·al·ize

vi·su·al·iz·er

vi·su·al·ly

vi·ta
pl vi·tae

vi·tal

vi·tal·i·ty

vi·tal·iza·tion

vi·tal·ize

vi·tal·ly

vi·tals

vi·ta·min

vi·ti·ate

vi·ti·a·tion

vi·ti·a·tor

vi·ti·cul·ture

vit·re·ous

vit·ri·fi·ca·tion

vit·ri·fy

vit·ri·ol

vit·ri·ol·ic

vit·tles

vi·tu·per·ate

vi·tu·per·a·tion

vi·tu·per·a·tive

vi·va

vi·va·ce

vi·va·cious

vi·vac·i·ty

vi·va vo·ce

vi·var·i·um
pl vi·var·ia *or* vi·var·i·ums

viv·id

viv·i·fi·ca·tion

viv·i·fi·er

viv·i·fy

vi·vip·a·rous

vivi·sect

vivi·sec·tion

vix·en

viz·ard

vi·zier

vo·ca·ble

vo·cab·u·lary

vo·cal

vo·cal·ic

vo·cal·ist

vo·cal·ize

vo·cal·ly

vo·ca·tion

voc·a·tive

vo·cif·er·ate
vo·cif·er·ous
vod·ka
vogue
vogu·ish
voiced
voice·less
void·able
void·er
voile
vol·a·tile
vol·a·til·i·ty
vol·ca·nic
vol·ca·nism
vol·ca·no
pl vol·ca·noes *or* vol·ca·nos
vo·li·tion
vol·ley
vol·ley·ball
volt·age
vol·ta·ic
vol·ta·me·ter
volt-am·pere
volte-face
volt·me·ter
vol·u·bil·i·ty
vol·u·ble
vol·u·bly
vol·ume
vol·u·met·ric
vo·lu·mi·nous
vol·un·ta·ri·ly
vol·un·tary
vol·un·teer
vo·lup·tu·ary
vo·lup·tuous
vo·lute
vom·it
voo·doo
vo·ra·cious
insatiable (*see* veracious)
vo·rac·i·ty
vor·tex
pl vor·ti·ces *also* vor·tex·es
vor·ti·cal
vo·ta·ry
vot·er
vo·tive
vouch·er
vouch·safe
vow·el
vox po·pu·li
voy·age
voy·ag·er
voy·eur
vul·ca·ni·za·tion
vul·can·ize
vul·can·iz·er
vul·gar
vul·gar·i·an
vul·gar·ism
vul·gar·i·ty
vul·gar·iza·tion
vul·gar·ize
vul·gar·iz·er
vul·ner·a·bil·i·ty
vul·ner·a·ble
vul·ner·a·bly
vul·ture
vul·tur·ous
vul·va
pl vul·vae

W

wad
wad·ded
wad·ding
wad·able
or wade·able
wad·ding
wad·dle
wad·er
wa·di
wa·fer
waf·fle
waft
wag
wagged
wag·ging
wa·ger
wa·ger·er
wag·gery
wag·gish
wag·gle
wag·gly
wag·on
wag·on·ette
wa·gon-lit
pl wa·gons-lits *or* wa·gon-lits
wa·hi·ne

wa·hoo
pl wa·hoos

waif

wail
cry (*see* wale, whale)

wain·scot
wain·scot·ed
or wain·scot·ted
wain·scot·ing
or wain·scot·ting

wain·wright

waist
middle (*see* waste)

waist·band

waist·coat

waist·line

wait·er

wait·ress

waive
give up (*see* wave)

waiv·er

wake
waked
or woke
waked
or wo·ken
wak·ing

wake·ful

wak·en

wale
ridge, texture (*see* wail, whale)

walk·away

walk·er

walk·ie-talk·ie

walk-in

walk-on

walk·out

walk·over

walk-up

walk·way

wal·la·by

wall·board

wal·let

wall·eye

wall·flow·er

wal·lop

wal·lop·ing

wal·low

wall·pa·per

wal·nut

wal·rus
pl wal·rus *or* wal·rus·es

waltz

wam·pum

wan
wanned
wan·ning

wan·der

wan·der·lust

wan·gle

wan·i·gan
or wan·ni·gan

want·ing

wan·ton

wan·ton·ness

wa·pi·ti
pl wa·pi·ti *or* wa·pi·tis

wap·per-jawed

war
warred
war·ring

war·ble

war·bler

war·bon·net

war·den

ward·er

ward·robe

ward·room

ware·house

war·fare

war·head

war-horse

wari·ly

wari·ness

war·like

war·lock

war·lord

warm-blood·ed

warmed-over

warm·heart·ed

war·mon·ger

warmth

warm-up

warn·ing

warp

war·path

war·plane

war·rant

war·rant·able

war·ran·tor

war·ran·ty

war·ren

war·rior
war·ship
wart
war·time
wary
wash·able
wash·ba·sin
wash·board
wash·bowl
wash·cloth
washed-out
wash·er
wash·er·wom·an
wash·house
wash·ing
Wash·ing·ton
wash·out
wash·room
wash·stand
wash·tub
washy
wasp·ish
was·sail
wast·age
waste
refuse (*see* waist)
waste·bas·ket
wast·ed
waste·ful
waste·ful·ly
waste·land
waste·pa·per
wast·rel
watch·band
watch·case
watch·dog
watch·ful
watch·ful·ly
watch·mak·er
watch·mak·ing
watch·man
watch·tow·er
watch·word
wa·ter
wa·ter·borne
Wa·ter·bury
wa·ter·col·or
wa·ter-cool
wa·ter·course
wa·ter·craft
wa·ter·cress
wa·ter·fall
wa·ter-fast
wa·ter·fowl
wa·ter·front
wa·ter·i·ness
wa·ter·leaf
pl wa·ter·leafs
wa·ter·less
wa·ter·line
wa·ter·logged
wa·ter·loo
pl wa·ter·loos
wa·ter·mark
wa·ter·mel·on
wa·ter·pow·er
wa·ter·proof
wa·ter-re·pel·lent
wa·ter-re·sis·tant
wa·ter·scape
wa·ter·shed
wa·ter·side
wa·ter-ski
wa·ter-ski·er
wa·ter-soak
wa·ter·spout
wa·ter·tight
wa·ter·way
wa·ter·wheel
wa·ter·works
wa·ter·worn
wa·tery
watt·age
watt-hour
wat·tle
watt·me·ter
wave
flutter, sea swell (*see* waive)
wave·length
wave·let
wa·ver
wav·i·ly
wav·i·ness
wavy
wax·en
wax·i·ness
wax·ing
wax·wing
wax·work
waxy
way
route, method (*see* weigh, whey)
way·bill
way·far·er

way·far·ing
way·lay
way·laid
way·lay·ing
way-out
way·side
way·ward
weak·en
weak·fish
weak·heart·ed
weak-kneed
weak·ling
weak·ly
weak·mind·ed
weak·ness
weal
well-being, welt (*see* wheal, wheel)
wealth·i·ly
wealth·i·ness
wealthy
wean
weap·on
weap·on·ry
wear
wore
worn
wear·ing
wear·able
wear·er
wea·ri·ly
wea·ri·ness
wea·ri·some
wea·ry
wea·sel
weath·er
atmospheric conditions (*see* whether)
weath·er·abil·i·ty
weath·er-beat·en
weath·er·board
weath·er-bound
weath·er·cock
weath·er·glass
weath·er·ing
weath·er·man
weath·er·proof
weath·er-strip
weath·er-wise
weath·er·worn
weave
wove
or weaved
wo·ven
or weaved
weav·ing
weav·er
web
webbed
web·bing
web-foot·ed
wed
wed·ded
also wed
wed·ding
wedge
Wedg·ies
wed·lock
Wednes·day
weed·er
weedy
week·day
week·end
week·ly
wee·ny
also ween·sy
weep
wept
weep·ing
weep·er
weepy
wee·vil
weigh
measure weight (*see* way, whey)
weight·i·ly
weight·i·ness
weight·less
weighty
weird
wel·come
weld·er
weld·ment
wel·fare
wel·far·ism
well
bet·ter
best
well-ad·vised
well-ap·point·ed
well-be·ing
well-be·loved
well·born
well-bred
well-con·di·tioned

well-de·fined
well-dis·posed
well-done
well-fa·vored
well-fixed
well-found·ed
well-groomed
well-ground·ed
well-han·dled
well·head
well-heeled
well-knit
well-known
well-mean·ing
well-nigh
well-off
well-or·dered
well-read
well-set
well-spo·ken
well·spring
well-thought-of
well-timed
well-to-do
well-turned
well-wish·er
well-worn
wel·ter
wel·ter·weight
welt·schmerz
wench·er
were·wolf
  pl were·wolves
wes·kit
west·bound
west·er·ly
west·ern
West·ern·er
west·ern·iza·tion
west·ern·ize
West·ern Sa·moa
West Vir·gin·ia
wet
  moist (*see* whet)
  wet·ter
  wet·test
wet
  wet
    or wet·ted
  wet·ting
wet·back
wet·land
wet·ness
wet·tish
whale
  sea animal (*see* wail, wale)
whale·back
whale·boat
whale·bone
whal·er
wharf
  pl wharves *also* wharfs
wharf·age
wharf·in·ger
what·ev·er
what·not
what·so·ev·er
wheal
  skin welt (*see* weal, wheel)
wheat
whee·dle
wheel
  disk (*see* weal, wheal)
wheel·bar·row
wheel·base
wheel·chair
wheel·er
wheel·er-deal·er
wheel·horse
wheel·house
wheel·wright
wheeze
wheez·i·ly
wheez·i·ness
wheezy
whelp
whence
when·ev·er
when·so·ev·er
where·abouts
  also where·about
where·as
where·at
where·by
where·fore
where·from
where·in
where·of
where·on
where·so·ev·er
where·to

where·up·on
wher·ev·er
where·with
where·with·al
wher·ry
whet
sharpen (*see* wet)
whet·ted
whet·ting
wheth·er
if (*see* weather)
whet·stone
whey
watery part of milk (*see* way, weigh)
which·ev·er
which·so·ev·er
whiff
while
time (*see* wile)
whim
whim·per
whim·si·cal
whim·si·cal·i·ty
whim·si·cal·ly
whim·sy
or whim·sey
whine
cry (*see* wine)
whin·er
whin·ny
whip
whipped
whip·ping
whip·cord
whip·lash
whip·per·snap·per
whip·pet
whip·poor·will
whip·saw
whip·stitch
whip·stock
whip·worm
whir
also whirr
whirred
whir·ring
whirl
whirl·i·gig
whirl·pool
whirl·wind
whirly·bird
whisk
whisk·er
whis·key
or whis·ky
whis·per
whis·tle
whis·tler
whis·tle-stop
whis·tling
whit
bit (*see* wit)
white·bait
white·cap
white-col·lar
white·face
white-faced
white·fish
White·hall
white-hot
white-liv·ered
whit·en·er
white·ness
whit·en·ing
white·wall
white·wash
whith·er
where (*see* wither)
whith·er·so·ev·er
whit·ing
whit·ish
whit·tle
whiz
or whizz
whizzed
whiz·zing
whiz
or whizz
pl whiz·zes
whiz·zer
who·dun·it
or who·dun·nit
who·ev·er
whole·heart·ed
whole·ness
whole·sale
whole·sal·er
whole·some
whol·ly
whom·ev·er
whom·so·ev·er
whoop-de-do
or whoop-de-doo
whoop·ee

whoop·la
whop·per
whop·ping
whore
whorl
who·so·ev·er
Wich·i·ta
Wich·i·ta Falls
wick·ed
wick·er
wick·er·work
wick·et
wick·i·up
wide-an·gle
wide-awake
wide-eyed
wid·en
wide·mouthed
wide·spread
wid·geon
also wi·geon
wid·get
wid·ish
wid·ow
wid·ow·er
width
wield
wieldy
wie·ner
wife
pl wives
wife·less
wife·li·ness
wife·ly
wig·an
wig·gle
wig·gly
wig·let
wig·mak·er
wig·wag
wig·wam
wil·co
wild·cat
wild·cat·ted
wild·cat·ting
wild·cat·ter
wil·de·beest
wil·der·ness
wild-eyed
wild·fire
wild·fowl
wild·life
wild·wood
wile
trick (*see* while)
wil·i·ly
wil·i·ness
will·ful
or wil·ful
will·ful·ly
wil·lies
will·ing
wil·li·waw
will-o'-the-wisp
wil·low
wil·low·ware
wil·lowy
will·pow·er
wil·ly-nil·ly
wily
wim·ple
win
won
win·ning
wince
wind
detect by scent, rest
wind·ed
wind·ing
wind
blow, sound
wind·ed
or wound
wind·ing
wind
bend
wound
also wind·ed
wind·ing
wind·age
wind·bag
wind·blown
wind·break
wind·burn
wind·er
wind·fall
wind·i·ly
wind·i·ness
wind·ing-sheet
wind·jam·mer
wind·lass
machine
wind·less
without wind
wind·mill
win·dow

win·dow-dress
win·dow·pane
win·dow-shop
win·dow-shop·per
win·dow·sill
wind·pipe
wind·proof
wind·row
wind·shield
Wind·sor
wind·storm
wind·swept
wind·up
wind·ward
wind-wing
windy
wine
beverage (*see* whine)
wine·glass
wine·grow·er
wine·press
win·ery
wine·shop
wine·skin
wing·back
wing·ding
wing-foot·ed
wing·span
wing·spread
win·kle
win·na·ble
win·ner
win·ning
Win·ni·peg

win·now
win·some
Win·ston-Sa·lem
win·ter
win·ter·green
win·ter·iza·tion
win·ter·ize
win·ter·tide
win·ter·time
win·try
or win·tery
wip·er
wir·able
wire·draw
wire·hair
wire·haired
wire·less
Wire·pho·to
wire-pull·er
wir·er
wire·tap
wire·work
wire·worm
wir·i·ness
wir·ing
wiry
Wis·con·sin
wis·dom
wise·acre
wise·crack
wise·ly
wish·bone
wish·ful
wish·ful·ly
wishy-washy

wispy
wis·te·ria
or wis·tar·ia
wist·ful
wist·ful·ly
wit
ingenuity (*see* whit)
witch·craft
witch·ery
witch-hunt
witch·ing
with·al
with·draw
with·drew
with·drawn
with·draw·ing
with·draw·al
with·drawn
with·er
dry up (*see* whither)
with·ers
with·hold
with·held
with·hold·ing
with·in
with·out
with·stand
with·stood
with·stand·ing
wit·less
wit·ness
wit·ti·cism
wit·ti·ly
wit·ti·ness

wit•ty
wiz•ard
wiz•ard•ry
wiz•en
wob•ble
wob•bly
woe•be•gone
woe•ful
also wo•ful
woe•ful•ly
wolf
pl wolves *also* wolf
wolf•hound
wol•ver•ine
wom•an
pl wom•en
wom•an•hood
wom•an•ish
wom•an•kind
wom•an•li•ness
wom•an•ly
womb
wom•en•folk
also wom•en•folks
won
pl won
currency
won•der
won•der•ful
won•der•ful•ly
won•der•land
won•der•ment
won•der-work•er
won•drous
wood•bin
wood•bine
wood-carv•er
wood•chuck
wood•cock
wood•craft
wood•cut
wood•cut•ter
wood•ed
wood•en
wood•en•head
wood•en•ware
wood•land
wood•peck•er
wood•pile
wood•shed
woods•man
woodsy
wood•wind
wood•work
woody
woo•er
woof•er
wool•en
or wool•len
wool•gath•er•ing
wool•li•ness
wool•ly
also wooly
wool•ly-head•ed
wool•pack
woo•zi•ly
woo•zi•ness
woo•zy
Worces•ter
word•age
word•book
word•i•ly
word•i•ness
word•ing
word•less
word•mon•ger
word-of-mouth
word•play
wordy
work
worked
or wrought
work•ing
work•abil•i•ty
work•able
work•a•day
work•bas•ket
work•bench
work•book
work•day
work•er
work•horse
work•house
work•ing•man
work•man
work•man•like
work•man•ship
work•out
work•room
work•shop
work•ta•ble
work•week
world-beat•er
world•li•ness
world•ly

world·ly-wise
world-shak·ing
world-wea·ri·ness
world·wide
worm-eat·en
worm·hole
worm·wood
worn-out
wor·ri·er
wor·ri·ment
wor·ri·some
wor·ry
wor·ry·wart
worse
wors·en
wor·ship
  wor·shiped
    or **wor·shipped**
  wor·ship·ing
    or **wor·ship·ping**
wor·ship·er
wor·ship·ful
wor·ship·ful·ly
worst
wor·sted
wor·thi·ly
wor·thi·ness
worth·less
worth·while
wor·thy
would-be
wound
wound·wort
wrack
wraith
wran·gle
wran·gler
wrap
  cover (*see* **rap**)
  wrapped
  wrap·ping
wrap·around
wrap·per
wrap·ping
wrap-up
wrath·ful
wrath·ful·ly
wreak
  inflict (*see* **reek**)
wreath
  noun
wreathe
  verb
wreck·age
wreck·er
wren
wrench
wrest
wres·tle
wres·tler
wres·tling
wretch
  miserable person (*see* **retch**)
wretch·ed
wrig·gle
wrig·gler
wring
  squeeze (*see* **ring**)
  wrung
  wring·ing
wring·er
wrin·kle
wrin·kly
wrist·band
wrist·let
wrist·lock
wrist·watch
writ
write
  wrote
  writ·ten
    also **writ**
  writ·ing
write-down
write-in
write-off
writ·er
write-up
writhe
wrong·do·er
wrong·do·ing
wrong·ful
wrong·ful·ly
wrong·head·ed
wrong·ly
wrought
wrung
  past of **wring** (*see* **rung**)
wry
  contorted (*see* **rye**)
wry·ly
Wy·o·ming

X

x

x-ed
also x'd *or* xed

x-ing
or x'ing

x-ax·is

X-dis·ease

xe·bec

xe·no·phobe

xe·no·pho·bia

xe·ric

xe·ro·graph·ic

xe·rog·ra·phy

xe·roph·i·lous

xe·roph·thal·mia

xe·ro·phyte

Xmas

x-ray
verb

X ray
noun

xy·lo·phone

xy·lo·phon·ist

Y

yacht

yacht·ing

yachts·man

ya·hoo
pl ya·hoos

yam·mer

Yan·kee

yap

yapped

yap·ping

yard·age

yard·arm

yard·bird

yard·man

yard·mas·ter

yard·stick

yarn-dye

yar·row

yawl

yawn

yaws

y-ax·is

yea

year·book

year·ling

year·long

year·ly

yearn

year-round

yeasty

yel·low

yel·low-dog

yel·low·ish

yelp

Ye·men

Ye·me·ni

Ye·men·ite

yen
pl yen
currency

yen
pl yens
longing

yeo·man

ye·shi·va
or ye·shi·vah
pl ye·shi·vas *or* ye·shi·voth

yes-man

yes·ter·day

yes·ter·year

yew
tree (*see* ewe)

yield

yield·ing

yo·del

yo·deled
or yo·delled

yo·del·ing
or yo·del·ling

yo·del·er

yo·ga

yo·gi
or yo·gin

yo·gurt
or yo·ghurt

yoke
couple (*see* yolk)

yo·kel

yolk
yellow of eggs (*see* yoke)

Yom Kip·pur

yon·der

Yon·kers

youn·ger

young·ish

young·ster

Youngs·town

your·self

your•selves
youth•ful
youth•ful•ly
yowl
yo-yo
  pl yo-yos
yu•an
  pl yu•an
yuc•ca
Yu•go•slav
Yu•go•sla•via
Yu•go•sla•vi•an
Yu•kon
yule•tide

Z

Zaire
Zam•bia
Zam•bi•an
za•ni•ly
za•ni•ness
zany
zar•zue•la
z-ax•is
zeal
zeal•ot
zeal•ous
ze•bra
  pl ze•bras *also* ze•bra
zeit•geist
Zen
ze•nith
ze•o•lite
zeph•yr
zep•pe•lin
ze•ro
  pl ze•ros *also* ze•roes
zest•ful
zest•ful•ly
zig•zag
  zig•zagged
  zig•zag•ging
zil•lion
Zim•bab•we Rho•de•sia
zinc
  zinced
    or zincked
  zinc•ing
    or zinck•ing
zin•nia
Zi•on•ism
zip
  zipped
  zip•ping
zip•per
zip•py
zir•con
zith•er
zlo•ty
  pl zlo•tys *also* zlo•ty
zo•di•ac
zo•di•a•cal
zom•bie
  also zom•bi
zon•al
zon•al•ly
zoo
zoo•ge•og•ra•pher
zoo•ge•o•graph•ic
  or zoo•ge•o•graph•i•cal
zoo•ge•o•graph•i•cal•ly
zoo•ge•og•ra•phy
zoo•log•i•cal
  also zoo•log•ic
zoo•log•i•cal•ly
zo•ol•o•gist
zo•ol•o•gy
zoy•sia
zuc•chet•to
zuc•chi•ni
  pl zuc•chi•ni *or* zuc•chi•nis
zwie•back
zy•gote
zy•mase
zy•mol•o•gy
zy•mot•ic
zy•mur•gy

ABBREVIATIONS

Most of the abbreviations included in this list have been normalized to one form. Variation in the use of periods, in typeface, and in capitalization is frequent and widespread (as *mph*, mph, MPH, m.p.h., Mph)

a acre, alto, answer
A ace, argon, assists
AA Alcoholics Anonymous, associate in arts
AAA American Automobile Association
A and M agricultural and mechanical
ab about
AB able-bodied seaman, at bats, bachelor of arts
ABA American Bar Association
abbr abbreviation
ABC American Broadcasting Company
abl ablative
abp archbishop
abr abridged, abridgment
abs absolute
abstr abstract
ac account
Ac actinium
AC alternating current, ante Christum (*Latin*, before Christ), ante cibum (*Latin*, before meals)
acad academic, academy
accel accelerando
acct account
ack acknowledge, acknowledgment
act active, actual
A.C.T. Australian Capital Territory
actg acting
A.D. after date, anno Domini (*Latin*, in the year of our Lord)
addn addition
addnl additional
ad int ad interim
adj adjective, adjutant
ad loc ad locum (*Latin*, to [at] the place)
adm admiral
admin administration
adv adverb, advertisement
ad val ad valorem (*Latin*, according to value)
advg advertising
advt advertisement
AEF American Expeditionary Force
aeq aequales (*Latin*, equal)
aet, aetat aetatis (*Latin*, of age)
AF air force, audio frequency
AFB air force base
afft affidavit
AFL-CIO American Federation of Labor and Congress of Industrial

Organizations
Afr Africa, African
Ag argentum (*Latin*, silver)
AG adjutant general, attorney general
agcy agency
agric, agr agricultural, agriculture
agt agent
AID Agency for International Development
AK Alaska
Al aluminum
AL Alabama
Ala Alabama
ALA American Library Association, Automobile Legal Association
alc alcohol
ald alderman
alg algebra
alk alkaline
alt alternate, altitude
Alta Alberta
alter alteration
a.m. ante meridiem (*Latin*, before noon)
Am America, American, americium
AM amplitude modulation, master of arts
AMA American Medical Association
amb ambassador
amdt amendment
AME African Methodist Episcopal
Amer America, American
amp ampere
amt amount
anal analogy, analysis, analytic
anat anatomy
anc ancient
and andante
ann annals, annual
anon anonymous
ans answer
ant antonym
anthrop anthropology
a/o account of
ap apothecaries'
AP additional premium, Associated Press
APO army post office
app apparatus, appendix
appl applied
appnt appointment
approx approximate, approximately
appt appoint, appointment
Apr April
apt apartment
aq aqueous
ar arrival, arrive
Ar Arabic, argon
AR Arkansas
ARC American Red Cross
arch architecture
archeol archeology
archit architecture
arith arithmetic
Ariz Arizona
Ark Arkansas
arr arranged, arrival, arrive
art article, artificial, artillery
ARV American Revised

Version
As arsenic
AS Anglo-Saxon, antisubmarine
assn association
assoc associate, association
ASSR Autonomous Soviet Socialist Republic
asst assistant
astrol astrology
astron astronomer, astronomy
ASV American Standard Version
At astatine
Atl Atlantic
atm atmosphere, atmospheric
att attached, attention, attorney
attn attention
attrib attributive
atty attorney
Au aurum (*Latin*, gold)
aud audit, auditor
Aug August
AUS Army of the United States
Austral Australian
auth authentic, author, authorized
aux auxiliary
av avenue, average, avoirdupois
AV ad valorem (*Latin*, according to value); audiovisual, Authorized Version
avdp avoirdupois
ave avenue
avg average
AZ Arizona

b bass, book; born
B bachelor, bishop, boron
Ba barium
BA bachelor of arts
bal balance
bar barometer
Bart baronet
BB bases on balls, best of breed
BBA bachelor of business administration
BBB Better Business Bureau
BBC British Broadcasting Corporation
bbl barrel
B.C. before Christ, British Columbia
BCS bachelor of commercial science
bd board, bound
BD bachelor of divinity, bank draft, bills discounted, brought down
bdl bundle
Be beryllium
BE bill of exchange
BEF British Expeditionary Force
Belg Belgian, Belgium
bet between
bf boldface
BF brought forward
bg bag
bhd bulkhead
Bi bismuth
bib Bible, biblical
bibliog bibliographer,

bibliography
BID bis in die (*Latin,* twice a day)
biochem biochemistry
biog biographical, biography
biol biologic, biological, biology
bk bank, book
Bk berkelium
bkg banking
bkgd background
bkt basket, bracket
bl bale, blue
B/L bill of lading
bldg building
bldr builder
blk black, block
blvd boulevard
BM basal metabolism, bowel movement
B/M bill of material
BMR basal metabolic rate
BO body odor, branch office, buyer's option
BOD biochemical oxygen demand
BOQ bachelor officers' quarters
bor borough
bot botanical, botany
bp bishop, boiling point
BP bills payable, blood pressure, British Pharmacopoeia
bpl birthplace
BPOE Benevolent and Protective Order of Elks
br branch, brass, brown
Br British, bromine
BR bills receivable
brig brigade, brigadier
Brit Britain, British
bro brother
bros brothers
BS bachelor of science, balance sheet, bill of sale
BSA Boy Scouts of America
BSc bachelor of science
bskt basket
Bt baronet
Btu British thermal unit
bu bushel
bull bulletin
bur bureau
bus business
BV Blessed Virgin
BWI British West Indies
bx box
BX base exchange

c cape, carat, cent, centimeter, century, chapter, circa, copyright, cup
C carbon, centigrade
ca circa
Ca calcium
CA California, chartered accountant, chief accountant, chronological age
CAF cost and freight
cal calendar, caliber, calorie
calc calculating
Calif, Cal California
Can Canada, Canadian
Canad Canada, Canadian
canc canceled
C and F cost and freight
cap capacity, capital,

capitalize, capitalized
caps capitals, capsule
capt captain
card cardinal
CARE Co-operative for American Remittances to Everywhere
cat catalog
CATV community antenna television
CBC Canadian Broadcasting Corporation
CBD cash before delivery
CBS Columbia Broadcasting System
CBW chemical and biological warfare
cc cubic centimeter
CC carbon copy
CCC Civilian Conservation Corps
CCTV closed-circuit television
ccw counterclockwise
cd cord
Cd cadmium
cdr commander
Ce cerium
CE chemical engineer, civil engineer
cen central
cent centigrade, central, century
cert certificate, certification, certified, certify
cf confer (*Latin*, compare)
Cf californium
CF carried forward, cost and freight
CFI cost, freight, and insurance
cg, cgm centigram
CG coast guard, commanding general
ch chain, champion, chapter, church
CH clearinghouse, courthouse, customhouse
chap chapter
chem chemical, chemist, chemistry
chg change, charge
Chin Chinese
chm, chmn chairman
chron chronicle, chronological, chronology
Chron Chronicles
CI cost and insurance
cía compañía (*Spanish*, company)
cie compagnie (*French*, company)
CIF cost, insurance, and freight
C in C commander in chief
cir circle, circular
circ circular
cit citation, cited, citizen
civ civil, civilian
ck cask, check
cl class
Cl chlorine
CL carload
cld called, cleared
clk clerk
clo clothing
clr clear
cm centimeter

CM Congregation of the Mission
cml commercial
CN credit note
CNO chief of naval operations
CNS central nervous system
co company, county
c/o care of
Co cobalt
CO cash order, Colorado, commanding officer, conscientious objector
COD cash on delivery, collect on delivery
C of C Chamber of Commerce
C of S chief of staff
cog cognate
col colonel, colony, column
Col Colossians
coll college
collat collateral
colloq colloquial
Colo Colorado
com commander, commerce, commissioner, committee, common
comb combination, combining
comdg commanding
comdr commander
comdt commandant
coml commercial
comm commission, commonwealth
commo commodore
comp comparative, compiled, compiler, composition, compound
compar comparative
comr commissioner
con consul, contra (*Latin*, against)
conc concentrated
conf conference
Confed Confederate
cong congress
conj conjunction
Conn Connecticut
cons consonant
consol consolidated
const constant, constitution, constitutional
constr construction
cont containing, contents, continent, continental, continued, control
contd continued
contg containing
contr contract, contraction
contrib contribution, contributor
cor corner
Cor Corinthians
CORE Congress of Racial Equality
corp corporal, corporation
corr corrected, correction, correspondence, corresponding, corrugated
cos companies, counties
COS cash on shipment, chief of staff
cp compare, coupon
CP chemically pure,

Communist party
CPA certified public accountant
cpd compound
CPFF cost plus fixed fee
cpl corporal
CPO chief petty officer
CPS cycles per second
CQ charge of quarters
cr credit, creditor, crown
Cr chromium
cresc crescendo
crit critical, criticism
cryst crystalline
cs case, cases
c/s cycles per second
Cs cesium
CS chief of staff, civil service
CSA Confederate States of America
CSSR Congregatio Sanctissimi Redemptoris (*Latin,* Congregation of the Most Holy Redeemer)
CST Central standard time
ct carat, cent, count, court
CT Central time, Connecticut
ctge cartage
ctn carton
ctr center
cu cubic
Cu cuprum (*Latin,* copper)
cum cumulative
cur currency, current
cw clockwise
CWO cash with order, chief warrant officer
cwt hundredweight
cyc cyclopedia
cycl cyclopedia
cyl cylinder
CYO Catholic Youth Organization
CZ Canal Zone

d date, daughter, day, degree, died, penny
D Democrat, Democratic, diameter, doctor, dollar, Dutch
DA days after acceptance, deposit account, district attorney, don't answer
Dan Daniel, Danish
DAR Daughters of the American Revolution
dat dative
dau daughter
db decibel
dbl double
DC da capo (*Italian,* from the beginning), decimal classification, direct current, District of Columbia, doctor of chiropractic, double crochet
DD days after date, demand draft, dishonorable discharge, doctor of divinity
DDD direct distance dialing
DDS doctor of dental science, doctor of dental surgery
DE Delaware
dec deceased, decrease

Dec December
def definite, definition
deg degree
del delegate, delegation
Del Delaware
dely delivery
Dem Democrat, Democratic
Den Denmark
dep depart, departure, deposit, deputy
depr depreciation
dept department
deriv derivation, derivative
det detached, detachment, detail
Deut Deuteronomy
dev deviation
DEW distant early warning
DF damage free
DFC distinguished flying cross
DFM distinguished flying medal
DG Dei gratia (*Late Latin*, by the grace of God), director general
dia diameter
diag diagonal, diagram
dial dialect
diam diameter
dict dictionary
diff difference
dig digest
dil dilute
dim dimension, diminished, diminutive
dir director
disc discount
dist distance, district
distn distillation
distr distribute, distribution, distributor
div divided, dividend, division
dk dark, deck, dock
DLit doctor of letters, doctor of literature
DLitt doctor of letters, doctor of literature
DLO dead letter office
DMD doctor of dental medicine
dn down
do ditto
DOA dead on arrival
doc document
dol dollar
dom domestic, dominant, dominion
doz dozen
DP domestic prelate, double play
dpt department
dr debit, debtor, dram, drive, drum
Dr doctor
DR dead reckoning, dining room
DS dal segno (*Italian*, from the sign), days after sight
DSC distinguished service cross, doctor of surgical chiropody
DSM distinguished service medal
DSO distinguished service order
dsp decessit sine prole (*Latin*, died without issue)

DST daylight saving time
Du Dutch
dup, dupl duplicate
DV Deo volente (*Latin*, God willing), Douay Version
DVM doctor of veterinary medicine
dwt pennyweight
DX distance
dz dozen

E east, eastern, einsteinium, English, errors, excellent
ea each
E and OE errors and omissions excepted
EC east central
eccl ecclesiastic, ecclesiastical
Eccles Ecclesiastes
Ecclus Ecclesiasticus
ecol ecological, ecology
econ economics, economist, economy
Ecua Ecuador
ed edited, edition, editor, education
EDT Eastern daylight time
educ education, educational
EE electrical engineer
eff efficiency
e.g. exempli gratia (*Latin*, for example)
Eg Egypt, Egyptian
ehf extremely high frequency
el elevation
elec electric, electrical, electricity
elect electric, electrical, electricity
elem elementary
elev elevation
embryol embryology
emer emeritus
EMF electromotive force
emp emperor, empress
emu electromagnetic unit
enc enclosure
encl enclosure
ency encyclopedia
encyc encyclopedia
ENE east-northeast
eng engine, engineer, engineering
Eng England, English
engr engineer, engraved, engraving
enl enlarged, enlisted
ens ensign
entom entomology
entomol entomology
env envelope
EOM end of month
Eph Ephesians
eq equal, equation
equip equipment
equiv equivalent
ER earned runs
ERA earned run average
erron erroneous
Es einsteinium
ESE east-southeast
esp especially
ESP extrasensory perception
esq esquire
est established, estimate, estimated

EST Eastern standard time
Esth Esther
ET Eastern time
ETA estimated time of arrival
et al et alii (*Latin,* and others)
etc et cetera (*Latin,* and so forth)
ETD estimated time of departure
ethnol ethnology
et seq et sequens (*Latin,* and the following one), et sequentes *or* et sequentia (*Latin,* and those that follow)
ety etymology
Eu europium
Eur Europe, European
EV electron volt
EVA extravehicular activity
evap evaporate
ex example, express, extra
exc excellent, except
exch exchange, exchanged
ex div without dividend
exec executive, executor
Exod Exodus
exor executor
exp expense, export, exported, express
expt experiment
exptl experimental
ext extension, exterior, external, extra, extract
Ezek Ezekiel
f female, feminine, filly, focal length, folio, following, forte, frequency
F Fahrenheit, fair, false, fellow, fluorine, French, Friday, furlong
fac facsimile, faculty
FAdm fleet admiral
Fahr Fahrenheit
FAO Food and Agricultural Organization of the United Nations
FAS free alongside
fath fathom
FB freight bill
FBI Federal Bureau of Investigation
fcp foolscap
fcy fancy
FDIC Federal Deposit Insurance Corporation
Fe ferrum (*Latin,* iron)
Feb February
fec fecit (*Latin,* he [she] made it)
fed federal, federation
fedl federal
fedn federation
fem feminine
FEPC Fair Employment Practices Commission
ff folios, following
FICA Federal Insurance Contributions Act
FIFO first in, first out
fig figurative, figuratively, figure
fin finance, financial, finish
Finn Finnish

FIO free in and out
fisc fiscal
fl flourished, fluid
FL Florida
Fla Florida
Flem Flemish
fm fathom
Fm fermium
FM frequency modulation
fn footnote
fo folio
FOB free on board
FOC free of charge
fol folio
for foreign, forestry
FOR free on rail
FOS free on steamer
FOT free on truck
fp freezing point
FPC fish protein concentrate
fpm feet per minute
FPO fleet post office
fr father, friar, from
Fr francium, French, Friday
freq frequent, frequently
Fri Friday
front frontispiece
FRS Federal Reserve System
frt freight
frwy freeway
FSLIC Federal Savings and Loan Insurance Corporation
ft feet, foot, fort
fur furlong
furn furnished, furniture
fut future
fwd forward
FYI for your information

g acceleration of gravity, gauge, gram, gravity
G German, good
ga gauge
Ga gallium, Georgia
GA general agent, general assembly, general average, Georgia
Gael Gaelic
gal gallon
Gal Galatians
galv galvanized
gar garage
GAR Grand Army of the Republic
GAW guaranteed annual wage
gaz gazette, gazetteer
GB games behind, Great Britain
GCA ground-controlled approach
GCT Greenwich civil time
Gd gadolinium
gds goods
Ge germanium
gen general, genitive
Gen Genesis
genl general
geog geographic, geographical, geography
geol geologic, geological, geology
geom geometrical, geometry
ger gerund
Ger German, Germany

GHQ general headquarters
gi gill
GI general issue, government issue
Gk Greek
gloss glossary
gm gram
GM general manager
Gmc Germanic
GNP gross national product
GOP Grand Old Party (Republican)
Goth Gothic
gov governor
govt government
gox gaseous oxygen
gp group
GP general practitioner
GPO general post office, Government Printing Office
GQ general quarters
gr grade, grain, gram, gravity, gross
grad graduate
gram grammar
gro gross
GSA Girl Scouts of America
gt great, gutta (*Latin,* drop)
GT gross ton
Gt Brit Great Britain
gtd guaranteed
GU Guam

h hard, hardness, hour, husband
H hits, hydrogen
ha hectare
Hab Habakkuk
Hag Haggai
handbk handbook
Hb hemoglobin
HBM Her Britannic Majesty, His Britannic Majesty
HC Holy Communion, House of Commons
HCL high cost of living
hd head
HD heavy-duty
hdbk handbook
hdkf handkerchief
hdqrs headquarters
hdwe, hdwre hardware
He helium
HE high explosive, His Eminence, His Excellency
Heb Hebrew, Hebrews
hf half, high frequency
Hf hafnium
Hg hydrargyrum (*Latin,* mercury)
HG High German
hgt height
HH Her Highness, His Highness, His Holiness
hhd hogshead
HI Hawaii
hist historian, historical, history
HJ hic jacet (*Latin,* here lies)—used in epitaphs
HL House of Lords
HM Her Majesty, His Majesty
HMS Her Majesty's Ship, His Majesty's Ship
Ho holmium
hon honor, honorable,

honorary
hor horizontal
hort horticultural, horticulture
Hos Hosea
hosp hospital
hp horsepower
HP high pressure
HQ headquarters
hr hour
HR home run, House of Representatives
HRH Her Royal Highness, His Royal Highness
HS high school, house surgeon
hse house
ht height
HT high-tension
Hung Hungarian, Hungary
HV high voltage
hvy heavy
hwy highway
hyp, hypoth hypothesis, hypothetical

I iodine, island, isle
Ia Iowa
IA Iowa
ib, ibid ibidem (*Latin,* in the same place)
IBM intercontinental ballistic missile
ICBM intercontinental ballistic missile
ICJ International Court of Justice
id idem (*Latin,* the same)
ID Idaho, identification
i.e. id est (*Latin,* that is)
IE Indo-European
IF intermediate frequency
IGY International Geophysical Year
IHP indicated horsepower
IHS Iesus Hominum Salvator (*Latin,* Jesus, Savior of Men)
IL Illinois
ill illustrated, illustration
Ill Illinois
illus, illust illustrated, illustration
ILS instrument landing system
imit imitative
imp imperative, imperfect, imperial, import, imported
imperf imperfect
in inch
In indium
IN Indiana
inc incorporated, increase
incl including, inclusive
incog incognito
incr increase
ind independent, index, industrial, industry
Ind Indiana
indef indefinite
indic indicative
inf infantry, infinitive, information
infl influenced
INP International News Photo
INRI Iesus Nazarenus Rex Iudaeorum (*Latin,*

Jesus of Nazareth, King of the Jews)
ins inches, insurance
insol insoluble
insp inspector
inst instant, institute, institution
instr instructor, instrument
int interest, interior, internal, international
interj interjection
interrog interrogative
intl international
intrans intransitive
introd introduction
inv invoice
IOOF Independent Order of Odd Fellows
IP innings pitched
IPA International Phonetic Alphabet
i.q. idem quod (*Latin,* the same as)
IQ intelligence quotient
Ir iridium, Irish
IRBM intermediate range ballistic missile
Ire Ireland
irreg irregular
IRS Internal Revenue Service
Isa Isaiah
isl island
Isr Israel, Israeli
It Italian
ital italic, italicized
Ital Italian
IUCD intrauterine contraceptive device
IUD intrauterine device
IV intravenous
IWW Industrial Workers of the World

J jack, journal
Jam Jamaica
Jan January
Jap Japan, Japanese
Jas James
JCC Junior Chamber of Commerce
JCS joint chiefs of staff
jct junction
Je June
Jer Jeremiah
jg junior grade
Jn John
jnt, jt joint
Josh Joshua
jour journal
JP jet propulsion, justice of the peace
jr junior
JRC Junior Red Cross
Judg Judges
Jul July
jun junior
Jun June
junc junction
juv juvenile
JV junior varsity

k karat, knit
K kalium (*Latin,* potassium), king
Kans Kansas
kc kilocycle
KC king's counsel, Knights of Columbus
kc/s kilocycles per second
KD kiln-dried, knocked down
kg kilogram

kgm kilogram
KKK Ku Klux Klan
km kilometer
kn knot
K of C Knights of Columbus
KS Kansas
kt karat, knight
kw kilowatt
Ky Kentucky
KY Kentucky

l left, length, line, liter
L lake, large, Latin, libra (*Latin,* pound)
La Louisiana
LA law agent, Los Angeles, Louisiana
Lab Labrador
lam laminated
Lam Lamentations
lang language
lat latitude
Lat Latin
lb pound
LC letter of credit, Library of Congress
LCD lowest common denominator
lcdr lieutenant commander
LCL less than carload
LCM least common multiple
ld load, lord
LD lethal dose
ldg landing, loading
lect lecture
leg legal, legislative, legislature
legis legislative, legislature
LEM lunar excursion model
Lev Leviticus
lf low frequency
lg large
LG Low German
lge large
LGk Late Greek
LH left hand, lower half
li link
Li lithium
LI Long Island
lib liberal, librarian, library
lieut lieutenant
LIFO last in, first out
lin lineal, linear
liq liquid, liquor
lit liter, literal, literally, literary, literature
LitD doctor of letters, doctor of literature
lith, litho lithography
LittD doctor of letters, doctor of literature
Lk Luke
ll lines
LL Late Latin
LLD doctor of laws
LOB left on bases
loc cit loco citato (*Latin,* in the place cited)
log logarithm
Lond London
long longitude
loq loquitur (*Latin,* he [she] speaks)
LP low pressure
LS left side, letter signed, locus sigilli (*Latin,* place of the seal)
lt lieutenant, light

LT long ton, low-tension
ltd limited
LTL less than truckload
ltr letter
lub lubricant, lubricating
lv leave

m male, mare, married, masculine, meridian, meridies (*Latin*, noon), meter, mile, mill, minute, month, moon
M master, medium, mille (*Latin*, thousand), Monday, monsieur
MA Massachusetts, master of arts, mental age
mach machine, machinery, machinist
mag magazine, magnetism, magneto, magnitude
maj major
Mal Malachi
man manual
Man Manitoba
manuf manufacture, manufacturing
mar maritime
Mar March
masc masculine
Mass Massachusetts
math mathematical, mathematician, mathematics
MATS Military Air Transport Service
max maximum
mc megacycle
MC master of ceremonies, member of congress
Md Maryland
MD doctor of medicine, Maryland, months after date
mdnt midnight
mdse merchandise
Me Maine
ME Maine, mechanical engineer, Middle English, mining engineer
meas measure
mech mechanical, mechanics
med medical, medicine, medieval, medium
mem member, memoir, memorial
mer meridian
Messrs messieurs
met metropolitan
meteorol meteorology
MEV million electron volts
Mex Mexican, Mexico
mf medium frequency
MF Middle French
mfd manufactured
mfg manufacturing
mfr manufacture, manufacturer
mg milligram
Mg magnesium
MG machine gun, military government
MGk Middle Greek
mgr manager, monseigneur, monsignor
mgt management
mi mile, mill
MI Michigan, military

intelligence
MIA missing in action
Mic Micah
Mich Michigan
mid middle
mil military
min minimum, mining, minister, minor, minute
mineral mineralogy
Minn Minnesota
misc miscellaneous
Miss Mississippi
mixt mixture
mk mark
Mk Mark
ML Middle Latin
MLD minimum lethal dose
Mlle mademoiselle
mm millimeter
MM Maryknoll Missioners, messieurs
Mme madame
Mn manganese
MN Minnesota
mo month
Mo Missouri, molybdenum
MO mail order, medical officer, Missouri, money order
mod moderate, modern
modif modification
mol molecular, molecule
mol wt molecular weight
MOM middle of month
Mon Monday
Mont Montana
mos months
mp melting point
MP member of parliament, metropolitan police, military police, military policeman
mpg miles per gallon
mph miles per hour
Mr mister
Mrs mistress
MS manuscript, master of science, Mississippi, motor ship
msg message
msgr monseigneur, monsignor
MSgt master sergeant
msl mean sea level
MSS manuscripts
MST Mountain standard time
mt mount, mountain
Mt Matthew
MT metric ton, Montana, Mountain time
mtg, mtge mortgage
mtl metal
mtn mountain
mun, munic municipal
mus museum, music
MV mean variation, motor vessel
mythol mythology

n net, neuter, new, noon, note, noun, number
N knight, nitrogen, normal, north, northern
Na natrium (*Latin*, sodium)
NA no account
NAACP National Association for the Advancement of Colored People

Nah Nahum
NAS naval air station
nat national, native, natural
natl national
NATO North Atlantic Treaty Organization
naut nautical
nav naval, navigable, navigation
Nb niobium
NB nota bene (*Latin*, note well)
N.B. New Brunswick
NBC National Broadcasting Company
NBS National Bureau of Standards
NC no charge, North Carolina
N.C. North Carolina
NCE New Catholic Edition
NCO noncommissioned officer
Nd neodymium
ND no date, North Dakota
N.D. North Dakota
N. Dak. North Dakota
Ne neon
NE Nebraska, New England, northeast
Neb Nebraska
NEB New English Bible
Nebr Nebraska
NED New English Dictionary
neg negative
Neh Nehemiah
NEI not elsewhere included, not elsewhere indicated
NES not elsewhere specified
Neth Netherlands
neurol neurology
neut neuter
Nev Nevada
NF no funds
Nfld Newfoundland
NG National Guard, no good
NGk New Greek
NH New Hampshire
N.H. New Hampshire
NHG New High German
NHI national health insurance (*Brit.*)
Ni nickel
NJ New Jersey
N.J. New Jersey
nk neck
NL New Latin, night letter, non liquet (*Latin*, it is not clear)
NLT night letter
NM nautical mile, New Mexico, night message, no mark, not marked
N.M. New Mexico
N. Mex. New Mexico
NNE north-northeast
NNW north-northwest
no north, northern, nose, number
No nobelium
NOIBN not otherwise indexed by name
nol pros nolle prosequi (*Latin*, to be unwilling to prosecute)
nom nominative
non seq non sequitur

Norw Norway, Norwegian
NOS not otherwise specified
Nov November
Np neptunium
NP no protest, notary public
NPN nonprotein nitrogen
nr near, number
NS not specified
N.S. Nova Scotia
NSF not sufficient funds
N.S.W. New South Wales
NT New Testament
N.T. Northern Territory
NTP normal temperature and pressure
nt wt net weight
NU name unknown
Num Numbers
numis numismatic, numismatics
NV Nevada
NW northwest
NWT Northwest Territories
NY New York
N.Y. New York
NYC New York City
N.Z. New Zealand

o ocean, ohm
O oxygen
o/a on account
OAS Organization of American States
ob obiit (*Latin,* he [she] died)
Obad Obadiah
obj object, objective
obl oblique, oblong
obs obsolete
obv obverse
OC overcharge
occas occasionally
OCS officer candidate school
oct octavo
Oct October
o/d on demand
OD officer of the day, olive drab, overdraft, overdrawn
OE Old English
OED Oxford English Dictionary
OES Order of the Eastern Star
OF Old French
ofc office
off office, officer, official
OFM Order of Friars Minor
O.F.S. Orange Free State
OG original gum
OH Ohio
OK Oklahoma
Okla Oklahoma
ON Old Norse
Ont Ontario
op opus, out of print
OP Order of Preachers
op cit opere citato (*Latin,* in the work cited)
opp opposite
opt optical, optician, optional
OR Oregon, owner's risk
orch orchestra
ord order, ordnance
Oreg, Ore Oregon
org organization, organized

orig original, originally
ornith ornithology
o/s out of stock
Os osmium
OS ordinary seaman
OS and D over, short, and damaged
OSB Order of St. Benedict
OT Old Testament, overtime
OTS officers' training school
oz ounce

p page, participle, past, penny, per, pint, purl
P pawn, phosphorus, pressure
pa per annum
Pa Pennsylvania
PA passenger agent, Pennsylvania, power of attorney, press agent, private account, public address, purchasing agent
Pac Pacific
paleon paleontology
pam pamphlet
Pan Panama
P and L profit and loss
par paragraph, parallel, parish
parl parliament, parliamentary
part participial, participle, particular
pass passenger, passive
pat patent
path, pathol pathology
payt payment
Pb plumbum (*Latin*, lead)
pc percent, percentage, piece, postcard, post cibum (*Latin*, after meals)
PC petty cash, privy council, privy councillor
pct percent
pd paid, pond
Pd palladium
PD per diem, potential difference
PE professional engineer, Protestant Episcopal
ped pedal
P.E.I. Prince Edward Island
pen peninsula
penin peninsula
Penn Pennsylvania
Penna Pennsylvania
per period
Per Persian
perf perfect, perforated
perh perhaps
perm permanent
perp perpendicular
pers person, personal
Pers Persia, Persian
pert pertaining
Pet Peter
pf preferred
pfc private first class
pfd preferred
pg page
PG postgraduate
pharm pharmaceutical, pharmacist, pharmacy
PhD doctor of philosophy

Phil Philippians
Phila Philadelphia
Philem Philemon
philos philosopher, philosophy
phon phonetics
photog photographic, photography
phr phrase
phys physical, physician, physics
physiol physiologist, physiology
P.I. Philippine Islands
pinx pinxit (*Latin,* he [she] painted it)
pk park, peak, peck
pkg package
pkt packet
pkwy parkway
pl place, plate, plural
pm premium
p.m. post meridiem (*Latin,* afternoon)
Pm promethium
PM paymaster, police magistrate, postmaster, postmortem, prime minister, provost marshal
pmk postmark
pmt payment
PN promissory note
pnxt pinxit (*Latin,* he [she] painted it)
Po polonium
PO petty officer, postal order, post office, putouts
POC port of call
POD pay on delivery
POE port of embarkation, port of entry
Pol Poland, Polish
polit political, politician
polytech polytechnic
pop popular, population
POR pay on return
Port Portugal, Portuguese
pos position, positive
poss possessive
POW prisoner of war
pp pages, past participle, pianissimo
PP parcel post, post position
PPC pour prendre congé (*French,* to take leave)
ppd postpaid, prepaid
PPS post postscriptum (*Latin,* an additional postscript)
ppt precipitate
pptn precipitation
PQ Province of Quebec
pr pair, price
Pr praseodymium
PR payroll, public relations, Puerto Rico
prec preceding
pred predicate
pref preface, preference, preferred, prefix
prelim preliminary
prem premium
prep preparatory, preposition
pres present, president
prev previous
prf proof
prim primary, primitive
prin principal
PRN pro re nata (*Latin,*

for an occasion that has arisen, as occasion arises)
PRO public relations officer
prob probable, probably, problem
proc proceedings
prod production
prof professor
pron pronoun, pronounced, pronunciation
prop propeller, property, proprietor, proposition
pros prosody
Prot Protestant
prov province, provincial, provisional
Prov Proverbs
prp present participle
Ps Psalms
PS postscriptum (*Latin*, postscript), public school
pseud pseudonym
psi pounds per square inch
PST Pacific standard time
psych psychology
psychol psychologist, psychology
pt part, payment, pint, point, port
Pt platinum
PT Pacific time, physical therapy, physical training
PTA Parent-Teacher Association
pte private (*Brit.*)
ptg printing
PTO please turn over
PTV public television
Pu plutonium
pub public, publication, published, publisher, publishing
publ publication, published
pvt private
PW prisoner of war
PX post exchange

q quart, quarto, query, question, quire
Q queen
QC Queen's Counsel
qd quaque die (*Latin*, daily)
qda quantity discount agreement
QED quod erat demonstrandum (*Latin*, which was to be demonstrated)
QEF quod erat faciendum (*Latin*, which was to be done)
QEI quod erat inveniendum (*Latin*, which was to be found out)
QID quater in die (*Latin*, four times a day)
Q'land Queensland
Qld Queensland
QM quartermaster
QMC quartermaster corps
QMG quartermaster general
qq v quae vide (*Latin*, which [pl] see)

qr quarter, quire
qt quart
q.t. quiet
qto quarto
qty quantity
quad quadrant
Que Quebec
quot quotation
q.v. quod vide (*Latin*, which see)
qy query

r rare, right, river, roentgen
R rabbi, radius, Republican, resistance, rook, runs
Ra radium
RA regular army, royal academy
RAAF Royal Australian Air Force
rad radical, radio, radius
RAdm rear admiral
RAF Royal Air Force
R and D research and development
Rb rubidium
RBC red blood cells, red blood count
RBI runs batted in
RC Red Cross, Roman Catholic
RCAF Royal Canadian Air Force
RCMP Royal Canadian Mounted Police
rd road, rod, round
RD rural delivery
re reference, regarding
Re rhenium
REA Railway Express Agency
rec receipt, record, recording, recreation
recd received
recip reciprocal, reciprocity
rec sec recording secretary
rect rectangle, rectangular, receipt, rectified
ref referee, reference, referred, reformed, refunding
refl reflex, reflexive
refr refraction
refrig refrigerating, refrigeration
reg region, register, registered, regular, regulation
regt regiment
rel relating, relative
relig religion
rep report, reporter, representative, republic
Rep Republican
repl replace, replacement
rept report
req require, required, requisition
res research, reserve, residence, resolution
resp respective, respectively
retd retained, retired, returned
rev revenue, reverend, reverse, review, reviewed, revised, revision, revolution
Rev Revelation

RF radio frequency
RFD rural free delivery
Rh rhodium
RH right hand
RI Rhode Island
R.I. Rhode Island
RIP requiescat in pace (*Latin,* may he [she] rest in peace)
riv river
rm ream, room
RMA Royal Military Academy (Sandhurst)
RMS root mean square
Rn radon
RN registered nurse, Royal Navy
rnd round
RNZAF Royal New Zealand Air Force
ROG receipt of goods
Rom Roman, Romance, Romania, Romanian, Romans
ROTC Reserve Officers' Training Corps
rpm revolutions per minute
RPO railway post office
rps revolutions per second
rpt repeat, report
rr rear
RR railroad, rural route
RS recording secretary, revised statutes, right side, Royal Society
RSV Revised Standard Version
RSVP répondez s'il vous plaît (*French,* please reply
RSWC right side up with care
rt right, route
RT radiotelephone
rte route
Ru ruthenium
Rum Rumania, Rumanian
Russ Russia, Russian
RW radiological warfare, right worshipful, right worthy
rwy railway
ry railway

s second, section, semi, series, shilling, singular, son, soprano
S sacrifice, saint, Saturday, senate, small, south, southern, sulfur, Sunday
Sa Saturday
SA Salvation Army, sex appeal, sine anno (*Latin,* without date), South Africa, subject to approval
S.A. South Australia
SAC Strategic Air Command
Sam Samuel
sanit sanitary, sanitation
SAR Sons of the American Revolution
Sask Saskatchewan
sat saturate, saturated, saturation
Sat Saturday
S. Aust South Australia
sb substantive
SB bachelor of science,

stolen base
sc scale, scene, science, scilicet (*Latin,* that is to say), small capitals
Sc scandium, Scots
SC South Carolina
S.C. South Carolina
Scand Scandinavia, Scandinavian
ScD doctor of science
ScGael Scottish Gaelic
sch school
sci science, scientific
scil scilicet (*Latin,* that is to say)
Scot Scotland, Scottish
script scripture
sctd scattered
sculp, sculpt sculpsit (*Latin,* he [she] carved it), sculptor, sculpture
SD sea-damaged, sine die, South Dakota, special delivery
S.D. South Dakota
S. Dak South Dakota
Se selenium
SE southeast
SEATO Southeast Asia Treaty Organization
sec second, secondary, secretary, section, secundum (*Latin,* according to)
sect section
secy secretary
sel select, selected, selection
sem seminary
sen senate, senator, senior
sep separate
sepn separation
Sept, Sep September
seq sequens (*Latin,* the following [singular])
seqq sequentia (*Latin,* the following [plural])
ser serial, series
serg sergeant
sergt sergeant
serv service
sf science fiction
SF sacrifice fly
sfc sergeant first class
sg senior grade, singular, specific gravity
SG solicitor general, surgeon general
sgd signed
sgt sergeant
sh share, show
Shak Shakespeare
shpt, shipt shipment
shr share
sht sheet
shtg shortage
Si silicon
S.I. Sandwich Islands, Staten Island (N.Y.)
sig signal, signature
sigill sigillum (*Latin,* seal)
sing singular
SJ Society of Jesus
Skt Sanskrit
SL salvage loss
s.l.a.n. sine loco, anno, vel nomine (*Latin,* without place, year, or name)
sld sailed, sealed
sm small
Sm samarium
SM master of science,

Society of Mary
Sn stannum (*Late Latin,* tin)
so south, southern
SO seller's option, strikeouts
soc social, society
sociol sociology
sol solicitor, soluble, solution
Sol Solomon
soln solution
sop soprano
SOP standard operating procedure
soph sophomore
sp special, species, specimen, spelling, spirit
Sp Spain, Spanish
SP shore patrol, sine prole (*Latin,* without issue)
Span Spanish
SPCA Society for the Prevention of Cruelty to Animals
SPCC Society for the Prevention of Cruelty to Children
spec special, specialist
specif specific, specifically
sp. gr. specific gravity
spp species (plural)
sq squadron, square
sr senior
Sr sister, strontium
SR shipping receipt
SRO standing room only
SS saints, steamship, Sunday school, sworn statement
SSE south-southeast
SSgt staff sergeant
ssp subspecies
SSR Soviet Socialist Republic
SSS Selective Service System
SSW south-southwest
st saint, stanza, start, state, stitch, stone, straight, strait, street
ST short ton
sta station
stat statute
stbd starboard
std standard
STOL short takeoff and landing
STD doctor of sacred theology
stg, ster sterling
stk stock
STP standard temperature and pressure
str stretch
stud student
subj subject, subjunctive
suff sufficient, suffix
suffr suffragan
Sun Sunday
sup superior, supplement, supplementary, supply, supra (*Latin,* above)
superl superlative
supp, suppl supplement, supplementary
supt superintendent
surg surgeon, surgery, surgical
surv survey, surveying,

surveyor
SV sub verbo *or* sub voce (*Latin*, under the word)
SW shipper's weight, shortwave, southwest
S.W.A. South-West Africa
Switz Switzerland
syll syllable
sym symbol, symmetrical
syn synonym, synonymous, synonymy
syst system

t teaspoon, temperature, tenor, ton, troy
T tablespoon, Thursday, true, Tuesday
Ta tantalum
tan tangent
Tas, Tasm Tasmania
taxon taxonomy
Tb terbium
TB trial balance, tuberculosis
tbs, tbsp tablespoon
TC teachers college
TD touchdown
Te tellurium
tech technical, technically, technician, technological, technology
tel telegram, telegraph, telephone
teleg telegraphy
temp temperature, temporary, tempore (*Latin*, in the time of)
ten tenor
Tenn Tennessee
ter terrace, territory
terr territory
Tex Texas
Th thorium, Thursday
ThD doctor of theology
theat theatrical
theol theological, theology
therm thermometer
Thess Thessalonians
thou thousand
Thu Thursday
Thur Thursday
Thurs Thursday
Ti titanium
TID ter in die (*Latin*, three times a day)
Tim Timothy
tinct tincture
Tit Titus
tk tank, truck
TKO technical knockout
tkt ticket
Tl thallium
TL total loss
TLC tender loving care
Tm thulium
TM trademark
TMO telegraph money order
tn ton, town
TN Tennessee
tnpk turnpike
TO telegraph office, turn over
topog topography
tot total
tp title page, township
tpk turnpike
tr translated, translation, translator, transpose
trans transaction, transitive, translated, translation, translator,

transportation, transverse
transl translated, translation
transp transportation
treas treasurer, treasury
trib tributary
trig trigonometry
TSgt technical sergeant
tsp teaspoon
Tu Tuesday
Tue Tuesday
Tues Tuesday
Turk Turkey, Turkish
TV television
TVA Tennessee Valley Authority
TX Texas

u unit
U university, uranium
UAR United Arab Republic
UFO unidentified flying object
UH upper half
uhf ultrahigh frequency
UK United Kingdom
ult ultimate
UMT Universal Military Training
UN United Nations
UNESCO United Nations Educational, Scientific, and Cultural Organization
univ universal, university
UNRWA United Nations Relief and Works Agency
UPI United Press International
u.s. ubi supra (*Latin,* where above [mentioned]), ut supra (*Latin,* as above)
US United States
USA United States Army, United States of America
USAF United States Air Force
USCG United States Coast Guard
USES United States Employment Service
USIA United States Information Agency
USM United States mail, United States Marines
USMA United States Military Academy
USMC United States Marine Corps
USN United States Navy
USNA United States Naval Academy
USNG United States National Guard
USNR United States Naval Reserve
USO United Service Organizations
USP United States Pharmacopeia
USS United States Ship
USSR Union of Soviet Socialist Republics
usu usual, usually
UT Utah
UV ultraviolet
UW underwriter

v vector, velocity, verb, verse, versus, vide

(*Latin*, see), voice, volume, vowel
V vanadium, victory, volt, voltage
Va Virginia
VA Veterans Administration, vice admiral, Virginia
VAdm vice admiral
val value
var variable, variant, variation, variety, various
vb verb
VC vice-chancellor, vice-consul
VD venereal disease
veg vegetable
vel vellum, velocity
ven venerable
vert vertical
vet veterinarian, veterinary
VF video frequency, visual field
VFD volunteer fire department
VFW Veterans of Foreign Wars
VG very good, vicar-general
vhf very high frequency
vi verb intransitive, vide infra (*Latin*, see below)
VI Virgin Islands
vic vicinity
Vic Victoria
vil village
VIP very important person
vis visibility, visual
viz videlicet (*Latin*, namely)
VL Vulgar Latin
vlf very low frequency
VNA Visiting Nurse Association
VOA Voice of America
voc vocative
vocab vocabulary
vol volume, volunteer
vou voucher
VP vice-president
vs verse, versus, vide supra (*Latin*, see above)
vss verses, versions
V/STOL vertical short takeoff and landing
vt verb transitive
Vt Vermont
VT Vermont
VTOL vertical takeoff and landing
Vulg Vulgate
vv verses, vice versa

w water, watt, week, weight, wide, width, wife, with
W Wednesday, Welsh, west, western, wolfram
WA Washington
war warrant
Wash Washington
W. Aust. Western Australia
WB water ballast, waybill
WBC white blood cells, white blood count
WC water closet, west central, without charge
WCTU Women's Christian Temperance Union

Wed Wednesday
wf wrong font
wh which
whf wharf
WHO World Health Organization
whol wholesale
whs, whse warehouse
whsle wholesale
WI Wisconsin
W.I. West Indies
wid widow, widower
Wis Wisconsin
Wisc Wisconsin
wk week, work
WL wavelength
wmk watermark
WNW west-northwest
w/o without
WO warrant officer
wpm words per minute
wrnt warrant
WSW west-southwest
wt weight
WV West Virginia
W. Va. West Virginia
WW World War
WY Wyoming
Wyo Wyoming

X experimental
xd without dividend
x div without dividend
Xe xenon
x in, x int without interest
XL extra large
Xn Christian
Xnty Christianity

y yard, year
Y YMCA, yttrium
Yb ytterbium
yd yard
yld yield
YMCA Young Men's Christian Association
YMHA Young Men's Hebrew Association
YO yarn over, year-old
yr year, your
yrbk yearbook
Yt yttrium
YT Yukon Territory
YW Young Women's Christian Association
YWCA Young Women's Christian Association
YWHA Young Women's Hebrew Association

z zero
Zech Zechariah
Zeph Zephaniah
ZIP Zone Improvement Plan
Zn zinc
zool zoological, zoology
Zr zirconium

A Handbook of Style

Punctuation

The English writing system uses punctuation marks to separate groups of words for meaning and emphasis; to convey an idea of the variations of pitch, volume, pauses, and intonations of speech; and to help avoid ambiguity. English punctuation marks, together with general rules and examples of their use, follow.

Apostrophe ’

1. indicates the possessive case of nouns and indefinite pronouns

   Mrs. Cenacci's office — the boy's mother
   the boys' mothers — her mother-in-law's car
   It is anyone's guess how much it will cost.

   NOTE: The use of an *'s* with words ending in \s\ or \z\ sounds usually depends on whether a pronounceable final syllable is thus formed: if the syllable is pronounced, the *'s* is usually used; if no final pronounceable syllable is formed, the apostrophe is retained but the *s* is usually not added.

   Knox's products — the bus's brakes
   Aristophanes' play — for righteousness' sake

2. marks omissions in contracted words

   didn't — o'clock

3. marks omission of numerals

   class of '91

4. often forms plurals of letters, figures, and words referred to as words

   You should dot your *i*'s and cross your *t*'s.

His *l*'s and his *7*s looked alike.

She has trouble pronouncing her *the*'s.

Brackets [ ]

1. set off extraneous data such as editorial interpolations especially within quoted material

   He wrote, "I ain't [sic] going."

   "But there's one thing to be said for it [his apprenticeship with Samuels]: it started me thinking about architecture in a new way."

2. function as parentheses within parentheses

   Bowman Act (22 Stat., ch. 4, § [or sec.] 4, p. 50)

Colon :

1. introduces a clause or phrase that explains, illustrates, amplifies, or restates what has gone before

   The sentence was poorly constructed: it lacked both unity and coherence.

2. directs attention to an appositive

   He had only one pleasure: eating.

3. introduces a series

   Three countries were represented: England, France, and Belgium.

4. introduces lengthy quoted material set off from the rest of a text by indentation but not by quotation marks

   I quote from the text of Chapter One:

5. separates elements in page references, bibliographical and biblical citations, and in set formulas used to express ratios and time

Journal of the American Medical Association 48:356
Springfield, Mass.: Merriam-Webster Inc.
John 4:10   8:30 a.m.   a ratio of 3:5

6. separates titles and subtitles (as of books)

    The Tragic Dynasty: A History of the Romanovs

7. follows the salutation in formal correspondence

    Dear Sir or Madam: Dear Dean Alvarez:
    Dear Ms. North:

8. punctuates memorandum and government correspondence headings, and some subject lines in general business letters

    TO: VIA: SUBJECT:
    REFERENCE:

Comma ,

1. separates main clauses joined by a coordinating conjunction (as *and, but, or, nor,* or *for*) and very short clauses not so joined

    She knew very little about him, and he volunteered nothing.
    I came, I saw, I conquered.

2. sets off an adverbial clause (or long phrase) that precedes or interrupts the main clause

    When she discovered the answer, she reported it to us.
    The report, after being read aloud, was put up for consideration.

3. sets off from the rest of the sentence transitional words and expressions (as *on the contrary, on the other hand*), conjunctive adverbs (as *consequently, furthermore, however*), and expressions that introduce an illustration or example (as *namely, for example*)

    Your second question, on the other hand, remains unanswered.

They will travel through two countries, namely, France and England.

He responded as completely as he could; that is, he answered each individual question specifically.

4. sets off contrasting and opposing expressions within sentences

The cost is not $65.00, but $56.65.

He changed his style, not his ethics.

5. separates words, phrases, or clauses in series

He was young, eager, and restless.

Her job required her to travel often, to dress expensively, and to be self-sufficient.

NOTE: Commas separate coordinate adjectives modifying a noun.

She spoke in a calm, reflective manner.

6. sets off from the rest of the sentence parenthetical elements (as nonrestrictive modifiers and nonrestrictive appositives)

Our guide, who wore a blue beret, was an experienced traveler.

We visited Gettysburg, the site of a famous battle.

The author, Marie Jones, was an accomplished athlete.

7. introduces a direct quotation, terminates a direct quotation that is neither a question nor an exclamation, and encloses split quotations

Mary said, "I am leaving."

"I am leaving," Mary said.

"I am leaving," Mary said with determination, "even if you want me to stay."

NOTE: If the quotation is used as a subject or as a noun phrase that follows a linking verb or if it is not being presented as actual dialogue, a comma is not used.

"The computer is down" was the reply she feared.

The fact that he said he was about to "leave this instant" doesn't mean he actually left.

8. sets off words in direct address, absolute phrases, and mild interjections

   You may go, John, if you wish.

   Our business concluded, we adjourned for lunch.

   Ah, that's my idea of an excellent dinner.

9. introduces a direct question that starts in the middle of a sentence

   It's a fine day, isn't it?

   I wondered, What is going on here?

   The question is, How do we get out of here?

10. indicates the omission of a word or words, and especially a word or words used earlier in the sentence

    Common stocks are preferred by some investors; bonds, by others.

NOTE: When the meaning of the sentence is quite clear without the comma, the comma is omitted.

   He was in love with her and she with him.

11. is used to avoid ambiguity and also to emphasize a particular phrase

    To Mary, Jane was someone special.

    The more embroidery on a dress, the higher the price.

12. is used to group numbers into units of three in separating thousands, millions, etc; however, it is generally not used in numbers of four figures, in pagination, in dates, or in street numbers

    Smithville, pop. 100,000

    but

3600 rpm	the year 1983
page 1411	27509 Alameda Drive

13. punctuates an inverted name

    Morton, William A.

14. separates a proper name from a following corporate, academic, honorary, governmental, or military title

    Sandra H. Cobb, Vice President

15. sets off geographical names (as state or country from city), items in dates, and addresses from the rest of a text

    Shreveport, Louisiana, is the site of a large air base.
    On Sunday, June 23, 1940, he was wounded.
    Number 10 Downing Street, London, is a famous address.

NOTE: When just the month and the year are given, the comma is usually omitted.

    She began her career in April 1983 at a modest salary.

16. follows the salutation in informal correspondence and follows the complimentary close of a formal or informal letter

    Dear Mark,
    Affectionately,
    Very truly yours,

Dash —

1. usually marks an abrupt change or break in the continuity of a sentence

    When they heard about it, they—well, let's just say they weren't too pleased.

2. is sometimes used in place of other punctuation (as the comma) when special emphasis is required

    The presentations—and especially the one by Ms. Dow—impressed the audience.

3. introduces a summary statement that follows a series of words or phrases

    Oil, steel, and wheat—these are the sinews of industrialization.

4. often precedes the attribution of a quotation

   My foot is on my native heath. . . . —Sir Walter Scott

5. may be used with the exclamation point or the question mark

   The faces of the crash victims—how bloody!—were shown on TV.

   Your question—it was *your* question, wasn't it, Mr. Jones?—just can't be answered.

6. removes the need for a comma if the dash falls where a comma would ordinarily separate two clauses

   If we don't succeed—and the critics say we won't—then the whole project is in jeopardy.

Ellipsis . . . .

1. indicates the omission of one or more words within a quoted passage

   I never knew any man . . . who could not bear another's misfortunes —Alexander Pope

2. indicates the omission of one or more sentences within a quoted passage or the omission of words at the end of a sentence by using four dots, the first of which represents the period

   That recovering the manuscripts would be worth almost any effort is without question. . . . The monetary value of a body of Shakespeare's manuscripts would be almost incalculable —Charlton Ogburn

   It will take scholars years to determine conclusively the origins, the history, and, most importantly, the significance of the finds. . . . —Robert Morse

3. usually indicates omission of one or more lines of poetry when ellipsis is extended the length of the line

   It little profits that an idle king,
   . . . .
   Matched with an aged wife, I mete and dole
   Unequal laws unto a savage race,

That hoard, and sleep, and feed,
and know not me.
—Alfred Tennyson

4. indicates halting speech or an unfinished sentence in dialogue

"I'd like to . . . that is . . . if you're sure you don't mind. . . ."

Exclamation Point !

1. terminates an emphatic phrase or sentence

Get out of here!

2. terminates an emphatic interjection

Encore!

Hyphen -

1. marks end-of-line division of a word when part of the word is to be carried down to the next line

mill-
stone

pas-
sion

2. is used between some prefix and root combinations:

(prefix + proper name)

pre-Renaissance

(prefix ending with a vowel + root word beginning often with the same vowel)

co-opted re-ink

(stressed prefix + root word, especially when this combination is similar to a different word)

re-cover a sofa
but
recover from an illness

3. is used in some compounds, especially those containing prepositions

   president-elect — sister-in-law
   attorney-at-law — good-for-nothing

4. is often used between elements of an attributive compound modifier in order to avoid ambiguity

   traveling in a fast-moving van
   She has gray-green eyes.
   He looked at her with a know-it-all expression.

5. suspends the first part of a hyphenated compound when used with another hyphenated compound

   a six- or eight-cylinder engine

6. is used in writing out compound numbers between 21 and 99

   thirty-four — one hundred and thirty-eight

7. is used between the numerator and the denominator in writing out fractions especially when they are used as modifiers; however, fractions used as nouns are often styled as open compounds especially when either the numerator or the denominator already contains a hyphen

   a two-thirds majority of the vote
   one seventy-second of an inch

8. serves as an arbitrary equivalent of the phrase "(up) to and including" when used between numbers and dates

   pages 40-98 — the decade 1980-89

9. is used between capitalized names to replace the word "to" or to indicate linkages

   the New York-Paris flight
   the Dempsey-Tunney fight

Parentheses ( )

1. set off supplementary, parenthetic, or explanatory material when the interruption is more than that indicated by commas and when the inclusion of such material does not essentially alter the meaning of the sentence

   Three old destroyers (all now out of commission) will be scrapped.

2. enclose Arabic numerals which confirm a written number in a text

   Delivery will be made in thirty (30) days.

3. enclose numbers or letters in a series

   We must set forth (1) our long-term goals, (2) our immediate objectives, and (3) the means at our disposal.

4. enclose an abbreviation that immediately follows its spelled-out form or may enclose a spelled-out form that follows its abbreviation

   a ruling by the Federal Communications Commission (FCC)

   the manufacture and disposal of PVC (polyvinyl chloride)

5. indicate alternative terms and omissions (as in form letters)

   Please indicate the lecture(s) you would like to attend.

6. are used with other punctuation marks in the following ways:

   (if the parenthetic expression is an independent sentence standing alone, its first word is capitalized and a period is included *inside* the last parenthesis; however, if the parenthetic expression, even if it could stand alone as a sentence, occurs within a sentence, it needs neither capitalization nor a final period but may have an exclamation point or question mark)

   The discussion was held in the boardroom. (The results are still confidential.)

Although we liked the restaurant (their Italian food was the best), we seldom went there.

After waiting in line for an hour (why do we do these things?), we finally left.

(parenthetic material within a sentence may be internally punctuated by a question mark, a period after an abbreviation only, an exclamation point, or a set of quotation marks)

Years ago, someone (who was it?) told me about it.

The conference was held in Vancouver (that's in B.C.).

He was depressed ("I must resign") and refused to do anything.

(no punctuation mark should be placed directly before parenthetical material in a sentence; if a break is required, punctuation should be placed *after* the final parenthesis)

I'll get back to you tomorrow (Friday), when I have more details.

Period .

1. terminates sentences or sentence fragments that are neither interrogatory nor exclamatory

   Give it your best. I gave it my best.

   He asked if she had given it her best.

2. follows some abbreviations and contractions

Dr.	A.D.	ibid.	i.e.
Jr.	etc.	cont.	

3. is used with an individual's initials

   F. Scott Fitzgerald

   T. S. Eliot

4. is used after Roman and Arabic numerals and after letters when they are used in outlines and enumerations

I. Objectives
  A. Economy
    1. low initial cost
    2. low maintenance cost
  B. Ease of operation

Required skills are:
  1. Shorthand
  2. Typing
  3. Transcription

Question Mark ?

1. terminates a direct question

   How did she do it?

   "How did she do it?" he asked.

2. terminates an interrogative element that is part of a sentence; however, indirect questions should not be followed by a question mark

   How did she do it? was the question on each person's mind.

   He wondered, Will it work?

   He wondered whether it would work.

3. punctuates each element of an interrogative series that is neither numbered nor lettered; however, only one such mark punctuates a numbered or lettered interrogative series

   Can you give us a reasonable forecast? back up your predictions? compare them with last quarter's earnings?

   Can you (1) give us a reasonable forecast, (2) back up your predictions, (3) compare them with last quarter's earnings?

4. indicates the writer's ignorance or uncertainty

   Geoffrey Chaucer, English poet (1340?-1400)

Quotation Marks, Double “ ”

1. enclose direct quotations in conventional usage, but not indirect quotations

   He said, "I am leaving."

   He said that he was leaving.

2. enclose words or phrases borrowed from others, words used in a special way, and often slang words when introduced into formal writing

   As the leader of a gang of "droogs," he is altogether frightening, as is this film. —Liz Smith

   He called himself "emperor," but he was really just a dictator.

3. enclose titles of poems, short stories, articles, lectures, chapters of books, short musical compositions, and radio and TV programs

   Robert Frost's "Dust of Snow"

   Katherine Anne Porter's "That Tree"

   The third chapter of *Treasure Island* is entitled "The Black Spot."

   "America the Beautiful"

   Ravel's "Bolero"

   NBC's "Today Show"

4. are used with other punctuation marks in the following ways:

   (the period and the comma fall *within* the quotation marks)

   "I am leaving," he said

   Her camera was described as "waterproof," but "moisture-resistant" would have been a better description.

   (the colon and semicolon fall *outside* the quotation marks)

   There was only one thing to do when he said, "I may not run": promise him a large campaign contribution.

   He spoke of his "little cottage in the country"; he might better have called it a mansion.

(the dash, the question mark, and the exclamation point fall *within* the quotation marks when they refer to the quoted matter only; they fall *outside* when they refer to the whole sentence)

He asked, "When did she leave?"

What is the meaning of "the open door"?

The sergeant shouted "Halt!"

Save us from his "mercy"!

5. are not used with *yes* or *no* except in direct discourse

She said yes to all our requests.

6. are not used with lengthy quotations set off from the text

He took the title for his biography of Thoreau from a passage in *Walden:*

I long ago lost a hound, a bay horse, and a turtle-dove, and am still on their trail. . . . I have met one or two who had heard the hound, and the tramp of the horse, and even seen the dove disappear behind a cloud, and they seemed as anxious to recover them as if they had lost them themselves.

However, the title *A Hound, a Bay Horse, and a Turtle-Dove* probably puzzled some readers.

Quotation Marks, Single ' '

1. enclose a quotation within a quotation in American usage

The witness said, "I distinctly heard him say, 'Don't be late,' and then heard the door close."

2. are sometimes used in place of double quotation marks especially in British usage

The witness said, 'I distinctly heard him say, "Don't be late," and then heard the door close.'

NOTE: When both single and double quotation marks occur at the end of a sentence, the period typically falls *within* both sets of marks.

The witness said, "I distinctly heard him say, 'Don't be late.' "

Semicolon ;

1. links main clauses not joined by a coordinating conjunction

   Some people have the ability to write well; others do not.

2. links main clauses joined by conjunctive adverbs (as *consequently, furthermore, however*)

   Speeding is illegal; furthermore, it is very dangerous.

3. separates phrases and clauses which themselves contain commas

   The country's resources consist of large ore deposits; lumber, waterpower, and fertile soils; and a strong, rugged people.
   Send copies to our offices in Portland, Maine; Springfield, Illinois; and Savannah, Georgia.

4. often occurs before phrases or abbreviations (as *for example, for instance, that is, that is to say, namely, e.g.,* or *i.e.*) that introduce expansions or series

   As a manager she tried to do the best job she could; that is, to keep her project on schedule and under budget.

Virgule /

1. separates alternatives

   Each applicant should have this form signed by his/her parent.

2. separates successive divisions (as months or years) of an extended period of time

   fiscal year 1991/1992 May/June issue

3. serves as a dividing line between one line of poetry and the next when each is not set on its own line

   Say, sages, what's the charm on earth/Can turn death's dart aside? —Robert Burns

4. often represents *per* in abbreviations

   9 ft/sec 20 km/hr

Italicization

The following are usually italicized in print and underlined in manuscript and typescript.

1. titles of books, magazines, newspapers, plays, movies, works of art, and long musical compositions (but not musical compositions identified by the nature of the musical form in which they were written)

   Eliot's *The Waste Land*
   Christian Science Monitor
   the movie *High Noon*
   Mozart's *Don Giovanni*
   but
   Fantasy in C Minor
   Saturday Review
   Shakespeare's *Othello*
   Gainsborough's *Blue Boy*

   NOTE: Plurals of such italicized titles have roman, not italic, inflectional endings.

   hidden under a stack of *Saturday Reviews*

2. names of ships and aircraft, and often spacecraft

   M. V. *West Star*
   Lindbergh's *Spirit of St. Louis*
   Apollo 13

3. words, letters, and figures when referred to as words, letters, and figures

The word *receive* is often misspelled.
The *g* in *align* is silent.
You should dot your *i*'s and cross your *t*'s.
The first *2* and the last *0* are barely legible.

4. foreign words and phrases that have not become established as part of English

aere perennius *che sarà, sarà*
sans peur et sans reproche *ich dien*
but
pasta ad hoc ex officio

NOTE: The decision as to whether or not a word or phrase has become established in English will vary according to the subject matter and the expected audience of the passage in which it appears. In general, any word entered in the main A-Z vocabulary of a general dictionary need not be italicized.

5. New Latin scientific names of genera, species, subspecies, and varieties (but not groups of higher rank, as phyla, classes, or orders) in botanical or zoological names

a thick-shelled American clam *(Mercenaria mercenaria)*
a cardinal *(Richmondena cardinalis)*
but
the family Hominidae

6. case titles in legal citations, both in full and shortened form ("v" for "versus" is set in roman, though)

Jones v. *Massachusetts* the *Jones* case
Jones

Capitalization

Capitals are used for two broad purposes in English: they mark a beginning (as of a sentence) and they signal a proper noun, pronoun, or adjective. The following principles describe the most common uses of capital letters.

Beginnings

1. The first word of a sentence or sentence fragment is capitalized.

   The play lasted nearly three hours.

   How are you feeling?

   Bravo!

   "Have you hand grenades?"
   "Plenty."
   "How many rounds per rifle?"
   "Plenty."
   "How many?"
   "One hundred fifty. More maybe."
   —Ernest Hemingway

2. The first word of a sentence contained within parentheses is capitalized if it does not occur within another sentence; however, a parenthetical sentence occurring in the midst of another sentence does not begin with a capital.

   The discussion was held in the boardroom. (The results are still confidential.)

   Although we liked the restaurant (their Italian food was the best), we seldom ate there.

   After waiting in line for an hour (why do we do these things?), we finally left.

3. The first word of a direct quotation is capitalized; however, if the quotation is interrupted in the middle of a sentence, the second part does not begin with a capital.

   The President said, "We have rejected this report entirely."

   "We have rejected this report entirely," the President said, "and we will not comment on it further."

NOTE: When a quotation, whether a sentence fragment or a complete sentence, is syntactically dependent on the sentence in which it occurs, the quotation does not begin with a capital.

   The President made it clear "that there is no room for compromise."

4. The first word of a direct question within a sentence is capitalized.

The question is: Is man an ape or an angel?
—Benjamin Disraeli

My first thought was, How can I avoid this assignment?

5. The first word of a line of poetry is conventionally capitalized.

The best lack all conviction, while the worst
Are full of passionate intensity.
—W. B. Yeats

6. The first word following a colon may be lowercased or capitalized if it introduces a complete sentence; while the former is the more usual styling, the latter is common when the sentence introduced by the colon is fairly lengthy and distinctly separate from the preceding clause.

The advantage of this particular system is clear: it's inexpensive.

The situation is critical: This company cannot hope to recoup the fourth-quarter losses that were sustained in five operating divisions.

7. When a sentence or phrase introduces a listing of items, the first word in each item is capitalized if the items are complete sentences themselves or if each item is set on its own line. Otherwise, the first word of each item is not capitalized.

Do the following tasks at the end of the day: 1. Clean your typewriter. 2. Clear your desktop of papers. 3. Cover office machines. 4. Straighten the contents of your desk drawers, cabinets, and bookcases.

This is the agenda:
Call to order
Roll call
Minutes of the previous meeting
Treasurer's report

On the agenda will be (1) call to order, (2) roll call, (3) minutes of the previous meeting, (4) treasurer's report. . . .

8. The first word in an outline heading is capitalized.

I. Editorial tasks
II. Production responsibilities
  A. Cost estimates
  B. Bids

9. The first word of the salutation of a letter and the first word of a complimentary close are capitalized.

Dear Mary,	Ladies and Gentlemen:
Sincerely yours,	Cordially,

Proper Nouns, Pronouns, Adjectives

The essential distinction in the use of capitals and lowercase letters beginning words lies in the particularizing or individualizing significance of capitals as against the generic or generalizing significance of lowercase. A capital is used with proper nouns, that is, nouns that distinguish some individual person, place, or thing from others of the same class, and with proper adjectives, that is, adjectives that take their descriptive meaning from what is named by the noun.

ARMED FORCES

1. Branches and units of the armed forces are capitalized, as are easily recognized short forms of full branch and unit designations; however, the words *army, navy,* etc., are lowercased when standing alone, when used collectively in the plural, or when they are not part of an official title.

   United States Army
   a contract with the Army
   Corps of Engineers
   a bridge built by the Engineers
   allied armies

AWARDS

2. The names of awards and prizes are capitalized.

   the Nobel Prize in medicine
   Distinguished Service Cross
   Academy Award

DERIVATIVES OF PROPER NAMES

3. Derivatives of proper names are capitalized when used in their primary sense. However, if the derived term has taken on a specialized meaning, it is usually not capitalized.

Roman customs	Shakespearean comedies
Edwardian era	

but

quixotic
pasteurized milk
cesarean section

GEOGRAPHICAL REFERENCES

4. Divisions of the earth's surface and names of distinct areas, regions, places, or districts are capitalized, as are derivative adjectives and some derivative nouns and verbs.

the Eastern Hemisphere
Tropic of Cancer
Springfield, Massachusetts
the Middle Eastern situation
Midwest
an Americanism

but

a japan finish
a green jersey

5. Popular names of localities are capitalized.

the Corn Belt
the Loop
The Big Apple
the Gold Coast
the Eastern Shore

6. Words designating global, national, regional, or local political divisions are capitalized when they are essential elements of specific names; however, they are usually lowercased when they precede a proper name or stand alone.

the British Empire
Washington State
Bedford County
New York City
Ward 1

but

the fall of the empire
the state of Washington
the county of Bedford
the city of New York
fires in three wards

NOTE: In legal documents, these words are often capitalized regardless of position.

the State of New York
the County of Bedford
the City of New York

7. Generic geographical terms (as *lake, mountain, river, valley*) are capitalized if they are part of a specific proper name.

Hudson Bay　　Long Island
Niagara Falls　　Crater Lake

8. Generic terms preceding names are usually capitalized.

   Lakes Michigan and Superior
   Mounts Whitney and Rainier

9. Generic terms following names are usually lowercased, as are singular or plural generic terms that are used descriptively or alone.

   the Himalaya and Andes mountains
   the Missouri and Platte rivers
   the Atlantic coast of Labrador
   the Hudson valley　　the Arizona desert
   the river valley　　the valley

10. Compass points are capitalized when they refer to a geographical region or when they are part of a street name, but they are lowercased when they refer to simple direction.

    up North　　back East　　the Northwest
    West Columbus Avenue
    but
    west of the Rockies　　the west coast of Florida

11. Adjectives derived from compass points and nouns designating the inhabitants of some geographical regions are capitalized; when in doubt consult a dictionary.

    a Southern accent　　Northerners

12. Terms designating public places are capitalized if they are part of a proper name.

    Brooklyn Bridge　　Lincoln Park
    the Dorset Hotel　　Independence Hall
    but
    Fifth and Park avenues
    the Dorset and Drake hotels

GOVERNMENTAL AND JUDICIAL BODIES

13. Full names of legislative, deliberative, executive, and administrative bodies are capitalized, as are easily recognized short forms of these names; however, nonspecific noun and adjective references to them are usually lowercased.

    the U.S. House of Representatives — the House
    the Federal Bureau of Investigation
    but
    both houses of Congress — a federal agency

14. Names of international courts, the U.S. Supreme Court, and other higher courts are capitalized; however, names of city and county courts are usually lowercased.

    The International Court of Arbitration
    the Supreme Court of the United States
    the Supreme Court
    the United States Court of Appeals for the Second Circuit
    the Michigan Court of Appeals
    Lawton municipal court — Newark night court

HISTORICAL PERIODS AND EVENTS

15. The names of congresses, councils, and expositions are capitalized.

    the Yalta Conference
    the Republican National Convention

16. The names of historical events, some historical periods, and some cultural periods and movements are capitalized.

    the Boston Tea Party
    Renaissance — Prohibition
    Augustan Age — the Enlightenment
    but
    space age — cold war — neoclassicism

17. Numerical designations of historical time periods are capitalized when they are part of a proper name; otherwise they are lowercased.

the Third Reich — Roaring Twenties

but

eighteenth century — the eighties

18. Names of treaties, laws, and acts are capitalized.

Treaty of Versailles
The Controlled Substances Act of 1970

ORGANIZATIONS

19. Names of firms, corporations, schools, and organizations and their members are capitalized; however, common nouns used descriptively and occurring after the names of two or more organizations are lowercased.

Merriam-Webster Inc.
University of Wisconsin
European Economic Community
Rotary International
Kiwanians
American and United airlines

NOTE: The word *the* at the beginning of such names is only capitalized when the legal name is referred to.

20. Words such as *group, division, department, office,* or *agency* that designate corporate and organizational units are capitalized only when used with a specific name.

while working for the Editorial Department of this company

but

a notice to all department heads

PEOPLE

21. The names of persons are capitalized.

Noah Webster
Sir Arthur Thomas Quiller-Couch

NOTE: The capitalization of particles (as *de, della, der, du, l', la, ten, van*) varies widely especially in names of people in English-speaking countries.

Thomas De Quincy | Willem de Kooning
Werner Von Braun | Gerald ter Hoerst

22. Titles preceding the name of a person and epithets used instead of a name are capitalized; however, titles following a name or used alone are usually lowercased.

President Roosevelt | Professor Harris
Queen Elizabeth | Old Hickory

but

Henry VIII, king of England

23. Corporate titles are capitalized when referring to specific individuals; when used in general or plural contexts, they are lowercased.

Laura Jones, Vice President
The sales manager called me.

24. Words of family relationship preceding or used in place of a person's name are capitalized; however, these words are lowercased if they are part of a noun phrase that is being used in place of a name.

Cousin Julia | Grandfather Jones
I know when Mother's birthday is.

but

I know when my mother's birthday is.

25. Words designating peoples, tribes, races, and languages are capitalized.

Canadians | Iroquois
Afro-American | Indo-European

NOTE: Designations based on color or local usage are variously capitalized or lowercased by different writers; however, style manuals usually recommend lowercasing such words.

black | white

PERSONIFICATIONS

26. Personficiations are capitalized.

She dwells with Beauty—Beauty, that must die;
And Joy, whose hand is ever at his lips
Bidding adieu.

—John Keats

obey the commands of Nature

PRONOUNS

27. The pronoun I is capitalized. For pronouns referring to the Deity, see rule 29 below.

. . . no one but I myself had yet printed any of my work —Paul Bowles

RELIGIOUS TERMS

28. Words designating the Deity are capitalized.

An anthropomorphic, vengeful Jehovah became a spiritual, benevolent Supreme Being. —A. R. Katz

29. Personal pronouns referring to the Deity are capitalized by some authors only when such words are not closely preceded by their antecedents; other writers capitalize these words regardless of their distance from their antecedents.

The principal group that disagreed with them . . . did so only in an even greater faith—that when God chose to save the heathen He could do it by Himself. —Elmer Davis

Allah will not subject any believer to eternal punishment because of His readiness to yield to the Prophet's intercession. —G. E. Grunebaum

The Almighty has his own purposes. —Abraham Lincoln

so lonely 'twas, that God himself scarce seemed there to be. —S. T. Coleridge

all Thy works, O Lord, shall bless Thee. —*Oxford Amer. Hymnal*

God's in His heaven—all's right with the world! —Robert Browning

30. Traditional designations of revered persons, as prophets, apostles, and saints are often capitalized.

our Lady the Prophet the Lawgiver

31. Names of creeds and confessions, religious denominations, and monastic orders are capitalized, as is the word *Church* when used to designate a specific body or edifice.

Apostles' Creed   Society of Jesus
the Thirty-nine Articles of the Church of England
Hunt Memorial Church
but
a Baptist church

32. Names for the Bible or parts, versions, or editions of it and names of other sacred books are capitalized.

Authorized Version   New English Bible
Old Testament   Apocrypha
Gospel of Saint Mark   Koran   Talmud

NOTE: Adjectives derived from the names of sacred books are irregularly capitalized or lowercased; when in doubt, consult a dictionary.

SCIENTIFIC TERMS

33. Names of planets and their satellites, asteroids, stars, constellations, and groups of stars and other unique celestial objects are capitalized; however, the words *sun, earth,* and *moon* are usually lowercased unless they occur with other astronomical names.

Venus   Ganymede   Sirius
Pleiades   the Milky Way
probes heading for the Moon and Mars

34. Genera in binomial scientific names in zoology and botany are capitalized; names of species are not.

a cabbage butterfly *(Pieris rapae)*
a common buttercup *(Ranunculus acris)*
a robin *(Turdus migratorius)*

35. New Latin names of classes, families, and all groups above genera in zoology and botany are capitalized; however, their derivative adjectives and nouns are not.

Gastropoda *but* gastropod

Thallophyta *but* thallophyte

36. Geological eras, periods, epochs, strata, and names of prehistoric divisions are capitalized.

Silurian period	Pleistocene epoch
Age of Reptiles	Neolithic age

TIME PERIODS AND ZONES

37. The names of days of the week, months of the year, and holidays and holy days are capitalized.

Tuesday June Thanksgiving
Independence Day Easter
Yom Kippur

38. The names of time zones are capitalized when abbreviated but usually lowercased when spelled out except for words that are proper names. See also rules 16 and 17 above.

CST
central standard time
Pacific standard time

TITLES OF PRINTED MATTER

39. Words in titles are capitalized with the exception of internal conjunctions, prepositions, and articles.

The Lives of a Cell
Of Mice and Men
"The Man Who Would Be King"
"To His Coy Mistress"
"Acquainted with the Night"

NOTE: In some publications, prepositions of five or more letters (as *about, toward*) are capitalized also.

40. Major sections (as a preface, introduction, or index) of books, long articles, or reports are capitalized when they are specifically referred to within the same material. The word *chapter* is usually capitalized when used with a cardinal number.

See the Appendix for further information.
The Introduction explains the scope of this book.

discussed later in Chapter 4
but
discussed in a later chapter

Capitalization of the titles of movies, plays, and musical compositions follows similar conventions. For more details, see the Italicization section above.

TRADEMARKS

41. Registered trademarks are capitalized.

Dubonnet Orlon

VEHICLES

42. The names of ships, aircraft, and spacecraft are capitalized.

M. V. *West Star*
Lindbergh's *Spirit of St. Louis*
Apollo 13

Forms of Address

Address Styling	Salutation Styling
Clerical and Religious Orders	
abbot	
The Right Reverend John R. Smith, O.S.B. Abbot of ______	Right Reverend and dear Father Dear Father Abbot Dear Father
archbishop	
The Most Reverend Archbishop of ______	Your Excellency
or	
The Most Reverend John R. Smith Archbishop of ______	Your Excellency Dear Archbishop Smith
bishop, Catholic	
The Most Reverend John R. Smith Bishop of ______	Your Excellency Dear Bishop Smith
bishop, Episcopal	
The Right Reverend The Bishop of ______	Right Reverend Sir
or	
The Right Reverend John R. Smith Bishop of ______	Right Reverend Sir Dear Bishop Smith
bishop, Protestant (excluding Episcopal)	
The Reverend John R. Smith	Reverend Sir Dear Bishop Smith
brotherhood, member of	
Brother John, S.J. *(or other initials for the order)*	Dear Brother John
cardinal	
His Eminence John Cardinal Smith	Your Eminence Dear Cardinal Smith
or	
His Eminence Cardinal Smith	(same)
clergyman, Protestant	
The Reverend Amelia R. Smith	Dear Ms. Smith
or if having a doctorate	
The Reverend Dr. Amelia R. Smith	Dear Dr. Smith

Address Styling	Salutation Styling
monsignor, domestic prelate	
The Right Reverend Monsignor John R. Smith	Right Reverend and dear Monsignor Smith
or	
The Rt. Rev. Msgr. John R. Smith	Dear Monsignor Smith
mother superior (of a sisterhood)	
The Reverend Mother Superior Convent of ______	Reverend Mother Dear Reverend Mother My dear Reverend Mother Mary Angelica
or	
Reverend Mother Mary Angelica, O.S.D. *(or other initials of the order)* Convent of ______	(same)
patriarch (of an Eastern Orthodox Church)	
His Beatitude the Patriarch of ______	Most Reverend Lord
pope	
His Holiness the Pope	Your Holiness Most Holy Father
or	
His Holiness Pope John	(same)
president, Mormon	
The President Church of Jesus Christ of Latter-day Saints	My dear President Dear President Smith
priest, Catholic	
The Reverend Father Smith	Dear Father Smith
or	
The Reverend John R. Smith	(same)
rabbi	
Rabbi John R. Smith	Dear Rabbi Smith
or if having a doctorate	
Rabbi John R. Smith, D.D.	Dear Dr. Smith
sisterhood, member of	
Sister Mary Angelica, S.C. *(or other initials of the order)*	Dear Sister Dear Sister Mary Angelica

Address Styling	Salutation Styling
College and University Faculty and Officials	
chancellor (of a university)	
Dr. Amelia R. Smith Chancellor	Dear Dr. Smith
dean (of a college or university)	
Dean Amelia R. Smith	Dear Dr. Smith Dear Dean Smith
or	
Dr. Amelia R. Smith Dean	(same)
president	
Dr. Amelia R. Smith President	Dear Dr. Smith
or	
President Amelia R. Smith	Dear President Smith
president, priest	
The Very Reverend John R. Smith President	Dear Father Smith
professor, assistant (or **associate**)	
Dr. Dale R. Smith Assistant (or Associate) Professor of ______	Dear Dr. Smith Dear Professor Smith Dear Mr. Smith Dear Ms. Smith
professor, full	
Professor John R. Smith	Dear Professor Smith
or	
Dr. John R. Smith Professor of ______	Dear Dr. Smith
Consular Officers	
consul, American (covers all consular grades such as *Consul, Consul General, Vice-Consul,* and *Consular Agent*)	
The American Consul (foreign city, country)	Sir Sir or Madam
or if in Latin America or Canada	
The Consul of the United States of America	(same)
or if individual name is known	

Address Styling	Salutation Styling
Amelia R. Smith, Esq.	Madam
American Consul	Dear Ms. Smith
or if in Latin America or Canada	
Amelia R. Smith, Esq.	(same)
Consul of the United States of America	
consuls, foreign (covers all consular grades)	
The ______ Consul	Sir
(U.S. city, state, zip code)	Sir or Madame
or	
The Consul of ______	(same)
(U.S. city, state, zip code)	
or if individual name is known	
The Honorable John R. Smith	Sir
______ Consul	Dear Mr. Smith
Diplomats	
ambassador, American	
The Honorable Dale R. Smith	Sir (or Madam)
American Ambassador	Dear Mr. (or Madam) Ambassador
or if in Latin America or Canada	
The Honorable Dale R. Smith	(same)
Ambassador of the United States of America	
ambassador, foreign	
His Excellency John R. Smith	Excellency
Ambassador of ______	Dear Mr. Ambassador
or	
Her Excellency Amelia R. Smith	Excellency
Ambassador of ______	Dear Madame Ambassador
chargé d'affaires, American	
Dale R. Smith, Esq.	Sir (or Madam)
American Chargé d'Affaires	Dear Mr. (or Ms.) Smith
or if in Latin America or Canada	
Dale R. Smith, Esq.	(same)
United States Chargé d'Affaires	
chargé d'affaires, foreign	
Mr. John R. Smith	Sir
Chargé d'Affaires of ______	Dear Mr. Smith
or	

Address Styling	Salutation Styling
Ms. Amelia R. Smith Chargé d'Affaires of ______	Madame Dear Ms. Smith
minister, American The Honorable Dale R. Smith American Minister	Sir (or Madam) Dear Mr. Minister Dear Madam Minister
or if in Latin America or Canada The Honorable Dale R. Smith Minister of the United States of America	(same)
minister, foreign The Honorable Dale R. Smith Minister of ______	Sir (or Madame) Dear Mr. Minister Dear Madame Minister

Foreign Heads of State: A Brief Sampling

Address Styling	Salutation Styling
premier His Excellency John R. Smith Premier of ______	Excellency Dear Mr. Premier
or Her Excellency Amelia R. Smith Premier of ______	Excellency Dear Madame Premier
president of a republic Her Excellency Amelia R. Smith President of ______	Excellency Dear Madame President
or His Excellency John R. Smith President of ______	Excellency Dear Mr. President
prime minister His Excellency John R. Smith	Excellency Dear Mr. Prime Minister
or Her Excellency Amelia R. Smith	Excellency Dear Madame Prime Minister

Address Styling	Salutation Styling
Government Officials—Federal	
attorney general	
The Honorable Amelia R. Smith The Attorney General	Dear Madam Attorney General
cabinet officer (other than attorney general)	
The Honorable Dale R. Smith Secretary of ______	Sir (or Madam) Dear Mr. (or Madam) Secretary
or The Secretary of ______	(same)
chairman of a (sub) committee, U.S. Congress (stylings shown apply to House of Representatives & Senate)	
The Honorable Dale R. Smith Chairman Committee on ______ United States Senate	Dear Mr. (or Madam) Chairman Dear Senator Smith
chief justice—see SUPREME COURT, FEDERAL; STATE	
commissioner	
The Honorable Amelia R. Smith Commissioner	Dear Mr. (or Madam) Commissioner Dear Mr. (or Ms.) Smith
congressman—see REPRESENTATIVE, U.S. CONGRESS	
director (as of an independent federal agency)	
The Honorable John R. Smith Director ______ Agency	Dear Mr. Smith
district attorney	
The Honorable Amelia R. Smith District Attorney	Dear Ms. Smith
federal judge	
The Honorable John R. Smith Judge of the United States District Court of the ______ District of ______	Sir My dear Judge Smith Dear Judge Smith

Address Styling	Salutation Styling
justice—see SUPREME COURT, FEDERAL; STATE	
librarian of congress	
The Honorable Amelia R. Smith Librarian of Congress	Madam Dear Ms. Smith
postmaster general	
The Honorable John R. Smith The Postmaster General	Sir Dear Mr. Postmaster General
president of the United States	
The President The White House	Mr. President My dear Mr. President Dear Mr. President
or	
The Honorable Amelia R. Smith President of the United States The White House	Madam President My dear Madam President Dear Madam President
representative, United States Congress	
The Honorable Amelia R. Smith United States House of Representatives	Madam Dear Representative Smith
or for local address	
The Honorable Amelia R. Smith Representative in Congress	Dear Ms. Smith
senator, United States Senate	
The Honorable Amelia R. Smith United States Senate	Madam Dear Senator Smith
speaker, United States House of Representatives	
The Honorable The Speaker of the House of Representatives	Sir (or Madam)
or	
The Honorable Speaker of the House of Representatives	(same)
or	
The Honorable Dale R. Smith Speaker of the House of Representatives	Sir (or Madam) Dear Mr. (or Madam) Speaker Dear Mr. (or Ms.) Smith

Address Styling	Salutation Styling
supreme court, associate justice	
Mr. (or Ms.) Justice Smith The Supreme Court of the United States	Sir (or Madam) Mr. (or Madam) Justice My dear Mr. (or Madam) Justice Dear Mr. (or Madam) Justice Smith
supreme court, chief justice	
The Chief Justice of the United States The Supreme Court of the United States	Sir (or Madam) My dear Mr. (or Madam) Chief Justice Dear Mr. (or Madam) Chief Justice
or The Chief Justice The Supreme Court	Sir (or Madam) My dear Mr. (or Madam) Chief Justice Dear Mr. (or Madam) Chief Justice
vice president of the United States	
The Vice President of the United States United States Senate	Sir (or Madam) My dear Mr. (or Madam) Vice President Dear Mr. (or Madam) Vice President
or The Honorable Dale R. Smith Vice President of the United States Washington, DC (zip code)	(same)

Government Officials—Local

Address Styling	Salutation Styling
alderman (or **councilman** or **selectman**)	
The Honorable Dale R. Smith	Dear Mr. (or Ms.) Smith Dear Alderman Smith
or Alderman Dale R. Smith	(same)
city attorney (includes city counsel, corporation counsel)	
The Honorable Amelia R. Smith	Dear Ms. Smith
councilman—see ALDERMAN	

Address Styling	Salutation Styling
county clerk The Honorable John R. Smith Clerk of ______ County	Dear Mr. Smith
county treasurer—see COUNTY CLERK	
judge The Honorable Amelia R. Smith Judge of the ______ Court of ______	Dear Judge Smith
mayor The Honorable Dale R. Smith Mayor of ______	Sir (or Madam) Dear Mayor Smith
selectman—see ALDERMAN	

Government Officials—State

Address Styling	Salutation Styling
assemblyman—see REPRESENTATIVE, STATE	
attorney (as commonwealth's attorney, state's attorney) The Honorable Amelia R. Smith (title)	Dear Ms. Smith
attorney general The Honorable John R. Smith Attorney General of the State of ______	Sir Dear Mr. Attorney General
clerk of a court Amelia R. Smith, Esq. Clerk of the Court of ______	Dear Ms. Smith
delegate—see REPRESENTATIVE, STATE	
governor The Honorable Dale R. Smith Governor of ______	Sir (or Madam) Dear Governor Smith
or in some states His Excellency, the Governor of ______ Her Excellency, the Governor of ______	(same)
judge, state court The Honorable John R. Smith Judge of the ______ Court	Dear Judge Smith

Address Styling	Salutation Styling
judge/justice, state supreme court—see SUPREME COURT, STATE	
lieutenant governor	
The Honorable Lieutenant Governor of ______	Madam
or	
The Honorable Amelia R. Smith	Madam
Lieutenant Governor of ______	Dear Ms. Smith
representative, state (includes assemblyman, delegate)	
The Honorable John R. Smith	Sir
House of Representatives (or The State Assembly or The House of Delegates)	Dear Mr. Smith
secretary of state	
The Honorable Secretary of State of ______	Sir (or Madam)
or	
The Honorable Dale R. Smith	Sir (or Madam)
Secretary of State of ______	Dear Mr. (or Madam) Secretary
senate, state, president of	
The Honorable John R. Smith	Sir
President of the Senate of the State (or the Commonwealth) of ______	Dear Mr. Smith Senator
senator, state	
The Honorable Amelia R. Smith	Madam
The Senate of ______	Dear Senator Smith
speaker, state assembly, house of delegates, or house of representatives	
The Honorable John R. Smith	Sir
Speaker of ______	Dear Mr. Smith
supreme court, state, associate justice	
The Honorable Amelia R. Smith	Madam
Associate Justice of the Supreme Court of ______	Dear Justice Smith
supreme court, state, chief justice	
The Honorable Dale R. Smith	Sir (or Madam)
Chief Justice of the Supreme Court of ______	Dear Mr. (or Madam) Chief Justice

Address Styling	Salutation Styling
Military Ranks	
for any rank	
full rank+full name+comma+abbreviation of the branch of service	*Dear+full rank+surname*
or	
abbreviation of rank+full name +comma+abbreviation of branch of service	(same)

(A small sampling of address formats for military ranks is shown here. Abbreviations for each rank and the branches of service using them are shown at individual entries.)

admiral [coast guard, navy (ADM)]

Admiral Amelia R. Smith, USCG (etc)	Dear Admiral Smith
or	
ADM Amelia R. Smith, USCG (etc)	(same)

— a similar pattern is used for **rear admiral** (RADM) and **vice admiral** (VADM) with the full rank given in the salutation line.

airman [air force (AMN)]

Airman John R. Smith, USAF	Dear Airman Smith
or	
AMN John R. Smith, USAF	(same)

— a similar pattern is used for **airman basic** (AB) and **airman first class** (A1C) with the full rank given in the salutation line.

captain [air force, army (CPT); coast guard, navy (CAPT); marine corps (Capt.)]

Captain John R. Smith, USAF (etc)	Dear Captain Smith
or	
CPT John R. Smith, USAF (etc)	(same)

chief petty officer [coast guard, navy (CPO)]

Chief Petty Officer Dale R. Smith, USN (etc)	Dear Chief Smith
or	
CPO Dale R. Smith, USN (etc)	(same)

chief warrant officer [army, navy, marine corps] (covers all grades of chief warrant officers, CWO2-CWO4)

Address Styling	Salutation Styling
Chief Warrant Officer Dale R. Smith, USA (etc)	Dear Mr. Smith Dear Ms. Smith Dear Chief Warrant Officer Smith
or	
CWO4 Dale R. Smith, USA (etc)	(same)
colonel [air force, army (COL); marine corps (Col.)]	
Colonel Amelia R. Smith, USMC (etc)	Dear Colonel Smith
or	
Col. Amelia R. Smith, USMC (etc)	(same)
commander [coast guard, navy (CDR)]	
Commander John R. Smith, USN (etc)	Dear Commander Smith
or	
CDR John R. Smith, USCG (etc)	(same)
corporal [army (CPL); marine corps (Cpl.)]	
Corporal Amelia R. Smith, USA (etc)	Dear Corporal Smith
or	
CPL Amelia R. Smith, USA (etc)	(same)

— a similar pattern is used for **lance corporal** [marine corps (L/Cpl.)] with the full rank given in the salutation line.

Address Styling	Salutation Styling
ensign [coast guard, navy (ENS)]	
Ensign Dale R. Smith, USN (etc)	Dear Ensign Smith Dear Mr. Smith Dear Ms. Smith
or	
ENS Dale R. Smith, USN (etc)	(same)
first lieutenant [air force, army (1LT); marine corps (1st Lt.)]	
First Lieutenant Amelia R. Smith, USMC (etc)	Dear Lieutenant Smith
or	
1st Lt. Amelia R. Smith, USMC (etc)	(same)
general [air force, army (GEN); marine corps (Gen.)]	
General Amelia R. Smith, USAF (etc)	Dear General Smith
or	
GEN Amelia R. Smith, USAF (etc)	(same)

Address Styling	Salutation Styling
— a similar pattern is used for **brigadier general** [air force, army (BG); marine corps (Brig. Gen.)], **major general** [air force, army (MG); marine corps (Maj. Gen.)], and **lieutenant general** [air force, army (LTG); marine corps (Lt. Gen.)] with the full rank given in the salutation line.	
lieutenant [coast guard, navy (LT)] — see also FIRST LIEUTENANT, SECOND LIEUTENANT; LIEUTENANT JUNIOR GRADE	
Lieutenant Dale R. Smith, USN (etc)	Dear Lieutenant Smith Dear Mr. Smith Dear Ms. Smith
or	
LT Dale R. Smith, USN (etc)	(same)
lieutenant junior grade [coast guard, navy (LTJG)] — see also LIEUTENANT	
Lieutenant (j.g.) Dale R. Smith, USCG (etc)	Dear Lieutenant Smith Dear Mr. Smith Dear Ms. Smith
or	
LTJG Dale R. Smith, USCG (etc)	(same)
major [air force, army (MAJ); marine corps (Maj.)]	
Major John R. Smith, USAF (etc)	Dear Major Smith
or	
MAJ John R. Smith, USAF (etc)	(same)
master chief petty officer [coast guard, navy (MCPO)]	
Master Chief Petty Officer Amelia R. Smith, USN (etc)	Dear Master Chief Smith
or	
MCPO Amelia R. Smith, USN (etc)	(same)
petty officer first class [coast guard, navy (PO1)]	
Petty Officer First Class John R. Smith, USN (etc)	Dear Petty Officer Smith
or	
PO1 John R. Smith, USN (etc)	(same)
— similar pattern is used for **petty officer second class** (PO2) and **petty officer third class** (PO3).	
private [army (PVT); marine corps (Pvt.)]	
Private John R. Smith, USMC (etc)	Dear Private Smith
or	
Pvt. John R. Smith, USCM (etc)	(same)

Address Styling	Salutation Styling
— a similar pattern is used for **private first class** [army (PFC)].	
seaman [coast guard, navy (SMN)]	
Seaman Amelia R. Smith, USCG (etc)	Dear Seaman Smith
or	
SMN Amelia R. Smith, USCG (etc)	(same)
— a similar pattern is used for **seaman apprentice** and **seaman recruit** [coast guard, navy].	
second lieutenant [air force, army (2LT); marine corps (2nd Lt.)]	
Second Lieutenant John R. Smith, USA (etc)	Dear Lieutenant Smith
or	
2LT John R. Smith, USA (etc)	(same)
senior chief petty officer [coast guard, navy (SCPO)]	
Senior Chief Petty Officer John R. Smith, USCG (etc)	Dear Senior Chief Smith
or	
SCPO John R. Smith, USCG (etc)	(same)
sergeant [air force, army (SGT)]	
Sergeant Amelia R. Smith, USAF (etc)	Dear Sergeant Smith
or	
SGT Amelia R. Smith, USAF (etc)	(same)
— a similar pattern is used for other sergeant ranks, including **first sergeant** [army (1SG); marine corps (1st Sgt.)]; **gunnery sergeant** [marine corps (Gy. Sgt.)]; **master sergeant** [air force (MSGT); army (MSG)]; **sergeant first class** [army (SFC)]; **staff sergeant** [air force (SSGT); army (SSG); marine corps (SSgt.)]; and **technical sergeant** [air force (TSGT)] with the full rank given in the salutation line.	
sergeant major [army (SGM); marine corps (Sgt. Maj.)]	
Sergeant Major Amelia R. Smith, USMC (etc)	Dear Sergeant Major Smith
or	
Sgt. Maj. Amelia R. Smith, USMC (etc)	(same)
warrant officer [army, coast guard, navy (WO1)] — see also CHIEF WARRANT OFFICER	
Warrant Officer Dale R. Smith, USA (etc)	Dear Warrant Officer Smith Dear Mr. Smith Dear Ms. Smith
or	
WO1 Dale R. Smith, USA (etc)	(same)

Address Styling	Salutation Styling

United Nations Officials

representative, American (with ambassadorial rank)

The Honorable Dale R. Smith United States Permanent Representative to the United Nations	Sir (or Madam) Dear Mr. (or Madam) Ambassador

representative, foreign (with ambassadorial rank)

His Excellency John R. Smith Representative of ______ to the United Nations	Excellency My dear Mr. Ambassador Dear Mr. Ambassador
or	
Her Excellency Amelia R. Smith Representative of ______ to the United Nations	Excellency My dear Madam Ambassador Dear Madam Ambassador

secretary-general

Her Excellency Amelia R. Smith Secretary-General of the United Nations	Excellency My dear Madam (*or* Madame) Secretary-General Dear Madam (*or* Madame) Secretary-General
or	
His Excellency John R. Smith Secretary-General of the United Nations	Excellency My dear Mr. Secretary-General Dear Mr. Secretary-General

undersecretary

The Honorable John R. Smith Undersecretary of the United Nations	Sir Dear Mr. Smith

WEIGHTS AND MEASURES

Unit	Equivalents in Other Units of Same System	Metric Equivalent
	length	
mile	5280 feet 320 rods 1760 yards	1.609 kilometers
rod	5.50 yards 16.5 feet	5.029 meters
yard	3 feet 36 inches	0.914 meters
foot	12 inches 0.333 yards	30.480 centimeters
inch	0.083 feet 0.027 yards	2.540 centimeters
	area	
square mile	640 acres 102,400 square rods	2.590 square kilometers
acre	4840 square yards 43,560 square feet	0.405 hectares 4047 square meters
square rod	30.25 square yards 0.006 acres	25.293 square meters
square yard	1296 square inches 9 square feet	0.836 square meters
square foot	144 square inches 0.111 square yards	0.093 square meters
square inch	0.007 square feet 0.00077 square yards	6.451 square centimeters
	volume	
cubic yard	27 cubic feet 46,656 cubic inches	0.765 cubic meters
cubic foot	1728 cubic inches 0.0370 cubic yards	0.028 cubic meters
cubic inch	0.00058 cubic feet 0.000021 cubic yards	16.387 cubic centimeters
	weight *avoirdupois*	
ton		
short ton	20 short hundredweight 2000 pounds	0.907 metric tons
long ton	20 long hundredweight 2240 pounds	1.016 metric tons
hundredweight		
short hundredweight	100 pounds 0.05 short tons	45.359 kilograms
long hundredweight	112 pounds 0.05 long tons	50.802 kilograms
pound	16 ounces 7000 grains	0.453 kilograms
ounce	16 drams 437.5 grains	28.349 grams
dram	27.343 grains 0.0625 ounces	1.771 grams

grain	0.036 drams 0.002285 ounces	0.0648 grams

troy

pound	12 ounces 240 pennyweight 5760 grains	0.373 kilograms
ounce	20 pennyweight 480 grains	31.103 grams
pennyweight	24 grains 0.05 ounces	1.555 grams
grain	0.042 pennyweight 0.002083 ounces	0.0648 grams

apothecaries'

pound	12 ounces 5760 grains	0.373 kilograms
ounce	8 drams 480 grains	31.103 grams
dram	3 scruples 60 grains	3.887 grams
scruple	20 grains 0.333 drams	1.295 grams
grain	0.05 scruples 0.002083 ounces 0.0166 drams	0.0648 grams

capacity

U.S. liquid measure

gallon	4 quarts (231 cubic inches)	3.785 liters
quart	2 pints (57.75 cubic inches)	0.946 liters
pint	4 gills (28.875 cubic inches)	0.473 liters
gill	4 fluidounces (7.218 cubic inches)	118.291 milliliters
fluidounce	8 fluidrams (1.804 cubic inches)	29.573 milliliters
fluidram	60 minims (0.225 cubic inches)	3.696 milliliters
minim	1/60 fluidram (0.003759 cubic inch)	0.061610 milliliters

U.S. dry measure

bushel	4 pecks (2150.42 cubic inches)	35.238 liters
peck	8 quarts (537.605 cubic inches)	8.809 liters
quart	2 pints (67.200 cubic inches)	1.101 liters
pint	1/2 quart (33.600 cubic inches)	0.550 liters

British imperial liquid and dry measure

bushel	4 pecks (2219.36 cubic inches)	0.036 cubic meters
peck	2 gallons (554.84 cubic inches)	0.009 cubic meters
gallon	4 quarts (277.420 cubic inches)	4.545 liters

quart	2 pints (69.355 cubic inches)	1.136 liters
pint	4 gills (34.678 cubic inches)	568.26 cubic centimeters
gill	5 fluidounces (8.669 cubic inches)	142.066 cubic centimeters
fluidounce	8 fluidrams (1.7339 cubic inches)	28.416 cubic centimeters
fluidram	60 minims (0.216734 cubic inches)	3.5516 cubic centimeters
minim	1/60 fluidram (0.003612 cubic inches)	0.059194 cubic centimeters